# HIZB-UT-TAHRIR

T0333647

REZA PANKHURST

# Hizb-ut-Tahrir

## *The Untold History of the Liberation Party*

HURST & COMPANY, LONDON

First published in hardback the United Kingdom in 2016 by
C. Hurst & Co. (Publishers) Ltd.,
41 Great Russell Street, London, WC1B 3PL

This paperback edition published in 2023 by
C. Hurst & Co. (Publishers) Ltd.,
New Wing, Somerset House, Strand, London WC2R 1LA

A Cataloguing-in-Publication data record for this book
is available from the British Library.

ISBN: 9781787389694

This book is printed using paper from registered sustainable
and managed sources.

**www.hurstpublishers.com**

بسـم الله الرحمن الرحيـم

IN THE NAME OF ALLAH, THE MOST MERCIFUL, THE MOST BENEFICENT

اللهـم انـى أسـألك حبك وحب من يحبك وحب كـل عمل يقربنـى الـى حبك

O ALLAH, I ASK YOU FOR YOUR LOVE, AND THE LOVE OF WHOMEVER LOVES YOU, AND THE LOVE OF EVERY ACTION THAT BRINGS ME CLOSER TO YOUR LOVE

*As the young man sat with Sheikh Taqiudeen al-Nabhani, he asked him, what is the difference between us and the other movements that work for revival? Al-Nabhani threw the question back at him to hear his view before replying. So he enumerated the differences as he understood them—we understand Islam better than any other movement, we have a unique culture, our political opinions are stronger, we are more politically aware, more sincere, and so on.*

*Al-Nabhani rejected all his points, and gave his explanation.*

*None of them is what differentiates the party from others... There are many others who have political awareness; there are thousands of others that have this understanding of Islam. As for sincerity—all the Muslim Umma is sincere, believing and good.*

*The idea that we are sincere, have understanding, are aware—none of this is the distinguishing feature of Hizb-ut-Tahrir. Rather, what distinguishes the party, is not these other characteristics, but the real distinguishing feature is the will and belief, and its confidence in itself, that it can achieve this idea, works seriously for this idea, and that it works to achieve its goal.*

*Its awareness, its understanding, and its work are all on the level of working to achieve this goal. This is an intellectual issue—born out of true sensation and deep research, which resulted in conviction, not simply academic knowledge of the matter.*

A discussion between Fayiz Taha and Sheikh Taqiudeen al-Nabhani

# CONTENTS

# CONTENTS

اللهـم يا مقلب القلوب ثبت قلوبنا علـى دينك

*O Allah, the One who changes hearts, keep our hearts*
*firm upon your din (religion/way of life)*

*For my wife and children, for their patience throughout*

# FOREWORD

Writing this book has been both fulfilling and challenging. As an academic and a historian, I felt the acute lack of any material in any language that gave an accurate insight into the history of the Hizb-ut-Tahrir in detail since its establishment. Even among members of the party, there were internal rumours and stories that spread, sometimes without basis.

While there was still an opportunity to talk directly to some remaining members of the first and second generations who joined around the period of its establishment or under the leadership of Sheikh Taqiudeen al-Nabhani, I felt it necessary that an authoritative history of Tahrir be written before losing all record of those who witnessed and participated in it first-hand.

Writing about the group from an academic rather than personal perspective has had its own challenges, in particular striking the balance between personal bias and objective analysis. This book is not an official account in any sense, but a personal academic endeavour encouraged initially by my publishers.

Writing the book has not been without its controversies—many consider that history, whether written in books or not, remains history, while the present requires activism. The group's founder himself, Sheikh Taqiudeen al-Nabhani, didn't see the point in having his biography written, a mentality and viewpoint that remains present among some.

My view was, and remains, that it is important to preserve the history of such a movement, given the breadth of its presence and influence, and the fact that others have made claims upon it.

My intention is that along with my previous book, *The Inevitable Caliphate?*, these works set down another academic perspective on issues of Muslim and Islamic politics, and political movements, from within—as a counterbalance to much that has been written in ignorance, whether deliberately or with the best of intentions, from the outside looking in.

As a result, if any student, scholar, or other person wishes to know what the caliphate is, what it means to the movements who call for it, and the history of the movement which has become synonymous with it, there now exist alternative academic accounts that will enrich their understanding and provide some much-needed informed perspective.

# INTRODUCTION

و اصدعوا بالأمر، فالعبء خطير     يا دعاة المبدأ الخالد سيروا

مرهف: فكر، عميق، مستنير     و احملوا دعوتكم فهي سلاح

و به يحرق بهتان، و زور!     بسناه يهتدي الحائر، طوعا،

*'O callers to the eternal ideology, go forth and proclaim that which you have been commanded, for it is a heavy burden*

*So carry your call for it is a sword that is sharp, A thought...deep, enlightened. With its light the undecided are wilfully guided, the falsehood and lies are vanquished.'*

Amin Shinnar, verses 148–50 from *'The Radiance of Belief'*[1]

*'[Hizb-ut-Tahrir's] is a potentially far more destructive method of operation [than al-Qaeda's]. They target minds instead of strategic installations and personnel, using the power of the intellect instead of road-side bombs. They have a self-perpetuating influence'*

Anonymous Pakistani intelligence official, October 2012[2]

On 2 September 2005, a man stood on a platform in front of the historic seventeenth century Wazir Khan mosque in Lahore, Pakistan, and read out an address in front of a crowd of people gathered after the weekly Friday congregational prayers. The date of the address corresponded with the eighty-fourth lunar anniversary of the formal abolition of the Ottoman caliphate by Mustafa Kemal, marked as 28 Rajab 1342 according to the Islamic *hijri* calendar.[3] In a speech lasting at least twenty minutes, he addressed the Muslims as the descendants of Salahudin Ayyubi,[4] Saif al-Din Qutuz,[5] Muhammad al-Fatih[6] and other celebrated figures of a collective Islamic history, reminding them of past glory while identifying their current weakness as a result of the absence of the political unity of the past, a unity represented in the normative orthodox theory of the caliphate.[7] The address called Muslims worldwide, in par-

1

ticular those who were 'from the people of power', to recognise that the geopolitical situation was favourable to the re-establishment of the caliphate, given the weakened US leadership as a result of its wars in Iraq and Afghanistan, paired with the lack of serious international rivals. He concluded by advising them to take the opportunity to work seriously at this time to gain the reward of the hereafter, advising them that the return of a righteous Islamic state was an inevitability prophesied by their religion, so they should not miss out such reward, given that 'participation in the work to establish the caliphate, is not equivalent to applauding the work after its establishment.'[8]

The following day a report was carried in *The News International* entitled 'Call to revive Khilafat', which mentioned that various demonstrations had been organised by the Islamic political party Hizb-ut-Tahrir—the Liberation Party—and included the central address in Lahore delivered by the man on the platform, Naveed Butt, the spokesman for its Pakistan branch at the time. It also stated that the leader of Hizb-ut-Tahrir had delivered the speech address through internet radio to members and the general public all over the world.[9] Another Pakistani newspaper wrote that the call was also read out and distributed in several other Muslim countries.[10]

In actual fact, the call was delivered as a speech after the Friday prayer in fourteen countries including Lebanon, Sudan, Turkey, Kazakhstan, Indonesia and elsewhere. It was printed and distributed in a further eleven Muslim countries including Egypt, Syria, Tunisia and Afghanistan.[11] Even though the Uzbek branch of the group was not asked by the central leadership to deliver the call openly, due to the harsh crackdown on its members by the regime there, its members decided to take their own initiative to record the speech onto tapes and then play the tapes on a stereo in front of the prayer congregations, despite the risk involved. In some locations the speech was read out without interruption; in others activists were stopped and arrested before completion.

National media covered the event in many of these countries, though reference to it was minimal and often critical, and in international media such as the BBC the reports were mainly regarding the arrests carried out in Jordan and Lebanon.[12] According to one researcher's calculation, around 400–500 people were arrested as a result of the call. Some of those arrested were released the same day, some were detained for a period before release, and others were jailed and received prison sentences, with the majority of the arrests taking place in Jordan, Turkey and Uzbekistan.[13]

Two years later, in the summer of 2007 during the same Islamic lunar month of Rajab, the central leadership of Hizb-ut-Tahrir co-ordinated a series of conferences and rallies that spread across diverse locations from the Australia to the UK with several countries in between, culminating in a conference that filled Jakarta's Gelora Bung Karno Stadium with a crowd of 100,000 people, the majority of whom were women. Held on the actual anniversary of the abolition of the caliphate, this event garnered wide international media coverage, with the 'push for the creation of a single state across the Muslim World'[14] being reported on the BBC World Service, Al-Jazeera and Fox News among others.

This international activity was all carried out by members of the same group, Hizb-ut-Tahrir, a global Islamic political party officially established in Jerusalem in 1953, with the expressed goals of initiating an intellectual revival that would restart the Islamic way of life and of conveying Islam to the world[15] through the re-establishment of the caliphate. As a political party it adopted a methodology of political and intellectual struggle to achieve its aims, while at the same time eschewing military action. Its three-stage methodology derived from its reading of the various actions of the Prophet Muhammad to establish Islam as a temporal power during the period before he became the political leader of the Muslim community in Medina. The methodology involved the enculturation (*tathqif*) of individuals who would embrace the party's ideas and opinions; then interacting with wider society to spread the movement's ideas and opinions until they became dominant; before establishing a radical form of Islam, meaning the establishment of a system that would implement Islam in a comprehensive and complete manner, while discarding any other system in place.[16]

Since its establishment in 1953, Hizb-ut-Tahrir has spread to more than forty countries internationally, with members found from the US to China. Despite its rejection of violence and insistence that it is a political party, government repression has often forced its activities underground and it is considered illegal in several countries. Treatment of its members and supporters varies from harassment and arrest to imprisonment and torture. Between 2000 and 2010 there were numerous news reports of arrests of alleged party members in Muslim-majority countries as well as countries with large Muslim minorities, including Jordan, Egypt, Lebanon, Syria, Kuwait, Turkey, Tunisia, Pakistan, Bangladesh, Uzbekistan, Kyrgyzstan, Tajikistan, Kazakhstan, Russia and China, with the numbers varying from tens to thousands depending on the location.

As a result of the glimpse of an opening of political space in the post-Arab-uprising Middle East, the party operates legally in Tunisia, and briefly maintained a public profile in Egypt before the counter-coup, which officially returned the army to power in Egypt at the expense of the elected president, Mohamed Morsi.

The group has a large and publicly accessible corpus of literature outlining its thoughts and methodology, including books detailing its proposed systems of governance, along with a prepared constitution. Alongside this is the regular output of pamphlets and articles, published centrally and from its branches around the world, which address intellectual and political issues as they arise. And yet very little is actually known about Hizb-ut-Tahrir and its history, despite the movement's international presence and the apparent contemporary attraction of some of the core components of its call: poll results from interviews in Egypt, Morocco, Pakistan and Indonesia published in 2007[17]—coincidentally just a year after the co-ordinated speeches and distribution of Hizb-ut-Tahrir's call—indicated 74 per cent support for the strict application of Sharia law in Muslim countries and 71 per cent support for the unification of Muslim countries into a single Islamic state or caliphate.

As of 2015, Hizb-ut-Tahrir operates legally in the US and European Union (EU) countries, with the exception of Germany, where it was prohibited from public activity by a 2003 Ministry of Interior ruling.[18] Attention on the movement in the West increased after 9/11, while the US was trying to build stronger relations with potential allies in Central Asia such as the regime of Islam Karimov in Uzbekistan.

There was a concerted effort by Western think-tanks to work with officials in Central Asia, specifically but not limited to the Uzbek regime, on combating the ideas and activities of Hizb-ut-Tahrir, which were seen as a threat to the stability of the governments in the region. The human rights records of the regimes were considered unhelpful in resolving the problem of opposition to the regime, but were seen as secondary to keeping the Uzbek regime onside because of its strategic importance. The research was largely politically driven, a natural consequence of its emerging from the highly politicised think-tank network, resulting in reports with titles such as *Hizb ut Tahrir: An emerging threat to US interests in Central Asia*,[19] *Uzbekistan & The Threat From Islamic Extremism*[20] and *The Challenge of Hizb-ut-Tahrir*[21] coming out of the Heritage Foundation, the Conflict Studies Research Center and the Nixon Center.[22]

Another example of a Western ally seen to be at threat from Hizb-ut-Tahrir is the government of Pakistan, where according to military sources the party has made at least three attempts to infiltrate the army since the turn of the century, the last involving Brig. Ali Khan, who was convicted by a military court for having links to the party in August 2012.[23] The group operated legally until 2003, when it was proscribed by the then military government. Successive British governments have pledged to proscribe Hizb-ut-Tahrir, with former prime minister Tony Blair first announcing his intention to outlaw the party shortly after the July 7/7 bombings in London in 2005. During a trip to Pakistan in November 2006 Blair gave personal assurances to former president of Pakistan Pervez Musharraf that the ban would go ahead, something Musharraf saw as a priority.[24]

However, British Labour and Conservative governments have stepped back from promises to proscribe the movement on the basis of legal advice, with private Foreign Office emails recording that '[there] is no apparent case to proscribe HuT [Hizb-ut-Tahrir] because its activities abroad include involvement in terrorism. Indeed, it is not entirely clear whether the movement would be caught under a future criterion of 'justifying or condoning violence', Much of their literature explicitly rejects the use of violence.'[25] This has not convinced the Pakistani authorities, who continued to lobby the British government to ban the movement in 2015.[26]

As a result of the highly politicised environment around the group and its stated goal of replacing the current governments in the Muslim world with a single Islamic state, one of the avowed aims of Osama bin Laden and al-Qaeda, it is easy to draw certain similarities between the two movements. Therefore it is perhaps not surprising that much of the media coverage and research about the group is firmly rooted in debates over security and terrorism, driven by the burgeoning anti-extremism industry that developed post-9/11 as America has pursued its so-called 'war on terror'. Consequently, much of what has been published about the movement has been considered inaccurate, polemical in nature and rarely undertaken academically, with unverified internet sources, interviews with unnamed sources and unsubstantiated claims the norm. The result of the research or—if one accepts that the research was politically driven—the goal of this research can be summed up in the conclusion of Zeyno Baran that Hizb-ut-Tahrir is a 'conveyor belt' to terrorism,[27] a theory which, though without any empirical evidence, has become popular in Western political circles, with the scope widened to extremism being a conveyor belt to violent extremism.

With very few experts on the group and its history, it has been easy to make claims about Tahrir for political purposes. As an example, numerous figures have been linked to the party, such as the former leader of al-Qaeda in Iraq, Abu Mus'ab al-Zarqawi, and Khalid Sheikh Muhammad, the alleged mastermind behind 9/11, who it was claimed were members of Hizb-ut-Tahrir; this is typical of un-sourced attributions that serve as evidence for the 'conveyor belt' theory.[28] As noted by Jean-François Mayer, Hizb-ut-Tahrir is the 'perfect candidate' for being seen as a threat, since there are no known experts on it and yet it has a radical discourse that can be used judiciously by commentators.[29]

A few attempts have been made at critical studies of the group in the same period, but they have generally been undertaken within the same paradigm of assessing the security threat it poses. The most well informed in this genre is Emmanuel Karagiannis's work *Hizb-ut-Tahrir al-Islami*, with its subtitle, *Evaluating the Threat by a Radical Islamic Group That Remains Nonviolent*, highlighting its focus. Karagiannis compared the group with the Islamic Movement of Uzbekistan, an armed resistance group fighting against the Uzbek government, concluding that although both groups use similar frames of discussion and worldviews, understanding the difference in their ideas is critical to 'understanding why Hizb-ut-Tahrir remains peaceful',[30] with ideology being the determining factor. Before the terms of the debate were set post-9/11, the main work on Hizb-ut-Tahrir was Suha Taji-Farouki's *A Fundamental Quest*,[31] which remains the most complete work in English giving an overview of the historical background, ideological foundations and internal structuring of the group.

Work on the group in the Arabic language is slightly broader based, varying between doctoral studies written from sectarian viewpoints to serious attempts at interpreting the group's political literature,[32] though the majority of work, whether academic or journalistic, up until the Arab uprisings of 2011 remained within the formulaic 'extremism threat' mould because of the politics in the Middle East. The best of the Arabic works available is Auni al-Ubaidi's *Hizb-ut-Tahrir al-Islami*,[33] which was the only accurate historical study of the movement at the time of its publication in 1993 and has remained so until now.

*The untold history*

As noted earlier, despite the previous attempts of al-Ubaidi and Taji-Farouki, an authoritative history of Hizb-ut-Tahrir has not been written, in any language, beyond generalities. There are several important reasons for this, one being the geographical scope of such a work, given that the party is not localised in one country, but is an international movement with branches across the Middle East and beyond. The most critical barrier has been a lack of access to interviews with prominent members of the group. Such access is all the more paramount given that the group has been forced to operate underground across the Middle East since the late 1950s, when its leadership went into hiding.

Political circumstances in the Middle East and the security considerations of members of the movement meant that no access was granted to senior members for interviews prior to the 1990s, and even with the opening of a (short-lived) more permissive environment in Jordan after the parliamentary elections of 1989, access to senior members for interviews regarding historical accounts of activity such as that written by al-Ubaidi and Taji-Farouki were limited to a handful of activists within Jordan itself. The security considerations and lack of access can also be coupled with a lack of desire by senior members of the movement at the time to concern themselves with having the history of the party written. This had its precedence in the example of the founder of the movement, Sheikh Taqiudeen al-Nabhani, who rejected a request for his autobiographical details from a supporter of the party who intended to write a thesis on the history of the group. The request elicited a written response that 'if we reach power, then everyone will rush to write about us, and if not—then we do not deserve to be written about.'[34]

Nevertheless, though several decades after its establishment in the 1950s, Hizb-ut-Tahrir has yet to see its goal achieved of resuming the Islamic way of life by re-establishing the caliphate in the manner it envisages, the contemporary international profile of the party and the emergence of the idea of re-establishing the caliphate in political discourse mean that it warrants attention irrespective of the views of its founder. Since the turn of the century, the party has emerged across the globe under radically differing conditions. In the more permissive environment of Indonesia, the 2007 conference filled a stadium with a 100,000 person capacity in Jakarta to the surprise of observers, who did not consider the party capable of mobilising such numbers. Despite living under the harsh repression of the dictatorial Karimov regime in Uzbekistan, some experts have estimated that Hizb-ut-Tahrir has between 10,000 and 15,000 members and many more supporters,[35] with thousands in prison. Across Central Asia the party's activity and government responses have also been notable, such as in Kyrgyzstan where it is estimated there are tens of thousands of supporters in Osh alone, with arrests of activists commonplace, for instance the arrest in 2000 of almost 300 in southern Kyrgyzstan for distributing religious materials.[36]

In the Middle East the party has also become more active and public in a manner not seen since its establishment and regional growth in the early to mid-1950s. Though the opening of a media office in Jordan at the beginning of the 1990s, coupled with a strident open stance against US intervention in the Gulf at the same time, heralded the beginning of the re-emergence of its public profile, that possibility was stifled by a series of court cases and the imprisonment of its spokesman Ata' bin Khalil Abu al-Rashta (who subsequently became the leader of the party after ill-health led to the resignation of its second leader Sheikh Abdul Qadeem Zallum in 2003), and it was not until around the turn of the century that the Hizb-ut-Tahrir began making a greater impression in the media.

This was in part because of a number of high-profile arrests involving hundreds of supporters across the Middle East. For example, more than 500 people were arrested in Syria in 1999;[37] and more than 100 were arrested in Egypt in 2002,[38] including numerous non-Egyptians—among them four British Muslims, the author being one of them, a Russian, a Palestinian and even a Japanese Muslim convert. This was accompanied by the legitimisation of the party in Lebanon following a decision in 2006 by former interior minister Ahmad Fatfat,[39] which was considered controversial locally and apparently caused enough consternation internationally for Fatfat to have to address it during an official visit to the United States.[40]

In Tunisia the main factor that has led to Hizb-ut-Tahrir's emergence on a public level is the more permissive politics and civil space that emerged as a result of the uprisings across the region that started in Tunisia, triggered by the self-immolation of Muhammad Bouazizi on 17 December 2010. Having been under strict surveillance during the years of former president Zine el-Abidine Ben 'Ali, the party took advantage of the unrest and participated with their own marches, gathering a few thousand supporters under their banner in early January.[41] Since the revolution and removal of Ben 'Ali the party has been legalised and its spokesman, Reda Belhaj, is a regular participant in mainstream media, in print and on television.

After the removal of Hosni Mubarak from the presidency in Egypt, the local branch of Hizb-ut-Tahrir established a public profile, garnering a lot of attention in national press, such as a ten-page pull-out published in *Al-Wathiqa* newspaper, ahead of the movement's July 2012 conference, explaining the party's manifesto and methodology.[42] Its members also presented a weekly show entitled 'And then there will be caliphate'[43] on Egyptian satellite channels during the period until the coup led by Gen. Abdel Fattah el-Sisi, after which the public space for any form of dissent was radically reduced.

The party was particularly involved in the Syrian uprising, with Al-Ikhbariyya al-Suriyya television news profiling the group on 28 March 2011 soon after the start of the revolution and quoting Syrian security sources that Hizb-ut-Tahrir had a major role in instigating the initial protests.[44] As the opposition protests developed into armed resistance as a defence against the harsh crackdown by the Syrian regime, opposition brigade spokesmen have openly declared that in the eventuality of coming to power they hope to establish a state based on 'what is written in the books of Hizb-ut-Tahrir, who have presented a complete and comprehensive political program and constitution.'[45]

In 2014, the region witnessed a declaration of the re-establishment of the caliphate. However, the declaration was not made by Tahrir or its supporters but rather by the group known as the Islamic State in Iraq and Syria (ISIS). At the time, the vast majority of Muslim scholars, academics, politicians and thinkers, as well as Tahrir, swiftly rejected the declaration, claiming that it did not meet the conditions required of such a state. Hizb-ut-Tahrir and its supporters continued its call for a caliphate based on what they considered to be a Prophetic example.

The changing situation in the Middle East is clearly unsettled, much as it has been since the onset of colonialism and particularly the post-First World War settlement in the region. Whatever immediate political outcomes may emerge from the upheavals that began with the Tunisian revolution and spread across the region, the influence and reach of Hizb-ut-Tahrir may expand within the Middle East in the same manner that it has done internationally, despite the attention currently given to ISIS. Alternatively, it may be further sidelined, as was the case in other periods of intensified conflict such as during the Lebanese civil war. The members of the party may or may not reach executive positions of power themselves, but it is possible that at a minimum they may have an influence on the political actors and direction taken.

This book is not intended as a contribution to the wealth of literature that can be classified as current affairs analysis, written in reaction to any recent events. Rather, it is intended to fill the gap in knowledge of the party and its history—to help others understand why and how it emerged, what led to its extremely rapid spread in the 1950s followed by a reversal in fortunes that forced it to operate underground in its sphere of work. While its ideas can be easily accessed in the contemporary era of the internet, with its books, pamphlets and other range of materials openly available online, looking at the political actions it has undertaken historically gives life to the theory and demonstrates practically how it has understood and acted on its adopted methodology to achieve its aims.

As already mentioned, this untold history is partly the result of the party being denied legal status at the time of its formation at the beginning of 1953, with the government issuing an explicit order banning the group on 23 March 1953. Pursued and harassed by the region's security services, the party leadership had gone into hiding by the end of the 1950s, with membership of the party leading to jail time across the Middle Eastern countries it operated in. However, members of the party ran for elections in Jordan during two parliamentary elections in the 1950s, and also competed in elections in Lebanon in 1957 and 1964.

After being driven underground and denied any public space for its ideas, the party attempted to take power through coup attempts, with two occurring in Jordan in the late 1960s, and members affiliated to the party in competition to take power with the Ba'athists in Iraq during the early 1970s. Among prominent political actions undertaken during the leadership of its second leader are the various delegations sent to political actors, notably to the Libyan leader Muammar Gaddafi in 1978, and numerous delegations sent to the Ayatollah Ruhollah Khomeini prior to and after the Iranian revolution in 1979. The reason and manner of the spread of the party beyond the Middle East, and its growth in Indonesia and Central Asia in particular, are largely unknown. This is alongside the party's internal history, its establishment and development and subsequent leadership disputes that afflicted the first and second leaders of the party.

Another part of this untold history is how the party developed and influenced major personalities of the time. Prominent former members included people such as Nimr al-Masri, an original member of the initial three-man leadership committee who subsequently became an influential member of the Palestinian Liberation Organisation (PLO), and his friend Khalid al-Hasan who was one of the founding members of Fatah with Yasser Arafat in Kuwait. Scholarly figures included Sheikh Asad Buyoud al-Tamimi who more than two decades after being expelled from Tahrir was one of the founders of the Palestinian Jihad movement; Sheikh Izz al-din al-Khatib al-Tamimi, who was made the minister for religious endowments (*al-awqaf*), as well as being appointed the mufti for Jordan; and Sheikh Abdul Aziz al-Khayyat, who also held the position of minister for religious endowments and became internationally renowned for his Islamic scholarship. Thinkers and activists included Amin Shinnar, who became a renowned Palestinian poet and writer; Samih Atif al-Zain, who became a prolific author and thinker in Lebanon; and Sheikh Abdul Aziz al-Badri who was possibly the most prominent anti-establishment leader in Iraq during the 1960s.

The party has also had a wide influence on other movements, with Islamic parties being set up by former members or those influenced by the party's thoughts. These included the above-mentioned Palestinian Jihad, set up by al-Tamimi in 1980. Other groups include the Iraqi Hizb al-Dawa, established as the Shia alternative to Hizb-ut-Tahrir, led by Sheikh Muhammad Baqr al-Sadr, whose introductory chapters to his work *Falsafatuna (Our Philosophy)* are striking in their resemblance terminologically and conceptually to the works of al-Nabhani. Outside of the Middle East, the founder of the Pakistani movement Tanzeem-e-Islami, Dr Israr Ahmad, established the Tahreek-e-Khilafat Pakistan in 1991 after becoming convinced of the correctness of making the revival of the caliphate the 'vital issue' for the Muslims, as a result of discussions with members of Hizb-ut-Tahrir he had met while visiting the US.[46]

*Bringing history to life*

This book aims to uncover the untold history of Hizb-ut-Tahrir, based on a diverse array of internal documents, multiple interviews and other materials, to build an authoritative account of the party as told from within. Beyond the interviews, much of the other primary source material is also unique; for example, the use of the early first and second editions of the books published by al-Nabhani, as well as rare materials he published prior to the establishment of the party.

The greatest drawback has been that the work has come perhaps ten to fifteen years later than would have been optimal, given that at that time members who had worked closely with al-Nabhani since the establishment of the party were still alive. The death of Zallum, the second leader of the party, in 2004 deprived this work of a wealth of information that would only have been known to him in his role as close companion to al-Nabhani and part of his leadership committee for more than twenty years.

However, until recently, security would not have permitted such meetings, even for members of the party such as myself, and as the next best option more than forty extensive interviews were undertaken in 2012 in numerous locations, including four countries in the Middle East, many with senior members who had been involved in leadership positions. This was only achievable in a moment of opportunity afforded briefly after the Arab uprisings, which allowed for easy access to the countries involved and to the required individuals, coupled with their willingness to talk candidly about the events they had witnessed and participated in with the party, many having been involved from the early years. These interviews took place in perhaps the only window available for such wide-reaching research, given the age of some of the participants, and the difficulty of arranging such access. The breadth of documentary resources made available for this book brings the events and people involved to life in a manner not achieved previously and unlikely to be replicated in the future.

The interviews include meetings with family members of party leadership, those who participated in leadership roles at different times and locations for the party, including three of the four leadership candidates in the elections for party leader in 2003 (the exception being the winning candidate, al-Rashta), and those who accompanied the leadership for extended periods, including close associates of al-Nabhani and Zallum. Interviews were also undertaken with two of the three members who were part of the delegation sent to Gaddafi in 1978, with numerous members covering the entirety of delegations sent to visit Khomeini both prior to and after the Iranian revolution, as well as with members who took part in other specific delegations such as those to former prime minister of Jordan Wasfi Tel and Egyptian president Anwar Sadat. Given that the party is international, these interviews took place across several countries, including the historical base of the party in Jordan, and in Lebanon where the party's central media office is based.

Though the effect of time on memory coupled with the inherent bias of personal recollections can lead to the possibility of inaccuracies in any narrative dependent on oral history, this has been compensated for by corroborating information and cross-referencing. For example, multiple separate interviews were held with numerous participants of the same delegations, or witnesses to the same events, such as the work of the party in Iraq in the period of the late 1960s and early 1970s when the leadership considered itself close to taking power there, providing ample cross-referencing of information.

The bulk of information gleaned from the interviewees were personal accounts of events and issues they were involved in rather than second-hand narratives, increasing accuracy and aiding easy resolution in resolving conflicting information. Additionally the wealth of internal documents regarding particular events and other primary source material that has emerged recently—such as publicly available written and oral biographical accounts of various people who either interacted with or were part of Tahrir—has been essential in helping create a comprehensive, accurate picture.

For the sake of brevity and simplicity in referencing, rather than giving references for every explicit statement or sentence to the interview it was taken from, a single reference at the end of a paragraph may be used from which the information in the paragraph was based. Though not an optimal solution, this was considered more suitable than the excessive amount of footnotes that would have resulted from associating every line with its source. Often the information in one interview is consolidated by information from separate interviews, but for the aforementioned reasons the most relevant source is normally preferred rather than mentioning all possible sources. Similarly, if a number of consecutive points in a paragraph are sourced from the same book or article, the footnote will appear at the end of the final point or paragraph.

As this book will show, understanding the formation of Tahrir revolves around understanding the personality of its founder and pivotal figureal-Nabhani. The first chapter of this book sets the scene for the emergence of the party, giving an insight into the environment al-Nabhani emerged from, having been born in Palestine shortly before the outbreak of the First World War. His personal upbringing in a household with two parents from scholarly backgrounds, and his close association with his grandfather Sheikh Yusuf al-Nabhani, are explored as part of his formative years, which included travel to Egypt to study at two major institutions concurrently before returning to Palestine soon after the death of his grandfather in the mid-1930s. His professional history is outlined, but more importantly his political positions during the tumultuous events in Palestine in the 1930s and 1940s are examined, along with his views on the Palestinian revolt against the British and his political activity up until leaving Palestine as a refugee after the war in Palestine in 1947–8.

The following chapter is about the birth of Hizb-ut-Tahrir, beginning after the loss of Palestine as the catalyst for shaping the views of many in the region towards the Arab rulers and how al-Nabhani's increased political activism led to early conflict with authority. It also engages with questions about the development of al-Nabhani's thinking, while interacting with the political trends of the time such as Arab nationalism that ultimately led to Tahrir coming into being, before outlining the early days, highlighting how the intellectual culture and methodology of the party was solidified and expanded until it began to settle into a corpus of adopted materials. With the emergence of the party into the public sphere, there was an almost immediate reaction and rejection by the Jordanian regime leading to the banning of the party from the time of its launch and making prison a common destination for its members from the start.

In the third chapter the party's great success in its early years is described and explained, as it rapidly became the foremost Islamic party in the region covering Jordan, Syria and Lebanon,[47] competing in elections and succeeding in getting one of its members into two consecutive Jordanian parliaments. However, its growth and popularity was soon stunted by a combination of internal conflicts over leadership and political currents moving decisively towards Arabism with the emergence of Gamal Abdul Nasser as the second president of the Egyptian republic in 1956, four years after the Free Officers coup of 1952. As the party itself moved into a phase where it adopted what it termed as 'political struggle', the initial expansion was reversed as its members were shunned by society while being pursued by the state. By the end of the 1950s the leadership of the party felt compelled to go into hiding in Lebanon, with their traditional Islamic scholars' garb discarded and beards shaved.

In the face of the restrictions on the party, which impeded any attempts to create a public political platform on which to build its influence and achieve its goals, a period of reflection over its methodology in the beginning of the 1960s led to the introduction of the concept it named as 'seeking *nusra*' (material help). This was considered a clarification of the manner in which it could achieve its objectives through taking power, and the fourth chapter covers the next stage in the party's history as it sought to practically establish an Islamic state once it believed that society was ready.

Despite failing at the first real attempt to take power, al-Nabhani continued to work to achieve his aims. The international focus of the party's work and willingness to undertake activities regionally without any consideration of borders meant that these efforts encompassed countries beyond Jordan including, but not limited to, Iraq and Syria. Covering these events in the fifth chapter, including material from extensive interviews with key members who participated in the heightened efforts to take power in these countries, brings together a picture of how al-Nabhani came closer than is realised to establishing the caliphate he aimed for, but ultimately saw his aim left unfulfilled, and how the lack of results affected him and the party he set up.

Zallum took over as the leader of Hizb-ut-Tahrir after al-Nabhani's death in 1977, and the sixth chapter describes how the new leadership came into being, the changes it brought about and the challenges it faced as it reassessed the state of the party and the reality it faced. A number of critical political actions that took place are covered in detail, including the delegations to the Libyan and Iranian governments and how the party faced further crackdowns, such as the execution of several members of the party by the Gaddafi regime and the Iraqi regime of Saddam Hussein in the 1980s.

It was initially intended that the book would cover the history of Tahrir up until the end of the 1980s, focusing on its core work in Middle Eastern countries, but it was felt that the story was incomplete without trying to give an overview of the progress of the group since that time. Numerous factors make it impossible to cover the period from the 1980s to 2012 in the same detail as the earlier period, but mainly because the spread of the party far beyond its intended homeland means that there is too much material involved. The final chapter therefore covers the international growth of the party from the 1990s but in less detail than previous chapters, relying more on overview with selective attention given to specific countries and events, with valuable insights from interviews and other primary sources used. At the same time, it is possible for other contemporary studies of Tahrir to be easily carried out if the researcher is willing to expend the necessary effort, with Emmanuel Karagiannis's *Political Islam in Central Asia*[48] and Claudio Nef's *Promoting the Caliphate on Campus*[49] examples of regionally based studies of the party.

Zallum also faced perhaps the greatest internal challenge to the party in the mid-1990s, when a group that included a member of his leadership committee as its figurehead attempted to declare his leadership illegitimate and appoint an alternative leader, threatening to destroy the party through internal divisions. Yet during the time the internal ruptures were being resolved, alongside the external pressures on the party in the Middle East, with arrests of hundreds of members in Egypt, Tunisia and elsewhere at the end of the 1980s and 1990s, its call spread beyond the Middle East, particularly eastwards towards Indonesia and the Central Asian republics of Uzbekistan and Kazakhstan—to the point that it now claims to operate in more than forty Muslim countries. How the party reacted to 9/11 and how the West reacted to the party is also covered, along with an overview of Hizb-ut-Tahrir during and after the Arab uprisings.

As far as is possible, the book also tries to situate ideas in the historical context in which they are expressed, rather than simply theorising the views of the party, or narrating party history without situating it within the broader events of the time. Although the importance of the context in which ideas are generated and expressed is not neglected, it should also be realised that while the context may serve to explain ideas it cannot serve to make them understood, and so the ideas may not merely be products of a particular reality but rather the result of thought that seeks to treat and change it.

At the same time this is not intended to be a comprehensive analysis of the party's literature, views about the systems of government it would implement, political analyses and so on, as this would require separate studies, while the books of the party are readily available in several languages including English. Rather, the aim here is to give an insight into the key aspects of its political culture and programme, while also addressing the various competing interpretations and analysis of the movement's ideas and the various assertions that have been made by some elements. Elements of intellectual history are covered, with reference to early copies of the party's core literature explaining how its materials developed and any differences that emerged over time.

In summary, this work has been compiled as a comprehensive and detailed history of Hizb-ut-Tahrir as told from within and is the most authoritative account written to date. It does not attempt to explicitly address all of the inaccuracies and misconceptions around the group—such as claims that it believes in the excommunication of all Muslims in the Middle East, that it is sectarian, that its leadership is based in the West, or historical inaccuracies such as false claims to membership or actions undertaken and so on. The intention is that by establishing an authoritative account of the group such questions will be answered naturally.

The material has been gathered, analysed and presented in order for this account to also be a valuable contribution to the history of Islamic social and political movements. The final product is a mix of political, intellectual and personal history, moving from regional events to personal accounts, situating Tahrir's history within the wars, coups, counter-coups and revolutions in the Middle East, explaining ideas and activities as they occurred.

It is necessary to present the untold histories of individuals and movements such as al-Nabhani and Hizb-ut-Tahrir, situating them within the history of the struggle against post-colonial dictatorial regimes, largely seen by those under their rule as Western puppets who have dominated the Middle East for decades.

# 1

# TAQIUDEEN AL-NABHANI

## (1911–1948)

عظيم بأعلى الخلد أصبح ثاويا     وأكبر أن يُرثى بلفظ وأحــــرف

بسمط سجاياه الحسان قوافيـــــا     ولكن جُوم الليل تأتي أصوغها

*Too great to be lamented by word or letter, one who is now present with the Everlasting,*
*But, when the night stars appear, I will thread them into rhyme with his beautiful character.*

Taqiudeen al-Nabhani, verses of poetry printed in *al-Karmil* newspaper, 1932

*Only a few months ago, the guiding sun set in the sky of knowledge and literature, and today something unexpected arose from the darkness of the horizon of literary genius and poetry.*

*Yesterday, the Professor Scholar Yusuf al-Nabhani died, after serving knowledge, religion, and the judiciary through his published works and rulings, and today his grandson Taqiudeen al-Nabhani has emerged in the world of literary genius by graduating with a diploma in higher education at the top of his class. He is the first Palestinian to graduate with this diploma since the Dar al-Ulum university (Cairo) was established, and the years he spent there were an advertisement of his intelligence and genius.*

*Al-Karmil*, Haifa, Palestine, 6 July 1932[1]

In 1948, war between the local Arab inhabitants and Jewish immigrants raged throughout Palestine. Ijzim was a relatively large and prosperous village of about 3,000 Palestinian inhabitants, located on a hill close to the Haifa-Jaffa road and close to the city of Haifa itself. It had been drawn decisively into a

17

conflict that would subsequently be known locally as the Kerem Maharal war, named after the Jewish settlement later established on the site of the village. According to oral histories of the Arabs of Ijzim, a bus carrying a teacher and nurse on the main road to Haifa was attacked by assailants in a jeep from a nearby Jewish settlement, killing the two passengers. The teacher, Tawfiq al-Murad, was a member of the al-Madi family, one of the historically influential families in Ijzim.

The next day, the driver and owner of the bus, Sa'id al-Madani, saw the same vehicle while on the road. He informed his passengers to hold tight before hurtling into the vehicle killing its occupants. Al-Madani was arrested and taken to trial by the British authorities—who had yet to abandon Haifa—where his supporters crowded around the courthouse to prevent any harm to him. Along with the kidnapping of local Arabs these events drew the majority farming population of Ijzim directly into armed conflict, and the local forces put up prolonged resistance against better armed Jewish forces, despite unrealised promises of support from external neighbouring and regional Arab countries.

Fighting continued for months after the fall of Haifa itself in April. The Ijzim fighters put up steadfast resistance, even though their morale was shaken in May by the massacre of between seventy and 200 villagers in nearby Tantura, along with men from the neighbouring villages of Jaba and Ein Ghazal. These three villages, called the 'Little Triangle' by Jewish sources, were the last in the Mount Carmel area to fall. The defeat of Ijzim came after a period of two weeks of air bombing in July—Jewish forces dropped bombs by hand from cargo planes—which preceded the second truce between the Arabs and Jews on 19 July. However, the truce was not respected with regards to Ijzim, which was attacked on 24 July. After two days of fighting, the remaining fighters had run out of ammunition and any hope that the United Nations mediator, Count Bernadotte, would intervene to enforce the truce on the Jewish side. They abandoned the village, making it one of the approximately 400 Palestinian villages depopulated during the 1948 war.[2]

The history of the region that Haifa and Ijzim belong to is long and rich, in part due to its significance for the three Abrahamic religions—Judaism, Christianity and Islam—as well as its fertile lands, amenable weather and geographical location. The Byzantine Empire had historically governed the area before being superseded by the Sasanian Persian empire, quickly supplanted by Muslim rule in the first half of the seventh century, during the era of the second caliph of Islam, Umar bin al-Khattab. The eagerness of the first generation of Muslims to quickly spread Islamic rule to the region can partially be explained by Jerusalem and the al-Aqsa mosque, which are given extra significance in Islam, with the mosque being the site of the night journey mentioned in the Qur'anic verse translated as 'Glory to (Allah) Who did take His Servant (the Prophet Muhammad) for Journey by night from the Sacred Mosque to the Farthest Mosque whose precincts We did bless—in order that We might show him some of Our Signs.'[3] According to accounts attributed to the Prophet, considered authentic by normative orthodoxy, the mosque is mentioned as one of only three that should be travelled to with the intention of visiting it,[4] and the region of al-Sham, which comprises modern-day Syria, Lebanon, Palestine and Jordan, is also praised in numerous Prophetic narrations such as one that mentions 'How blessed is al-Sham.'[5]

Though the modern-day conflict is commonly viewed as a Jewish-Muslim struggle, the area around Palestine and al-Sham saw heightened conflict in the twelfth and thirteenth centuries, with cities like Haifa passing between Christian and Muslim rule multiple times during the period of the Crusades before the final expulsion of the crusader forces. During the period of the Ottoman Caliphate, the area around Haifa remained under its rule after being absorbed by the state at the beginning of the sixteenth century, until defeat by British forces in the region of Syria and surrounding areas in the First World War.

Alongside the existence of sites of great religious significance and their linkage to Islamic beliefs, which meant that the Palestinians had a deep connection with Islam, it also had a historically strong connection and loyalty to the Ottoman Caliphate, with several high positions in the state coming from the region. Notably, the story of Sultan Abdul Hamid II's rejection of the advances of the Zionist Theodore Herzl to provide diplomatic and financial support for the Ottoman state in exchange for lands in Palestine only reinforced that sense of commitment. While the call for an Arab caliphate or Arab independence was growing in other areas at the beginning of the twentieth century, it was considered an innovation in Palestine up until the onset of the First World War.[6] After the war, the British took official control of Palestine following the ratification of the British mandate by the League of Nations in 1923.

Ijzim sits about 20 km from the city of Haifa, and Ottoman records from the end of the sixteenth century note that it had fifty-five inhabitants at the time.[7] By 1948, the major families of the approximately 3,000 inhabitants of Ijzim were the al-Madis and the al-Nabhanis. The al-Nabhani family was descended from *bani Nabhan* (the Nabhan tribe) of Bedouin Arabs who settled in northern Palestine. The village's original inhabitants, including the al-Nabhanis, were either expelled or fled as a result of the conflict in 1948, and were not permitted to return thereafter, with Ijzim falling on the Israeli side of the armistice lines drawn in 1949.

Soon after the turn of the twentieth century, Taqiudeen al-Nabhani was born in the village. The year of his birth is disputed and sources vary, putting it between 1905 and 1914, with 1909 being the most common.[8] However, according to family sources al-Nabhani himself, along with other relatives, confirmed that he was in fact born in 1911.[9] Both his parents were religious scholars: his father Ibrahim became a teacher of Sharia (Islamic law)[10] in Palestine after working as a judge in Damascus, and his mother Taqiyya was a memoriser of Prophetic narrations.[11]

The family had a reputation among the people of the region as being highly regarded for their Islamic knowledge, piety and trustworthiness during a time when some considered that many in central and northern Palestine were more influenced by secularism and lack of concern for their religion. His mother was reported to have stood out among the women of the area as someone known not to indulge in the common pastimes of gossiping and backbiting.[12]

Taqiudeen was raised in a household dominated by a culture of Islamic learning and teaching that his family nurtured. His father had wanted to send him to live for a period with the Bedouin Arabs in the area, a practice dating back to pre-Islamic times when people would send their children outside of their villages or towns to learn the Arabic language from them while also developing the self-sufficiency that such an upbringing gives. His mother, however, opposed this idea and so he stayed in Ijzim, where he memorised the whole of the Qur'an by heart under his father's instruction, at some point between the ages of seven and ten.[13]

Taqiudeen's family was known to be loyal to the Ottoman state, which was the norm at that time. His maternal grandfather Yusuf al-Nabhani was a well-known state figure in the region, having worked as a judge in several Ottoman provinces, as well as having written many works that supported the caliphate and the ruling Osmanli family.

Yusuf remained loyal to the Ottoman caliphate even after Abdul Hamid II's removal, and when Sharif Hussein sided with the British against the Ottomans in the First World War he left Medina and returned to his birthplace in Ijzim,[14] and divided his time between his home village and Beirut. This close proximity to his family meant that he had a great influence on the upbringing of his grandson Taqiudeen, who spent time with him as a young boy. It was with his grandfather's encouragement and financial backing that Taqiudeen was sent to complete his studies at the al-Azhar University in

Cairo, where he also attended the lessons by various scholars whom his grandfather had recommended.[15]

## Sheikh Yusuf al-Nabhani

Yusuf was born in Ijzim in 1849. Like his grandson, he memorised the whole of the Qur'an at a young age and was taught by his father, Ismail al-Nabhani, who also taught him numerous other texts in Islamic sciences before sending him to Egypt at the age of 17 to study at al-Azhar University. After seven years of study in Egypt, he returned to Palestine where, after a year, he was appointed as a judge in Jenin. The following year he travelled to the capital of the Ottoman state, Constantinople (Istanbul), where he spent about two and a half years before being appointed as a judge in the governorate of Mosul.

After less than eighteen months in Mosul Yusuf travelled to Baghdad and then to Beirut, where he worked for two years and wrote a book entitled *al-Sharaf al-Mu'abad li Aal Muhammad* (The Everlasting Honour for the Family of Muhammad). He subsequently returned to work as a judge, this time in Latakia, a principal port city in Syria. He was then appointed as the head of the criminal court in Jerusalem, before being appointed as the head of the court of rights in Beirut.

At this point Yusuf settled in Beirut, where he stayed for more than twenty years after his return around 1888, and he remained in this position until he was removed following the deposition of Abdul Hamid II. During his working life he also travelled to several other cities and made the pilgrimage to Mecca during his second period of work in Beirut. He was finally removed as judge after Abdul Hamid II was deposed by the Committee of Union and Progress (also known as the Young Turks) in 1909, at which point he travelled to Medina, where he spent much of his time in the Prophet's mosque, and it appears some of his contemporaries who saw him there were impressed with his habits and consistency in worship.

However, despite the upheavals in the Ottoman state at the time, Yusuf remained loyal to the caliph and the institution of the caliphate, and therefore moved from Medina after Sharif Hussein began to fight against the Ottomans during the First World War. It was at this point that he returned to his place of birth of Ijzim in Palestine.[16] He withdrew entirely from public life after the British occupation of Palestine, and died in 1932.

Like many other prominent scholars of the Ottoman caliphate, Yusuf was a follower and staunch supporter of Sufism, and particularly the political pan-

Islamic support the various Sufi sheikhs could provide the institution of caliph, as promoted by Abdul Hamid II to build support across the diverse territories under his control[17] at a time of the dual threat of physical foreign encroachment and the growth of the seeds of nationalism. What stands out is the diverse travel and work experience that Yusuf accrued in the service of the Ottoman state, which made him one of the foremost figures of the caliphate of the time. He claimed that throughout his work across the various courts and geographies in his time as a judge, he could not recall a single judgment he made that went against Sharia as far as his ability and power were able to discern.[18]

As with the vast majority of the scholars, including the many Sufi sheikhs of the period, Yusuf asserted that loyalty to the caliph was a religious obligation, and considered the caliphate to be the symbol and executive power of Islam. This is made apparent throughout his written work, specifically in a book he wrote that collected forty Prophetic narrations related to religious obedience to the leader of the believers (itself another title given to the individual political leader of the Islamic community and used interchangeably with the title of caliph), to which he appended a short article he had written in praise of Abdul Hamid II and his ancestors.[19]

During his lifetime Yusuf wrote a number of books across several disciplines of Islamic sciences, as well as volumes of poetry. These works vary from collections of stories of reported miracles that occurred at the hands of *awliya* (those close to God),[20] to collections of Prophetic narrations regarding the obligation of and preference for military jihad and those who undertake it.[21] His poetry was exclusively of a religious nature, and varied from his four-volume work of poetry praising the Prophet,[22] to poems written in support of what he considered to be Islamic orthodoxy and against the agenda advanced by prominent reformers Jamaluddin al-Afghani and Muhammad Abdu in the latter part of the nineteenth and the early twentieth centuries.[23] Though the nature of topics covered was narrow in scope, literary experts of the time such as Shakib Arslan considered him to be among the most well-known and eloquent poets of the period, and also mentioned how some said he would have been the equal of Ahmad Shawky, one of if not the most celebrated Egyptian poets of the early twentieth century, had his work been more diverse.[24]

Throughout his time living under the Ottoman state, Yusuf took a prominent and vocal stance in support of the caliphate as well as mainstream Sufism and its practices. The period he lived in was one of weakness in both the Ottoman state and the institution of the caliphate, and he was caught between three competing trends of the time (nationalism, Islamic reformism and pan-

Islam), each emerging as a reaction to the decline of the region in political and material terms.

The first was the nationalist trend, which up until the end of the nineteenth century had not garnered much support, with the possible exception of areas under colonial occupation.

The second trend was that of Islamic reformism, which encompasses many strands within itself but here refers to the beginning of modernist trends calling for the reinterpretation of the Qur'an, the Prophetic narrations and the canonised schools of thought regarding legislation in light of modernity. Common aspects include the refutation of Sufism, seen as encouraging a parochial outlook reliant on spiritualism while neglecting material advancement; calling for a rational approach to interpretation of religious texts including the Qur'an; and advancing ideas encouraging the practise of *ijtihad*[25] (juristic reasoning), while not being bound to follow the four dominant canonised schools of thought (known as *mathab;* plural *mathahib*).

The final trend was that of pan-Islam, which was promoted in particular during the time of Abdul Hamid II in an attempt to prevent the disintegration of the state through reviving it on the basis of Islamic unity.

In the face of a weakening Ottoman state, which was threatened by the military of European powers on its borders and the import of ideas such as nationalism and secularism, which served as the ideological basis that encouraged their material progress under what is often termed modernity, Yusuf was a prominent figure among those who believed that the return of Islamic power was dependent on greater adherence to classical orthodoxy. He was not unaware of the weaknesses of the Islamic world at the time, but considered that a reversal of the decline was dependent on what he considered to be a revival rather than a reformation of the religion. This meant that his political views included two focal aspects.

The first was Yusuf's support for the Ottoman caliphate, and the call for all Muslims to unite under its banner and to answer its call to take up arms against European encroachment on Ottoman territory. In his book of Prophetic narrations regarding jihad, he wrote an introduction articulating his anti-colonialism and explaining his motivation for writing on the subject of jihad, at that time stating:

'it is not possible that anyone today does not know about the transgressions of the enemy against the people of belief, and how they have occupied most of the Islamic lands,... and so when the order of the caliph is issued... to fight holy Jihad against the Russians, English and the French in order to raise the Word of Allah most high,

23

it becomes obligatory upon the Muslims to join under the flag of the caliph of the Muslims and the leader of the believers.[26]

The second aspect was his staunch position against the ideas of reformism, which included that advocated by modernists such as al-Afghani or by what he termed *Wahhabi* thought based on the teachings of Muhammad bin Abdul Wahhab, an eighteenth century scholar from Najd. Though there are fundamental differences between the two, both called for a return to original sources of Islam and the exercise of *ijtihad* in any issue (*ijtihad mutlaq*), and were against *taqlid* (the practice of following a previously formed opinion by another scholar). Both were also against what they deemed to be the excesses of certain Sufi practices. Yusuf was fiercely opposed to both modernist and *Wahhabi* trends, and campaigned against the two.

The poem *al-Ra'iya al-Sughra* (The Brief Insight) was a fierce denunciation of al-Afghani along with his student Muhammad Abdu, and Abdu's student Rashid Rida. It declaimed their reformist agenda as being a cut-and-paste version of Protestant reformism, which took aim at the Catholic Church in the sixteenth century and was therefore specific to the circumstances in Europe and Christian philosophy at that time, while being completely alien to Islamic thought and inappropriate. It rejected their call for any new *ijtihad* on resolved issues, and mocked their claim to be capable of such *ijtihad* in the first place because of their ignorance in the basics of the religion.

The poem went beyond this to decrying their irreligious nature, a theme al-Nabhani apparently addressed when meeting Rashid Rida personally while in Lebanon, asking him, 'why do you take Muhammad Abdu as your teacher while he is someone who does not fulfil his obligations. He stayed with me last year and did not pray the obligatory prayers despite having no excuse not to.'[27] This lack of trust even in the religious nature of these personalities stemmed from their philosophical and rational approach, which al-Nabhani claimed resulted in neglect of the Islamic sources by re-interpreting them without justification to become compatible with the modern world.

His opposition against *Wahhabi* thought was similar in nature, even though the reality of the two trends is that while both were calling for *ijtihad* there was qualitative difference between the two. While al-Afghani saw *ijtihad* in the loosest possible framework giving free rein to interpret Islamic sources as he saw fit without recourse to any of the normative systems which regulated the process, the *Wahhabi* scholars took a literalist approach to the texts and so their approach was at the opposite end of the spectrum to al-Afghani's. In contemporary terms, someone who adopted an approach similar to al-

Afghani's today would probably be labelled as a 'moderate' in the West, while the *Wahhabi* would be given the now popularised term *salafi*.[28] However, in the nineteenth century, both strains of reformist thought laid claim to the title of *salafi*, and both were heretical to al-Nabhani.

A second, equally important reason for his opposition to the *Wahhabi* trend was that it was seen as rebellious, in part due to its view that the Ottoman caliphate was implementing and promoting heretical views and therefore lacked Islamic legitimacy. Though the movement's major figures in Arabia were geographically and politically marginalised at the time, they were not simply seen as heretics but also considered by the Ottoman authorities a threat to the unity and stability of the state, requiring numerous state campaigns to re-establish order in areas they attempted to take over militarily.

Given the forceful public stance taken by Yusuf, it is not surprising that he became a polarising figure. A prominent scholar who wrote refutations against Yusuf was Iraqi Sheikh Mahmud Shukri al-Alusi. The stance he took against Yusuf was part of the oppositional stance taken by the *salafi* trend in his area against the expansion of Sufi brotherhoods, which the Ottoman state often encouraged. Al-Alusi made an interesting opponent because although he was accused of being a *Wahhabi* by local administrative authorities, who attempted to exile him from Baghdad because of his beliefs, he was actually against what he considered was the excessive *Wahhabi* tendency to proclaim *takfir* (excommunication) against anyone who disagreed with their beliefs.

Al-Alusi was not an opponent of the Ottoman state as *Wahhabi* scholars often were, and while he disdained the corruption and decline that characterised the final years of the caliphate, he hoped for its reform and remained loyal to it rather than abhorring it as a heretical entity. This is highlighted by his participation in a diplomatic mission sent to Riyadh during the First World War in what was an ultimately futile attempt to convince Abdul Aziz ibn Saud to enter the war on the Ottoman side.[29] Al-Alusi was one of a number of scholars who replied in verse to Yusuf's poetry, refuting his contentions that *ijtihad* was no longer permitted,[30] as well as authoring a two-volume book in which he vigorously attacked Yusuf's Sufi beliefs and what he considered to be Yusuf's political opportunism in promoting Sufism while in the employ of the Ottoman state.[31]

It is clear that Yusuf was actively involved in some of the major debates of his time, and like those he debated with he was in part hostage to circumstance. The vigorous debates and disputes were more pronounced because it was a period of rapid decline in the political fortunes of the Ottoman state, which eventually resulted in its defeat in the First World War, followed by dismemberment and abolition at the hands of Mustafa Kemal in 1924. In such circumstances, the competing narratives as to why the the representative of the Islamic world's political unity had been overtaken by non-Muslim nations naturally led to serious introversion, to understand the reasons for the decline and the medicine that would cure the so-called 'sick man of Europe'. Given what was at stake, it is not surprising that emotions appeared to run high through the writings of many of those involved.

By the time Yusuf had returned to Ijzim, the First World War was raging and he had been in retirement for a number of years in Medina. Although he no longer played a central or prominent role in the politics of the Ottoman caliphate, the experience and worldview he carried with him back to his village would affect those around him. In this way, it is of little surprise that he would play an influential role in the life of his grandson Taqiudeen.

Among the anecdotes that Taqiudeen would tell about his grandfather, two in particular indicate some of the influence Yusuf played in shaping his grandson's personality. The first relates to the Baha'i faith, a recent offshoot sect from Islam which began in nineteenth-century Persia, rejected as heretical and entirely outside of the Islamic faith by Muslims. This is because of the claims by its founder Bab (Syed Ali Muhammad Shirazi) and one of its other main figures Bahaullah (Mirza Husain Ali-Nuri) to be messengers from God, which contradicts the finality of the Prophethood of Muhammad, which is a principal foundation of Islamic belief.

Both Haifa and the nearby town of Akka (Acre) are sites of pilgrimage for members of the Baha'i community, because of the existence of shrines where their founders' remains are kept. This meant that there were sometimes members of the community who would also visit the surrounding areas, carrying the call to their religion with them. One such person visited Yusuf's house while his grandson was with him and gave him papers proselytising the Baha'i faith. Yusuf called Taqiudeen to bring him some matches to burn the papers, provoking the young child to question why he was destroying them without reading them first. Yusuf replied, 'because it is too contemptible to be worth looking at.'[32]

The second anecdote relates to when an older Taqiudeen was spending one of his summers back in Ijzim during his period of study in Egypt between 1928 and 1932. On one occasion, one of his colleagues from university visited him at his village, and Taqiudeen took him out for the day in Haifa before later returning to his grandfather. At this point his grandfather called him over and told him that when he and his friend had left, the two of them had visited such and such places, after which Taqiudeen had taken them to a specific restaurant, where he ordered this specific food for his friend, after which he had ordered these specific fruits for the two of them. Taqiudeen said that it was true, bewildered as to how his grandfather had known all of these details before Taqiudeen had told him about them.

Yusuf replied that this was the result of *karamat*—a word used to refer to miraculous events gifted to the Prophets or seemingly miraculous events gifted to those who were considered to have a close relationship with God. He then explained what he meant by outlining how he arrived at his seemingly miraculous knowledge—that since Taqiudeen's friend was visiting the region for the first time it was natural that Taqiudeen would take him to the famous attractions in the town, after which it would be lunch time. Yusuf continued by explaining to Taqiudeen that due to the desire to honour your guest, you would take him to the best restaurant and order the best food, and once lunch was finished you would invite him to eat some fruit and given this is the season for such and such fruits they must have been the fruits that you ordered; all of this is *karamat*, in other words, knowledge, intelligence and deduction, which can sometimes lead to correct insight and sometimes be incorrect. Though Taqiudeen had previously heard of this understanding in al-Azhar, where many of the scholars would in fact go further and reject entirely the notion of miraculous *karamat* for anyone except Prophets, in this instance he understood the concept through its practical manifestation and his grandfather's explanation.[33]

These two examples give a small insight into the influence that Sheikh Yusuf al-Nabhani had on his grandson, such as his certainty that Islam was the truth and other belief systems were false or how he explained the process of rational deduction in a practical manner. His political stance in support of the Ottoman caliphate, firm belief in the obligation for the Muslim community to be united behind a single leader and the need to implement Sharia in its pure form would all have played a part in the environment Taqiudeen grew up in. This does not, however, mean that Taqiudeen adopted everything inherited from his grandfather or that there are no differences in their beliefs—there are some quite substantive differences between the two and their methodologies.

While Taqiudeen's parents and siblings adopted the political Sufism commonly associated with this latter period of the Ottoman state, which his grandfather promoted, Taqiudeen himself was largely unaffected.[34] The example of his understanding of *karamat* highlights this. He later wrote that miracles were specific to Prophets as a way of confirming the message they were being sent with, and so *karamat* could not be miraculous in nature unless they were confirmed by an Islamic text from the Qur'an or Prophetic narrations.[35] On the other hand, his grandfather had written a two-volume book narrating various *karamat* reported to have been performed by religious Muslim figures throughout time, with his stated belief that any miracle a Prophet performed could also be repeated as a miracle for those close to God as a further proof of the Prophethood and the truth of the message of Islam.[36]

Indeed, while the elder al-Nabhani was involved in sectarian disputes over creedal issues with those he considered *Wahhabi* scholars, Taqiudeen would later form Hizb-ut-Tahrir on a non-sectarian basis, considering Muslims as one in terms of their essential belief (referred to as *aqida* or *usul al-Iman*), whereas detailed creedal issues related to the branches of the belief would never be resolved and in fact were the result of misunderstanding the nature of Islamic belief. Somewhat ironically, the non-sectarian stance of Tahrir has resulted in it being labelled as a sect by others, as will be discussed in more detail later.

Sheikh Yusuf al-Nabhani's forceful stance against the modernism of al-Afghani and others is reflected clearly in the unapologetic views advanced by Taqiudeen. For example, Taqiudeen rejects most modern exegesis of the Qur'an, such as the one written by Rashid Rida, being of the opinion that it was in contradiction with the fundamentals of the religion in numerous places.[37] However, while Yusuf was against the principle of anyone claiming to practise *ijtihad* outside of the established four schools of thought[38] and denied the permissibility of anyone to claim they were capable of undertaking *ijtihad* in the modern age, Taqiudeen believed that *ijtihad* was a necessity for the religion to be able to give verdicts on new issues such as modern technologies, and that as long as the person fulfilled the conditions of being deeply knowledgable in the Arabic language, the sources of Islamic jurisprudence and the methodologies of deriving Islamic edicts, there was no problem with practising *ijtihad* unrestricted by previous juristic rulings of the established schools of thought.

As a result, Taqiudeen lay somewhere between modernists such as al-Afghani and traditionalists such as his own grandfather. He believed firmly in the need and right to practise *ijtihad* and that its neglect was a factor in the decline of Muslims; but also that *ijtihad* did not simply mean free rein to reinterpret according to one's own interpretation, but had to be grounded solidly in the traditional Islamic science of *usul al-fiqh* (the foundations of jurisprudence), which laid down conditions and principles for any *ijtihad* to be considered valid. In application, this meant that while he would have disagreed with his grandfather on the issue of the necessity of *ijtihad*, he agreed that what was being touted by modernists such as al-Afghani and Abdu was not a valid form of it.

In this way it can be seen that while Sheikh Yusuf al-Nabhani played a central influential role in the upbringing and direction of his grandson, conceptually and politically, perhaps the area in which he had the greatest influence was in giving Taqiudeen confidence in his religion as well as his ability and intellect. It was that confidence and independent thinking, coupled with his forceful personality, that proved to be the foundation of the character of his grandson, who eventually established a political party that aimed to reverse the decline that had exercised the minds of many others who came before him.

*Taqiudeen al-Nabhani: the formative years and the end of the Ottomans*[39]

As mentioned previously, Taqiudeen was born in 1911, and memorised the Qur'an with his father at a young age. While he was receiving his Islamic education at home, he also used to attend primary school in Ijzim. He then travelled to the nearby town of Akka for his secondary schooling. His grandfather encouraged the family to send Taqiudeen to university in Cairo to follow the same educational journey he himself had taken, and gave the young Taqiudeen five gold coins to finance his study and expenses.[40] With his father's agreement, Taqiudeen travelled to Egypt in 1928, where he completed his secondary education at al-Azhar the same year. At this point he enrolled at the newly established Cairo university, Dar al-Ulum, where he pursued a formal degree in the new education system, while simultaneously participating in the old system of attending lessons held by different scholars in the precincts of al-Azhar.[41]

In 1932, the same year as the death of his grandfather, Taqiudeen graduated from both Dar al-Ulum and al-Azhar among the top of the graduation class. Some of his teachers commented how he had garnered the respect of colleagues and teachers from the moment he had entered Dar al-Ulum, an indication of his personal ability as well as the preparation that his upbringing had given him in terms of his knowledge of the Arabic language and Islamic studies.[42]

Taqiudeen left Egypt permanently that year and returned to Palestine, coming back holding four certificates: the al-Azhar high school certification, a certificate equivalent to a degree in Sharia from al-Azhar, the Dar al-Ulum degree in Arabic language and literature, and the *Ijaza* (permission) certificate from the Higher Institute for Islamic Jurisprudence (connected to al-Azhar), which confirmed his status as someone capable to work as a judge in Sharia.[43]

The period of Taqiudeen's formative years was one of unprecedented upheaval for the Islamic world in general and the Middle East in particular. During his early childhood, Palestine had fallen under British control in 1917, with the draft of the mandate for British colonial control of Palestine being agreed by the council of the League of Nations in 1922 before being ratified in 1923. Jewish immigration into Palestine continued to increase, leading to conflict and resentment, and rioting in 1929 that a British-commissioned report explained as the result of the Arab feeling of animosity and hostility towards the Jews consequent upon the disappointment of the former's political and national aspirations and fear for their economic future.[44]

Parallel and key to this series of events, by the time the young Taqiudeen reached thirteen years of age, the Ottoman caliphate that his grandfather had been intimately associated with no longer existed, having been officially consigned to history in 1924 by the pen of the president of the new Turkish republic, Mustafa Kemal, a decision that had international ramifications. Across various parts of former Ottoman territories, from Jeddah to Tripoli in Libya, Damascus to Kabul, the decision to abolish the institution of the caliphate was greeted with general dismay and disbelief,[45] the formal end of a political entity that according to some was 'considered by the generality of Moslems and Islamic thinkers to be one of the essential Islamic institutions, and to be an excellent means for securing the unity of Islam and a most important instrument for the conclusion of political alliances.'[46]

In Egypt the immediate reaction was similar, despite Kemal being widely considered a Muslim hero for his military campaigns against the British and responsible for maintaining the independence of Turkey from imperial powers after the war. This support had even extended to his decision two years earlier in 1922 to separate the position of caliphate from the temporal power of the sultanate, which basically reduced the caliph to a kind of constitutional monarch. But the abolition was an irreligious step too far, and newspapers that had previously supported the decision regarding the separation of the powers were dismayed, asking questions regarding Muslim unity and solidarity and what the removal of the most prominent symbol of Islamic political unity meant.[47] Islamic scholars such as Muhammad Shaker, who had previously vocally supported Kemal and came out after the abolition comparing the decision to abolish the caliphate to a violent hurricane, lamented what they considered to be a crazy decision.[48] Most other newspapers such as *Masr* and *al-Siyassa* carried similar opinions, a rare moment of unity in the fractious environment of Egyptian politics in that period.

The scholars of al-Azhar in Cairo gathered at a somewhat tardy council meeting three weeks after the official abolition on 25 March, issuing a notice in which they restated the normative orthodox view that the caliphate was the 'general leadership in the *din* (religion or way of life) and worldly affairs,' and the Prophet's representative in 'the protection of the *din* and the implementation of its laws.'[49] In other words, it was a religious obligation to establish the rules of Islam in all spheres of life, which requires a political entity that has the coercive power to implement, defend and promote it, and this was the caliphate. Numerous efforts were made to re-establish the caliphate, with calls to competing conferences emanating from Mecca and Cairo with the aim of electing a new caliph. Both were complete failures.[50]

Once regular politics resumed in Egypt the caliphate became an issue of contention between various competing factions, used as a prop in a struggle involving King Fu'ad and his opponents of the time, the Liberal Constitutionalists. At the same time, a book published in 1925 entitled *al-Islam wa Usul al-Hukm* (Islam and the Fundamentals of Ruling)[51] became a major source of conflict between the secular liberal and religious conservative establishments. Written by Ali Abdul Raziq, an al-Azhar graduate who was part of the political family that founded the Liberal Constitutionalists, the book challenged the prevailing orthodoxy regarding the caliphate in Islam by denying it had any religious significance at all. He went further by basically claiming that Islam was secular and had nothing to do with politics at all.

Raziq's book caused uproar, particularly because up until that point secularism had been considered a European solution to a European problem (namely that of the conflict between religion and science in Christendom), and was not promoted in the Middle East except by a small section of the society fond of Western culture.[52] The fact that he was doing so while wearing the garb of an al-Azhar scholar made it even more bitter for his opponents, notwithstanding his year of study abroad in Oxford, meaning that he was also Western educated. His former colleagues from al-Azhar were not impressed, and several wrote stinging refutations of his book, all the while reaffirming that Islam was political and its politics was supposed to be led by a caliph, and that this normative ideal had to be upheld as orthodoxy. In the end Raziq was summoned before the Council of Grand Scholars made up of senior al-Azhar authorities, which published a unanimous ruling to censure his book and strip him of his university certification and permission to act as a judge.

Several Islamic scholars from al-Azhar and beyond, as well as writers and others, lined up against Raziq, among them Tunisian scholar Sheikh Muhammad al-Khidr Hussein. A prolific writer and activist, al-Khidr Hussein had previously spent time in Syrian jails for agitating against the French. He counted himself as a personal friend of Raziq, but this did not prevent him from publishing a comprehensive critique of his book, dismissing Raziq's attempt to superimpose European political theories onto the caliphate, given that it was not a theocracy as the term was commonly understood in the West.

As an example, he stated that while Western philosopher Thomas Hobbes believed that it was the duty of every individual to submit to the authority of the king, Islamic scholars stated that the ruler was not to be obeyed unless he ruled within the bounds of Islamic scripture. Whereas Hobbes claimed that for the ruler to submit to one of his subjects contradicted the necessary nature of hierarchy, the Islamic scholars said that it was the duty of the ruler to submit to the lowest of the people in stature if that person ordered him to act justly and refrain from oppression And where Hobbes made religion submit to the king, the Islamic scholars said that it was imperative that rulers submitted to the rule of Islam.[53] This line of argument is found throughout the various rebuttals of Raziq's book, along with the refutation of his work as a valid *ijtihad* and the declaration that it rather fell well outside of normative orthodoxy.[54]

Support for Raziq's book came from his family's political party, the Liberal Constitutionalists, and he was vigorously defended by secular intellectuals such as Taha Hussein, one the most influential Egyptian writers of the twentieth century. After failing to graduate from al-Azhar University, Hussein had then gone on to study at Dar al-Ulum subsequently achieving doctoral degrees in Egypt and France. He married a French woman he met during his studies in France, and returned as an advocate of modernity, secularism and nationalism. While some rebuttals of Raziq's work speculated that his book had been written by a European, because of its lack of familiarity with Islamic principles and reliance upon Western political theory, it turns out that Hussein may have in fact played a role in writing the work, apparently claiming to have amended it for Raziq several times as they passed the manuscript between one another before it was eventually published.[55]

Hussein's own book on pre-Islamic poetry[56] was a cause for further conflict when it was initially published (and quickly banned) in 1926, with the accusation that he was insulting Islam, which led to a court case being brought against him. This was in part over his questioning of the historical accuracy of stories within the Qur'an, treating it as a historical document rather than revelation. His defenders came from the Liberal Constitutionalists, while the main political party of the time, al-Wafd (with whom the Liberals were regularly at loggerheads), lined up with his opponents in al-Azhar (Hussein would subsequently swap political allegiance and joined the al-Wafd party in the 1930s after being offered a job to edit *Kawkab al-Sharq*, a journal published by the party). That the trial collapsed and the book was re-published the following year was characterised by some as a victory for secularism and freedom of speech at the time, though given that Egyptian society largely remained conservative it would be more accurate to say that the victories were bureaucratic and legal rather than ideological.[57]

The subject matter of the two books by Hussein and Raziq were ostensibly different, one a literary critique and the other a work of political science and theology, but both were both considered shots fired against the legitimacy of religion in public political life. At the forefront of this debate, alongside his rebuttal of Raziq's theories al-Khidr Hussein also wrote a similarly detailed criticism of Taha Hussein's book on pre-Islamic poetry soon after its publication. In its introduction, al-Khidr Hussein claimed that the colonialists had a hatred for any Islamic revival that was aiming for liberation, and that while they supported oppression and spilling the blood of colonised peoples, they would hypocritically champion 'freedom of thought' when what was intended was to undermine this revival by attacking its religious basis. In this case, Hussein and his book were among the weapons used as the means to achieve this objective by attacking the Qur'an to try to remove the respect and reverence the Muslim nation had towards its source of guidance.[58]

Taqiudeen arrived in Cairo in 1928 as a young man of 16 or 17, and while these debates and discussions had possibly peaked between 1925 and 1928, he was stepping into a political environment of heightened tension where al-Azhar and some of its scholars felt under threat from the wave of secularism that was in vogue after the failure of the caliphate as a religious polity had been brutally undermined by its formal abolition. Though he was just entering his teen years when the caliphate was abolished, and in practical terms, living in British-occupied Palestine, it may not have had a direct effect on him, his household and that of his grandfather would have engendered a sense of the religious obligation of the Islamic state and what its decline and removal meant. Upon entering al-Azhar, one of the teachers he studied under on his grandfather's recommendation was in fact Sheikh Muhammad al-Khidr Hussein,[59] meaning he had not only entered al-Azhar during these ideological battles, but was learning under one of their main protagonists.

During his time in Cairo, Taqiudeen would also spend time in poetry recital sittings held by Ahmed Shawky. Shawky was the most celebrated Arab poet of his time, nicknamed *amir al-shu'ura'*, meaning the prince of poets, and a nemesis of Hussein, who admitted to his feud with him in the introduction to his book, critiquing the work of Shawky and another major poet of the time, Hafiz Ibrahim, which he wrote a year after the two of them had died.[60] He too had spent a few years in France to study towards the end of the nineteenth century, and remained in Egypt after his return in 1894 up until the British forced him into exile in 1914. On his return to Egypt in 1920, he began to compose more religious poetry in praise of Islam and its Prophet, including a eulogy to the Ottoman caliphate after its abolition in 1924. It can be seen that the struggle over the caliphate, religion and the place of Islam in politics and society was not restricted to al-Azhar; the whole cultural environment was involved, with students and thinkers taking sides between the two. Taqiudeen would mention how he was of those who were identified as the supporters of Shawky, as opposed to Hussein.[61]

However, most of his time in Egypt was spent in study, and Taqiudeen claimed to have read 16,000 books while at al-Azhar. Though the number was surely not meant to be an accurate figure, several accounts indicate that he was naturally gifted and could read and digest information quickly, as well as write prolifically as indicated by the amount of literature he produced in later years. This is confirmed by his simultaneous study and graduation from al-Azhar and Dar al-Ulum near or at the top of his class in both universities. One of his colleagues from al-Azhar, Sheikh Subhi al-Mu'aqat, stated that Taqiudeen caught the attention of students and teachers because of his depth of thinking and strength in argumentation, with reference to proofs while participating in the debates and intellectual discussions taking place in the heated student environment of the time.[62]

It was during this period of reading that he developed more independent thinking, because his approach was not the typical rote learning associated with religious learning at the time. Instead he read opposing views with the intention of evaluating the difference and reconciling which was the more correct opinion based on the strength of argument and evidence used. This approach would naturally have given him an inclination towards the next stage, which would have been *ijtihad* and the process of exercising his own judgement on the sources of Islamic law directly.

Due to the time he spent studying and at the libraries in Cairo, and possibly in part due to the warnings he had received from his grandfather regarding politically active reformists such as Rashid Rida (who were in any case viewed with suspicion by scholars and students at al-Azhar generally), Taqiudeen did not join any political party or movement during his time in Egypt. The extent of his organised political activity during his four years in Egypt appears to have been his involvement with a group of Palestinian students at al-Azhar who sent a telegram to the British ambassador in Egypt to oppose and complain about British policy on Palestine.[63]

Though he did not join or participate in any activities of the nascent Muslim Brotherhood, established by Hasan al-Banna in Egypt in 1928, Taqiudeen visited al-Banna with one of his fellow Palestinian students Sheikh Ahmed al-Da'ur. Al-Da'ur first met al-Nabhani in Egypt while studying at al-Azhar between 1930 and 1934, suggesting the meeting took place between 1930 and 1932, placing it sometime after the formation of the group but before it had emerged to interact politically. Al-Banna made a positive impression on Taqiudeen at the time for his intelligence and views regarding Islamic revival.[64]

Although he may not have engaged in organised political activity while in Egypt, he was known to be an active debater of politics among the students and teachers at al-Azhar, with one of his Egyptian colleagues Prof. Jad al-Rabb Ramadan (head of the faculty of Sharia and law, 1973) mentioning how he would stress the need for religious scholars to take an active role in the revival of the Islamic nation.[65] Additionally, the connections he made with other students and scholars, particularly those from Palestine, would help Taqiudeen in the future when he began to look to form a political party.

### The return to Palestine, working life and the Nakba (Catastrophe)

Taqiudeen returned to Palestine after completing his studies in Egypt in 1932. He initially began work as a school teacher, and taught in numerous schools in the area where he lived for the next six years.[66] During his time as a teacher he also taught in mosques, such as the historic Ibrahimi mosque in Hebron where he would regularly give lessons to children. In this period he was not known for any unusual political activity or views other than being an Islamic teacher, and though respected as teachers generally were, particularly in the Middle East, he was not considered extraordinary or unusual in any respect.[67]

In 1938, Taqiudeen applied to work in the Sharia court system on the advice and with assistance of former colleagues from his days at al-Azhar. There is speculation that this was because of his dislike of working within an education system that was strongly influenced by the British, and so he preferred to instead work in a field where he could apply Islamic law, working on cases linked to family law such as inheritance and divorce. He was initially appointed as a clerk before he sent a request to the Higher Islamic Council to work as a judge, informing the Council of his qualifications and capabilities.

After looking into his request, the council promoted him to the position of head clerk in the central court in Haifa, before he was appointed as an assistant judge in 1940.[68] It is around this time that Taqiudeen's family situation also changed, with the birth of his eldest son and first child Ibrahim—having earlier married a member of the al-Mayasi family from Haifa—who would be the first of four children, three sons and one daughter.

In 1945, he was transferred to work in Jerusalem, where he remained for only forty days before being transferred to al-Ramla. The family believe that his initial transfer was because of a conflict with one of the heads of council in Hebron, Muhammad Ali Jabari, who had a case in Taqiudeen's court at the time. Jabari had visited Taqiudeen at his home to discuss the case with him, only for Taqiudeen to refuse to discuss any of the issues related to the case outside of court. Soon after, he was transferred from his position to Jerusalem without explanation. Apparently, those in the area were upset over his transfer, because he had built a reputation for fairness in issues relating to marital dispute resolution.[69]

Irrespective of the reality behind the suspicions over the reason for his transfer, given Taqiudeen's position as a respected Islamic figure from an established family and with a reputation growing with experience, it is not surprising that he should have the sympathy of his community if they felt he had been treated unjustly in such a situation. A small indication of his profile at the time is given by his son's recollection of attending congregation prayers on the religious festival of Eid with his father as a small child, and Taqiudeen withdrawing his own hand from people attempting to kiss it,[70] a common sign of respect shown either towards religious or elderly figures in Arab society (Taqiudeen would have been younger than forty years old at the time).

Throughout this period, there was no indication of his prominent participation in organised political activity. Taqiudeen was, like many other Palestinians, concerned with the fate of his home under the British mandate, with Jewish emigration affecting the demographics dramatically at the time. During his time as a teacher, he sought to build a spirit of resistance in his students and inflame them against Western colonialism.[71] He also admired the political thought of an emerging scholar activist in Haifa, Izz al-Din al-Qassam, and sometimes used to give speeches to his followers with his approval, though how often this would take place and the extent of this activity is not clear.[72]

Qassam, after whom the Hamas military wing the al-Qassam Brigade is named, had emerged in Haifa as an influential leader agitating to start an armed insurgency against the British. He was born in Syria in 1882 to a religious family and his father was a court official for the Ottomans as well as the leader for the local branch of the Qadari Sufi Brotherhood. He studied at al-Azhar for a time at the turn of the twentieth century, and had experience of organising armed resistance in Libya and Syria against the Italians and French respectively before moving to Haifa in Palestine by early 1921.[73] He is credited with introducing the idea of armed struggle to modern Palestinian politics, and uniquely encouraged the participation of the poor, illiterate and dispossessed, who were those who had lost the most during the period of the British mandate.[74]

His social concern was one of the characteristics that separated him from the other prominent figure of the time, Hajj Amin al-Husseini, the grand mufti of Jerusalem and head of the Higher Islamic Council, who was descended from a land-owning family and represented elite politics. Another of their differences in the late 1920s and early 1930s was that Qassam agitated for direct conflict against British occupation, seeing Britain as the root of the problem, whereas al-Husseini has been accused of deliberately directing his energies and activities against the Jewish presence to avoid conflict with the British authorities as much as possible.[75]

It is this particular aspect that led Taqiudeen to admire Qassam as a 'great hero' whose struggle was a 'correct Jihad',[76] believing him to have identified correctly the root of the problem, and that the British were the main enemy and not the Jews. At the same time he was wary of Husseini, whom he considered to be under the influence of the British,[77] given his role in recruiting for the Arab army to fight against the Ottomans at British instigation during the First World War.[78]

Qassam declared jihad against the British in 1935, a move which Husseini rejected because he supported taking a diplomatic approach.[79] Qassam was killed the same year after a shoot-out with British police, with some claiming that his death inspired the revolt that engulfed Palestine between 1936 and 1939.[80] Husseini fled Palestine in 1937, and is well known for his support and propaganda on behalf of the Axis powers during the Second World War. It appears that although Taqiudeen admired Qassam, and had some interaction with him given their close geographical proximity, he was not meaningfully involved with Qassam's efforts at the time, nor is there any suggestion that he played any noticeable political role during the Arab revolt.

Despite some suggestions that Taqiudeen had close connections with Husseini, this seems difficult to reconcile with his view of Husseini as effectively a British agent and Husseini's role in eventually fighting against the Ottomans (though other leading members of Hizb-ut-Tahrir did have such connections, particularly Zallum, who became the leader of the party after Taqiudeen's death in 1977).[81] While Taqiudeen was politically active, it seems that up until at least 1940 his political activity was on an individual basis rather than through affiliation to any group or person.

Taqiudeen did join an association named *al-I'tisam* (guarding/preservation) during the early 1940s and became its vice-head. Sheikh Muhammad Nimr al-Khatib had established the association in Haifa in 1941, with the aim of combating societal ills such as drinking and gambling. The al-Khatib family had a long history of Islamic scholarship, and Nimr al-Khatib continued the family tradition of studying at al-Azhar before returning to Palestine, where he promptly joined the secret circles that had been established in and around Haifa by Qassam (with whom he had studied before leaving to study in Egypt). Khatib participated in the uprisings during the revolts and was jailed for close to a year. After his release from prison he continued his activism, which included establishing the association.

During the same period the Muslim Brotherhood was beginning to spread in Palestine and opened its first official branch in Jerusalem in 1945, at which point a delegation of senior Muslim Brotherhood members from Egypt visited Haifa. The delegation included Said Ramadan, the son-in-law of Hasan al-Banna, and they visited the association to encourage its members to join their party. Most of the members of the association accepted the invitation, but Khatib and Taqiudeen declined.[82] It was soon after, in 1946, that Taqiudeen met one of the key Palestinian members of the Muslim Brotherhood, Sheikh Abdul Aziz al-Khayyat, who spoke with him at length about revising and reviewing the work for Islamic revival by benefitting from the experience of mistakes made in political and party matters by other movements of the day.[83]

Taqiudeen's only other registered political activity was at the beginning of 1947, when he was recorded as attending a conference in Haifa held by a group called al-Qawmiyyin al-Arab (The Arab Nationalists). The group originally began in Beirut in 1929 and spread to Palestine, where it remained limited in its membership. The gathering in Haifa was an open meeting that was attended by members and non-members, and according to the records of attendees Taqiudeen was registered as not being affiliated to the movement.[84] In this period, Taqiudeen is reported to have been concerned about how to revitalise the work for Islamic revival and was attempting to learn from mistakes previously made by other movements. At this time his own ideas on the necessary path for Islamic revival had a lack of clarity and were also influenced by the ideas and vocabulary of Arabism;[85] therefore his attendance as a non-member at a locally held conference would be unsurprising, considering he was not on a definitive path and was concerned to investigate and learn from the political trends around him.

War broke out in Palestine soon after, in 1947, and Taqiudeen's main efforts at the time were to acquire heavy weapons, in his role as part of an independent group of fighters who took part in the defence of the area around Lydda. The Palestinians had a shortage of weapons in large part because of the harsh punishment the British would apply to any Arab found to be armed, even with a bullet casing.[86] From the time of the revolts in the mid- to late 1930s up until 1947 the British authorities had confiscated large quantities of firearms and ammunition from the Arabs, putting them at a military disadvantage at the time of the outbreak of hostilities.[87]

Taqiudeen first travelled to Syria, where he attempted to meet members of the government to make the purchases required. Instead of help with the provision of military equipment, he was offered financial assistance, which he considered of no use. He thus returned to Palestine empty handed, before travelling to Egypt where he received a similar response. As a result, he believed that the Arab rulers had in effect betrayed the Palestinian cause.[88] When fighting broke out, he continued advising and working with the group that he had attempted to purchase weapons for, with his family house occasionally used to deposit their finances for safekeeping.[89]

The population of Ijzim was expelled by the Jewish forces in July 1948. Al-Ramla and Lydda fell the same month. Taqiudeen and his family were officially refugees, victims of the *Nakba* (catastrophe). He left for Jerusalem, then travelled through Syria before arriving in Beirut, where he had previously left his wife and children in an apartment block occupied by his in-laws. The shock of defeat, the displacement from home and the sense of betrayal by their Arab rulers caused agitation in the minds of many Palestinians. The questions of how, why and what could be done would lead Taqiudeen and others to form their responses.

# 2

# THE BIRTH OF HIZB-UT-TAHRIR

## (1948–1953)

*'...because the movements up until this time misunderstood the true meaning of "tahrir" (liberation), by seeking liberation of land from occupation alone, limiting it to a struggle against the occupier. They did not oppose the conditions the occupier established, or the concepts they created, or the systems and laws they implemented.*

*To be more specific, they did not oppose the intellectual leadership which was carried by the occupier—the separation of din (religion) from life's affair—which was carried in order to implant the occupation's foot in the land from its roots'.*

Nimr al-Masri, Foreword to The System of Islam (1953)[1]

*'In the beginning, this aware band of individuals will be worried and uncertain. They will see numerous paths and will be uncertain as to which path to follow. The degree of awareness within this group will vary amongst its members... Out of this aware group, a select and distinguished band will arise. This band will embrace one path after deep and thorough research. It will perceive both the objective that this path leads to as well as the clarity of the way, so it will follow it towards its objective. Thus, this band of individuals will discover the ideology with both its idea and its method and will embrace it as a deeply rooted 'aqida (belief). This group will embody the ideology and the 'aqida, which together with the party culture, will be the bond that binds the individuals in this group.'*

Taqiudeen al-Nabhani, theorising the emergence of Hizb-ut-Tahrir[2]

The *Nakba* redrew the political map of the region, and the creation of the state of Israel created approximately 700,000 dispossessed who had to remake their lives elsewhere, as refugees living in various conditions away from their homes.

41

Spared the trauma of being forced to live in the camps created to cope with the displaced across the region, Sheikh Taqiudeen al-Nabhani did not remain with his family in Beirut for long. Later that year in 1948 Anwar al-Khatib, a personal friend of al-Nabhani and the head of the newly formed administration for Eastern Jerusalem under the authority of the Jordanian government (Transjordan), sent a message to al-Nabhani asking him to return to Jerusalem to work as a judge in the Sharia courts. Although he had been offered Lebanese citizenship by the mufti of Lebanon, Sheikh Muhammad Tawfiq Khalid, to enable him to work as a judge in Lebanese courts,[3] al-Nabhani responded to al-Khatib's request.

Soon after his return to his former role in Jerusalem al-Nabhani was appointed a member of the Sharia appeals court by its head, Sheikh Abdul Hamid al-Sa'ih. He remained as a member of the court for more than two years, until 1951,[4] when he resigned to (unsuccessfully) run for parliament in August the same year. After this interlude he was invited to deliver lectures to students at the Islamic College in Amman, a role he continued in from 1951 until 1953, at which point he stopped to dedicate his full time to politics as the leader of Hizb-ut-Tahrir.[5]

It was during this period that the idea of establishing a new party was discussed between al-Nabhani and acquaintances such as Sheikh Dawud Hamdan and Nimr al-Masri. As previously noted, Sheikh Abdul Aziz al-Khayyat mentioned how al-Nabhani was concerned about how to reinvigorate the work for an Islamic revival before 1948, but the loss of Palestine and the Palestinians' from their homes increased his concern. In particular, his view of the rulers of the time was influenced by their lack of sincere efforts to fight for Palestine, and in some cases clear indications of their collaboration with the Jews to divide the land between them. King Abdullah of Jordan had negotiated the idea of a Greater Transjordan with the Jews prior to the commencement of hostilities, suggesting that Transjordan annex the land for the Arab state proposed by the UN after the end of the British Mandate and that any Jewish state should occupy the rest.[6]

This became the basis of British policy towards the Arab-Israeli conflict in 1948, and was formulated during the Anglo-Transjordan negotiation in February 1948. A series of meetings between Abdullah and the head of the Political Department of the Jewish Agency, Golda Meir, confirmed this agreement.[7] Other Arab leaders were wary of Abdullah's ambitions, and though there were supposed to be seven Arab armies participating in the war for Palestine, which was internationalised in May 1948, they only sent expeditionary forces to aid efforts while keeping the bulk of their armies at home.[8] As a result, there was widespread disillusionment with the Arab regimes of the time, as well as discontent, which led to a period of coups and counter-coups as the region simmered in the context of the withdrawal of colonialism and the birth of Israel.

*'When severe shocks in the society produce a common feeling'[9]*

The political environment was alive with discussion about how to liberate Palestine and return the dignity of the Arabs. In his position as a member of the appeals court in Jerusalem, al-Nabhani had the opportunity to move in political circles. Soon after he had returned to Palestine and taken up his new position al-Nabhani began to make contact with the various personalities and scholars he knew across the Arab region, travelling to Egypt and elsewhere to discuss the idea of establishing a new political party with the aim of Islamic revival. He also travelled to Syria in May 1949 on behalf of the military governor of Jerusalem, Abdullah al-Tall, as part of an attempt to overthrow the Jordanian monarch and connect the two countries together, and remove British influence as represented by head of the Arab Legion John Bagot Glubb (also known as Glubb Pasha).

Al-Tall had been involved in negotiations between King Abdullah and the Jews over the division of Palestinian land at the beginning of 1949, and had been embarrassed by the inept and servile manner in which the king had conducted the talks.[10] Virulently anti-British, Al-Tall had been impressed by the actions of Husni al-Za'im, who had launched a coup in Syria in April 1949 (with apparent support from the CIA).[11] Through secret communication between his supporters and al-Za'im in Egypt the same month, al-Za'im requested that al-Tall send him a verbal message with a messenger who was to come bearing al-Tall's diplomatic passport as the agreed sign between them. Al-Tall appointed two men he had deep trust in at the time for the job, and between whom there was a deep friendship: al-Nabhani and Abdullah al-Rimawi.

Al-Rimawi was committed to the ideals of pan-Arabism and a vocal opponent of the Hashemite ruling family in Jordan. With the encouragement and tacit protection of al-Tall, in March 1948 he began publishing a weekly political paper entitled *al-baa'th*, even though he was not officially a member of the Ba'ath party at the time.[12] The paper was highly critical of the Jordanian regime and was eventually closed by the end of May 1949. When al-Rimawi and al-Nabhani travelled to Syria on 7 May 1949 to meet with al-Za'im their cover story was that they were intending to purchase paper needed for the printing of *al-baa'th*.[13]

The plan itself never came to fruition, with al-Za'im executed in August the same year after a second coup attempt had removed him, hoist by his own petard. Glubb had become aware of al-Tall's attempts to overthrow King Abdullah, and although he did not appear to have specific details of a plot he submitted a report to the king in June 1949, which resulted in al-Tall's removal from his position and eventual exile to Egypt in October of that year.

During the same period, al-Nabhani is reported to have given fiery speeches in the al-Aqsa mosque in Jerusalem, among other large mosques, speaking against Western imperialism and exposing the role of the Arab rulers in surrendering Palestine and allowing continued colonial influence in the region.[14] As a result of one speech given in Nablus, he was allegedly summoned before King Abdullah, when, according to one account, he was reminded how his grandfather Sheikh Yusuf had been a friend of the monarchy, after which Abdullah extended his hand to al-Nabhani and asked him to pledge allegiance to him. Al-Nabhani eventually responded, 'I have already pledged allegiance to Allah to be the ally of His and His Messenger's allies, and the enemy of His and His Messenger's enemies,' leading to his being jailed for a short period before the intervention of other scholars on his behalf led to his quick release.[15] Al-Rimawi was also jailed for a period in August 1949, as a result of a campaign of harassment of opposition figures and the closure of anti-regime papers such as *Filastin*, which he edited at the time.

The relationship between al-Nabhani and individuals such as al-Rimawi and al-Khatib, both of whom became Ba'ath party members in the early 1950s, has led to speculation regarding the influence that Arab nationalism and socialism had on al-Nabhani. For example, according to Taji-Farouki, al-Nabhani's role in the al-Tall coup plot and his closeness to al-Tall are proof that he was committed to the platform of the coup, which was based on a belief in revolutionary change across the Arab world, with a removal of the old regimes and unification under a single Arab state, which could then liberate Palestine.[16] At the same time, there is no evidence that al-Nabhani was ever a member of the Ba'ath party, and indeed even those associates such as al-Rimawi who went on to become a part of the Ba'ath party were not members until the early 1950s. Other close associates who were engaged in discussions with al-Nabhani at the time, such as al-Khayyat, were adamant that al-Nabhani was not a member of any other political group at the time.[17]

Al-Nabhani's support for the coup plot could also be understood from two other angles. The first was that al-Nabhani considered the removal of the borders between Arab Muslim countries and unification between them as a natural obligation required by Islam, irrespective of the platform of the ruler. This principle remained with al-Nabhani as part of the adopted policies of Hizb-ut-Tahrir after its formation, with the party, for example, calling for the unification of Jordan with the United Arab Republic (UAR) in 1960, despite being an avowed enemy of Nasser and considering him an American agent.[18]

The second is that al-Nabhani was going through a process of discovery at the time, and while he was seeking to establish a party for the sake of Islamic revival and the liberation of Palestine he had not yet formulated his own solution in detail. Although he was critical of other movements such as the Muslim Brotherhood, his own ideas were not settled or clear. The fall of the caliphate and division of Muslim lands had led to calls for unity that were split between those who supported unity through Arabism and those who supported unity on an Islamic basis.

Al-Khayyat considered al-Nabhani's rhetoric somewhere between the two, and felt that initially his discourse when he first met him was closer to that of Arabism than to that of Islam.[19] It was the severe shock of the loss of Palestine that produced a 'common feeling' among people with differing viewpoints that something had to be done in its immediate aftermath. Initial efforts to find a solution saw people with disparate or vague ideas co-operating towards reactionary goals, before going their separate ways based on the development of their differing ideologies.

Al-Nabhani wrote three works that indicate the progression of his thought between 1949 and 1951. The first was the book *Inqath Filistin* (Saving Palestine) which was published in 1950, with the introduction dated January 1950 stating that the book covers events of the twentieth century up until the end of 1949. The first important point is the philosophy al-Nabhani adopted, with a call to action based on thought rather than preceding it, in order to be productive.[20] The second important point is that the loss of Palestine, and not the fall of the Ottoman caliphate, is at this time identified as the worst event to have happened to the Arabs in modern history, and the prime enemy behind the loss and continued situation was the British, with the Jews and the Americans also playing their roles.[21] The third important point is that Arabism is continually linked to Islam throughout the book, with the Ottoman caliphate praised when it recognises the philosophy that the 'Arabs are one people who possess an eternal message, Islam, and the Turks are partners in that message since it became their message.[22] To further confirm the point, the idea of Arabism and Arab nationalism stripped of ideology, and left as a nationalism or identity by itself, is considered an incorrect, sterile idea, which would not lead to any progress for the Arabs and had proved to be a failure.[23]

The book certainly did not look at the Ottoman caliphate in a romantic manner, with support for the actions of Muhammad Ali in trying to establish an Arab caliphate in the nineteenth century and narrating the story of Sharif Hussein's decision to side with the British against the Ottomans dispassionately.[24] Al-Nabhani praised Izz al-Din al-Qassam as a hero for identifying the British as the real enemy and fighting a true jihad against them,[25] and also narrated how the Arabs at the time had rejected the idea of reducing Palestine to a national identity rather than its remaining an Arab issue.[26] The white paper of 1939 (also referred to as the MacDonald White Paper) that the British government at the time adopted favoured the idea of an independent Palestine rather than the previous proposal to partition the mandate. Al-Nabhani considered it to be positive, but he criticised Arab countries for their inaction and inability to avail themselves of the opportunities it had produced.[27]

The book also talked about al-Nabhani's rebuffed efforts to purchase weapons from neighbouring Arab countries in preparation for war in 1947,[28] and how the Arab governments only entered the war as a result of popular pressure and therefore their presence was merely a superficial façade to give the impression they were engaged in a real battle.[29] Israel was identified as a European entity established as a bridgehead for continued Western imperialism in the region.[30] It should be the goal of all Arabs—whether male or female, adult or child, from the general public or the ruling classes—to save Palestine from the Zionists.[31] Saving Palestine would only be achieved through jihad, which relied on the Arab countries remaining under a state of war,[32] and would require Arab unity through a method other than that of the failed Arab League.[33] Al-Nabhani here proposed a United Arab States, with each country representing a *wilaya* (governorate) with its own local assembly, and a higher assembly at the state level headed by an elected leader who would have the powers of legislation and governance for the whole entity.[34]

Reading *Inqath Filistin*, al-Khayyat's description of al-Nabhani as not yet having clarified his ideas seems accurate. But although there was a lack of clarity in discourse and ideas with a mixture of Arabism and Islam, it is clear that the underlying basis and reference point was Islam. Ziyad Salama, an author and expert on Islamic movements and individuals, considers al-Nabhani's ideas of Arabism to be intrinsically linked with Islam at the root rather than as a cultural adage, which put al-Nabhani at odds with the ideas of Arab nationalism and Ba'athism even at this early stage.[35]

Al-Nabhani saw Islam as having Arab roots due to the centrality of the Arabic language to Islam, and identified Islam as the eternal message of the Arabs. This understanding fits with his upbringing and all accounts of his personality, whether from family or colleagues at the time. It is likely that just as al-Nabhani was developing his ideas, so too were those colleagues involved in the coup attempt, such as al-Rimawi, and while they shared ideas on unity of the Arabs and liberation from imperial influences, their differing basis led to a separation of paths thereafter.

The second work, *Risala al-Arab* (The Message of the Arabs), was a lecture al-Nabhani was invited to deliver to the cultural committee of the Arab League in August 1950. He was prevented from travelling to the conference by the government, indicating that there were clearly tensions between him and the authorities at the time. Instead he sent the lecture in writing to be delivered on his behalf. In it, he identified the revival of the Arabs as being linked to Islam, because it was Islam that revived the Arabs in the seventh century.

The decline of the Arabs was due to two external factors: the first was the Western cultural attack, which led to blind imitation of the West rather than making their own *ijtihad*; the second was the absence of carrying a message to the world, where he defined message as *din* in historical terms, considered equivalent to the modern term 'system of life.' The main problem was therefore not a military one in essence, but rather the cultural colonialism that prevented true revival. It stated that

> 'the message of the Arabs is the message of Islam, and this is the only message that the Arabs should adopt, particularly the Muslims from among them, in consideration that it is an ideological message which solves their problems.'

In closing, al-Nabhani called for the Arab League to adopt Islam as the eternal message of the Arabs, and to overhaul their respective education systems, putting in place a programme he alluded to in the lecture that would build the Arab mentality and mindset based on *ijtihad* rather than blind imitation.[36]

By May 1951 a short article in a journal showed al-Nabhani expressing his ideas regarding Arabism unequivocally and clearly within the context of Islamic culture, highlighting the importance of completely mixing the 'energy' of the Arabic language (which is the sole language that the revelation to the Prophet Muhammad came in) with the energy of Islam. In other words, the consideration of Arabic is purely linked to the linguistic aspect, which is only important due to its role in the original conveyance of Islam. The loss or lack of importance given to the Arabic language leads to weakness among the Muslim nation, because it is the key to understanding Islam and without it there can be no *ijti-had*. The article was explicit that Islamic politics was from the same genus as Islamic thought, and so modern political ideas such as the end justifies the means were rejected as alien to Islam and its political philosophy.

Al-Nabhani's ideas regarding state were also much more developed by this stage, and after outlining different aspects of the system in a basic form (such as the social system, political system and so on), he urged the reader that it was imperative to recognise that the Islamic system must be identified as unique in its own right.[37] Though his ideas were not yet as detailed as found in the initial literature produced after 1952 under the name of Hizb-ut-Tahrir, the evolution of thought was clear and the foundations had been clearly set.

Tracing the development in thought between *Inqath Filistin* in the beginning of 1950, and the journal article 'al-Nitham al-Islami' (The Islamic System), three major aspects can be noted. The first is that al-Nabhani had moved on from simply looking at the issue of Palestine, which became a starting point for thinking about the reasons for the decline of the Arabs and Muslim nation rather than an independent problem that needed resolution. Secondly, *al-Nitham al-Islami* highlighted the emergence of a clearer understanding of a comprehensive Islamic system, whose ultimate aim was not simply the liberation of occupied land (as understood in *Inqath Filistin*), but rather sought to carry Islam to the whole of humanity through its political state. The third aspect was one of continuation, because the message of Islam formed the basis of the message of the Arabs in all three publications. As mentioned by al-Ubaidi, al-Nabhani's early publications were Islamic in origin, and in al-Ubaidi's opinion had no element of nationalism to them.[38] This is based on the fact that even in *Inqath Filistin* it was made clear that Arabism stripped of the Islamic ideology was a false and failed idea.

This idea was developed in more detail by 'al-Nitham al-Islami', where Islam is explained in terms of being unique in its *fikra* (thought) and *tariqa* (method), or in other words in terms of its beliefs and rules (its thought), and the system which would protect and promote those beliefs while implementing its rules (its method). This was not a new concept to al-Nabhani, but he began to articulate it more clearly over time. Of his three works, only *Risala al-Arab* was initially adopted as part of the literature of Hizb-ut-Tahrir and was mentioned as such in the first editions of the party's literature published in 1952; but this was only for one year and was duly removed from mention by the time second editions were printed in 1953.[39] With respect to *al-Nitham al-Islami*, the basic outlines for the unique Islamic systems are developed further in his books published initially in 1952. As for *Inqath Filistin*, it was never considered as party literature and was fully repudiated by al-Nabhani, who told his son to 'throw it in the garbage' rather than read it after seeing him with a copy one day.[40]

## Al-Nabhani and the Muslim Brotherhood

It was around the same period in the late 1940s and early 1950s that al-Nabhani was sitting and studying privately with Dawud Hamdan and Nimr al-Masri, in what was to become the initial leadership of Hizb-ut-Tahrir. During this time, they were seeking to create a new Islamic party that would benefit from the experience of previous movements' failed efforts to revive the Arab and Muslim nations. Al-Nabhani's role as a senior member of the judiciary gave him the platform to organise and participate in conferences and meetings with other scholars with the same aim from across Palestine.[41] Nimr al-Masri had helped him with the publication of *Inqath Filistin*, which had made al-Nabhani a well-known figure among activists due to its wide distribution in the region (it was originally printed in Damascus).[42] Among the prominent young scholars and activists attracted to their ideas and involved from the beginning (before any publications) was Sheikh Abdul Aziz al-Khayyat.

Al-Khayyat was born in 1924 in Nablus to a middle-class family involved in trade. At a young age his uncle, Sheikh Fayad al-Khayyat, would take him to meetings involving other Islamic scholars. After he had completed his secondary education in Palestine, he travelled to Egypt to study in al-Azhar university from 1939 until 1946, whereupon he returned to Palestine having completed studies that qualified him to act as a Sharia judge.[43] While in Egypt he was active with the Muslim Brotherhood, joining the group in 1942 but keeping his membership unofficial in order not to adversely affect his visa status. Al-Khayyat stated that during this period he learnt politics directly from the office of the head of the Muslim Brotherhood, Hasan al-Banna, for whom he developed a lot of respect.[44]

After leaving Egypt he remained in almost daily contact with the head office of the Brotherhood, because he had been appointed to lead the internal enculturation process of the group to develop more Islamic understanding among its members. He was also responsible for starting up Muslim Brotherhood activity and cells in the region of Syria, Lebanon, Palestine and Jordan.[45] Al-Khayyat recounted how al-Banna, like al-Nabhani, also lost any faith in the rulers as a result of their inaction with respect to Palestine, telling him during a meeting in Damascus that 'there is no benefit in them, we need to rely upon ourselves'.[46] Consequently he was personally involved in the fighting in Nablus during the war for Palestine in 1947–8, and was responsible for a group of fifty local fighters, while liaising with the Iraqi army that was supposed to be in charge of defence of the area.

Though an active member of the Muslim Brotherhood both while in Egypt and after leaving, al-Khayyat also harboured some disillusionment with the movement, because it would accept members on a very loose association basis. Anyone who wanted to work for the sake of Islam could join, irrespective of their (lack of) understanding of what that would entail. According to al-Khayyat, most members had a very simple understanding of the religion, and only a superficial idea of what political Islamic work entailed, and therefore they were ill-equipped to face any pressures from the authorities.[47] In particular, he felt the weakest aspect of the Muslim Brotherhood was that it gathered people around it on the basis of prominent personalities rather than ideas,[48] and after the assassination of al-Banna al-Khayyat even began to have doubts regarding some of these personalities, believing that they were receiving direction and funding from British sources.[49]

According to al-Khayyat the other result of the assassination was that it left a void within the Brotherhood leadership as far as Islamic knowledge was concerned.[50] He raised this with the local leadership in Jordan first, and attempted to rectify the matter through his own cultural circles, but found they turned into social rather than study gatherings, confirming in his mind the problem of having no firm basis for membership. He then tried to contact the central leadership in Egypt to resolve these problems, but was unsuccessful.[51]

As al-Khayyat was struggling personally with his position in the Muslim Brotherhood, Al-Nabhani's ideas were becoming clearer and more defined. Al-Khayyat was particularly attracted to the idea of a single Islamic party that would operate across the *al-Sham* region (Syria, Lebanon and Jordan), as well as Egypt and Iraq, which had recognised and overcome the mistakes of previous movements that had been established during the period of Western colonisation. Although he felt that initially al-Nabhani's ideas were unclear and his discourse was inclined towards Arabism, he claims to have been able to reconcile al-Nabhani's Arabism with Islamic discourse through the expression that Islamic unity was dependent on the Arabic language and therefore on the Arabs. Therefore any Islamic revival would naturally start among the Arabs and within the Arab lands, and then spread to the non-Arab-speaking

Muslim countries.[52] This is expressed by al-Nabhani in *al-Takattul al-Hizbi* as follows:

> *'The entire world is suitable for the call to Islam; however, since the people in the Islamic lands are Muslims, the call must start there. Also, since the people in Arab territories (being part of the Islamic world) speak Arabic, and since Arabic is an essential part of Islam and its culture, the priority must be given to the Arab territories. Furthermore, combining the power of the Arabic language with that of Islam is necessary... Therefore, it is only natural for the Islamic State to be re-established in the Arab territories, so that it will serve as a nucleus for the Islamic State which will encompass all Islamic lands.'[53]*

As discussions between al-Khayyat and al-Nabhani deepened, al-Khayyat began to invite al-Nabhani to deliver lectures in the various Muslim Brotherhood centres he was linked to between the years 1949 and 1951,[54] and published articles by al-Nabhani and Hamdan in his journal *al-Wa'i al-Jadid* (The New Awareness). Ibrahim Ghosha, a former official spokesman for the Palestinian movement Hamas, was a young member of the Muslim Brotherhood in Jerusalem at the beginning of the 1950s when the first set of Islamic circles that he attended consistently were being run by al-Nabhani in the Brotherhood centre. Al-Nabhani's behaviour convinced Ghosha that he was a strong personality, and he would read to them from a book entitled *Hayat Muhammad* (The Life of Muhammad), written by Muhammad Hussayn Haykal, connecting the stories of battles during the early Islamic era to the reality facing the Muslims in the contemporary era.

As a result of al-Nabhani's regular invitations to speak at the centre, Ghosha assumed that al-Nabhani was a member of the Muslim Brotherhood at the time. He also heard rumours that al-Nabhani was offered a position as regional leader of the Muslim Brotherhood, but refused and instead went on to establish Hizb-ut-Tahrir.[55] Other rumours include a meeting between al-Nabhani and Sayyid Qutb in Jerusalem, when Qutb is alleged to have tried to dissuade al-Nabhani from separating from the Brotherhood—the source being a book published in 1979, two years after the death of al-Nabhani, under a pseudonym, which narrates the event without reference to anyone at the apparent meeting.[56] This is despite the fact that al-Khayyat and other senior members deny such a meeting ever took place,[57] and that the timings of the alleged meetings were impossible given that al-Nabhani was not in Amman during the periods Qutb was there.[58] For his own part, al-Nabhani stated that he had never had the opportunity to meet Qutb at all, whatever the circumstances.[59]

Similar rumours are quite common among Muslim Brotherhood activists, and a number of authors have made the assertion that al-Nabhani was an active member of the movement and quit over a difference of opinion.[60] This is not surprising given that al-Nabhani regularly delivered lectures in their centres, and both he and Hamdan contributed to al-Khayyat's journal while al-Khayyat was a prominent member of the Muslim Brotherhood. Hamdan even wrote an article in 1951 entitled 'Hasan al-Banna, the Reformer of the Era' in which he identified the failings or shortcomings of previous reformers while praising al-Banna for his understanding of Islam.

What is particularly interesting is that al-Banna's ideas were interpreted in a way that matched the philosophy of Hizb-ut-Tahrir, which had not yet officially been established. So al-Banna was praised as having a clear call, having understood Islam as *fikra* (thought) and *tariqa* (method), recognising that Islam had a unique set of systems, and following a methodology that began with building individuals who would then win the trust of the people. These individuals would be elected as the people's rulers, at which point they would implement Islam in a revolutionary manner in one go rather than the misunderstood gradualism of previous reform attempts, all of which corresponds to the ideas of Hizb-ut-Tahrir.[61] This was clearly different to any understanding of the Muslim Brotherhood from the post-Sadat era onwards, with the modern version of the movement more easily characterised by pragmatism, gradualism and assimilation into the existing systems in place, but it was possible that Hasan al-Banna's intellectual heritage could be interpreted in such a revolutionary manner, as Sayyid Qutb had done.[62]

The accuracy of Hamdan's assessment (and parts were clearly disputable) was less important than its evident appeal to a constituency of Muslims seeking revival, whether within the Brotherhood or not. The article went on to talk about how the Muslim Brotherhood was not limited to the Muslim Brotherhood group, but was rather a political liberation movement seeking to liberate Muslims and Arabs.[63] In other words, the article could be interpreted as part of the preparation for the emergence of Hizb-ut-Tahrir, which would represent a renewal from within the constantly progressing revivalist trend, benefitting from the experiences of previous failed movements.

For his part, al-Nabhani explicitly denied ever being part of the Muslim Brotherhood, and as far as he was concerned if he was given the opportunity to address people with his ideas then it was only natural that he would take it.[64] While young members of the Muslim Brotherhood, such as Ghosha, who would have been in his mid-teens at the time, may have looked up to al-Nabhani and assumed he was a member, there are no direct reports confirming this, whereas al-Khayyat provides the most reliable and clear primary source from within the Brotherhood leadership at the time. Al-Khayyat explicitly denied al-Nabhani ever being a member, but rather was himself the main conduit trying to reach a resolution between the two sides on his own initiative. He believed that al-Nabhani's ideas were much clearer than those of the Muslim Brotherhood at the time; Hizb-ut-Tahrir adopted rules based on Islamic jurisprudence (*fiqh*), with clear political thought coupled with a clear method to achieve its goals.

The scholarly background of al-Nabhani, as well as having been involved in many of the discussions himself as an Islamic scholar, was an attractive alternative to what al-Khayyat felt was a substantial deficit in knowledge in the Muslim Brotherhood leadership post-al-Banna. Importantly, al-Nabhani's fledgling party recognised that it was vital that membership was based on understanding and agreement with core party culture, rather than on an associative basis through paying a membership fee or simply signing up to a vague commitment to work for Islam.

As a senior member of the Muslim Brotherhood in Palestine at the time, al-Khayyat took it upon himself to try to convince his leadership of the shortcomings he perceived in the Brotherhood and encourage them to unify with al-Nabhani under a single Islamic party for the region. However, his efforts ultimately failed, with al-Khayyat laying the blame firmly at the door of al-Banna's son-in-law Said Ramadan, who apparently began to wage a public campaign against al-Nabhani at the time.[65]

In 1952 al-Khayyat left the Muslim Brotherhood and joined Hizb-ut-Tahrir. In his opinion, what separated the party from other movements was a combination of four aspects: that its call was clearly focused on restarting the Islamic way of life; that it adopted Islamic concepts and understandings, which it detailed in its literature regarding the different systems of Islam such as the economic and ruling systems, and did not allow individual members to hold contradictory opinions leading to disunity or lack of clarity; that it was concerned with political awareness built from an Islamic basis; and that it had a party structure to organise its membership rather than a loose, associative basis such as that adopted by the Muslim Brotherhood.[66] He claims to have been a victim of a campaign of slander by the Brotherhood as a result and was, for example, accused of being a freemason.[67]

There was a lot of conflict between the two groups, in part because many prominent members of the Muslim Brotherhood in the *al-Sham* region left and joined al-Nabhani, particularly those who were graduates from al-Azhar such as al-Da'ur and Zallum. Additionally, they were both aiming for the same constituency, and given that the Muslim Brotherhood had what could be considered a monopoly on political Islamic movements at the time it could have irked the Brotherhood that there was an alternative idea and party being promoted, especially since establishing an Islamic state was one of its own major proclaimed objectives. While the rumoured attempts regarding unifying the two parties appear correct, the evidence indicates that it was done on the personal initiative of al-Khayyat, as he stated and was confirmed by others.[68]

It is also notable that none of the original three who made up the first leadership committee of Hizb-ut-Tahrir—al-Nabhani, Hamdan and al-Masri—were members of the Brotherhood, and though some senior members and others did indeed leave the Brotherhood—with a source used by the British embassy stating that '[al-Nabhani's] theories have attracted many of the Ikhwanis to his party'[69]—by all internal accounts they made up a minority proportion of the membership of the party from the start.

## *The beginnings*

On 17 November 1952 a formal application for permission to establish a new political party was submitted to the interior ministry in Amman. Although this was the date for the formal application, there is debate over when al-Nabhani and his colleagues began to work as a party unofficially, with estimates dating back as far as 1949 for the year that the group was set up on the basis of the same broad fundamental beliefs.[70] The evidence used for these estimates includes speculative points such as *Risala al-Arab*, which was published in 1950, being included in the initial lists of publications of the party, and that al-Nabhani was prevented from travelling to Egypt in 1950, indicating political activity that had led to conflict with the government.

Other indications include early activists being referred to as the *nabahaniyyun* (literally, followers of al-Nabhani) around 1951 and early 1952 before the party was officially established,[71] as well as party members arriving in Iraq to win over supporters by 1952, suggesting that there was organised party activity before the application in November.[72] The original group of three—namely al-Nabhani, Hamdan and al-Masri, who would subsequently form the initial leadership committee—had been meeting and having discussions since the late 1940s, and it is likely that they formed the initial leadership sometime in 1950–1, prior to al-Nabhani resigning from his position on the appeals court and then running for parliament in August 1951.

The parliamentary elections of August 1951 were held a month after the shooting dead of King Abdullah during Friday prayers in al-Aqsa mosque in

Jerusalem, a result of rumours that he was pursuing a separate peace deal with the Israelis at the time. Both Hamdan and al-Nabhani stood for election.[73] Al-Nabhani's campaign centred on the issue of the liberation of Palestine, and he believed that he had gained enough support, including among Christian Palestinians, to have won but for the intervention of Glubb to fix the results against him. Al-Nabhani had been arrested during the campaign period and claimed that Glubb, whose loyalty remained to Britain throughout his time in the Middle East, approached him while under arrest to try to reach an arrangement whereby al-Nabhani would take a less confrontational stance against the British and work in co-operation with the authorities in exchange for a political position.[74] Although unsubstantiated, it has been mentioned that al-Nabhani was not permitted to travel to Alexandria in Egypt on the 20 August, only nine days prior to the elections, indicating friction with the government.

After Hamdan and al-Nabhani failed to be elected, al-Nabhani took up a lectureship in the Islamic College in Amman, which gave him the opportunity to win over students to his ideas, while at the same time travelling across Transjordan trying to build support. In this initial phase, many gathered around al-Nabhani because of his prominent public profile as a member of the judiciary and author of *Inqath Filistin*.[75]

Among the initial supporters were prominent young al-Azhar scholars other than al-Khayyat, such as al-Da'ur, Hasan Sultani, Zallum and al-Tamimi. Al-Da'ur was from Qalqilya in the West Bank, a colleague of al-Nabhani from university and veteran fighter in the Palestinian revolt and the war for Palestine. Sultani was from Terah near Tulkarem, while Zallum and al-Tamimi were both from Hebron and also veterans of the 1948 war. All three (among others) were involved in winning over supporters to the group prior to the official application to establish a party in November 1952. Zallum in particular was involved in early discussions with al-Nabhani regarding forming the group and the methodology it should adopt, based on the example it could draw from the life of the Prophet Muhammad.

Consequently, numerous individuals and groups of like-minded activists were won over to the party prior to its official establishment. In Hebron, young Muslim Brotherhood members would often sit together and read the Qur'an, with Zallum among them. Some of them felt that their work with the local branch of the Brotherhood was limited to memorising the Qur'an, and so used to ask themselves whether this would aid them in liberating Palestine, or implementing the verses they were memorising. As Zallum's ideas developed in line with al-Nabhani's call to establish an Islamic state that would have the necessary power to wage war against occupation, many others were also won over. The Brotherhood gave them an ultimatum to choose between the two. Deciding that Qur'an recitation alone would not free Palestine, they left with Zallum to join al-Nabhani.[76]

As a result of the political earthquakes in the region from the First World War up until the *Nakba*, there were other new, less well-known groups that had collected together to work towards Islamic revival and the liberation of Palestine, which were ripe for being won over to this new call.

A group of men from Hebron and neighbouring areas had gathered in early 1952 led by Hamza Tahbub. They had come together as the result of reading the Qur'an and asking questions about how the different verses related to laws and punishments could be implemented without the executive power of a state. In reaction, the group said that they needed to form a state, which they believed would come about when they had 313 strong Muslims on the same level of the first Muslim generation. This number correlated to the estimates of the number of Muslims who took part in the famous battle of Badr, which was the first major military conflict between the nascent Islamic state in Medina and Meccan society, with the Muslims of Medina winning despite being outnumbered approximately three to one. Consequently, people used to refer to them as the 313 Group. There were approximately fifteen members from Hebron, and Zallum and al-Tamimi visited them until they convinced them of al-Nabhani's ideas.[77] All of the group's members subsequently joined Hizb-ut-Tahrir,[78] and so instead of being labelled the 313 Group they were then referred to as the *nabahaniyyun*.[79]

In Irbid, Qadri al-Nabulsi formed a group of approximately thirty to forty teenage friends who would train together in preparation for the fight to liberate Palestine. He was taken to meet al-Nabhani in early 1952 and was impressed with his knowledge and strength of character, returning to Irbid to convince his colleagues to join al-Nabhani's group. Although one of his friends resisted, and suggested that they should remain separate while cooperating with each other, al-Nabulsi insisted that it was better for them to work under al-Nabhani and his new movement. As a result, all of the group except for the dissenter ended up becoming convinced and followed their leader into Hizb-ut-Tahrir.[80]

In Amman, where al-Nabhani was based in his teaching job, members of the military used to attend a daily lecture given at 10 am, which was attended by many locals who were referred to as the *jama'a al-Nabhani* (Nabhani's group) and were known to be discussing issues around the need to establish an Islamic state.[81]

These and other early supporters, all generally referred to as the *nabahani-yyun* and who were identified by their explicit call to establish an Islamic state, would initially study from pamphlets made up of a small number of pages attached together. This is because the literature of Hizb-ut-Tahrir had not yet been published, and so the lectures that al-Nabhani gave were printed and given out for study as early as 1951.[82] The pamphlets were subsequently collated and published as books, explaining the origin of the subtitle 'from the leaflets of Hizb-ut-Tahrir' often found on the book covers, and also helping to understand how it was practically possible to publish such a large corpus of material at one time (including at least eight books written by al-Nabhani).

At the same time, students were encouraged to read more widely and to study from other authors' work. Among the works al-Nabhani advised them to study were Sayyid Sabiq's *Fiqh al-Sunna*, a work of comparative jurisprudence, Muhammad Asad's *Islam At the Crossroads*, Qutb's *Social Justice* and Haykal's *Life of Muhammad*.[83] They were also encouraged to study Islamic sciences such as *usul al-fiqh* (the principles of jurisprudence) and *tafsir* (exegesis of the Qur'an).[84]

During this period, al-Nabhani moved around a lot, travelling between Jerusalem, Amman, Damascus and Beirut, meeting people and delivering lectures, and helping to attract an initial following that would form the beginnings of Hizb-ut-Tahrir.[85] He was also working on the literature that would form the intellectual foundation of his new party. One of the first books published was *al-Shakhsiyya al-Islamiyya* (The Islamic Personality), which was used as the basis for his lectures at the Islamic College in Amman.

In the foreword written by Hamdan, it reiterated the theme that correct revival required definition, with a clear known aim and goal. Hamdan proceeded to criticise all previous attempts at revival, and specifically the Islamic revivalist attempts that either looked at the problem of decline from specific, limited angles, such as the spread of religious innovation or the lack of morals; or were apologist in nature, seeking to refute the idea that Islam was incompatible with modernity and therefore resulted in adopting modernity as a solution for the decline of the Muslims. He then called for an 'aware revival', built on an Islamic personality with a unified viewpoint of life, which had been lost over time due to the creeping influence of secularism that separated religion from life's affairs.[86]

Al-Nabhani began the book by differentiating between knowledge and culture, defining knowledge as universal while culture was specific to the people who produced it. That the Qur'an encouraged people to ponder over

God's creation in its entirety, and specific elements as evidence of the necessity of a Creator, had historically fostered enlightened thought among Muslims, which encouraged them to study all different manner of sciences and philosophies, while remaining informed from an Islamic basis. It was this basis, a viewpoint defined by the commands and prohibitions of God, which created the Islamic personality and revived the Arabs.[87] Though the book represented the second element of Hizb-ut-Tahrir's initial literature after *Risala al-Arab*, it was the first substantial publication that remained as part of the party's adopted literature beyond 1952—though it was radically altered and added to by the early 1960s when it was re-published as three volumes.

Al-Khayyat has claimed that the book was drawn out of notes he had written for al-Nabhani, which al-Nabhani then corrected and amended before compiling them in the finished publication.[88] According to other members, al-Nabhani would often share initial drafts of work with his supporters and other scholars at the time to gather feedback, before revising and publishing a final version that took into account criticisms and suggestions.[89] It was in this manner that numerous initial books that formed the intellectual material of the party were published in 1952, listed in the first edition of *al-Dawla al-Islamiyya* (The Islamic State) and including *Nitham al-Islam* (The System of Islam), *Nitham al-ijtima'i fi-l-Islam* (The Social System in Islam), *al-Nitham al-iqtisadi fi-l-Islam* (The Economic System in Islam), *al-Nitham al-hukm fi-l-Islam* (The Ruling System in Islam), *al-Shakhsiyya al-Islamiyya*, *Risala al-Arab* and the lone publication by someone other than al-Nabhani, Hamdan's *Usus al-Nahda* (Principles of Revival).[90]

The intention behind the publication of this wide corpus listing the various details of these systems derived from Islamic sources is outlined in one of the introductions written by al-Masri, stating that 'this work is not intended to be academic material to defend Islam... rather what is intended by these studies is to carry the call to Islam, and is part of the work to restart the Islamic way of life through the establishment of the Islamic state.'[91] The book covers had red titles on a plain white background, symbolising the belief that the Muslim nation would not move without sacrificing blood.[92]

Though a more collaborative approach to writing party material was used consistently in the early days, with al-Nabhani seeking feedback to improve and clarify the presentation of ideas, security made it much more difficult by the end of the 1950s. However, before the party was officially established al-Nabhani could generally travel locally and openly engage with others (though he had been prevented from travelling to Egypt in 1951 as previously explained), and despite friction between himself and the highest authorities he was treated with respect by the interior ministry prior to the application to establish a political party.[93]

While he gained a measure of support as some people invested hope that they would be able to liberate Palestine with him, many began to turn away as his ideas progressed from merely talking about the liberation of Palestine. Colleagues and other scholars, who were initially supportive of his general ideas, found that talking about the return of the Islamic way of life through the re-establishment of an Islamic state that would reverse the post-Sykes-Picot Middle East was too big a jump and unrealistic, and that al-Nabhani was either dreaming or mad.[94]

In the second edition of *Nitham al-Islam*, published in 1953, a proposed constitution containing eighty-nine articles was added to provide an example of the basis of a possible Islamic state the party was calling for. The first article stated that the Islamic belief was the basis for the state, constitution and legislation. The ruling system proposed was based on four principles found in the thirteenth article—namely that sovereignty was for the Sharia, authority belonged to the people, the appointment of a single caliph was obligatory and the aforementioned caliph had the sole right to adopt legislation.[95] A reading of the constitution outlined that the social contract was between the ruler and the people, whereby the people consented to be ruled by the caliph elected by them, on the agreement that he would govern them according to the constitution, which was derived from Islamic sources.

The proposed constitution could be described as a form of contractualism, with the Sharia providing its normative force in place of a rationally derived morality. Since the elected caliph had the final say in adopting legislation, it could be argued that the vision was an autocratic one with unrestricted power in the hands of the ruler. The counter-argument would posit that the caliphate was more closely related to a form of constitutionalism that would constrain the ruler, in that although he was responsible for taking the final decision on most constitutional and legislative matters, he was restricted by Islamic sources that could also be interpreted and challenged by any person, akin to a type of popular constitutionalism, though the final arbitration to determine whether an interpretation was ultimately valid or not if it was disputed would be referred to a court that could overrule the caliph, a form of legal constitutionalism.

As such, a form of accountability and balance existed, invested in the separate court system that would check the power of the caliph. The other critical aspect was that there was no concept of popular sovereignty in the legislative sense, but rather sovereignty lay in the Sharia, meaning that, as mentioned, any interpretations could be challenged by anyone and overturned if found to be invalid. This could be termed a type of Islamic constitutionalism, wherein the rule of law was paramount, state power was restricted and political participation was considered a duty under the overall Islamic tenets of enjoining good and forbidding evil.

## Making it official

There was enough support growing to warrant moving to the next stage of the party's development, which was to introduce it officially into the political arena by making the application in November 1952. The party opened offices in Jerusalem, and began printing a weekly publication entitled *al-Sarih* (The Clear/Frank). The application, which originally stated that the aim of the new party was to 'restart the Islamic way of life' through the establishment of 'the single Islamic State which implements Islam and calls the world to Islam'[96] was rejected by the government because it refused to acknowledge hereditary rule, rejected Arab nationalism, and emphasised that the Islamic bond was the basis of solidarity rather than the bond of nationality, which made it unconstitutional. Unable to get the government to accept the party's registration, despite communication that included the governor of Jerusalem mediating on the party's behalf, it was decided to register Hizb-ut-Tahrir as an association, which, under the still active Ottoman association law, simply meant announcing its establishment for it to be officially recognised.[97]

On 14 March 1953 Hizb-ut-Tahrir announced its establishment in *al-Sarih*, listing its organisation structure as Taqiudeen al-Nabhani (president), Dawud Hamdan (vice-president), Ghanim Abdu (treasurer), Adil al-Nabulsi (member) and Munir Shuqayr (member).[98] This led to an immediate reaction from the deputy interior minister, Ali Hasana, who sent a letter on the same day addressed to 'his honour, Sheikh Taqiudeen al-Nabhani and all of the respected founders of Hizb-ut-Tahrir', which said that after reading their announcement he had to inform them that any claim that the party had been officially recognised was 'without any truth.'[99] Within a fortnight a number of the respected founders were arrested, and on 1 April an order was issued to remove the party's signs from their office in Jerusalem, which was duly carried out.[100]

Initially, all of those mentioned in the organisational structure were detained other than al-Nabulsi. Al-Khayyat was arrested a few days later and taken to prison, where after three days he was met in the office of the prison warden by a delegation sent by Prime Minister Tawfiq Abu al-Huda. The three-man delegation discussed the party's activities with al-Khayyat, and indicated to him that if he were to leave the group he would be appointed mufti of Jordan, an offer he declined.

Another delegation met with al-Nabhani and the others, where they took the opportunity to explain that the party was not calling for violence or civil unrest but was rather using peaceful means to disseminate its ideas. While a number of members were being held, Zallum appealed for help to al-Nabhani's former colleague al-Sa'ih who was still the head of the appeals court, accusing him of sitting idly by while al-Nabhani was in jail. Al-Sa'ih took up the matter with the interior ministry and was given permission by Glubb to visit al-Nabhani in jail, where he attempted, unsuccessfully, to convince al-Nabhani to limit his activities to criticising the government and to abandon any call for change.[101]

In the meantime, other members had managed to collect thirty-seven prominent signatories, including members of parliament, lawyers and businessmen, to a letter to the authorities calling for the release of those arrested. The letter was then published in the newspaper *al-Difa'* (Defence) on 3 April. They were in fact released soon after, but al-Nabhani and Hamdan were then subject to enforced residency in Jerusalem, with Abdu and Shuqayr subject to the same conditions in Amman. The details of these orders were published in the newspaper *al-Urdun* (Jordan) newspaper on 10 April. This was only a temporary measure and al-Nabhani was able to return to work in Amman after eighteen days.[102]

Two months later, at the beginning of June, a document was presented to the Jordanian government requesting a reversal of the order to ban the party. It blamed the decision on 'the atmosphere produced by colonialism in the Islamic countries alongside a series of actions which have produced a blindfold upon the minds which prevent the correct understanding of the Islamic State, and resulting from that is the position taken vis-à-vis Hizb-ut-Tahrir.' The pamphlet then embarked on a long explanation that included the historical roots of European secularism, the decline of the Ottoman State leading to Western cultural invasion, and the difference between a theocratic state as understood by the West and an Islamic state as understood by Islam.

The analogy between a theocracy and an Islamic state was completely rejected, stemming from a rejection of the dichotomy between spiritual and material, meaning that in Islam there was no understanding of 'religion' and 'life' separated as understood by secularism, nor was there ever a formal religious clergy or Vatican-like entity. Consequently the laws implemented would not be considered sanctified or above question since they would be rules derived from Islamic jurisprudence, and therefore 'open to discussion' and to 'change, correction and removal according to correct *ijtihad*.'

The pamphlet went on to outline the motivation for the establishment of the party, explaining that 'when the society in the Islamic lands—and amongst them the Arab lands—is based upon foundations that contradict Islam... it is imperative to establish the Islamic State in order to restart the Islamic way of life, and carry its call to the World'. Therefore, the party was set up to re-establish the Islamic state to implement Islam through the ruling system, and given that the founders lived in Jordan it was 'natural for us to begin here, as a starting point for the call.'

It also clarified that any call to nationalism was in fact a 'call to imperialism', and indeed any call other than the Islamic call would be considered to be 'alien'. The pamphlet then mentioned that the party was obliged to express that 'any peace with the Jews, is a rejected crime, and the presence of any Jewish state or entity in any part of Palestine or other than Palestine, represents a great danger for the entity of the Islamic *Umma* (nation or people) and amongst them the Arab people.' It finally summarized that Hizb-ut-Tahrir 'works for the liberation of the Islamic *Umma*... from slavery... in all their affairs, and to revive them on the correct basis of the Islamic belief.'[103]

Given the lack of even a sense of willingness to compromise, along with unconditional rejection of the nation state, the pamphlet was likely to have further convinced the authorities that not only was it correct to ban the party, but that it was imperative to prevent its ideas spreading for the sake of the Jordanian regime's own survival. Al-Nabhani's stance, and hence the stance of his party, was seen as confrontational and threatening. Jordanian Prime Minister Abu al-Huda was rumoured to have commented that 'Hizb-ut-Tahrir is much more dangerous than the communists,' who were at the time themselves repressed by the government. According to al-Khayyat the government took as many measures as possible to prevent the spread of the party, including pressure on the media to deny it any publicity.[104]

The treatment of Hizb-ut-Tahrir stands in contrast to that of the Muslim Brotherhood, which successfully applied to be registered as an association in January of the same year, which may have been the inspiration behind al-Nabhani's attempt to do likewise. According to Taji-Farouki, the more sympathetic approach taken with the Brotherhood was down to a number of factors. Prime among them was that any political objectives of the Brotherhood branches in the West Bank and Amman were overshadowed by their social and moral reform projects. While the Brotherhood was more willing to take a more pragmatic approach vis-à-vis the government, al-Nabhani insisted on pushing his own revolutionary ideas, irrespective of official reaction.[105]

Despite the pressures on the founders and attempts to restrict travel and prevent the spread of the party, by the end of 1953 it had spread within Jordan and the West Bank, as well as to other countries in the region. With the publication of its literature, a more formal study process also took place alongside the larger talks and circles, which would take place in public.

The *halaqa* process was a weekly study circle where students read and discussed a party book paragraph by paragraph, under the supervision of a *mushrif* (literally, 'the one responsible') who had to be a party member, beginning with the first three central books.[106] When a student was considered to have sufficiently understood and embraced the ideas such that they affected his personality and activities, he would be offered official membership of the party, at which point they might deliver party materials to others as a *mushrif* himself.

Activities took place in a number of towns and cities including Amman, Jerusalem, Hebron, Jenin, Tulkarem, Irbid, Ramallah and Qalqilya among others. Lists of members at the time show that the party was attracting, and accepting, a wide range of people, including several Islamic scholars and judges, teachers, traders and barbers.[107] In Amman, activists described how every household knew someone who was studying with the party, with daily speeches in mosques in the capital where, in fiery political language, speakers would openly attack Glubb by name. This brazen approach attracted a number of people, with socialists reported to have come to the mosque and listened to the speeches from outside, as well as winning support among Christians who were impressed with the anti-imperialist stance taken.[108]

When al-Nabhani was in Amman he used to stay in a hotel close to the central al-Husseini mosque, where he would lead more in-depth study circles for supporters after morning prayers. He also used to give general talks and open circles to the public, and would spend time in the house of Ghanim Abdu where they would gather important personalities for discussions and debate.[109] In Jerusalem, al-Nabhani led regular circles that many there would attend, among them several secondary school students including Muhammad Dawud Owda, who subsequently became a member of the revolutionary council of Fatah, but was deeply affected by the ideas of al-Nabhani growing up and credits him with giving him a correct understanding of Islamic jurisprudence from that time.[110]

Based in Syria, Nimr al-Masri was one of the other three members of the leadership committee, who was very active in attracting new followers and influential in winning over apparently hundreds of supporters without resistance from the authorities at the time. Some of the first editions of al-Nabhani's books were printed in Damascus from where members would pick up copies and transport them into Jordan.[111]

There are claims that in Syria at that time Adib al-Shishakli made an offer to the party to take power in early 1953, during the period around the arrests of al-Nabhani and others. Although many of the younger activists from the period have no knowledge of this, and even consider it far-fetched due to al-Shishakli's politics, two members who were close to the leadership from the beginning, al-Khayyat[112] and Sheikh Fathi Salim,[113] have mentioned that the offer was made.

Al-Shishakli was a military ruler who had dissolved all political parties and banned all opposition newspapers before forming a one-party state, meaning that if his offer was serious he was in a position to deliver it. Ironically, his own brand of politics was nationalist, liberal and secular. The offer was conditional on al-Shishakli being president, or in other words caliph, something that al-Nabhani refused outright, believing him to be a wholly unsuitable candidate. Al-Shishakli went on to hold staged elections later in the year and was duly elected president, but he had lost most of his popular support and ended up fleeing the country after a counter-coup in 1954.

If accurate, his offer indicates the presence and impact of Hizb-ut-Tahrir among senior elements in Syria at that time, highlighting al-Masri's influence, as well as raising questions about either how serious al-Shishakli could have been, given his own political persuasion, or how far he understood what al-Masri and the party actually stood for—although, if true, he obviously believed that the party had sufficient support and credibility to lend him needed legitimacy.

In Lebanon, where al-Nabhani's family was based, the growth of the party extended into at least the second city of Tripoli by 1953, with al-Nabhani attending personally to take the oath of membership from attendees after they had studied sufficiently to be considered adept enough to teach others from the party books. When taking their oaths, al-Nabhani would also read *al-Fatiha* (the opening chapter of the Qur'an) over each person individually, after which they were informed that they were now permitted to hold circles with others and educate them in what they had learnt.[114] In addition, members from the party also travelled to Kuwait for work, leading to a natural presence, with the establishment of Hizb-ut-Tahrir in Jordan announced in a Kuwaiti journal in December 1952.[115] Students travelled to Egypt by 1954, and possibly as early as 1953, where they were also encouraged to spread the party's ideas.

While there was a natural expansion into these countries, al-Nabhani also deliberately sent members with specific assignments to complement this growth, as well as to other locations to promote the party. In particular, Iraq was targeted early on and a number of people travelled there including Khalid al-Hasan and Abdul Fattah Zayd al-Kilani.[116] They set about discussing their ideas and won over several Iraqis in Baghdad, including a large group under the leadership of Hussain Ahmed al-Salih who were previously connected to the Muslim Brotherhood in Iraq.

Another personality who was won over was Abdul Aziz al-Badri, an energetic and charismatic young scholar and imam. Al-Badri was born in 1932 and completed his Islamic studies under local scholars who granted him *ijaza* (permission) to teach by the early 1950s. Although the Muslim Brotherhood was present in Iraq at that time, its activities were mostly restricted to relaying information about its main headquarters in Egypt, and al-Badri did not consider their ideas to be clear in any case.

Before the members from Hizb-ut-Tahrir arrived in the country he was part of an association of scholars concerned with promoting Islamic morals. On meeting members of the group and hearing their ideas he, along with two others, decided to travel to Amman to meet al-Nabhani himself to discuss their ideas further.[117] After a successful meeting the group returned and al-Badri soon became one of the leaders of the party. Along with Hussain Ahmed al-Salih and six others, he presented a request to the government for an official permit to work as a recognised political party, which was submitted in 1954 and promptly rejected for being unconstitutional and contradictory to the hereditary system in place.[118]

Despite the restrictions on Hizb-ut-Tahrir, it was able to gain the beginnings of a foundation of support across the region within its first year. However, government pressure on al-Nabhani increased towards the end of 1953. When he received news that police had turned up at his office in Amman to arrest him he decided to leave the capital and Jordan. His departure deprived the party of its major personality in the main cities in Jordan and the West Bank where it was operating, and left a vacuum in the party leadership at the centre of the country's political life. Al-Nabhani initially travelled to Syria before returning to his family in Lebanon.

# 3

# TRYING TO ENTER SOCIETY

## (1954–1959)

*The poet is an individual from the Umma [Muslim nation], so it is essential that his poetry lives the issues that face his Umma. And the Umma is on its upwards journey, from the darkness of the night to the dawn of revival.*

Amin Shinnar, 11 August 1957, al-Bira[1]

*Freedom as understood by Islam is that people should not be enslaved to other people, and people should not be debased by others, and that the word of truth is used to empower the weak and to weaken the powerful. And that sovereignty belongs to the Sharia.*

Dawud Hamdan, 1953[2]

After arriving back in Lebanon, al-Nabhani chose Beirut as the centre for his personal activity and role as the head of the party. For several years, before being driven underground, he stayed with his family when not travelling to neighbouring Syria and elsewhere, as required. His usual daily routine as witnessed by his son began with pre-dawn prayers followed by reading the Qur'an, after which he would either read or write materials before taking breakfast. In the morning he would be busy with appointments and meetings, either at home or sometimes outside, before returning to have lunch. After a short nap of perhaps a quarter of an hour, he would again be busy with meetings and giving study circles until the evening. However, he always insisted on having dinner, believing that sleeping on an empty stomach would be unhealthy. In the evening, he would often sit at the table and write pamphlets and other party materials. Even at this early stage, he would not use the telephone at all for contact, believing it to be monitored, and would instead rely on messengers to receive instructions and send information.

Al-Nabhani's wife, Umm Ibrahim, who was originally from Haifa and like many Palestinian women at the time used to wear the *niqab* (face covering) when out in public, was entirely in charge of the running of the household. Despite being illiterate, she was also responsible for managing the family finances on behalf of her husband (al-Nabhani was famous for not being concerned about monetary issues, and was often out of pocket when out and about). This was in line with his understanding that a woman's primary role was to manage the household responsibly and to protect and support the husband, which Umm Ibrahim had plenty of opportunity to do during the time of Nasser's rule, due to the harsh criticism, even among close family, of Hizb-ut-Tahrir and al-Nabhani's stance towards him in the late 1950s. Al-Nabhani's son Ibrahim believed that in doing so Umm Ibrahim was fulfilling her obligation to the goals of the party.

Though a life of (largely underground) politics denied al-Nabhani's family his presence for extended periods of time, he was a parent who treated his children with a mixture of kindness and strictness according to the situation. Early recollections of his eldest son before the *Nakba* include sitting on his father's lap reading the newspaper to him at the table and correcting the four-year old's Arabic. After establishing Hizb-ut-Tahrir, al-Nabhani did not try to impose the party on his children, and instead used to talk to them in general terms about the political affairs of the day and the various activities he was involved in. His son rarely heard him talk about Hizb-ut-Tahrir to them directly, but would discuss and explain ideas to them and left it to them to decide on their own paths. Eventually, two of his three sons became members of the party[3] and one was a supporter.[4]

Even though al-Nabhani was forced away from the central area of the party's growth in Jordan and the West Bank, several accounts indicate numbers continued to increase for at the least the first year after its establishment. Academic and expert on Jordanian politics of the period Amnon Cohen notes that the party gained ground rapidly in 1953–4,[5] and that it was most successful in north-western towns of the West Bank including Tulkarem, Qalqilya and Jenin, while in the south Hebron and Jerusalem also witnessed noticeable growth.[6] Azzam al-Tamimi, a prominent Hamas sympathiser and critic of Hizb-ut-Tahrir, also stated that the party became the primary Islamic party in Palestine and Jordan during this initial period after its formation.[7]

Those who witnessed events at the time give similar accounts. Najib al-Ahmad, one of the founders of the National Socialist Party set up in Jordan in 1954, wrote that 'in the 1950s a religious Islamic party known as Hizb-ut-Tahrir al-Islami appeared on the scene, its leader being Sheikh Taqiudeen al-Nabhani, and through the use of religion this party spread in Jordan like fire through straw', and that 'this party displayed astonishing activity and its pamphlets were always found in people's hands.'[8] Munir Shafiq, whose father worked in the judiciary and was friends with al-Nabhani (who was particularly impressed with his knowledge of Islamic jurisprudence, despite being a Christian), mentions how the party imposed itself powerfully upon the political scene in its initial stages, and how as a young Marxist at the time (Munir later embraced Islam towards the end of the 1970s) he would debate with party members in terminological discussions over the meaning of state, ideology and so on.[9]

The party was particularly strong among the student population, in part due to its strength among teachers. Former Hamas spokesman Ibrahim Ghosha recalls how the majority of students were with Hizb-ut-Tahrir and only one or two were affiliated to the Muslim Brotherhood at the time, he believed mainly because the party had won over the majority of teachers and thinkers at the time, leading to their influence over their students.[10] According to Shafiq, the party was the strongest political group among students in Jerusalem until 1955, with 20 to 25 of his thirty-seven classmates aligned with it.[11] This is corroborated by activists at the time, with numerous accounts indicating how in towns such as Hebron and Tulkarem the majority of students attended party activities, with the young men particularly impressed with the first chapter studied in the party book *Tariq ila-l-Iman* (The Path to Belief), which explained the rational proofs behind the belief in a Creator and His Messenger, giving them a new confidence in their religious convictions. While the party had a strong presence among teachers, particularly those responsible for religious studies such as Sheikh Zallum, who was a teacher in Hebron, contrary to Ghosha's experience in Jerusalem, in other areas many teachers were more influenced by nationalist and socialist trends at the time.[12]

Soldiers and officers in the Arab Legion were also won over, with members claiming that in the early years in Jordan hundreds of them were studying with the party. Anyone from the army who was involved with the party was ordered to keep their affiliation hidden, since any suspicion of involvement with the political opposition would result in their expulsion from the army, which in fact happened to a number of members. The government issued directives to contain Hizb-ut-Tahrir's activities in the armed forces by the end of 1954.[13]

Glubb, who was the head of the Arab Legion and the 'mainstay' of the British position in Jordan,[14] wrote that while the 'Muslim Brethren' were 'fanatically anti-foreign and anti-Western', the 'Freedom Party' as he termed Hizb-ut-Tahrir was 'even more extremist' and 'narrower and more bitter in its xenophobia' than the Brotherhood, in his opinion. This contradicted an earlier assessment from Jordanian sources, which reported that the movement was similar to the Muslim Brotherhood 'but more civilized'.[15] Glubb's view became orthodoxy, as highlighted by the British Embassy in Amman describing the party as 'a group of Muslim extremists whose attitude towards such matters as cooperation with the West is hardly distinguishable from that of the Communists'.[16]

At the time, Glubb believed that the Russians were financing Hizb-ut-Tahrir, as opposed to the more common rumour that the US was funding the party. His stated viewpoint matches an account in which he was sitting with a group of Arab soldiers and mentioned that the party was established by Russia. Fathi Abdullah, a member of the party, was present and unable to restrain himself, raising his hand to debate Glubb on the issue. When allowed to speak, he asked Glubb how the group could have been established by Russia, when its stated goal was to establish Islam (which went against the atheism of communism). Glubb smiled and replied that perhaps Fathi was correct, but this is what he thought—a point that he emphasized in his biography where he asserted that 'Russia has often supported rival parties at the same time, merely in order to produce anarchy.'[17] Fathi Abdullah was retired from the Arab Legion two months later without explanation.[18]

The early popularity and spread of the party is generally attributed to its providing a new idea, emerging at a time when others in the Palestinian leadership were largely left-wing and/or nationalist, such as the Ba'ath party, the National Party and the National Socialist Party.[19] Shafiq stated how the idea of creating a new state first to liberate Palestine was innovative and won people over. This is an analysis shared by Ziyad Salama, who believes that as the Palestinians emerged from the trauma of the *Nakba*, the party offered a radical vision that which was wider than just Palestine, and the novelty of the idea won people over. With the weak presence of the Muslim Brotherhood and its lack of overt political involvement in society, Ghosha believed that al-Nabhani's constant talk about the comprehensive enculturation of Muslims was attractive,[20] and activists recall that they were largely alone in representing Islam in the political debates against the communists and nationalists that were dominant at the time.[21] This quick uptake apparently inspired great confidence among some leading members, with Hamdan reported to believe that the party would take power within as little as three months.[22]

Al-Nabhani's view was more measured, believing that it would take at least ten years, but no more than twenty-five, and the most realistic timescale for the party achieving the establishment of an Islamic state between thirteen and fifteen years.[23] At the same time, al-Nabhani initially believed that any movement that did not achieve its goal within twenty-five years had failed and should leave the work to others.[24] Activists varied, and while a number were not overly expectant, it appears that there were at least a few who threw themselves into travel and activity, sacrificing their studies, seeming to believe that they were on the verge of victory within the first years (which in turn led to despondency when this was not achieved).[25] Whatever the case, the spread of the party locally and across the region gave the leadership confidence that their ideas could lead to the revival of the society through the sparking of an intellectual and emotional revolution, but were wary of the obstacles that lay ahead.

### From emergence to lift-off

Although Tahrir had spread impressively in its first official year, a result of the combination of having strong personalities such as al-Nabhani and al-Masri and the novelty of its culture, many of the supporters were not fully cognizant of the party's ideas. This was highlighted in the perceived difference in the depth of understanding between al-Nabhani and the general members at the time, something that was unsurprising considering al-Nabhani's background and intellect, coupled with his process of discovery over years of debate, discussion and experience, before being primarily responsible for writing the corpus of the party's material.

Early activist Qadri al-Nabulsi recalls that he and his colleagues used to think that if they could understand even 5 per cent of what al-Nabhani was talking about it would represent a great amount of knowledge for them.[26] Others remember sitting as teenagers in their study circle reading *Nitham al-Islam*, which was the first book new recruits were taught from, with a limited understanding that they were studying Islam with an entity called Hizb-ut-Tahrir, and recall how the one responsible for teaching them would talk while they would sit there understanding nothing.[27]

This was not limited to the younger recruits, with more mature figures from the time also concurring that to begin with they found the ideas difficult to comprehend.[28] This lack of clarity and confusion is something that the party leadership had expected, accepting that the ideas they were delivering would be in terms and meanings that would be unfamiliar to what society was accustomed to, and that their understanding of Islam and its role in life's affairs would appear alien to begin with, after years of misunderstanding and foreign influences that preceded the party's establishment.[29] The books on their own were of little help, given that they were written with the intention that they would be taught and explained in the study circles, and so some of those who purchased them before knowing about or studying with the party found them difficult to understand and off-putting.[30]

Along with the leadership of al-Nabhani, Hamdan and al-Masri, it rested with senior members around them such as the scholars Zallum, al-Tamimi and Sultani, to explain these ideas to others. It is natural that some of the initial supporters and activists had more enthusiasm than understanding in the early days as more people were beginning to study the party's ideas in their formalised system of circles. Even though the number of actual members, who were the only ones qualified to lead a study circle, was not that high, there was a strong demand among people to study with the party, and so each member took responsibility for a large number of circles at one time. As an example, Faruq Habayib, a teacher from Tulkarem who fought alongside Sultani as a teenager in 1948 and was involved in the party well before its official establishment in 1952, was responsible for fourteen study circles every week in his area, two every day.[31] With each study circle at the time consisting of up to ten people, there could be many more students than members, and this was just the number of attendees within the private study circle system, quite apart from the greater numbers that would attend public talks and circles.

By early 1954 the activities and presence of the party were established across Jordan and the West Bank. In February 1954 internal statistics provided by party members estimated that in Nablus, Jericho, Jerusalem, Jenin and Tulkarem they had 70 per cent public support, while in Amman and Hebron that support reached 60 per cent.[32] Though the figures may have represented an over-optimistic evaluation rather than verified support—and it is unclear exactly what the public was supporting, other than the broad outline of the goal of establishing an Islamic state to then liberate Palestine, or what that support entailed—they indicate that the members at the time believed, and not without reason, that their call was beginning to reach the masses. In the same year, al-Nabhani released a short booklet that explained how the party had moved from its initial enculturation stage into what he termed as the *nuqta al-intilaq* (departure point).

From the beginning the party had defined the method it adopted to establish its aim, derived from its reading of the Prophet's life in Mecca where he faced resistance to his call to Islam up until he was able to establish his authority in Medina. This was articulated as passing through three phases: the first phase was enculturation to develop the party culture in the minds of individuals; the second phase would occur when the party structure entered into and interacted with wider society; and the third and final phase would be the 'ruling stage', which resulted from acquiring the authority throughout the *Umma* in order to impose the ideology upon the society, meaning the complete and comprehensive implementation of Islam in one radical and revolutionary shift.[33] At this point the party was seeking to move from its enculturation stage into interacting with wider society, and the booklet *Nuqta al-Intilaq li Hizb-ut-Tahrir* (The Departure Point of Hizb-ut-Tahrir) was to address how this was to be done.

Al-Nabhani felt the need to write the book at the time because he believed that the party was about to reach its most dangerous stage, just before it came into intellectual conflict with prevailing societal norms. He explained that the next stage would result in becoming a party that would impose itself on the society, sparking off a comprehensive intellectual and emotional revolution. The main obstacles at this point would include 'those enamored with foreign culture' as well as other organisations working within society pursuing other aims, but that the party should not 'aim for them nor busy themselves with them', believing that any issues resulting from them would be resolved naturally by engaging with society directly, leading either to the sidelining of other points of view or influence over them.

At this point, the party would extend its activities from general public talks and private, concentrated study circles to also include what al-Nabhani termed 'adopting the interests of the *Umma* and exposing the plans of the imperialists.'[34] In practical terms, this resulted in a more overtly political face addressing contemporary international events and policies in terms of their publications, with regular pamphlets addressing issues as they occurred over the coming years, such as the Baghdad Pact, the Eisenhower Doctrine and events in Suez.

The reality of society at the time was assessed to be that while 'all of the Islamic *Umma* know that they are in a bad situation and that they require a sincere, aware leadership', this realization was unclear due to society being 'an un-Islamic society, where the ideas of capitalism and democracy rule and western culture dominates' and the 'system of capitalism and democracy is implemented over it.' Rather than Islamic thoughts leading the people, they were instead led by 'patriotic and nationalistic feelings', whereas Islam remained as a spiritual inspiration rather than a practical solution, except in social areas regulating relations between men and women.[35]

These thoughts were not only dominant in society; other groups were also considered as being subject to the same confusion. The difference was that the party would carry the call of Islam 'as an intellectual leadership from which a system emanates' as an alternative to the intellectual leadership offered by the West, which was secularism, from which capitalism and democracy emanated. This meant that there would be an inevitable clash between the ideas of the party and the ideas dominant in society, and the only weapon the party carried was Islam alone. It was 'not correct to use any other weapon, and the intellectual aspect is the one which is necessary for the party to be armed with.'[36]

The booklet also explained the need to impress upon society the uniqueness of Islamic ideology, and the danger in trying to make false comparisons with dominant Western constructs, common in Islamic apologetics, which could confuse people as to the real nature of both. Therefore, it was incorrect

> 'to make the *Shura* (consultation) council comparable to the parliament, and not permitted to make the caliphate comparable to the President of the Republic, since this makes the visualization of the rule of Islam more distant. Rather it is necessary to rise above the reality, and explain the *Shura* council and the caliphate as they came in the Sharia rules.'

In the same manner, the use of the terms that in al-Nabhani's view were part of the hegemonic Western discourse such as ideas of 'social justice' and 'international peace' were to be avoided.

The practical lessons in how to present the party's ideology aimed at party members and supporters, was further detailed, with numerous examples regarding how to deal with various scenarios that they might commonly come across in their discussions with people. For example, if someone favoured the Western camp as opposed to the Soviets, due to the supposition that they were 'people of the book' as opposed to the atheist communists, it should be pointed out to them that the Western camp was entirely dominated by capitalism and not Christianity and so had nothing to do with religious background. If they heard people complaining about the moral degradation of society, with the spread of drinking, fornication and theft, they should be made aware that this was because of the lack of the implementation of Sharia punishments, since they were intended as harsh deterrent and preventative measures to protect society's values. This was all intended to impress upon the party's members that it was vital to make 'people see that these thoughts are meanings that can be touched' and that 'they should be dominated by the feeling that it is imperative for these thoughts to be present in the reality of their lives.'[37]

The need to radically change ways of thinking worldwide was also addressed, as was the fact that the party sought to make the Islamic way of thinking the basis internationally and replace the incorrectly sanctified position of science. Al-Nabhani believed that what he termed the 'rational way of thinking' was the correct root methodology for thinking, as opposed to the 'scientific way of thinking', which he considered to be a subset of rational thought.

While scientific thinking was suitable for testing out verifiable hypotheses under laboratory conditions and the like, al-Nabhani proposed that many things in life were not based on scientific thinking but rather rational thought. He explained that rational comprehension was that 'which comes about by the transfer of the reality via the senses to the brain', which, when coupled with 'previous information', led to an explanation of the reality that enabled the brain to issue a conclusion regarding it, and that this conclusion was 'the thought, or the rational comprehension' which was the true 'basis of thinking'. In this way, people think rationally looking at history to learn from past mistakes and experiences, or regarding logical realities, or when answering what al-Nabhani defined as the central question in any person's life: 'the comprehensive thought about man, life and the universe.'[38]

Most of these points were summaries extracted from party literature, which could be found in the books already published. It may be that the booklet was written to address the teachings of the party in a comprehensive manner at this early stage to either concentrate the minds of the members and supporters before embarking on what al-Nabhani believed would be a period of conflict—albeit of an intellectual nature—with society; or it could have been to ensure that all of its readers would have an understanding of the overview of the work and ideas of the party to remove or at least reduce any disparity in understandings. Though al-Nabhani and other senior activists had suffered some pressure from the authorities by this stage, including the arrest of numerous senior members at the start of 1954—Zallum, Hamdan, Abdu and others[39]—most members and supporters had not been involved in such conflicts.

Indeed, the ideas of the party were considered fashionable among the elite in Amman, where it was considered that its arguments and views were normally dominant in any debate given its intellectual nature.[40] A hint of the early appeal was recorded in August 1952 by Jordanian sources in Amman who believed that the group's objectives were similar to those of the Muslim

Brotherhood, 'but more civilized', seeking 'a state run on Western administrative methods, but with a religious background.'[41]

While theoretical, intellectual debates were one issue, taking on political issues and vested interests would be a different matter. Al-Nabhani seemed to recognise this, and made it clear that when antagonism against the generality of members spread, whether from the authorities, other movements in society or the general public, there was no place for individualism and defence of oneself, nor should members respond to abuse or being sworn at. Rather, the party had to 'avoid conflict with the people of the land completely, and make the conflict against colonialism as one between it and the *Umma* as a whole, not the party alone.'[42]

*Campaigning for an Islamic state*

The Jordanian general elections held in October 1954 were considered a good opportunity for Hizb-ut-Tahrir to interact with the wider society and introduce its ideas into popular consciousness. The idea was that the heightened political consciousness of the election campaign afforded ample chance to naturally win support for the party. Moreover, any victory would give the party a platform in the consultative council to address the government and promote its alternative message in public.

Not all were in agreement. Abdu, in particular, believed that it was not permissible to run in the elections, given that the system was un-Islamic, even with the proviso that the campaign call be purely Islamic, and that if elected the candidate only use his position to promote the call to Islam and not participate in government matters such as legislation. However, al-Nabhani insisted on running and taking a seat on the council if possible, considering it a platform for the party's call and ideas to reach as many people as possible, particularly other politicians and influential figures.[43] The campaign focused on speeches and meeting as many people as possible, rather than leafleting and party promotion asking for votes, and the activists would stress to people that the goal of the party for running was for 'the voice of Islam to be heard within the walls of parliament' as part of its work to call for the implementation of Sharia.[44]

In total, six members of the party ran as independents: Dawud Hamdan in Jerusalem, al-Da'ur in Tulkarem, Zallum and al-Tamimi in Hebron, and Muhammad Musa Abdul Hadi in Jenin.[45] Out of the six, only al-Da'ur met with success in the elections, with members believing that fraud prevented any others from victory. In his biography, Glubb admitted that election fraud was a regular occurrence in Jordan, but claimed that it was impossible to ascertain whether these particular seats were won through falsification of the results. Glubb's own account was more concerned with refuting the common rumour that he was responsible for manipulating election results, and indeed politics in general in Jordan.[46] In the case of al-Da'ur, people had surrounded the hall where the votes were collected and forced the count to take place in public to ensure that a true total was announced.[47] However, there were also real political considerations that led to al-Da'ur's victory.

Irrespective of any vote-rigging that occurred, there were substantive differences that led to al-Da'ur's comfortable victory at the ballot box in Tulkarem. Habayib nominated al-Da'ur as the party's candidate, which was practical politics, because al-Da'ur's family was very influential in Qalqilya, and the strength of the party in the town itself had reached such a level of popular support that people attending community celebrations such as wedding processions would chant 'long live Hizb-ut-Tahrir.'[48] Although they had no tribal leadership in Tulkarem, unlike in Qalqilya, the party's presence in Tulkarem was also strong, guaranteeing that it would win the majority of votes in both of these major voting locations. Given that the opposition was also considered to be strong, Habayib suggested that the party ran a single candidate rather than both al-Da'ur and Sultani, in order not to split the vote. Al-Nabhani agreed with Habayib's proposals, and al-Da'ur won through a combination of family ties, party support and because he was a well-known figure who had won the respect of the people in the area, due in part to his participation in the Palestinian uprising in the 1930s and the fighting in 1948.[49]

Substantive discussions revolved around the issue of working for the return of an Islamic state and ruling by what Allah had revealed, and how Islam was a complete ideology, meaning a comprehensive belief from which a complete system for life's affairs emanated. The word caliphate did not feature in the discussions with numerous sources, who mentioned that for the first few years the term Islamic state was preferred because of the word's connation at the time being more spiritual than political.[50] The election period saw most conflict emerging between the party and nationalists. Sometimes discussions were not taken to kindly, with younger members physically attacked by nationalists in some of the villages they visited to promote the party. The campaigns saw concerted efforts by the party, with candidates travelling to support one another across all areas and members returning from neighbouring countries such as Syria to lend their support.[51]

The political approach advocated by Habayib paid off in Tulkarem, and al-Da'ur's candidacy was apparently so strong that other candidates generally accepted that most voters would select him for one of the two seats available, and were reduced to asking people to vote for them as their second choice.[52] Given that many people voted according to parochial interests or tribal loyalties, the lack of success of Zallum in Hebron was surprising, given the strength of the family in the town, and it was not the first (or last) time that there were accusations of electoral fraud in the Middle East. Some members claimed that fraud was brazen, with entire ballot boxes being replaced.[53] At the same time, others conceded that while their campaigning for people to base their relations on Islamic brotherhood rather than tribal loyalty may have had some positive results, they were not necessarily successful in leveraging political realities in the manner that Habayib was able to, and if voting was close any manipulation of the results would not have been so apparent as to have caused a major outcry.[54]

Although the people of Tulkarem had managed to ensure that their vote was respected and al-Da'ur would take his place in parliament, the party faced further official restrictions when its new publication, *al-Raya*, was banned at the end of October, only a few months after it was started in place of the previously banned *al-Sarih*.[55] The magazine had been used to good effect in the region, with activists in Egypt receiving copies and keeping up to date with discussions and arguments through it, and it helped them spread their ideas in a difficult environment. Most of those involved with the party were graduates from the Islamic College in Amman who were studying in Cairo. While they used to read in local Egyptian papers that the party was dominant in the streets of Amman, the difficulty of combining study with party activities, coupled with the distance from the party centre and al-Nabhani in particular, resulted in the majority of members in Egypt at the time leaving the party.

As a result, the party began to support specific members financially to ensure they would be able to dedicate their time to party activities rather than studies or work. A number of capable members were encouraged to go to Cairo to aid activities there, among them al-Kilani, who had previously been in Iraq. Interestingly, given the animosity shown by the Muslim Brotherhood towards Hizb-ut-Tahrir in Jordan at the time, with its structure in Egypt largely decimated by Nasser a number of those associated with the Brotherhood met and talked with Hizb-ut-Tahrir members on various occasions, including prominent author Khalid Muhammad Khalid, as well as Jamal al-Banna, brother of the founder Hasan. Others, such as Salih Ashmawi, who was expelled from the Brotherhood following disagreement with the new leadership under Hasan al-Hudaybi,[56] studied in the party study circles in the same period. However, the political and security situation in 1954 after the clampdown on the Muslim Brotherhood was difficult terrain for the mostly Jordanian Palestinian activists, especially with the rising popularity of Nasser-style Arabism and socialism, and thus little headway was made in the mid 1950s.[57]

Meanwhile, in Iraq towards the end of 1954 six members applied to the interior ministry for an official permit for the party to be recognised and participate in political activity. The six members were Hussein Salih, Sheikh Abdul Aziz al-Badri, Abdul Ghani al-Mallah, Khalid Amin al-Khadara, Abdullah Ahmad al-Dabuni and Muhammad Hadi Abdullah al-Subayti. The government rejected the application for largely the same reasons as the Jordanian government had the previous year, namely that the party's platform contradicted the constitution and opposed the monarchical system.

If the sense of déjà-vu was not complete, the rejection was appealed, with the appeal duly rejected, resulting in the publication of a leaflet by the party explaining its stance. As the party grew in Iraq, it initially attracted several Shia members because of its non-sectarian approach and acceptance of the Ja'fari school of thought (the legislative juridical basis of what is commonly known as Twelver Shi'ism) as a legitimate opinion within Islamic jurisprudence. Al-Subayti was one of the most prominent Shia members and was in contact with leading Shia scholar Muhammad Baqr al-Sadr, among others, in Najaf, leading to interaction between the party and the activists among the clerical class there at the time.

The party took a strident position against the Baghdad Pact, which strengthened relations between Iraq and Turkey in early 1955, before the United Kingdom joined in April of the same year, considering it to be the British counterweight to the developing US-supported Egypt-Syria axis. This development was interpreted as part of the imperial Anglo-American struggle over control of the region, and the party labelled King Faisal II as a British agent (seen in the same light as the Jordanian monarchy). This led to the arrest of activists distributing leaflets in 1955, and the signatories to the application for an official permit being arrested and briefly jailed before they were all released, though some were forced to pay fines.[58]

In Lebanon, the party was also spreading in Beirut and the south, particularly among the Shia community. The presence and activity of the party was very strong between 1954 and 1955, in part because Nasser's influence had not yet reached its zenith and he did not enjoy broad popular support there.[59] When al-Nabhani had gone to Beirut he became acquainted with Samih Atif al-Zain during his time investigating the various groups and Islamic activities there. At the time, two of the major groups were 'Ibad al-Rahman (Slaves of the Merciful), which was an offshoot of the Muslim Brotherhood, and Jami'a al-Huda al-Islamiyya al-Shi'iyya (the Association of Islamic Shia Guidance) which was headed at the time by al-Zain. After a while, al-Nabhani apparently asked al-Zain tell him about the Shias' understanding of Islam, jurisprudence and Islamic government, along with their beliefs, because he did not know much about them. Ultimately, al-Zain ended up joining the party, and was the first person appointed to be in charge of the structure in Lebanon.[60] In its initial years in Lebanon, the majority of those who joined the party in Beirut were also Shia.

Despite apparently rejecting the advances of al-Shishakli in 1953, the party was managing to extend its support base in Syria through the efforts and contacts of al-Masri. The contacts were of sufficient importance that al-Nabhani would stay in Damascus to lead study circles for some of them. It was during one of these study circles in 1954 that he received a message that his eldest son Ibrahim had been badly burnt in an accident during a festival in Lebanon, leading to his hospitalisation. On hearing this, al-Nabhani left Damascus immediately after concluding the circle and returned to Beirut, where he found his son lying unconscious in a hospital bed. Ibrahim was later told that his father had stood at the door of his room, reduced to tears seeing the state his son was in.[61] His son recovered, but by 1955 the situation in Syria had become more difficult, with the first arrests of members there. Although the party had managed to gain support among some of the political and military circles it remained unofficial and had little impact among the general public beyond a few of the more religiously minded elements.[62]

While 1955 saw increased conflict with the authorities, particularly in Iraq, the situation was becoming much more difficult across the board back in Jordan. There were further legal restrictions, which affected the party's ability to spread its ideas. The government issued a prohibition on teaching political subjects in schools, which reduced the possibility of tapping into the student population as the party had been doing successfully up until that point.[63] In January of that year the government issued a 'law on preaching and guidance' stating that 'it is not permitted for anyone to teach or deliver a speech in any mosque if they are not an employee or previously permitted to do so by the Chief Justice',[64] which was intended to exclude party members from one of its most effective public platforms.

As a result, there were regular arrests of members as some of them attempted to continue their activity, despite the possible ramifications. The first to be arrested was al-Khayyat, who used to give twice-weekly lessons in the central mosque in Amman. Al-Khayyat protested his innocence, stating that he was neither preaching nor teaching, but simply explaining verses from the Qur'an. The judge, who was likely to have been sympathetic to the cause, as was the general case among the judiciary and other religious figures,[65] issued a not-guilty verdict and al-Khayyat was duly released. He was arrested a week later as a result of another lesson he gave, this time spending ten months behind bars.[66] Despite the restrictions, the party kept ordering its activists to deliver speeches in mosques, and some were so resigned to arrest that they would bring their bags packed with their pyjamas along with a copy of the speech they were to read out.[67]

*Parliament and beyond as a platform*

Meanwhile, in parliament al-Da'ur was delivering long speeches al-Nabhani wrote for him, such as one given on 24 January in which he criticised a government proposal to introduce a new civil law to replace the Ottoman codes in place. The proposed legislation was in effect a copy of the Syrian civil law code, which had been issued at the time of Husni al-Za'im in 1949, and was based on numerous sources including European law (from France and Italy, which also formed the basis of Syrian and Egyptian civil law), as well as Sharia. Al-Da'ur's speech was printed and distributed across Jordan and the West Bank to maximize exposure for the party's view. He focused specifically on what he considered to be the piecemeal nature of the current legislature, with reference to the oppposing positions of French (and other) civil law versus Islamic law resulting in internally contradictory legislation.

Al-Da'ur then went on to criticise democracy for giving 'the people the right to legislate laws', which he considered to be 'wrong, and impractical.' It was wrong because 'people are not able to encircle all the needs of the multiple people, nor the relationships between them, and therefore any system they law down will be deficient in treating the human problems and arranging their relationships, and so will be contradictory', which would then require constant change and correction as the shortcomings became apparent, and so it was required that the Creator lay down the system, given His all-encompassing knowledge. As for democracy's lack of practicality, in what can be considered a version of elite theory[68] al-Da'ur went on to explain that since a large number of people cannot draft laws, they have to appoint a parliament to do this on their behalf; a government is then formed from the parliament and a few individuals end up drafting legislation, which is then debated by a few others before a vote is held to pass it. Ultimately, he concluded that in reality only 'a few people draft the laws, not the people or the parliament.'[69]

The speech also debated the veracity of the idea of freedom, considering it to be an impractical utopian idea that was flawed in its basis, because people require society to be organised to avoid anarchy. He stated that the 'reality of life necessitates the protection of the weak from the strong, and to help those who are not able to get what they need for life,' and that 'there is no complete freedom for people except that at the expense of the interests of others, and this means the transfer of life to a barbaric state where the powerful rule, and take advantage of the weak', concluding with the admission that it was recognised that there was no practical reality to the idea of freedom and hence its advocates 'are forced to say that the freedoms are unrestricted as long as they do not impinge upon the freedom of others.'[70]

Another example of al-Da'ur's use of parliament to promote the alternative ideology of the party was his response, also printed and distributed, to a statement in August 1955 made by the relatively new government of Sa'id al-Mufti (who was appointed prime minister after Abu al-Huda in May and lasted until just November, before the even shorter-lived one-week government of Hazza Barakat al-Majali, who was brought down by popular protest against joining the Baghdad Pact at the end of 1955). The statement regarded Jordan's role as an Arab nation in the context of the continuing unresolved problem of Palestine, and announced that 'this government believes with a deep belief that the Jordanian people are a part of the Arab *Umma*'. Al-Da'ur called it meaningless, since according to him the meaning of *Umma* was a nation:

> gathered upon a single belief from which a system emanates—and the Arabs are not an *Umma*, rather they are a people (*shab*), and the *Umma* [in its true meaning] is the Islamic *Umma* [not the Arab *Umma*], and the Arabs are a people from the peoples who embraced Islam.

He went on to criticise nationalism, stating that 'it is not for any Muslim who believes in Islam to have nationalistic goals, since the one who believes in Islam does not believe in tribalism, and does not believe in race but rather in Islam, where every tribe and every race is equal,' and rejected the government's statement that Palestine was an Arab issue, identifying it rather as an Islamic one—an issue between Muslims and the West, not Arabs and the West. While he considered that it was as a result of US and British policy to treat the issue of Palestine as one of economics and refugees, he believed that 'in reality it is a political military issue'. Al-Da'ur noted the government's statement that it had a responsibility with respect to its sister Arab nations and the Palestinian question. He asked what exactly that entailed and whether the Jordanian government even had a point of view with respect to how to proceed to deal with the case.[71]

At the time, the monarchy felt under threat from the rise of Nasser in Egypt and the rising tide of a socialist Arabism, with Syria electing Shukri al-Quwatli president in 1955, which led the two countries to seek closer ties. This put pressure on the Hashemite monarchies in Iraq and Jordan, and as a result political circumstances in Jordan worsened for all illegal opposition to the king—basically the majority of the opposition—irrespective of its ideological bent, with communists, nationalists and Hizb-ut-Tahrir members all facing increased security service efforts over the next few years to prevent them establishing any kind of effective leadership.[72] While prior to 1955 jail had been the destination of a select few among the leading members, a wider crackdown on party activity was now felt by members and the public alike. A number of Tahrir members were arrested as a result of contravening the preaching and guidance law; others were charged after leaflet distribution.

Although it would not have made sense to punish people for distributing the words of al-Da'ur, given that he was saying them openly in the parliamentary council at the time, the first published political address of the party, issued in September 1955, regarding US Secretary of State John Foster Dulles's speech on 26 August regarding the 'Arab-Israeli' problem[73] led to the arrest and trial of activists in Amman, and ultimately resulted in an embarrassing loss for the government after the court found them innocent.[74] However, repeated arrests were enough to disrupt activity and dissuade others from joining the party. This was the view of Abu Mu'tasim, around the same period, who as a young man in a refugee camp in Ramallah heard about Hizb-ut-Tahrir. While he and others in the camp were sympathetic to the few party members there and their views, local activists such as Amin Shinnar, a teacher and poet, and Nitham Hussein, a tailor, were arrested often enough to intimidate others from joining.[75]

While members had to deal with confrontation with the authorities, their daily interaction—whether in public cafes or during visits to people seeking to win their support—found them engaged in public arguments and discussions that would naturally involve supporters of other political factions. In his memoirs *Sabili illa Allah* (My Path to Allah) Dawud Abdul 'Afw wrote how, as a Ba'athist at the time, new members of Hizb-ut-Tahrir would actively seek him and his colleagues out to test their new ideas against them, causing them a headache to the extent that they had to arrange their own private sessions to work out ways to refute the 'Tahriris' in argument. At the same time, 'Afw mentioned how the Muslim Brotherhood violently opposed Hizb-ut-Tahrir, but that members of the party avoided reciprocating, a matter he found surprising given their pursuit of debates with socialists and nationalists like himself.[76]

This is consistent with most accounts from activists at the time such as al-Khayyat, Zallum, Habayib and others, who claimed they were not concerned with the Brotherhood, despite the antagonism shown towards them. On the other hand, Cohen mentions that there was fierce competition between the two groups because they were both vying for a similar constituency, with Hizb-ut-Tahrir accusing the Brotherhood of lacking any coherent positions on economic and social issues, as well as of political opportunism, for working for and against the monarchy, according to their interests; with the Brotherhood's response being that the Hizb-ut-Tahrir members were a cause of disunity and falsely claiming religiosity and piety.[77]

Whatever the case, Brotherhood publications sometimes contained material that was scathing of Hizb-ut-Tahrir, such as in an article published in the Brotherhood journal *al-Muslimun* (The Muslims) that mocked Hizb-ut-Tahrir members for being overly concerned with the Islamic state, to the point that they were instructed to repeat it 11,111 times a day on rosary beads, after which it was imperative for them to seek out people for the rest of the day and tell them it was not permitted to do anything until the state was established, and some even said that anything from jihad to liberating Palestine to praying was not obligatory without an Islamic state.[78]

Although previously seen as a loyal opposition, the Muslim Brotherhood was heavily involved in protests against the Baghdad Pact that rocked the Jordanian monarchy at the end of 1955. Under popular pressure, King Hussein dissolved parliament and ordered new elections, but this did not calm the rioting, so he considered it impossible to join the alliance, despite British and Turkish encouragement.[79] As a result of growing pressure from the opposition, encouraged by Egypt, and looking for ways to appease the public, in March the king ordered Glubb and most other British officers out of the country and Arabised the military,[80] which was a blow to British interests. Hizb-ut-Tahrir members did not generally participate in mobilisation of the street and protests under what they considered to be vague banners and slogans, believing them to be ultimately fruitless, an emotional distraction from the work of changing people's ideas and done on the incorrect basis of a nationalist struggle. The party lost some popular support as a result of its stance distancing itself from the street.[81]

Open elections, which pro-Nasser elements in Jordan would participate in freely, were called for October 1956 to try to relieve the pressure that was building against the monarchy. The continued ascent of Nasser and growing optimism among the general populace over a unified and independent Arab renaissance were a concern for the establishment, as well as continued agitation against the young king by the Egyptian propaganda machine (especially the *Sawt al-Arab* radio channel), targeting him as a British agent. The elections were the first to be considered free and fair in Jordan, and once again the party chose six candidates to run, with the only change being that al-Khayyat ran in Irbid while Hamdan, who had run in Jerusalem in 1954, was dropped.[82]

There was no change in the outcome, with only al-Da'ur winning a seat after claiming 3,440 votes in Tulkarem. Al-Khayyat officially won 2,593 votes, which placed him fourth out of seventeen candidates who ran in Irbid. He was stunned to have lost and convinced that the results had been doctored. A friend in the judiciary apparently confirmed this to him later, explaining that those registering the vote totals would remove the first digit from the amounts coming in, thus depriving al-Khayyat of thousands of votes.[83] But another activist, Qadri al-Nabulsi, was not particularly shocked by the result and travelled to Lebanon where he told al-Nabhani that he had been misinformed about the strength of support the party enjoyed in Irbid, particularly because al-Khayyat was not from the area originally and other movements had a stronger presence on the ground.[84] As would happen on other occasions, identifying a balance between optimistic calculations and sober analysis became impossible due to the murky nature of the political systems at the time.

The king invited Sulayman al-Nabulsi (no relation to Qadri), the leader of left-wing opposition coalition the National Front, to form a government. Al-Nabulsi accepted, and as part of his negotiations with the different political factions proposed that one of the two members of Hizb-ut-Tahrir, al-Da'ur or al-Khayyat, be appointed as minister of education. While al-Khayyat was agreeable to the idea, al-Nabhani ordered that the offer be rejected, considering that it was not permissible to be part of a government that was not based solely on Islam.[85]

The unity government enjoyed the almost full support of the parliamentary council; al-Da'ur was the only member not to give it a vote of confidence. He announced that he refused to give his trust to the government because 'the imperialists and the disbelievers could not have found a better government than this for its interests and to betray the Muslims', to the astonishment of Najib al-Ahmad of the Nationalist Socialist Party and others, considering that al-

Nabulsi and his allies were Arab nationalists and pro-Nasser, and likely thought themselves impeccable anti-imperialists.[86] Hizb-ut-Tahrir on the other hand considered that anyone who promoted Western ideas like nationalism, even in its Middle Eastern version of Arabism, was an imperialist tool, whether they realised it or not. (In any case, al-Nabulsi was not averse to co-operating with the British in Jordan, as highlighted in Foreign Office dispatches).[87]

Al-Da'ur became known for his consistent stances against the government of the day in parliament. Aided by his friendly personality, he built a lot of personal support and even affection from others who were not normally supporters of the party. He was nicknamed the 'turbaned representative' because he often wore a turban, which was associated with Islamic scholars. Anecdotally, a judge in Amman informed members that he was a supporter of al-Da'ur, but not of al-Nabhani, who could alienate people due to his confrontational and stern manner in debates.[88] At the same time, he cut a somewhat lonely figure against the government during his time in parliament. Although there was plenty of other opposition to the monarchy, as has been pointed out previously it was generally secular and nationalist in orientation.

As far as the Muslim Brotherhood—the other Islamic party—was concerned, it appears that it was not averse to collaborating with the monarchy as a loyal opposition or with the anti-regime leftists when expedient to do so. The party first received 'enormous encouragement'[89] from the government in the 1956 elections, and then supported the al-Nabulsi government when it formed in 1957. It then subsequently supported the king's decision to remove al-Nabulsi as prime minister in 1958.[90] Backing the monarchy, the Brotherhood was left to expand its influence as the only legally recognised party.[91]

Hizb-ut-Tahrir rejected the Hashemite monarchy unconditionally,[92] as well as the secular opposition of any stripe—the former as a willing British agent and the latter as unwitting imperialist tools. As a result of his stance in parliament, al-Da'ur was considered the 'most convincing opposition candidate', but due to his ideological views he was 'ill-suited to day to day co-operation with secular "revolutionaries"',[93] meaning that he was unable to leverage his position for political gain.

On the other hand, the Brotherhood's pragmatism allowed it to operate under different circumstances, avoiding a major clash with the authorities, and ultimately giving the party the opportunity to embed itself in the country and grow. Al-Da'ur was eventually expelled from parliament in 1958 by a vote supported by all except one other member of the council, and, stripped of his immunity, he was subsequently given a two-year jail sentence for 'publis[h]ing reports intended to shake the confidence of the people in the government.'[94]

Soon after the elections, on 29 October 1956 Israeli, French and British forces launched a pre-planned assault against Egypt, known as the 'Tripartite aggression'. The campaign was in response to Nasser's decision to nationalise the Suez Canal in July 1955, and Egyptian forces were soon overwhelmed militarily. However, international pressure from the US and the Soviet Union through the UN forced hostilities to cease by 7 November. All British and French troops were withdrawn before the end of the year, and the Israelis by March 1957, to be replaced by a UN peacekeeping force. While Nasser had suffered a military defeat, he had been gifted a political victory as a result of his defiance in the face of aggression.[95] His star was rising even more rapidly, and pan-Arabism was becoming the de facto hope for the people in the region.

*Between leadership struggles and growing pains*

While Nasser was on an upwards trajectory, the same was not true of al-Nabhani and Hizb-ut-Tahrir, with 1955 appearing to be the high point before reversals began to occur. In early 1956 a scandal erupted with a claim that al-Nabhani had received a cheque for US $150,000 from US sources.[96] The news was widely propagated in newspapers and on the radio across Jordan and Lebanon in particular, and the rumour that al-Nabhani was in fact a US agent began to spread. Though the evidence was scant, it would have fitted neatly into the existing leftist narrative that Tahrir was against Nasser because the latter was anti-American, and that anyone who was against pan-Arabism, which was in their view a liberation ideology, must be an imperial agent of some sort.

According to party members the source of the rumour was a newspaper owner in Jerusalem, who spread the story on behalf of the Jordanian government in order to discredit them, and given the competition between Tahrir and other groups, whether from a socialist pan-Arab or Brotherhood leaning, some others were more than willing to spread the news irrespective of its authenticity.[97] The lack of any evidence, it now being established that the relationship between Nasser and the US was not one of antagonism as it might have superficially appeared,[98] and al-Nabhani's character and views all make the original claim highly implausible, but with the media coverage at the time there were suspicions and rumours around the party until at least the late 1950s.

Many members who joined the party around this time recall that before meeting Tahrir activists or reading any of their material, they had heard rumours that it was in fact a US-backed group.[99] Auni al-Ubaidi has a section in his book on the party in which he discusses the sources of its funding, including the rumour that al-Nabhani received money from America, as well as other rumours such as the claim that the party was funded by Amin al-Husseini. As an expert and biographer of al-Husseini himself, al-Ubaidi states that both claims are unfounded and far-fetched, concluding that the party was funded through internal contributions from its own membership base.[100]

This was the most prominent of the various rumours that swirled around the party, but while potential misconceptions and misunderstandings could be addressed through personal contact and perhaps resolved, internal fissures were also straining the party. In 1956, a dispute over the nature of leadership broke out between the three members of the leadership committee, namely al-Nabhani, Hamdan and al-Masri. Hamdan and al-Masri believed that the leadership committee should be consultative with the majority position binding, whereas al-Nabhani held that in Islamic jurisprudence leadership was always unitary and the final decision after consultation lay in the hands of the leader, in other words, himself in this case.

The reason for the debate lay over the role of Tahrir in Syria, with al-Masri and Hamdan suggesting that it should be excluded from the criticism by the party and instead kept as a neutral safe haven for its members. Al-Nabhani rejected this outright, believing that the party was a unitary whole and so its actions in the Middle East would be consistent across borders and consequently it would be wrong to make an exception for Syria or any other country they worked in politically. As a result of the argument, al-Nabhani expelled both al-Masri and Hamdan from the leadership and from the party as a whole.[101]

Senior members at the time stated that the real reason behind the argument was that al-Masri and Hamdan had personal interests in Syria that they were afraid would be threatened if the party stepped up its overtly political and confrontational actions there as it had in Jordan. Abdu believed that the pair were actually looking for a way out of the party to protect themselves from the potential consequences they would likely face from the authorities, while saving face by claiming that the disagreement in the leadership reached an impasse.[102] There is some merit in Abdu's analysis since, if Hamdan did previously consider that the Islamic state could be established after three months, it is likely that the growing confrontation with authorities, continued illegality of the party and increased arrests and harassment may have not been what he had in mind. However, without further information it is impossible to try to assess the intentions involved. Removing people from the party and applying administrative punishments such as freezing a member's activities were not alien to al-Nabhani, who was infamous among members for his strictness in internal disciplinary matters.

The fallout from the dispute was wide-reaching. To begin with, al-Masri had been in charge of party activity in Syria. He was an influential figure in his own right, with similar weight to al-Nabhani in the society due to his respected work in the aid agencies dealing with the Palestinian refugees, but more liked on a personal level due to his nature, as opposed to the more serious and confrontational al-Nabhani. When he left a combination of the fact that he did not pass over any details of the structure and his strong personal connection to the members in Syria meant that the membership body was decimated in one blow. Conversely in Jerusalem, where Hamdan was based and was reported to have had a good relationship with many of the members, not a single individual was reported to have left on his account. This is possibly explained by al-Masri building the party membership around him in Syria whereas, though Hamdan was well known to the membership in Jerusalem, he was not a pivotal personality there.

Al-Masri's close ties to others extended beyond Syria to members in other countries, in particular Khalid al-Hasan who was in Kuwait at the time of the conflict. Al-Hasan decided to leave the party on account of al-Masri, and was subsequently involved in the establishment of Fatah with Yasser Arafat, becoming a member of its central committee.[103] Al-Masri was also later to become a prominent figure within the Palestine Liberation Organization (PLO) and was a member of their Executive Committee for a period, both he and al-Hasan involving themselves in Palestinian nationalist politics. These ideas fundamentally clashed with original views they were expected to ascribe to as senior members in Tahrir, though they highlight their continued personal concern for the case of Palestine.

Al-Nabhani replaced the two with al-Da'ur and Zallum. Both of the new members of the leadership committee were al-Azhar graduates, from influential families, and enjoyed a good reputation among party members and public alike. They both also submitted to al-Nabhani's decisions as the leader of the party. The party soon tried to restart activity and rebuild in Syria, with al-Nabulsi and al-Tamimi from Jordan and al-Badri from Iraq travelling there later in 1956 where they lived together in a room in Damascus. They made some inroads, and though the number of members in Syria remained small at the time, they were all active in promoting the party. As activity across Syria grew the authorities took a harsher stance against it, and arrests and expulsions prevented them gaining large numbers at the time.[104]

Other senior members had been sanctioned prior to the expulsions of al-Masri and Hamdan. One such example was when al-Khayyat and al-Da'ur attempted to arrange a meeting with King Hussein in early 1956. They believed the King's rejection of the invitation to join the Baghdad Pact, efforts to cleanse the army of British influence and Hussein's outreach to the opposition meant that there may have been a window of opportunity to win him over, or at a minimum to open channels of communication. When al-Nabhani found out he punished them both with a three-month suspension from involvement in party administration.[105]

A few other members became concerned about al-Nabhani's leadership style. Ibrahim Makki, who had been in Kuwait with al-Hasan at the time of the leadership conflict, visited al-Nabulsi in Irbid along with al-Kilani to try to convince him that al-Nabhani was too hot-headed and impatient, and that it was necessary for them to either force al-Nabhani to agree to restrictions upon his actions as the leader, or to remove him from the leadership itself. Al-Nabulsi refused to countenance any such suggestion at the time, and insisted on loyalty to the leader. Both al-Kilani and Makki left the party soon after, while al-Nabulsi left for Germany in 1959, and though he remained in contact with al-Nabhani his party activity effectively ended at that point.[106]

Though activity in Syria had been damaged, the change in the leadership did not affect other activities elsewhere, such as the numerous campaigns run in the 1956 elections. In June 1957, two candidates ran in the Lebanese elections—Ali Fakhr al-Din in Beirut and Sheikh Ali Safi in Tripoli. The political environment was open at the time, and members of the party were optimistic that they were winning people over. A number of passionate speakers were brought over from Jordan to help the campaigns, with al-Tamimi and al-Khayyat both involved on the ground giving speeches to large crowds numbering thousands. Discussion focused around the obligation to rule by Islam, and immediate political issues such as bureaucratic corruption and the need to unify Lebanon with Syria as the Lebanese state was an artificial creation.

Al-Nabhani was based in Beirut at the time and was arrested during the campaign, and subsequently charged with inciting sectarianism. He spent three months in jail after which he was released on bail. When the results of the election were announced, neither candidate had succeeded. The members were stunned when each of their candidates was announced as having won approximately only 500 votes. Yusuf al-Ba'darani, a young man from a political family close to the first prime minister of Lebanon, Riad al-Sulh, couldn't comprehend how they had received so few votes given that they had received little opposition while discussing with the electorate.[107]

On this occasion acting the part of the sober realist, al-Khayyat believed that the party's refusal to run under another recognised political banner was the cause for downfall, since Lebanese elections were in his view based upon personality and party politics rather than campaign manifestos (al-Nabhani and Zallum had rejected his proposal as they believed that the party could not be seen to compromise its ideological principles by running under a different party platform that did not necessarily represent its ideas).[108] While Yusuf al-Ba'darani disagreed with al-Khayyat's analysis as to the reason for failure, he admitted that the fact that the candidate for Beirut, Ali Fakhr al-Din, was not actually from the city itself would only have compounded the problem.

There was also another election in Hebron the same year due to the death of one of the sitting representatives. The town was under emergency law at the time, and the situation was tense. The king had demanded al-Nabulsi's resignation less than six months after appointing him prime minister, and had expelled from the Arab Legion several officers he believed threatened his rule. The party nominated al-Tamimi to run in the by-election, but he immediately faced intense pressure from the authorities, with violence threatened if he did not remove his candidacy. The party saw the issue as a political struggle between themselves and the government, and in such circumstances to back down would be an inexcusable weakness.

The environment was potentially explosive, with parents of members of the party asking al-Tamimi to remove himself, asking whether he could continue to run in good conscience knowing the possible consequences. A distraught al-Tamimi publicly announced his withdrawal, stating, 'I am removing myself as a result of the pressure by the government, and with this action I have betrayed Allah', before leaving the town and living as a hermit for a short period.[109]

When al-Nabhani heard about his withdrawal, he wrote to the local leadership, stating, 'Asad [al-Tamimi] is dear to us, but Islam is dearer, and since the betrayal of Asad had been proven, it has been decided to [expel] him out of the [party]'.[110] Al-Tamimi was a big loss, having been active all over the region as a young Islamic scholar who was adept at public speaking. He remained close to the party and its members despite his expulsion, and played further critical roles in its history, before becoming a founding member of the Palestinian Islamic Jihad in 1980, a few years after the death of al-Nabhani.

The year was also to witness the party losing a substantial section of its structure in Iraq. Hussain Ahmed al-Salih in Iraq, who was previously connected to the Muslim Brotherhood and had brought all those under his responsibility with him into Tahrir when joining a few years earlier, decided to separate from the party in 1957 soon after meeting with al-Nabhani in Lebanon. When he did he once again took those under his responsibility with him. In the same year, some of the Iraqi members of the party from a Shia background had travelled to Najaf, one of the two major cities of Shia scholarship, the other being Qom in Iran, to try to establish a branch of the party there.

One of these members was al-Subayti, one of the six who originally applied for a permit to establish Tahrir as a political party at the end of 1954. As a result of interaction with Muhammad Baqr al-Sadr and other scholars, al-Subayti was convinced to leave Tahrir and instead join a Shia version of the party called Hizb al-Dawa which had been set up by another Tahrir activist, Talib Rifa'i, who was central to its establishment in 1957, along with Baqr al-Sadr and other Shia in Iraq at the time.[111] They were not the only founding members of Hizb al-Dawa who had been affiliated with Tahrir, with the two elder sons of one of the most prominent Shia scholars Ayatollah Muhsin al-Hakim, Sayyid Mahdi and Sayyid Baqer, as well as Sheikh Arif al-Basri having all been closely associated with the party before deciding to separate and establish their own specifically Shia version.[112]

Back in Lebanon, al-Nabhani had written a draft copy of a book he entitled *al-Khilafah* (The Caliphate) which basically laid out plainly his view of an Islamic state based upon his reading of primary sources, with the resulting conclusions falling within what would be normative orthodox Sunni jurisprudence opinion on the issue. In it, rather than relying upon a school of thought he addressed the Islamic proofs for it, based upon the Qur'an, *Sunna* (Prophetic narrations), *ijma'* (consensus of the companions of the Prophet) and juristic reasoning. The book also addressed the issue of how a caliph is to be appointed, with al-Nabhani explaining that the correct view was that the position was to be filled by one who had the consent of the people, or in other words by election.

Al-Nabhani implicitly refuted the Shia understanding of Islamic leadership, termed the *imama* (or 'imamate', literally meaning leadership), and struck at the fundamental tenet of Shia belief that the caliphate was decided by revelation rather than popular choice. It is upon that tenet that the Shia claim that the first caliph should have been Ali, the cousin of the Prophet Muhammad, and assert that he was ordained by God to be the successor. Al-Nabhani's intention is hinted at in the first line of the book, which stated that 'the caliphate is the general leadership for all the Muslims in the temporal life, in order to establish the Islamic Sharia laws and to carry the call to Islam to the World, and it is the *imama*, and so the caliphate and *imama* are one and the same.'[113]

Before publishing the book, al-Nabhani ordered al-Zain to take the draft to Najaf and present it to the scholars there in order to see their response.

Al-Zain decided instead to first travel to Syria, where he met with some of the Shia scholars before proceeding to Najaf. He spent a short time in Najaf presenting the book and its arguments to scholars there, but left after believing his life was under threat. The contents of the book would have struck a raw nerve, as it undermined the fundamental tenet of Shia belief which was the root from which all other subsequent branch differences emanated. Acceptance of al-Nabhani's views would have ultimately meant the reduction of modern Twelver Shi'ism to a difference of opinion in jurisprudence rather than a different sect.

Whether or not the threat was real, al-Zain left Najaf; rather than returning to Lebanon and informing al-Nabhani of the results of his discussion he decided to travel on to Qom in Iran, and remained there in discussions for a period before returning to Beirut a full two years after originally leaving. Al-Nabhani ended up publishing the book before his return, not expecting al-Zain to take so long.[114]

The majority of members around al-Nabhani in Lebanon at the time were from a Shia background, and publication resulted in a number of them leaving the party, complaining that by addressing the issue of the caliphate and its origins al-Nabhani was effectively forcing them out, as it conflicted with their beliefs.[115] (There remained a sizeable proportion of members from a Shia background in Lebanon up until the end of the 1970s, at which time the Iranian revolution and consequently the establishment of Hezbollah resulted in a much more difficult environment to win over supporters).

Though having suffered the losses of a not insignificant proportion of the party body across Iraq, Lebanon and Syria, and with senior members such as Hamdan, al-Masri, al-Tamimi, Hasan and others removed or leaving, al-Nabhani still remained confident that the party was making progress. Entering into public consciousness through art, Amin Shinnar composed a book of poetry entitled *al-Mash'al al-Khalid* (The Eternal Torch) which translated the party's ideas into verse.[116] Through his contacts who worked at the radio station, the whole of the book was recited on Jordanian radio in 1957.[117] In 1958, al-Nabhani published *Dukhul al-Mujtama'* (Entering the Society), stating that Hizb-ut-Tahrir had successfully addressed the society, was now recognised as a doctrinal, ideological party and had been able to make its presence felt among the people, and was at the point of attempting to enter society and impose itself as a political force within it.[118] But bigger troubles lay ahead.

*Entering society with Nasser at the doorway*

Amidst the challenges that he had faced as leader of Hizb-ut-Tahrir in 1957, after being released from jail al-Nabhani was also afflicted with a curious medical condition. One day after washing, he sat in front of a breezy window without drying. The draft upon the cold wetness caused a paralysis of half his face, and thinking that it was a temporary numbness he ignored the problem until realising that the feeling had not returned after a few days. At that time he went to a specialist who berated his tardiness in seeking medical advice, and instructed him to massage the face as treatment. After a while, he began to regularly apply an electric massager to his face. Though it returned some of the sensation his face remained semi-paralysed for the rest of his life despite continuing to use the machine up until his death.[119] Whilst the breeze in Lebanon caused paralysis in the face, the storm brewing from Egypt was to soon cause a much wider stagnation.

The next year was particularly tumultuous for the region. On 1 February 1958, unification between Egypt and Syria was announced, and the UAR was created, a result of the machinations of Ba'ath party supporters in the Syrian government and military looking to expand their power locally at the expense of the Communists. The union was the beginning of a new age of Arab unity winning the support of the public across the region, with adulation of Nasser reaching new heights, to the worry of other Arab leaders.[120] The Hashemite kingdoms of Iraq and Jordan were particularly susceptible to pressure, and announced their own unification to form the Arab Union (AU), a response to the UAR.

King Hussein's hold on power in Jordan had been teetering precariously for some time. A few months earlier in December 1957, after a royal visit to Nablus had not resulted in a spontaneous outpouring of expressions of devotion to the monarchy—acid was thrown in the face of an elderly man who had made a speech in his honour—five people were arrested in the town for 'communist activities.'[121] In the same month, martial law was declared across the country and five members of Hizb-ut-Tahrir were arrested in Jerusalem.[122]

Among those detained was al-Khayyat, who had been arrested three or four times over the previous two years as a result of his Tahrir activities. On this occasion he was taken to a military court, where he was charged with undermining the government and abusing the monarchy. He defended himself against the charges and was acquitted, but remained in jail, where he was visited by three ministers from the government who assured him that he would soon be released. Instead, two days after the visit, from behind closed doors the court issued a sentence of three years' hard labour. When the news reached him, he was shocked by the turn of events because the court had initially found him innocent, and his sense of oppression led him to write a poem appealing directly to Hussein, which he entitled 'To his majesty the glorified King'. The following three verses highlight the substance of the poem:

*O great King, you are the longing of hearts, the one sought by those who are hopeful*

*I have been imprisoned without a sin, are you content that who longs for you remains a prisoner [?]*

*I have been sentenced to the 3 years, after being found innocent by a just court*

It is somewhat more poetic in the original Arabic, but literary merit aside, the piece, dated 19 March 1958, had the desired effect, with the king ordering his release on receiving the poem. The king was in desperate need of potentially loyal subjects such as al-Khayyat, who visited the king after he was released to thank him for his clemency. Despite al-Khayyat's protestations to al-Nabhani that there was nothing in the poem that contradicted Sharia or Islamic belief, he recounted that he was suspended from party activity as a result of his actions. The suspension gave al-Khayyat an opportunity to quietly leave Hizb-ut-Tahrir, and he returned to work as a teacher in the Islamic College in Amman and separated himself from the party completely.[123] (Al-Khayyat went on to become the minister for religious endowments three times in his lifetime, starting in 1973, believing that it was permissible to be a minister in an non-Islamic government, as long as the role did not involve legislation.)[124]

Attempts to stymie the spreading influence of Nasser's supporters in Jordan were dealt a blow, and the precarious position of the Jordanian monarchy worsened, after a coup in Iraq overthrew King Faisal II on 14 July. There had been little popular support for the federation between the two countries in the first place, with most Jordanian politicians and public preferring to join the UAR. The Iraqi Free Officers had launched the coup, inspired by their Egyptian forerunners, and with it came the end of the Hashemite monarchy created and backed by the British since the post-First World War settlement. Hizb-ut-Tahrir considered the coup to be a US-backed endeavour to replace British influence in Iraq, similar to their analysis of the coup in Egypt. However, al-Badri apparently went on Iraqi radio and gave a positive speech in support of the Free Officers' actions and as a result al-Nabhani temporarily suspended him from the party as an administrative punishment.[125]

By that stage, al-Badri's reputation had become established in its own right in Iraqi society, and according to his biographer Muhammad al-Aleisi he had outgrown the party. He remained respectful of al-Nabhani and Hizb-ut-Tahrir and continued to promote their fundamental ideas. His brother was a party member until being executed by the Iraqi regime for his membership in the 1980s. Al-Badri did not publicly announce his separation from the group or inform the authorities, even though he was arrested numerous times because they believed he was still one of the party's leaders; they were surprised when they eventually found out that he was no longer a member.[126] Al-Badri remained a critic of non-Islamic authority generally and continued to call for the establishment of an Islamic state. He was eventually abducted, tortured and killed in 1969, reportedly by the Ba'ath party, which had come to power in Iraq following a coup in 1968, and which al-Badri subjected to intense open criticism in speeches from his pulpit.[127]

While al-Nabhani had lost al-Badri as a result of the coup, King Hussein had lost half of his Arab Union, and his throne was closer to being toppled. He had already faced two plots to overthrow him that year, including one uncovered by the CIA,[128] and had to take steps to prevent the revolution in Iraq spreading to Jordan. British forces were requested to help protect the sovereignty of the country—150 officers in the Arab Legion were arrested for their anti-government leanings. As the crisis escalated, the US assistant secretary of state suggested Hussein's position was untenable and that they should seek to manage some form of peaceful transfer of power. The British, however, were not willing to sacrifice their man at that stage and stubbornly stood behind him while the US issued orders for its citizens to leave the country. In August, it was agreed that a UN observer force would replace the British troops in Jordan, and the king managed to ride out the turmoil until the end of the year, at which point the situation had been sufficiently brought under control to allow for the lifting of emergency law.[129]

It is clear that the political temperature in 1958 was high across the region, and Hizb-ut-Tahrir saw the machinations of the UAR and Arab Union as part of the Anglo-American struggle over the Middle East, with the US seeking to remove British influence through the use of Nasser. The unions, coup attempts and revolutions opened peoples' minds to the potential possibilities of revolutionary change, and Lebanon was facing civil war as Muslims agitated for the country to join the UAR. This led Maronite Christian Prime Minister Camille Chamoun to ask for US help, which led to the first practical application of the Eisenhower Doctrine in the region, with US forces stationed in Lebanon between July and October 1958.

The atmosphere affected all opposition across the Middle East and security services were more vigilant than ever. In Jordan, even the simple act of applying for permission to study abroad became an interrogation. One Hizb-ut-Tahrir member was summoned to Nablus to be interrogated by an officer over seeking permission to travel to Egypt, a destination of heightened concern for the Hashemite kingdom. On arrival, the officer picked up a file from the table labelled 'Hizb-ut-Tahrir' and split into three sections—A, B and C. Glancing up, the officer said to him *'kamman alif?'* ('A? As well?') The division was to identify the level of commitment to the party cause, with A referring to membership, B to a student attending study circles, and C for supporters, highlighting the level of detail about Hizb-ut-Tahrir activists the security services were recording.[130]

In Egypt, the party was having little success spreading its call beyond the Palestinian student population and a few Islamically minded Egyptians; these included former Brotherhood members Sheikh Ali Raghib and Muhammad Abdu, who were in limbo because their leaders were in Nasser's jails. The region was being swept up in the adulation of the Egyptian leader as a modern Arab hero, more so in Egypt where the masses beyond Cairo were now receiving free university education and other benefits previously denied to them. The security forces there were also extremely vigilant, and having dealt large blows to the Muslim Brotherhood were not about to allow another Islamic movement to put down roots there.

The party continued sending members to try to win new supporters. Zallum travelled to Cairo in 1958, taking advantage of his history in al-Azhar to use his contacts among former students and teachers he had met while there in the 1940s. As a result of his discussions he came to the attention of the authorities, who arrested and interrogated him. The Egyptian authorities were apparently fully informed about the party because their embassy in Amman sent them detailed information regarding Hizb-ut-Tahrir as it emerged. They asked Zallum why a sheikh and teacher was associated with a US agent (referring to the claim made regarding the cheque from the US embassy). Zallum replied that given they had so much information about the party, surely it was their responsibility to warn the public away from them. This brought the response that they would not spread a word about the party, positive or negative, because this would only end up promoting it. Zallum was subsequently deported, but the idea that there was a deliberate attempt to enforce media silence regarding the party was implanted in his mind from this point and would influence his future thinking.[131]

The slow uptake of ideas in Egypt and the loss of al-Badri and al-Khayyat were in fact relatively insignificant issues for the party. Al-Nabhani's analysis of the Free Officers' coup in Egypt from the beginning was that it was US-backed. Nasser was in his opinion a US agent, the formation of the UAR being just another move to extend US influence and try to unbalance the British-backed Hashemite monarchies. Hizb-ut-Tahrir issued a pamphlet at the beginning of 1958 supporting the union of Egypt and Syria on the basis that all Islamic countries were one in origin and that the borders between them were artificial, which put the party in direct conflict with the Hashemite regimes. But it did not prevent al-Nabhani from continuing to issue pamphlets against Nasser and maintaining a stance against Arabism at the same time. The problem was that with the unification of Syria and Egypt, and the resulting adulation of its leaders among the public, practically nobody believed this analysis, including within his own party.

At the height of events in July 1958, al-Nabhani decided that the party was now in the process of attempting to 'enter society', and the publication of the booklet *Dukhul al-Mujtama'* (Entering Society) was to help encourage and explain to the members how they should proceed in the coming phase of interaction. In a nod to the problems regarding leadership disputes and differences over strategy, as well as perhaps internal discussions regarding the content of party teachings, the booklet began by stating that 'at this point... the ideas should be fixed' and that members should be 'content and convinced with them' and no longer debate or discuss such issues.

In this phase, the focus had to be on efforts to 'enter the society with its idea, method and styles', however long it might take. Al-Nabhani rejected the definition of society as simply being composed of individuals, and explained it as a collection of people, the ideas and emotions that bound them together, and the systems that regulated them. Therefore, what made a group of people a society were the relationships among them, and entering society was 'confronting the established relationships between people in society.' The specific relationships to be targeted were not those between common people, but rather between the people and the authorities, since the authorities were responsible for organising society's relationships and had the executive power to do so. The whole political class needed to be targeted and not simply the ruler, because many people were involved in the ruling system apart from its head. The success of the party would be measured by how far it came to influence the relationship between rulers and the ruled, and vice versa, on the basis of its adopted ideas.[132]

At this point, al-Nabhani expected members to engage in intellectual debate in all areas without requiring instruction from the party leadership, and that the party body would now be able to work independently of its leaders in the event that they became separated. With its work spread over numerous countries, the Hizb-ut-Tahrir had been structured into numerous *wilaya* councils, each country represented by its own *wilaya*, with the council responsible for executing instructions on behalf of the central leadership. Beneath each *wilaya* council sat local councils, which were responsible for the activities in their respective areas.

In this new phase, al-Nabhani stated that *wilaya* councils had to begin to take on social interaction and decide which issues to address locally on their own initiative and without prior permission from the leadership. He gave the *wilaya* councils the power to write and distribute their own pamphlets (as long as they did not bear the name of the party), and to adopt approaches that ranged from co-ordinated campaigns of visits to the publication of local news journals, which should focus on journalistic current news issues rather than being seen as party journals. Despite the new powers that the *wilaya* councils had, they were expected to send any publications back to the central leadership within two weeks of publication for the sake of quality control, and there was to be regular contact through letters to maintain party unity in progress and thought.

It was necessary for the party to now engage in a political struggle that would critically address the relationship between the ruler and general public in a manner to make the people recognise the necessity for their relationships to be organised by Islam and no other system of ruling. This meant that thoughts such as Arab nationalism, patriotism, socialism, secularism and democracy should be comprehensively attacked, as before. This political struggle would bring the party into greater conflict with the ruling class and those who supported it, but it should continue on its path no matter the potential responses and blows it received as long as it was able to avoid being dealt a 'death blow' as a political entity.[133] Deciding to confront the wave of Arabism and pro-Nasser emotion head-on at the height of their popularity tested this approach to its limits.

In Jordan and Lebanon, where the vast majority of party members were based, activists were often physically attacked while distributing pamphlets. The public vehemently rejected any accusation that Nasser was an agent for foreign powers, and indeed rejected the same accusations against any of the other rulers coming to power through what were seen as anti-imperial coups. Rather, those making the accusations were accused of being Western agents standing in the way of Arab liberation. Despite the consequences, al-Nabhani issued directives that members had to distribute pamphlets that were now overtly political and attacked the various rulers along with the dominant proclaimed ideologies of Arabism and democracy, in line with the method laid down in *Dukhul al-Mujtama'*. Pamphlet distribution had to be carried out by hand, with many leaving or being expelled from the party because they did not wish to do so.

Some believed that al-Nabhani was asking too much of them, with orders to give speeches in mosques or distribute leaflets leading to conflict with the general public, which resulted in their isolation and being ostracised by the people.[134] Al-Nabhani considered it to be a test of their convictions, a practical manifestation of how the call had to be carried out, and that compromising for the sake of appeasing public opinion would mean that Hizb-ut-Tahrir had compromised its ideology, which it considered to be its raison d'être. As al-Nabhani put it, he believed that it was 'imperative for the party members to adhere to the ideology alone' even if they were subjected to the '*Umma's* resentment', which would only be temporary, because 'their adherence to the ideology [would] win them the trust of the *Umma* again' in the long term.[135]

With an antagonistic public on one side, the party continued to come under scrutiny and pressure from the authorities. In Jordan, Al-Da'ur was expelled from parliament and jailed. From 1958 numerous activists had to report daily to police stations and pay bail, while others were expelled from the country from 1959.[136] At the same time, when people were arrested if they admitted to membership of the party they received an automatic two-year sentence. If members tried to remain silent, they would be forced to write a formal repudiation of the party, a tactic that the authorities used to try to reduce the number of party members because it was well known to them that such a position would lead to al-Nabhani expelling them. As it became clear that this was a deliberate action on the part of the authorities, it was decided that before expelling someone for writing such a statement the circumstances would be investigated to assess whether he had done so in a manner that reflected weakness or whether it was a true case of compulsion.[137]

The party's ranks were decimated in 1958 as a result of its stance in the face of the wave of support for Nasser. The highest estimate, from al-Nabhani himself, was that 97 per cent of party members left during that period. Some did not believe Nasser was a US agent; others left as a result of the public enmity towards the party; others because they were forced to choose between their job and the party; and others as a result of family pressure to leave. Many people advised al-Nabhani that attacking Nasser was self-defeating. Members questioned why it was necessary given that they were the ones losing out, and that it was like hitting their heads against a wall, with the result being broken heads while the wall remained standing.[138]

Although there were differences over the wisdom of the decision, and a minority view has persisted that instead of facing the storm of Arabism head on the party should have sidestepped it and waited for it to abate, al-Nabhani remained convinced of the correctness of his original analysis and the approach he had adopted. In response to a question put to him in 1970 regarding this analysis, an exasperated al-Nabhani replied that despite the fact that by then several thinkers and analysts had come to the same conclusion that Nasser was undoubtedly a US agent, as evidenced by the amount of material in terms of books and articles on the subject, which made it obvious to most people, it still was not obvious to some party members even after the 'hundreds' of leaflets 'full of evidences [sic.]' that the party had issued.[139]

In sum, the confrontational stance taken in relation to Nasser lost Hizb-ut-Tahrir the popular support it had been building since the 1950s, as well as the majority of its members. The difference over the three years from 1955 to 1958 was mentioned in US embassy reports from Amman, which in 1955 estimated the size of the party at up to 6000 members. The total is likely to have been inaccurate; even today US analysts would have difficulty differentiating between actual members, students and supporters. To put the figures into context, in the same year the Muslim Brotherhood was estimated to have a total of approximately 6000 members across the whole of Jordan and the West Bank, matched by Tahrir's Amman contingent alone according to estimates.[140] Three years later in 1958, the same source in Amman referred to Hizb-ut-Tahrir as merely 'a small grouping of... fanatic Islamic "fundamentalists"'.[141] On an anecdotal level, when a young Fayiz Taha joined Hizb-ut-Tahrir around 1960 he found just a handful of members in his home town of Qalqilya, most of whom kept their allegiances quiet out of fear. Qalqilya was al-Da'ur's home and had been a major hub of party support in the mid-1950s.[142]

Upheaval in Lebanon in 1958 meant that al-Nabhani never returned to court to face the charges brought against him in the wake of the 1957 election campaign. In 1959, police came to arrest him while he was staying in an apartment in Tripoli with Zallum. Having been warned that the police were on their way, the pair fled back to Beirut. Up until that point it had been al-Nabhani's practice to wear the turban and cloak associated with Islamic scholars in the region, in order to protect himself from the authorities if he was out giving speeches or meeting people; he thought that regular policemen would be more wary of attacking someone who was likely to have a position of respect and weight, such as a religious leader. However, it also sometimes attracted unwarranted attention, as had been the case in Tripoli, where the police had come to arrest the two men dressed in their scholarly attire as a result of information passed on by neighbours who had begun to spy on them. Al-Nabhani made the decision to shave off his beard and discard the hat and cloak permanently for security reasons, and moved into a separate apartment away from his family, going into hiding.[143]

# 4

# ESTABLISHING THE CALIPHATE

## (1960–1968)

صارحوها بالذي ساء , و سر!      خدم الأمة أنتم . فاعملوا

انما العزلة يأس , و خور!      و احذروا العزلة , و امشوا قدما

انما سعي بلا قصد خطر!      و ابتغوا الغاية في أعمالكم

*'You are servants of the Umma, so work—express to her what is wrong, openly and in secret!*

*Beware of isolating yourself, and march forward—isolation is only despondency, and weakness!*

*And seek the objective in your actions—proceeding without purpose is nothing but danger!'*

Amin Shinnar, verses 162–5 from *'The Radiance of Belief'*[1]

Back in Beirut, al-Nabhani proceeded to rent an apartment, separate from his family's dwellings. He maintained a complete separation for a period of time to evade any possible surveillance of where he and Zallum were staying, while food and clothing was delivered to him. Others would deliver newspapers, and he would receive and send letters via messengers to administer party issues. After a time, his wife cooked for him and the food was delivered by third parties, then he began quietly to attempt to visit the family regularly, while maintaining a low profile.[2]

When al-Nabhani issued his opinion that the party was now in a position to enter society it was based on his personal judgement. The provision of extra powers and responsibilities to the various *wilaya* councils across the region, most importantly in Jordan, Syria, Lebanon and Iraq coincided with the high point of Nasser's popularity. Coupled with al-Nabhani's personal situation soon after, which led to disruption in the normal administration of party matters as the leadership went underground, the result was that progress stalled, and the implementation of new measures was slow.

As activities in Jordan slowed due to increased government pressure such as forced expulsions or requiring activists to report daily to pay bail,[3] the party leaders in Beirut applied for official recognition on 23 April 1959 (probably before going underground), in compliance with the Ottoman Law of Associations, as they had done in Jordan in 1953. The application was submitted by five signatories who came from Sidon, Tripoli and Beirut, highlighting the presence of the party in the three main cities representing south, central and north Lebanon. They also represented diverse elements of society, being a student, landowner, merchant, bookshop manager and accountant.[4]

The application noted the goals of the party as resuming the Islamic way of life and bringing Islam to the world, while emphasising that all its methods were legitimate, including spreading ideas through discussion and the publication of books and pamphlets, holding public and private meetings, sending delegations to politicians, and general contact with rulers and the public, among others. There was no response from the government at the time, and according to the Ottoman Law of Associations the absence of an objection within one month meant that the party was thereby considered legal.

In Iraq a similar application was made on 1 February 1960 by ten members, believing it was worth a second attempt under the 1960 Societies Law, the first attempt having been made prior to the 1958 revolution which ultimately resulted in Abdul Karim Qasim taking power. Although Hizb al-Dawa was established by then, the Hizb-ut-Tahrir retained support and respect among the Shia community, even among some of the religious clergy in Najaf, as highlighted by the support for the application by Muhsin al-Hakim, who was one of the most prominent Shia scholars in Iraq.[5]

However, the interior ministry rejected the application, not because it contradicted the now non-existent monarchy, but somewhat ironically because the party believed in revolutionary change. Al-Subayti was not mentioned among the applicants, having formally left Hizb-ut-Tahrir in 1959 after being visited by Zallum, who had requested that he and three others renew their party oaths, a request that he declined to fulfill, making it apparent that he no longer considered himself a member. (In fact he had been involved in Hizb al-Dawa since its inception, something that would have conflicted with membership of Hizb-ut-Tahrir and vice versa).[6]

## Interacting with society

Despite the slow progress, al-Nabhani believed that Hizb-ut-Tahrir had managed to enter society and had begun the interaction phase from 1960—one reference gives the specific date as 23 April 1960[7] with another suggesting it was the second half of 1960.[8] It was intended that this final phase would add a critical element to the party's activities, which prior to then had been confined to explaining ideas to people or trying to address the relationship between the people and their rulers. At this point, the party was not only seeking to explain ideas to convince people of their correctness; but now there had to be a clear intention to address ongoing events in a way that motivated people to respond to these issues practically, alongside Hizb-ut-Tahrir and in accordance with its ideas. In other words, the interaction phase was to make the party into a true mass movement, defined by three new characteristics.

Firstly, by seeking to build a popular base, which could be motivated to act and express itself on the street, and would come to dominate public opinion. Secondly, it was expected that every member now had to be concerned with what was termed as partial actions and events, meaning day-to-day regular occurrences and life issues, and be sure to explain to people how an Islamic state would practically resolve these daily issues for them. In other words, members were expected to highlight the differences between the current system of ruling and administration with the party vision of how the state should be run by explaining the Islamic rules regarding specific matters. These could vary from economic issues, such as banking or insurance, to political ones such as bribery and government corruption or taxation and so on. This would naturally mean that party members would have to keep referring back to party literature to find the specific solutions for the issues to be addressed. Finally, as a result of this interaction the party directly aimed to take power. Previously the party consistently stated that it ultimately aimed to take power to implement its goals, but this was done without the intention of practically seeking to take power at that time.[9]

The issue of how reaching power was to be achieved practically was not clearly defined in the party's methods. It had been enough to state that it was seeking authority 'through the *Umma*' or society in numerous places in its works. As a result of questions from members in the mid-1950s about how this would happen it was explained that when society had accepted the party and its ideas—in other words, when the party had established a general awareness built on public opinion that it was necessary to resume an Islamic way of life through establishing Islamic rule—the party would then study the current reality and decide the most appropriate action to take. This might then entail encouraging a campaign of civil disobedience, mass protests, violent revolution, military coups or other means that would be used to replace the existing order with the new one demanded by the people, bringing the Islamic state into being as a result of a popular mandate.[10]

This was the state of play when entering the interaction stage in 1960. One obvious question is why it had been decided that the party should enter this new phase when it did, especially given the problems it had faced from 1958. By al-Nabhani's own estimation, even though the remaining members continued their activities after the formation of the UAR in February, it was as though the party was 'walking on the same spot.' However, al-Nabhani believed that despite the slowdown the party should continue in issuing its opinions, and as a result of the softening stance of people towards the party this resulted in Hizb-ut-Tahrir winning supporters and 'naturally' moving into the interaction phase.[11]

An alternative answer is that the 'departure point' was in fact deemed unnecessary. It had been announced in 1954 and entailed adding actions to expose colonialist plans against Muslims while continuing the enculturation of the public.[12] This is although the party believed it remained in the departure point stage for six years, the last two of which included the writing of *Dukhul al-Mujtama'* in 1958. In theory, the decision to enter the interaction phase, according to al-Nabhani's blueprint, could have occurred at any point from 1954, by ordering the additional actions of the interaction phase—namely building mass support, applying the party views to everyday life and seeking to establish the state through the *Umma*. The process stalled in 1958–9, between Nasser, the Lebanese civil war and the party leadership going underground, but an internal pamphlet in 1960 stated that every house in Lebanon had heard about the party, suggesting a confidence in the leadership that the worst was behind them.[13]

An interesting early manifestation of what the interaction stage entailed was a pamphlet on Jerusalem that was sent to all Jordanian parliamentarians in July 1960 and also distributed to the public. It analysed the situation through the prism of the Anglo-American struggle, and raised what it considered to be the US plan to internationalise Jerusalem, which would give the US more influence in the region at the expense of the British. But the address went beyond political analysis, calling on the representatives to live up to their responsibilities to the electorate by holding an emergency sitting of parliament to call on the king to abdicate and to join the Jordanian kingdom with the UAR to prevent the country 'being pulled apart'. If the king refused, it was up to them to convene, to take whatever necessary steps to remove him from the throne.

Explaining what could be considered quite an odd point of view, given Hizbut-Tahrir's views on Nasser, the pamphlet went on to confirm that Nasser was a US agent but that this was beside the point, because King Hussein was a British agent, 'who works like an employee not just an agent.' So while Egypt was under US influence, Jordan was practically under indirect British rule. Given the political reality, therefore, there was nothing to prevent Muslims from uniting Jordan with another Muslim country, since unification was obligatory as long as it did not lead to harm, such as 'uniting a liberated country with one that was under the influence of the colonialists.' In other words, although Nasser was a stooge, the king was an even bigger one, so the issue of being under the influence of foreign countries did not come into consideration.

The pamphlet went on to say that Nasser would not actually want to unite Egypt with Jordan, for fear of upsetting the US over Jerusalem and Israel, but that if the people of both countries demanded their unification this would compel the two sides to 'submit to the will of the *Umma*.' This would be a 'practical lesson' that what the people want comes before what the US or British want. Towards the end of the pamphlet, it talked about how the strength of the masses would ultimately be able to have the agents removed.[14]

Three points emerge from the pamphlet. Firstly, the party's adoption of the internationalisation of Jerusalem as a key political issue, which would be a recurring theme for the next four years. Secondly, the call to take practical action, and indications that there would be more attempts to call on the public to join the party's programme at this stage. Finally, the issue of unification between Jordan and the UAR, which highlighted al-Nabhani's understanding that unity was a goal in and of itself. Given that the Jordanian regime was still unstable, isolated from the UAR and weakened by the end of the Arab Union, it was also bound to elicit a reaction from the authorities, especially as the move to a more practical political call was obvious.

Reaction against the party was not limited to Jordan. In August and September a number of activists were arrested across Jordan, Syria and Lebanon, and in each country a number of cases were brought before state security courts (there were also arrests in Egypt the same year).[15] According to the case for the defence that Uthman Salhiyya presented before a court in Damascus on 6 December 1960, the party believed that it was no coincidence that more than one hundred activists in Jordan, thirty in Lebanon and twenty in Syria were all arrested and tried around the same period.

The court case was also another opportunity to highlight the political work of the party, and Salhiyya mentioned the stance it had taken against international loans provided by the US, the call to merge Jordan into the UAR and for parliament to ask the king to abdicate, that democracy was un-Islamic and so on. With respect to the unity that nationalists so prized, Salhiyya stated that 'even though Hizb-ut-Tahrir works to change the system of the UAR and other places via the *Umma* due to their being systems that contradict Islam, Hizb-ut-Tahrir are the most committed to unity and its preservation.'[16]

While the pamphlets and subsequent arrests indicate the party's continued political activity, the combination of facing an unresponsive society and members being chased by the authorities throughout the region led to a rethink. Beyond their detention, there was also a noticeable change in the treatment of those arrested, with torture of members in Jordan, for example, becoming common where previously it had been rare, possibly the result of a decision to eliminate the party in the region.[17]

These circumstances made the party leadership review its strategy, which resulted in the adoption of *talab al-nusra* (seeking support), which meant seeking help from the people in power directly rather than through the general public. This was justified by making the situation analogous to the Prophet's attempts to seek backing for his call from the heads of tribes outside Mecca, after his own tribe of the Quraish had rejected it. Accordingly, at the beginning of 1961, an instruction was issued to those responsible for running the various regional councils to seek support from those who could establish an Islamic state, whether they were the rulers themselves or their backers. This additional action was only made known to a handful of people in each region, who were specially charged with it, rather than the general membership, who remained largely unaware. The main activity of the bulk of the body was to continue to work among society as a whole to win people over to the party call.[18]

In response to a claim that there had been no progress to speak of, Al-Nabhani issued an internal document in May 1961 that reviewed the party's progress a year on from the announcement that it had entered the interaction phase. It concluded that the party had succeeded in its cultural phase in the early 1950s, when motivation and activity were high, but had failed in the first year of interaction in its attempt at leadership of the *Umma* because party members were still 'living in the atmosphere of 1958'. They remained inactive and were subsequently unable to carry out the new actions, which required daily contact with people to explain the party's views in relation to their ongoing issues. Members believed that there had been no development and that the party was static, even though the party leadership believed it was continuing to give its opinions on political and societal issues, addressing relations between the people and their rulers in a powerful manner; and had begun encouraging its members to increase contact with the public through writing articles for newspapers and magazines, as well as pushing them to meet with people regularly for discussion of the party's views on issues and the way forward.

The pamphlet appeared to be an attempt to substantiate party progress as a structure, while laying responsibility for the lack of results on individual members, stating that 'despite many members sensing that the personality of the party is growing in all areas, including those where it was not working such as Egypt, many of them still lack motivation.' Members were exhorted to make daily contact with people in order to expose them to the party's ideas directly, rather than simply being informed about the party's views through pamphlets, and to push the public to work for the sake of realising the party's goals while undertaking direct political actions themselves.[19]

The review came a few months after an earlier internal pamphlet published in January that had explained that leading the masses was completely different from theoretical intellectual leadership—the former involved leading the people and the latter simply required philosophers—and that leading people and politics was a complicated skill, which required expert performance. It also emphasised to members that the politician was in a constant battle that required bravery, moving onto the next battle even if he had lost the previous one because he was focused on winning the war.[20]

Clearly, the move from theory and intellectual debate over ideology to practical politics was proving problematic, and positive results were difficult to come by. In August, a pamphlet was published assessing the influence of the party in the style of a dialogue between two party members. The first asked whether the party had had any political effect. The second replied that governments were aware of the party and afraid of it, as evidenced by their pursuit of its members, and that the party had managed to attract the attention of 'some thinkers.' At the same time, the party could not influence the government politically in terms of altering its behaviour in line with the political actions it had proposed (such as the removal of King Hussein and the joining of Jordan with Syria). It had also been unable to influence the public, since they did not stand by the party in its demands, and this would only happen when public opinion supported the party and its ideas. When that occurred it would be considered proof that society had embraced the party, but this had not yet been achieved.[21]

The end of the UAR in September 1961 led to a natural subsiding of the cult of Nasser in the region, lessening one of the obstacles in the party's way, though problems with the level of activity still persisted. At the end of the year, the party published yet another booklet that attempted to explain to members what was required of them in the interaction phase. In it, al-Nabhani explained that one who wished to carry the call to Islam had to live among the people to transfer what was written on paper into reality. At this stage, it was necessary for the party to develop influential individuals who could lead the people, either building them up from within the party body, or winning them over from existing leading figures.

Personal contact with the public had to take a priority over anything else, particularly over simply distributing pamphlets. Without that, it would be impossible for the party to gain mass support and a popular platform for its ideas. Building a following would allow the party to bring about a change in the system, given that 'the *Umma* is the natural source of authority and it is the effective means for the removal of the unnatural support which props up the authority.' New measures were introduced to encourage interaction, with weekly meetings to discuss what topic should be addressed that week, with all the members expected to pass on what had been discussed to everyone that they knew. In this manner it was hoped that, over time, through practical implementation they would understand what was required of them and act accordingly on their own initiative.[22]

This was a recognition that the party membership had become overly reliant on the central leadership's issuing of pamphlets. The constant stream of publications had led to a dependency on distribution as an end in itself and a lack of personal initiative or originality. The centrality of al-Nabhani in all of these publications was a further problem, with comparatively little literature being produced by the general body of members or even the other two members of the leadership committee, Zallum and al-Da'ur. In other words, there was a reliance on one man, something that had been unwittingly encouraged by the manner in which the party had progressed until this stage. The party's singular leadership and al-Nabhani's dominating personality had unintentionally constrained the personal initiative of the membership.

Being in hiding restricted al-Nabhani's activities when in Beirut, meaning that he spent most of the day either reading or writing, and listening to the news on the radio, following events and then issuing comments on them. During this initial period of the interaction stage, while party members were unable to gain traction with the public, al-Nabhani wrote a number of new works, further developing the party's material. The one-volume *al-Shakhsiyya Islamiyya* was expanded and re-written as a three-volume collection. The first volume dealt with the basis of Islamic culture, the second was a complete overview of the principles of jurisprudence (*usul al-fiqh*), and the third was an application of the principles of aspects of law at state level, such as the rules related to jihad and foreign policy.

After writing the second volume, al-Nabhani left the written copy in the possession of one of the party members, a Saudi student at the American University of Beirut, to arrange for its publication. Unfortunately, the student was arrested and the authorities confiscated the book, resulting in the publication of the third volume as the second, in its place, and leaving al-Nabhani to worry about whether he would be able to re-write what would now become the third volume to the same level of detail. After rewriting it, he believed that the new edition had actually turned out better than his original, reaching almost 500 pages in length.[23]

Of particular note in the new publication of the second volume covering jurisprudence (which was originally intended to be the third), al-Nabhani further discussed the belief that the caliphate was to be divinely appointed, with a large section entitled 'The Sharia didn't appoint a specific person to the caliphate'[24] dedicated to exploring and ultimately rejecting all of the evidence from the Qur'an to support the position that Ali was divinely appointed, possibly as a result of the interaction with Shia scholars in Najaf and elsewhere.

These three volumes were written between 1959 and 1963, along with another book entitled *Muqadimma al-Dustur* (The Precepts of the Constitution), which was an explanation of the party's proposed constitution for an Islamic state, detailing the evidence used to derive each of the articles from Islamic sources.[25] These books were published under the name of al-Nabhani. From 1958 to 1965 a number of other publications appeared, including *al-fikr al-Islami*[26] (Islamic Thought), *ahkam al-Bayyinat*[27] (Rules of Evidence), *ahkam al-salah*[28] (Rules of Prayer), *nitham al-'uqubat*[29] (System of Punishments) and *naqd al-ishtirakiyya al-markziyya*[30] (Refutation of Socialist Marxism).

All of these books were attributed to various members of the party at the time of publication, such as Ghanim Abdu (*naqd al-ishtirakiyya al-markziyya*) and Ahmad al-Daʻur (*ahkam al-Bayyinat*), but according to multiple internal sources al-Nabhani wrote them all, which was confirmed by a number of the attributed authors. One of the justifications for the party publishing these books with other people's names on the front cover was that it was a means of trying to meet the objective of building prominent figures from among its membership by building their credibility.[31] Another reason given was to avoid the use of al-Nabhani's name for legal reasons,[32] though this seems unlikely given that the party would normally publish its own books.

Two points stand out from this. The first is the impressive volume and breadth of output of al-Nabhani, especially when taking into consideration that he was also writing regular political commentaries, party booklets detailing the practical steps to apply his vision for change, and even taking on writing the defence presented by members at court. The second is the possible effect on the membership, including those such as Ghanim Abdu who were thinkers in their own right and capable of producing their own work; or Ali Raghib who was a teacher at al-Azhar at the time—it is not inconceivable that he could have been capable of writing a similar book to the book on prayer attributed to him but in reality authored by al-Nabhani. That the party did not publish books of substance at the time other than those written by al-Nabhani, even though such writings were encouraged, possibly indicates that members were either complacent or intimidated by what they considered to be al-Nabhani's apparent genius, or were busy in other activites. This in turn reinforced the dependency on al-Nabhani, meaning that the whole exercise could be construed as counter-productive, as well as artificial.

*Mass support and 'caesarean sections'*

At the beginning of 1962, Hizb-ut-Tahrir was officially banned in Lebanon. President Fuʼad Shehab met with the cabinet on 3 January and decreed that the permission to form the party had been revoked on the grounds that the group had been founded on an illegitimate basis. Hizb-ut-Tahrir condemned the decision because it had stated on its application in 1959 that the party was based on Islam, and challenged the government to announce publicly that it believed that Islam was an illegitimate basis. The party also rejected the legitimacy of the decision, given that under Ottoman law the party was legal and therefore required a court decision to dissolve it.[33]

Part of the background to the Lebanese government's delayed response to the party's 1959 application was that for two years running Hizb-ut-Tahrir had distributed pamphlets attacking the fact that Prime Minister Rashid Karami and Head of the House of Representatives Sabri Hamada, among others, attended Christian church services on Christmas Day, though Muslims. This was considered to be an act of disbelief, because it was not permitted for a Muslim to pray in accordance with a different religion's rules. It was given a political significance because the confessional make-up of the Lebanese government divided political positions among the different religious groupings, and incumbents in these roles were expected to attend the various different confessional services. After warning the Muslim politicians in December 1960 that attending such services constituted an act of unbelief, in 1961 Hizb-ut-Tahrir addressed Christians directly. The party explained that expecting Muslim leaders to attend Christian services was equivalent to the *jizya* head tax that the Islamic state previously charged non-Muslims. In this case the *jizya* was being exacted in religious rather than financial terms by forcing the Muslims to pray alongside Christians, whereas the Islamic *jizya* was merely financial and people were free to follow their religion as they chose.[34]

The two pamphlets provoked more concerted campaigns by the authorities against the party in Lebanon, described by activists as 'very fierce', with numerous arrests, particularly because the publications were reportedly popular among the Muslim community.[35] Again, the party believed that there was regional cooperation against it and collaboration between the region's security services. Moreover, party members thought there were numerous indications that Western intelligence agencies were directing them. It is difficult to corroborate these claims with any degree of certainty, but Beirut in particular was a hub for multiple foreign intelligence agencies and it is unlikely that the type of activities and discussions Hizb-ut-Tahrir was involved in would have gone unnoticed.

Although the party's increased activity in Lebanon—in part a result of its leadership being based there—had resulted in continued campaigns of arrest by the government, and Jordan too was witnessing harsher treatment of Hizb-ut-Tahrir members, the first member to die for the cause was in Iraq. In February 1963, a coup there brought the Ba'ath party to power. Immediately, the Ba'athists moved against all other political movements, targeting the communists to eliminate them, and Hizb-ut-Tahrir for its statement that the US had driven the coup under the supervision of the US ambassador in Baghdad. Hizb-ut-Tahrir believed that the 1958 coup by the Iraqi Free Officers against King Faisal II was US-led, because it was against a British-backed monarchy. One of the coup leaders, Abdul Salam Arif, had close ties to Nasser and had expressed a desire for unity with the UAR, which buttressed Hizb-ut-Tahrir's opinion. But his co-leader Abdul Karim Qasim did not share the same pan-Arab vision and moved against Arif, while drawing closer to the communists.

The 1963 coup brought Arif to power on the back of the Ba'ath party, resulting in Qasim's execution and a subsequent assassination campaign against communist targets (apparently on a list provided by the CIA). It was reported in September that year that King Hussein of Jordan had stated that 'what happened in Iraq on 8 February had the support of American intelligence.' More importantly, former high-ranking officials in the US State Department confirmed that Saddam Hussein and other Ba'athists had made contact with the US in the late 1950s and were thought to be 'deserving of American support against Qasim and the communists.' The coup was forecast in great detail by the CIA, with insider knowledge about what was to occur; unsurprisingly, though (and somewhat unconvincingly), some still deny any active US involvement.[36]

After a series of arrests, around seven Tahrir members were taken to the Olympic Club where they were held and tortured. As a result of their interrogation, they identified the leader of the party in the Iraqi *wilaya* as Abdul Ghani al-Mallah. The Ba'athists turned their attention to him, which resulted in his death under torture.[37] Al-Mallah was the first martyr for the party, one of many opposition figures killed by the Ba'athists who had only been in power for nine months before Arif took a leaf out of Qasim's book and moved against his former allies, expelling them entirely from government in an internal coup on 11 November. This was only the first in a series of conflicts and competition between the Ba'athists and Hizb-ut-Tahrir in Iraq, and within a few years they would be vying with each other to win over officers to their respective causes.

Throughout 1962–3 the activity of the party across its areas of work was increasing, with measures to increase personal contact and reduce reliance on pamphlets beginning to take effect. The ability of the party to bring people out onto the streets of Jordan in January 1964 was attributed to personal contact between party members and the public, resulting in political action based on the views given in the party pamphlets. From the early 1960s Hizb-ut-Tahrir had decided that the issue of the internationalisation of Jerusalem, supported by a UN resolution in 1949 (still explicitly supported by, for example, the European Union), constituted one of the interests of the people that they would adopt, warning against it numerous times.

After Pope Paul VI announced in November 1962 that he intended to visit Jerusalem, a pamphlet was released titled 'The campaign of the crusader Pope for the sake of internationalizing al-Quds', which stated that the trip came 'under the cover of a visit and pilgrimage' to 'put pressure upon the Jordanian rulers to submit to the internationalization of al-Quds' and to 'terrify the Muslims into giving up' its defence.[38] Soon after, another pamphlet positioned the issue as the central goal of the struggle between Muslims and the West since the time of the crusades, with the attack this time coming in a political guise as a call to internationalise the city, as opposed to a military campaign.[39]

With personal contact, these views were disseminated throughout Jordan, and public opposition to the Pope's visit, scheduled for January 1964, once again led to arrests of activists, with a number being sent to the notorious Jafar desert prison, reserved for political opposition to King Hussein.[40] Despite the widespread clampdown, Tahrir still managed to bring demonstrators against the Pope's visit onto the streets,[41] with supporters being bussed into Amman from all over the East and West Bank, evidence of progress made in being able to move the public in support of the party's political viewpoints.

This event was retrospectively understood by al-Nabhani as a proof of Jordanian society's responsiveness to the party's call, and based on the feeling that 'at that point [the party] became sure that it had established the [Islamic] state already and there remained only the task of taking the power in order to complete this state.'[42] What was meant by the suggestion that an Islamic state had been established in 1964 was that the intellectual revolution required within society for the state to come into existence had occurred such that the people now wanted to be organised according to the rules of Islam. Evidence of this would be if the public embraced the party and its ideas, since the party was calling for the resumption of an Islamic way of life.

Al-Nabhani was not concerned with taking power per se, but with establishing Islam as the basis for rule. It was for that reason that he had apparently rejected previous offers to take power, such as the offer made by al-Shishakli in Syria, or his rejection of offers of support to take power by members of the military establishment in Jordan prior to 1964, because he 'felt that the society in Jordan had not embraced the party',[43] or in other words had not embraced its vision and goals.

The assessment that Jordanian society had indeed embraced these ideas appears particularly bold, especially given that according to members involved numerous other factions in Jordan at the time were against the papal visit and had helped mobilise public opposition.[44] That this single event was used as proof of society's adoption of the party ideology was questionable enough, but according to the party's understanding of the Muslim nation it was in origin a single entity and the borders between Muslims were artificial. By this reckoning, society across the whole area of the party's work in the region was now ready and waiting for the actualisation of the Islamic state, which would run their affairs and organise their relations according to Islamic beliefs.

However, the success in bringing people onto the streets to protest against the Pope's visit as a political expression against any move to attempt to internationalise Jerusalem was not repeated in any other political action of note over the next year. Soon after, the party tried to run in the 1964 elections in Lebanon (which took place between April and May), with the candidacy of Yusuf al-Ba'darani in Beirut a more local choice than the 1957 candidate Ali Fakhr al-Din. That his family was politically connected was also advantageous, lending credibility and name recognition to his candidacy. The campaign was more serious and concentrated than in 1957, with the party having enough members in Lebanon not to require outside support as previously, with figures such as al-Tamimi travelling to provide numbers.

Al-Ba'darani believed that the party had greater public support in 1964, that the idea of Islamic rule was clearer in the public's mind and that the call for the resumption of an Islamic way of life was better understood. The campaign also used the term *khilafa* (caliphate) explicitly, both in discussions and in slogans painted on walls, highlighting that it was a normal part of the discourse as opposed to being deliberately avoided, as had occurred in previous campaigns, particularly in Jordan. While this was received well among the public, the state clamped down on the campaign and party activists in an unprecedented manner, in particular in response to the campaign manifesto that al-Ba'darani published towards the end of March.

The manifesto was originally written by al-Nabhani, but he invited al-Ba'darani to amend it as he saw fit.[45] The manifesto outlined the five major points that al-Ba'darani was running on: for the president of the state to be Muslim; implementation of Islamic laws across society; the dismantling of the current concocted ruling system; implementation of an alternative, Islamic economic policy; and the removal of foreign influence from the country. The first and second points were detailed in a manner consistent with other similar statements derived from the normative Islamic viewpoints on ruling in Islam. The third point attacked the agreement establishing a confessional state, explaining that Lebanon had been artificially created within the *al-Sham* region to undermine Muslims through the creation of a sectarian state that would act as a Western base in the heart of the Muslim lands. Instead of continuing as a sectarian state, Lebanon would be united with other countries in the region under the rule of Islam, and under which its population had a 'history of contentment'. The manifesto also criticised the current economic policy, in particular taxation, which relied on universal and indirect taxes, while reducing direct tax on wealth, and outlined alternative industrial, international trade and tax policies. As for the issue of foreign interference, the conflicts in Lebanon were also identified as part of the wider Anglo-American struggle in the region, with various agents representing both sides' interests in the political arena.[46]

The campaign election slogans were Islamic in nature, using Prophetic narrations and verses from the Qur'an, while pamphlets were issued daily to build strong support. Dozens of activists were arrested during and after the elections, including al-Ba'darani himself, who was jailed for a year on charges of inciting sectarianism. The manifesto was banned, but there was a demand for it after the controversy and discussion it had sparked off; some took to printing and selling it on the black market. The official election tally was as poor as 1957, with al-Ba'darani only receiving a few hundred votes. The party was convinced that the results had been tampered with. The response to their delegations and individual visits been positive. Moreover, al-Ba'darani was from a well-known family. It was apparently confirmed to many of his family's connections that fraud had indeed occurred, not necessarily with the objective of denying him victory but rather to prevent any suggestion that the party had any significant support and to humiliate it.[47]

Towards the end of April, before the end of the election period, a second major publication was issued under al-Ba'darani's name, which addressed the regional political situation. Al-Ba'darani could not recall having written it, and the nature of the topics and manner in which they were addressed suggest that it was almost certainly written in its entirety by al-Nabhani, but issued as part of the election material to garner interest and attention. The pamphlet was remarkable in that it not only outlined the political views of the party at the time, but it also explained the positions of the various actors within the framework of the Anglo-American struggle, and outlined the practical political steps that needed to be taken to resolve the situation.

Syria at the time was under the rule of a Ba'ath military council that had risen to power after a coup in 1963, following two years of instability after breaking away from the UAR. The situation remained unstable as factions sought to consolidate their positions. The pamphlet placed the instability in Syria in the context of the regional struggle for influence, identifying the various players, and their motivations and roles within the upheavals taking place from Yemen to Lebanon. The main issue in the struggle was still about rooting out British colonialism and influence, to leave US influence in its place.

As mentioned above, the pamphlet also outlined a broad political programme and actions to resolve the issue. A number of points were raised with respect to ruling, the first being a call for the military to understand that its place was to protect the country, and not run it (a theme also found in the more locally addressed manifesto issued in March). Rather than ruling from a military council, a council should be set up to protect the country from outside influence. The second point was that in reality there was no such thing as collective rule, with ultimate executive power always having to be held by one individual (such as the president in the US, or the prime minister in the UK), and that those who had claimed they would implement such a system, such as the USSR's Nikita Khrushchev, never applied it due to its inapplicability.

The specific actions called for to remove foreign influence included closing the embassies of the UK, the US, France and the USSR (due to its overt and known attempts to involve itself in the struggle for influence in the Middle East), along with any other embassy or consulate where covert activity was known about. Any politicians who were known to be under the influence of the major international powers should be placed under enforced residency (prohibited from travel abroad), and those who were suspected but not proven agents would be placed under temporary restrictions until the situation stabilised. Additionally, every army officer that fell under suspicion had to be removed, and no politician or individual known to be a Western agent should be allowed into the country. At the same time, no foreign aid or loans should be accepted, because they constituted means of influence for creditors.

The document also repeated Hizb-ut-Tahrir's central theme of intellectual revival. A true revival had to be based on Islamic thought alone. For the Islamic thought to 'crystallize' in people's minds, it should be spread and debated among the public as a 'spiritual political idea' (rather than as a purely political or spiritual matter), which required everyone to participate. The focus of discussions would be around the ideas and not the system, since people needed to be convinced by the ideas from which the system would emanate. After discussions 'matured' there should be a council of thinkers and politicians that would gather on the basis of the discussions, and after a six-month interim period they should have elections for a council and president.[48]

The proposals had no practical impact, not surprisingly given that the party had minimal penetration in Syrian society. Activists there were unable to grow beyond a few, and although they were extremely active in distributing pamphlets and generating debates among the public, they were often arrested, which halted potential development and hindered their ability to take advantage of the opportunities created. Although the period after the separation from the UAR afforded them a more receptive audience, the arrival of the Ba'athists in 1963 meant harsher security conditions all round, and some of the few senior activists were soon deported, reducing their ranks even further.[49]

It may be surmised that al-Nabhani believed this was an opportunity to engage with the various intellectuals who were involved with the Syrian government at the time, but the political analysis within it would likely have been difficult for many such individual to stomach. In any case, the pamphlet represented an attempt to seek political backing through the established power players, the obvious problem being most of them were associated with leaders who had been labelled as one kind of agent or another. As part of the Lebanese campaign material, the pamphlet came a few months after the successful attempt to protest against the Pope's visit, and so theoretically speaking was issued at a time that al-Nabhani believed that the party had already achieved the establishment of the Islamic state and was now seeking power.

The failed election campaign and lack of any popular response to the jailing of al-Ba'darani and party activists, along with the lack of any meaningful response to the proposals made in the pamphlets issued, might have been a cause of concern, occurring as they did on al-Nabhani's doorstep. If society had truly 'embraced' the party, then the evidence ought to have been the ability to influence the political situation, something that was clearly not occurring. However, the party was not stagnant regionally in terms of growth of its membership, and progress was reported in several areas.

Along with growth over the past few years in Jordan and Lebanon, after Arif had removed the Ba'athists from government in Iraq, circumstances permitted the spread of activity across several cities and towns in that country, including Baghdad, Basra, Mosul, Fallujah and Najaf, each with between fifty and 200 active members.[50] New areas targeted by the party were also opening up, with membership growing in Turkey,[51] and the recruitment of a Sudanese al-Azhar student in Egypt had also presented the possibility of extending the party's work into Sudan after his return there in 1963.[52] Meanwhile, other members had travelled to Libya, Saudi Arabia and some of the Gulf countries, though al-Nabhani was not targeting these areas at that time. Party members were left to carry the ideas of Tahrir as individuals rather than in close coordination with the party leadership, and the same applied to those who had left the Middle East for Europe or elsewhere.

The apparent conundrum of how to achieve party growth and the party's success in mobilising the street in Jordan at the beginning of 1964, contrasted with the failure to make any meaningful political impact between 1961 and the end of 1964, led to a rethink by the beginning of 1965. To enable the practical establishment of an Islamic state, the public had to have an opinion on and general awareness about the idea of ruling by Islam, which would be made evident by society's embracing Hizb-ut-Tahrir and its programme, and the party's ability to assume power. As mentioned previously, al-Nabhani had always stated that the party would take power through the people, without specifying how that would be done. At this stage, the party was unable to mobilise the masses to engage in a revolution or strikes that would bring the government down, nor was it able to influence rulers to bend them to its goals.

Hizb-ut-Tahrir had two main options before it: either to re-assess whether society had in fact already established an Islamic state and was simply waiting for its birth to become a reality; or to accept that there were other factors preventing its birth such as government security measures and foreign support keeping rulers in place. In al-Nabhani's words, the party

> 'studied the situation of the society, the people, the area as a whole, and as a land which is under the influence of the disbelieving states, and it then came to the understanding that the birth of the Islamic state was difficult, and waiting for the birth was increasing the hardship, so it saw that a caesarean section was compulsory for the birth of the state.'[53]

In other words, after four years of seeking power through the rulers and those who backed them, it had been concluded that their support was not in fact derived from the society but rather they were artificially in place and refusing to move. At the same time society had no understanding that it was the source of authority and therefore acquiesced to having its leaders imposed upon it. It was decided that although there was evidence of a mass support for the party's ideas, and a leadership that represented those ideas, due to artificial 'material barriers' created by those in power—meaning the imperialists and their agents—there was no connection between the party leadership and the mass support that would enable it to lead the public to the natural destination of an Islamic state.

The material barriers were preventing party members from connecting with and consequently leading the public. Therefore there was the need for other actions that would seek to remove those barriers to taking power, which was to be pursued by those charged with seeking *nusra* (support)—this was referred to as the 'caesarean section,' by the then regular occurrence of a military coup. While this additional aspect was added to the party methodology, it was kept private among the leadership and those assigned to help, while the rest of the membership was to remain working as normal.

*Preparing for birth*

The attempts to seek support to establish an Islamic state continued through-out the area where the party worked, but the first serious attempt to convince a government or military to establish an Islamic state occurred in the unlikely location of Sudan. The first Sudanese member of Hizb-ut-Tahrir was an al-Azhar student called Abu Yusuf who returned to his homeland in 1963, which led to al-Nabhani's interest in the potential for development there. Al-Nabhani had originally intended to send a young Lebanese Palestinian, Abu Mahmoud, to help make preparations with Abu Yusuf, having pulled out a map in front of him during a visit where he outlined the strategic advantages that Sudan provided as the launching point for any potential Islamic state. Having only recently been released from jail, Abu Mahmoud ended up declining, and eventually former election candidates al-Ba'darani and Fakhr al-Din travelled there to help move the party's work along.[54]

It was during this period that the book *Nida' Harr Min Ila-l-Muslimin Min Hizb-ut-Tahrir* (A Warm Call to the Muslims from Hizb-ut-Tahrir) was re-published and distributed in Khartoum in 1965, three years after its original publication as part of the literature produced during the new interaction phase that sought to motivate society to take action on the party's ideas. The treatise sought to explain the causes of the decline of Islamic civilisation and the path for its revival, with its conclusion stating that the 'illness' of the Muslims had 'been diagnosed as being the shaken confidence in the thoughts and rules of Islam, and the cure has been clarified... as being the establishment of the Islamic caliphate with the thoughts and rules of Islam.'[55]

Its re-publication in the Sudanese capital was an indication of the party's presence and interaction there at that time. Along with generic party material, there was also a focus on the issue of southern Sudan due to its centrality to the politics of Sudan generally (an issue that Hizb-ut-Tahrir continued to address, stressing the importance of unity and opposition to international interests that aimed at the disintegration of the state for geo-political reasons, until the eventual separation of South Sudan in 2011). Though al-Ba'darani claimed that the attempts made were 'powerful' and the first of their kind by the party, in the end nothing came of their hopes and al-Nabhani's attention soon turned elsewhere.[56]

The mid-1960s saw increased activity across several countries where the party worked, particularly in Jordan, Syria and Iraq, as well as further afield in Turkey, the first non-Arab country targeted due to its position as the centre of the last Islamic state. Al-Nabhani sent Zallum to help establish the party there, but although by 1965 indigenous people were joining and studying with them in Turkey,[57] it appears that the majority of the members and leadership was made up of Palestinian Arabs who had travelled there to study and had spread the party's ideas among fellow students.[58]

According to original Turkish members from the period, the party was the first Islamic political party to publicly try to introduce ideas such as the necessity of the caliphate, the obligation of Islamic dress for women and so on during a period when socialism and Kemalism were dominant. Although such ideas were present in books that may have been found in Turkey at the time—for example, in the works of Sayyid Qutb—the claim is that the party was the first to carry such ideas there via a political vehicle. In April 1967, party books were sent to journalists, politicians and other prominent individuals across Turkey.[59] In the same period, the party was being discussed in newspapers, where even satirical responses such as caricatures mocking the party appeared, and was also mentioned in parliament by the head of the opposition, who apparently stood up with a copy of the party's book *Nitham al-Islam*, and asked rhetorically who had permitted such a book to be printed and distributed in Turkey.[60]

As a reaction to the party's actions in April, the security forces moved quickly to arrest Hizb-ut-Tahrir activists, with several Jordanian citizens as well as a group of Turkish members being detained. In August, an open letter was addressed to the Turkish prime minister, Suleyman Demirel, warning him that his stated belief in secularism was tantamount to unbelief in Islam, which did not recognise the separation of religion from politics,[61] but any significance in this challenge was reduced when in the same month the party leadership in Turkey was detained for the first time, hampering Hizb-ut-Tahrir's activity there and in effect removing it from any concerted continuous activity for a period.[62]

Rather than attempting re-establishment of the state where it last stood in Istanbul, there was also a particular focus on Iraq, itself the historical centre of the Abbasid caliphate. The expulsion of the Ba'athists from the government at the end of 1963 allowed Hizb-ut-Tahrir to operate more freely and build on its presence across the country. Arif, who had taken sole power, was personally known to some of the party members, and had a good relationship with Talib Samara'i, in particular, who was mayor of Baghdad during Arif's time in power.[63]

Al-Nabhani ordered a delegation to be sent to Arif to request his support for the party in establishing an Islamic state; but, apparently, instead the delegation simply explained the party's ideas to Arif, after which he told them they were free to promote their ideas in public. A series of letters passed between the party leadership in Iraq and al-Nabhani in Lebanon asking for direction on what to do, with each response from al-Nabhani leading to further excuses about what the party in Iraq was lacking and what it required. The lack of initiative from the Iraqi branch led to a back and forth where it became clear that they were waiting for every word to be explained before taking any action, and months passed without any real steps being taken to take advantage of the opportunity.[64]

According to Muhammad Ubaid, another of the Iraqi members of Tahrir who knew Arif personally, Arif had promised more than once to establish the caliphate in Iraq. Despite his connections with Nasser, there was some hope invested in him due to a story he divulged about his time in exile. After being expelled by Qasim, Arif had made the Islamic pilgrimage (*hajj*) to Mecca, where he took a vow that if he returned to power he would rule by Islam.[65] But coming to power on the back of a CIA coup undertaken with the Ba'athists would not seem to be ideal preparation for any such programme to be implemented. Even though he had out-manoeuvred the Ba'athists and removed them from government, Arif never fulfilled his promise.

In a suspected act of sabotage, Arif was killed in a helicopter crash in April 1966,[66] closing a wasted window of opportunity that had frustrated al-Nabhani to the point that he began to blame himself for trying to convey his directions to the leadership in Iraq in writing rather than simply going himself. This exasperation was summed up in his words that whoever wanted an action done needed to do it himself, something he would ultimately end up putting into practice.[67]

As quickly as one opportunity escaped the party's grasp in Iraq, circumstances meant that another presented itself immediately afterwards. Abdul Salam Arif's death resulted in his brother Abdul Rahman Arif—who was the head of the army at the time, a position given to him by his brother after the coup in 1963—being appointed as president by the Iraqi Revolutionary Command Council. While Abdul Salam was believed to be a strong character, having been involved in orchestrating two coups and eliminating political opponents, while being adept at playing politics, Abdul Rahman was considered a weak figure who was merely the figurehead of the regime. This left the field open for others to attempt to win over those who held the real power in Iraq, namely the other military officers.

Zallum was sent to Iraq to take control of the party there, and a good presence was built among the officer corps. At the request of some of these officers, to raise the profile of the party on the street and gain a mass support for any future state a team of ten activists from Lebanon, Kuwait, the Emirates and Jordan was sent to Baghdad with the single mission to engage in as much public activity as possible. Although the need for an external team to undertake such activity might fairly be questioned, it is likely that this was to protect local activists from any repercussions. If this was indeed the justification, it was a wise decision given that those involved were arrested no fewer than six times during the few months they were there, before finally being deported at the end of 1966.[68]

However, none of this activity impressed al-Nabhani, who wrote an internal pamphlet at the end of 1966 complaining that the party had no influence in Iraq—what he termed as being 'below zero', despite the fact that it had distributed 'millions' of pamphlets there. The diagnosis was severe and frank, a plain admission of frustration that even though one of its major goals was to be embraced by society in the Muslim world, Tahrir's opinions had no weight in affecting the actions and relations between the ruler and the ruled or within society. Clearly irritated at the lack of progress in making connections that were effective in building public support, al-Nabhani summarised his point with the statement that 'the party is a party of pamphlets, and in the society it is below zero [in other words, has no weight], without a doubt.' This was not just in Iraq. The same diagnosis was made generally and applied to other countries where the party's work was actively seeking to change the system, such as Syria and Jordan.[69]

Hizb-ut-Tahrir had tried to involve itself in political discussions in Syria following a coup in 1966, when a faction from the Ba'athist regime expelled the National Command, which had come to power in 1963. The National Command was originally led by prominent Ba'athist ideologue Michel Afleq and soon lost whatever little legitimacy it had by purging Nasserists from its ranks. It was also largely drawn from among religious minorities in Syria rather than the majority Sunni population, and although the Sunnis were largely pro-Arab nationalists they were alienated by the secular Ba'athist ideology and the clear push to monopolise power at the expense of all other factions.

The coup did not bring about any fundamental change in the basis of the state, but did introduce a more radical form of Ba'athism that sought to accelerate the socialist revolution in Syria. It forced out the more pragmatic old guard of Afleq and his supporters, while the new faction was led by General Salah Jedid. Although various land reforms were used to try to win over the rural poor, there was intense opposition to the regime, particularly in the capital and other urban areas. In particular, Islamic sentiments were offended and alienated by the heterodoxy of the regime.[70]

Trying to tap into the political conflict, Tahrir published a pamphlet at the end of July 1966 that called on the military to acknowledge that although Syria had been freed from the military occupation of the French, the colonial power had left behind the idea of secularism that had been the basis of the rule since liberation. This meant that while the country had been militarily liberated, it was still under intellectual occupation. It was this contradiction between the people's Islamic beliefs and the nature of secular rule that had caused political instability in the country.

In an echo of the proposals made in the name of al-Ba'darani two years earlier, the pamphlet called for the election of a body that would look into the basis of rule that the government was established on and to end the separation of religion from the state. Instead, it would make Islamic *aqida* (belief) the foundation of the state, from which all its rules would be derived. This demand was made 'in the name of the *Umma*', though the lack of response, as admitted by al-Nabhani, indicated that while the party could make its claims, they remained just words on paper.[71]

During the same year, in Jordan a number of pamphlets were published on the Palestinian question, warning that the government was planning to provoke a regional war at the behest of the UK, which would end with the surrender of the West Bank to Israel. It appears that there were also possibly two sources who worked in official circles who confirmed this analysis: the first was a 'trusted source' who had been informed by an employee in the Saudi embassy in Syria that Israel was going to occupy the West Bank either in the near future or after some time;[72] and the same information was also passed on by al-Tamimi to the party. It is possible that al-Tamimi was the unnamed source mentioned in one of the pamphlets.[73]

Conflict had been growing between King Hussein and Ahmad al-Shuqayri, who was the PLO's first chairman after it was established in 1964, over the ultimate clash of interests between the idea of establishing an independent Palestine including the West Bank or keeping the East and West Banks unified under Jordanian leadership. This was exacerbated by the independent military action against Israel carried out by Fatah and other armed factions aligned to the PLO, collectively known as the *fedayin*, which undermined the Jordanian state by taking liberation into their own hands. The competition between the two was summed up in al-Shuqayri's retort to King Hussein's customary assertion that 'Jordan is Palestine, Palestine is Jordan', with the claim that what happened in 1948 was in fact the annexation of the East Bank to Palestine, rather than the other way around.[74] Hussein tried to position himself as championing the unity of the East and West Banks, while painting al-Shuqayri as seeking their division.

In July 1966 al-Nabhani wrote a political analysis outlining Hussein's British-directed policy, which he believed aimed to manufacture a regional war that would lead to the humiliation of Nasser and al-Shuqayri, while also surrendering the West Bank to Israel. The first indication of this plan was a speech that Hussein had made in Ajloun on 14 June, when he had made it clear that he was withdrawing support for the PLO, a step of great political significance that al-Nabhani did not believe had originated from the Jordanian government, but which was rather a British decision. Hussein stated that 'hopes have vanished for the possibility of cooperation with this organization' and his speech included vehement expressions such as 'be the hand cut off that menaces the integrity of Jordan' and 'be the eye gouged,' language not normally associated with Hussein, leading historian Urial Dann to speculate that the Jordanian Prime Minister Wasfi al-Tall was the real speechwriter.[75] Al-Nabhani, however, believed that the language used was clearly translated from English, due to the existence of certain phrases and idioms that were unfamiliar in Arabic and likely to have been the result of literal translation, indicating that the speech had been written for Hussein by the British.

Following Hussein's announcement, the conflict with al-Shuqayri increased, and a series of festivals were held across Jordan, where the attendees were addressed by significant figures in the country, such as parliamentarians, scholars and tribal leaders, all in support of Hussein and against al-Shuqayri. The rumour from the Saudi embassy, the statements of Hussein and the festivals were tied together in light of the regional situation to mean that Hussein was preparing to surrender the West Bank to Israel, while passing the blame onto al-Shuqayri and Nasser, and in doing so preparing the ground for a normalisation of relations with Israel that was being promoted heavily at the time by Tunisian president Habib Bourguiba. The analysis ended by calling on the people in Jordan and the region to stand as one against this 'dirty English conspiracy' that Hussein had begun implementing, and instead to wage a real war against Israel and its supporters.[76]

Party members distributed this analysis as widely as possible, even among Arab students in Austria and Germany.[77] The party had re-established itself in Jordan by that time, with more than fifty study circles in Amman alone, and dozens in other major cities such as Irbid and Zarqa.[78] But there was a universal rejection of the party's point of view for the next year, most vehemently from army officers such as Shamsudin Shirkasi, who was based in Hebron, who believed that a military build-up in the area was defensive. Party members, however, countered that the build-up of arms on the border with Israel was in fact further proof that plans were under way, given that there had to be some form of justification for Israel to attack Jordan.[79]

This was despite the fact that on 13 November 1966 Israel attacked Samu', a West Bank village south of Hebron, in retaliation for the death of three soldiers who ran over a mine planted by Fatah, which led to huge demonstrations against Hussein due to belief that he had betrayed the Palestinians by allowing the Israeli attack to go unanswered.[80] The party issued another analysis soon after these events, in which it stated that the small attack appeared to be a test by the Israelis to gauge reaction in Jordan and internationally before attempting to widen the war to encompass Syria and Egypt. However, US intervention at the UN and the anti-Hussein response in Jordan led to the plans being postponed.[81]

Although the party believed that there was public anger directed at the Jordanian regime for the next month, the situation settled down, perhaps offering further proof to al-Nabhani regarding the lack of Tahrir's influence on political action and events beyond simply providing analysis. It did not help that around the same period two influential members had either left or been expelled from the party. Ghanim Abdu, whose name was on the original application for recognition of the party in Jordan and had been close to al-Nabhani from the start, left over ideological disagreements, the conflict over attempting to use parliament as a pulpit for the party's ideas apparently coming to a head.[82]

The other loss was the expulsion of al-Tamimi, who had graduated from al-Azhar in 1951 before returning to Palestine and was a popular figure among members. Al-Tall had given him a gun as a present as a result of their interaction and relations, something that al-Nabhani found unacceptable. He ordered al-Tamimi to return the gift to the prime minister in a stern manner to make it clear that members of the party could not be influenced or won over through such actions. Al-Tamimi was unwilling to do so, whether out of custom or fear, and was expelled from the party as a result (he went on to hold numerous official positions in Jordan from the 1990s onwards, including becoming mufti of Jordan and minister of religious endowments). While the event again highlighted aspects of al-Nabhani's nature when dealing with party issues, it also indicated the extent of party interactions with the highest levels of authority.

Prior to the war in June 1967 a party delegation met al-Tall to inform him that the party was aware of plans to surrender the West Bank to Israel and to warn him against carrying it out. Al-Tall obviously disagreed, pointing to Nasser's rhetoric and preparations against Israel as proof against such a plan actually being able to take place. The delegation countered that such evidence did not actually contradict the party's analysis. Regardless, al-Tall strongly rejected the allegations, and stated such an event would never happen while he remained prime minister.[83] (He in fact resigned soon after, just three months before the June 1967 war, and was succeeded by Saad Jum'aat.)

As it was, the regional temperature was rising rapidly and by the end of May Nasser's troops were in the Sinai, close to Israel, after he had requested UN troops leave there earlier in the month. While Syria was aligned with Egypt, theoretically under a unified command, Hussein was very much viewed as being reticent to get involved, given his conflict with both governments. In an unexpected step, Hussein travelled to Cairo at the end of May to join the unified Arab command, ensuring Jordan's involvement in any attack. Israel launched an attack a few days later on 5 June 1967, the beginning of what would become known as the Six Day War, which led to the destruction of the Egyptian air force on the first day, and the loss of the Sinai, the Golan Heights and the West Bank by the time the conflict ended on 11 June.

The motivations and intrigues behind the war are a study in their own right, with many different opinions regarding why it happened and its effects on the region. With respect to Hussein's role, he admitted afterwards that he did not believe that the Arabs would win. Nor could he have wanted them to, given that victory would have surely meant that Nasser and his supporters in Jordan would become irrepressible. When asked by the US Secretary of State Dean Rusk to stay out of the fighting after the outbreak of war, he insisted on participating with the statement that his honour left him no choice.[84]

Whether Hussein's assertion or Tahrir's unconventional analysis is the more believable is subjective. What is indisputable is that the war conclusively ended Nasser's image and reputation, dealing a massive blow to the viability of pan-Arab nationalism as a creed capable of uniting and liberating the Middle East. This meant the significant reduction of a major threat to the existence of the Hashemite kingdom in Jordan, with Hussein having long suffered propaganda aimed against him from Cairo's *Voice of the Arabs* radio station, and threats to his regime from Nasser supporters in the country. It also meant a change in the fortunes of Tahrir.

On 12 June, the day after the end of hostilities, the party distributed a pamphlet that labelled Hussein a traitor who had co-operated with the

British and Israelis in the war. It asserted that the king's sudden agreement to join the mutual defence pact at the end of May was a ploy to ensure that he would be embroiled in any hostilities and able to carry out the plan of surrendering the West Bank, which was duly carried out without a shot being fired in some areas.[85]

The authorities responded with a series of arrests that targeted members in positions of responsibility in Amman, with hundreds detained, including around seventy members who held administrative positions in the party. Only two senior members who were responsible for administering party activities and enculturation remained free, one of them being Fayiz Taha. They sent a message to al-Nabhani in Beirut asking how to proceed. He sent Abdul Halim Zallum, one of the younger brothers of Abdul Qadeem, who was working with him in Iraq at the time in their attempts to win over Iraqi officers to the party.

On Abdul Halim's arrival in Amman he met with Taha, who was in hiding, and began to investigate what remained of the body of members after the arrests. He was somewhat bemused to find that approximately fifty members (excluding students) remained at liberty, remembering his own experiences in Syria between 1961 and 1965 when a handful of activists had been able to at least stir up some public discussion around the party's ideas through their activities. The two set about re-organising study circles and local committees, and within a few months the structure had been re-built and was under control. At that point, they decided to publish a second pamphlet that would be harsher than the first, which had led to the widespread arrests in June, and that the distribution would take place by hand on the main streets in the centre of Amman—as opposed to other less risky approaches sometimes adopted, such as placing them on car windscreens and so on—as an open challenge to the government.

The pamphlet addressed the issue of discussions around the internationalisation of Jerusalem, which according to a newspaper report was the focus of a meeting between Hussein and British Foreign Secretary George Brown, which took place in London on 26 November. In it Hussein's surrender of Jerusalem and agreement to its internationalisation was characterised as one of 'the most despicable crimes done in history by the traitor.'[86] Prior to distribution, the party members in Amman gathered for a motivational speech, where Abdul Halim addressed them, saying that whoever was willing to distribute the pamphlets was welcome to participate, and if anyone was unwilling then they ought to leave the gathering at that point, an offer taken up by one. The distribution was carried out as planned and was likely to have caught the authorities off guard, given the mass arrests that had taken place earlier that year. In the aftermath, they only managed to arrest six of those involved in the distribution over the next two months, including Taha, Shahada Arar and Ali Ismadi, other prominent members, though Abdul Halim was not affected.[87]

Most of those arrested previously in 1967 had been released by this point, and many of them had been expelled from the party because they were considered to have taken a weak stance before the government, which had led to their release. To ensure that al-Nabhani was happy with the defence the newly arrested group presented in court, Arar wrote their statement and it was sent out of the prison for confirmation. Not content with it, al-Nabhani sent them an alternative statement, which Arar read out in the group's defence when they were brought to trial before the internal security court in Zarqa on 7 February 1968.

The defence stated that 'the surrendering [sic.] of the West Bank to Israel by King Hussein is a well known fact' which 'the people of Jordan, all politicians in general, and the rulers in the Muslim world, especially in the Arab world, are aware of.' Their arrest was due to distribution of a pamphlet that 'accused King Hussein of surrendering the West Bank' and so 'in other words, we accused him of being a traitor.' In closing, Arar requested that the court 'ask [him] to prove the treason of King Hussein through multiple witness statements in order to convince the judge of the truthfulness of [his] accusation against King Hussein', which would give him the opportunity to prove before the court that the accusation he made was true, thus concluding his defence that labelling the king a traitor was simply a statement of fact and could not be considered an insult. The court duly handed down the standard two-year jail sentence for membership of the party, which was reduced to one year on appeal, with the defendants leaving jail after serving nine months in accordance with administrative law.[88]

*Attempting 'caesarean section'*

The brazen attitude taken towards the regime won Tahrir admiration in some quarters of the public, as well as in the military, which was still smarting from the 1967 war. The result of the war had naturally led to a huge increase in the interest and credibility of the party, given that it had been openly predicting the chain of events for at least a year before they occurred. Its accusations chimed with officers such as Shirkasi, who had previously attacked party members for their pre-war analysis, but was then ordered to retreat from Hebron without a single bullet being fired. Others confirmed seeing the surrender as foretold by the party with their own eyes. The sense of indignation at the loss of Jerusalem as a result of what they considered to be a betrayal was palpable in the army—as much as if not more so than among the general public.

This presented an opportunity for the party to win more support from within the military, and so additional individuals were assigned to work on seeking support there in 1967. The key figure involved was Ahmad al-Faqir, a Bedouin Jordanian, which gave him easy access and the ability to win the trust of the Jordanian officers, who were mainly drawn from among Bedouin leaders. Visiting the various officers, he found among them people such as Salih Abulful, who remembered al-Nabhani from his time as a lecturer at the Islamic College in Amman in the early 1950s. Other Bedouin officers were won over, such as Arif al-Raqad, and Abdul Hadi Falah, who was a first lieutenant of an armoured division.

Al-Faqir used to meet the officers at his car showroom, where they would bring other potential recruits under the pretence of purchasing new vehicles. Whenever someone was convinced, they would take an oath to support the establishment of the Islamic state, sealed with a recitation of a verse from the Qur'an:

> 'Among the believers, there are men who came true to the covenant they had with Allah. So, some of them have fulfilled their vows [by sacrificing their lives in the way of Allah], and some of them are [still] waiting, and they did not change [their commitment] in the least.'[89]

Al-Faqir would then inform Abdul Halim, who would relay the information back to al-Nabhani, and a meeting would be arranged between al-Nabhani and the new recruits.[90] Other officers outside of the Bedouins included Abdul Halim's brother, Maj. Abdul Wahab Zallum, who was in an artillery battalion.

However, the party had never prioritised Jordan as the main target for establishing the Islamic state, believing that the country was not suitable on its own as a starting point, given its relatively weak army and geo-political situation.[91] The focus at that specific moment was firmly on Iraq, due to the space afforded by Abdul Rahman Arif's weak position, with Abdul Halim and others involved in trying to win over officers there. The party was not alone in such talks, with the Ba'athists also sensing the same opportunity to stage a comeback. Apparently, often the two groups were targeting the same individuals, with one offering Islamic ideals and the other focusing more on nationalist aspirations. Hizb-ut-Tahrir's efforts were bearing fruit, with key officers such as Revolutionary Guard leader Bashir Talib on board.

The increased activity within the party to seek support (*nusra*), which involved key members from the leadership, was likely to have been sensed by a few within the general party body, even though in theory and practice there was a clear separation between the handful of members charged with these specific duties and the main membership, whose role was to keep trying to win public support. In a reminder written in March 1968 titled 'Our issue is not taking power', al-Nabhani stressed that the role of the party was not to simply get into power, but rather to build a state based on Islamic revival. That revival had to be intellectual, and not based on economic strength, moral fortitude or simply a matter of the implementation of laws over people. This is what the West and the USSR had done when they adopted the ideas of secularism and materialism respectively, leading to their revival and emergence as leading nations.

For an Islamic revival, which would be the only correct revival as it also included a spiritual basis, the root issue was for the *Umma* to embrace the Islamic idea, and while the Muslims remained believers they needed to have their belief connected to their transactions and ruling. This required progress in the manner the party had outlined: building public support for the idea, getting people to embrace and carry it, and making the party recognised as a capable ruling entity. In other words, there was no point in simply taking power to implement Sharia if society was not ready. Instead, the party had to come to power organically through the steps mentioned.[92] As a document, the internal pamphlet indicated that until then the main body of the party remained officially uninformed regarding any possible 'caesarean section', and were being pushed to keep working to build public support, which would embrace radical change when it came.

Meanwhile, efforts in Iraq were continuing, with al-Nabhani in the country meeting officers in July to prepare to take power when a coup occurred on 17 July, which resulted in Abdul Rahman Arif being exiled and ultimately (after a short internal power struggle and a second coup within two weeks) the installation of the Ba'athists back in power. This meant an end to al-Nabhani's efforts there at that immediate time. Abdul Halim drove al-Nabhani out of Iraq by car soon after and said during the journey that if al-Nabhani had been an Iraqi then he would definitely have been installed as the caliph instead of leaving at that time, indicating their belief that although the party had won over key officers, others were ultimately swayed by those who were more familiar to them.[93]

Soon after, al-Nabhani wrote a short internal note regarding the events of the July coup, in which he mentioned that it took 'no more than a telephone call ordering Arif out of the country' to undertake the coup attempt, and that the real power behind the coup was nationalist officers who wanted to bring about a government involving all groups and had therefore included the Ba'athists with them. The Ba'athists then took advantage of circumstances to get their officers—who had been previously expelled by Arif—back into the army and took control of events immediately after the coup. According to al-Nabhani, the Ba'athists had no support among either the people or the army, and their short-sighted behaviour would ensure that the regime would not last long (one of al-Nabhani's less accurate predictions).[94]

Although events in Iraq had slipped out of their grasp for the time being, the party retained its presence there, with supporters in the army, and continued to try to gain further influence, considering the regime lacked any credibility. At the same time, further progress was being made in Jordan as far as army support was concerned, with concerted efforts to meet officers in the palace guard producing two recruits from within the heart of the regime itself. In August, al-Nabhani wrote another internal document titled *Marhala al-Tafa'ul* (The Interaction Phase), which explicitly stated that the party had succeeded in winning support (*nusra*). The analysis was very clear: the party had 'begun to look for *nusra* until the political events in the region occurred on top of each other, which caused the centers of leadership to fall one after another in front of people's eyes, which made it easy for the party to gain *nusra*', a clear reference to the loss of support and estimation of the regional leadership as a result of the events of 1967. *Nusra* was defined here as 'powerful people or factions who aid the call... meaning that they proceed with the call, support it and together with the party attempt to take advantage of any chance to get into power, or prevent anyone from harming the carriers of the call, or the two together.'

At this stage, all that remained according to al-Nabhani was 'success in taking the leadership of the *Umma*', and that the issue of assuming leadership was one that required the keen awareness of all the party members. It was therefore necessary for all members to be armed in three ways: firstly, with a comprehensive knowledge of party ideas; secondly, with practical experience of party actions; and finally, each member had to have limitless self-confidence, which would result from constant interaction with people through individual visits and participation in delegations, which would engender in them a sense of responsibility as politicians.

Yet again, great emphasis was placed on public discussions and attempts to address the masses, whether in mosques or other public arenas. At the same time, however, party members were warned off giving their own political analysis on any new event that had taken place before the party had given its opinion on it, to ensure a conformity of opinion and not reduce their credibility in the eyes of the people by contradicting one another. Rather, they should deal with the situation before them and explain it in accordance with Islamic law. Hence, for example, the Ba'athist coup in Iraq should not be discussed from the angle of whether it was a British- or US-backed event before the party had issued its opinion on it. Instead, party members should focus on the political statements made after the coup to expose how the political agenda was not in accordance with Islam.

In effect, despite the level of detail in the pamphlet, which is beyond the discussion here, it appears to have been a final motivational push to ensure the whole membership engaged with society in a coherent manner, while al-Nabhani made his final preparations to establish the Islamic state. The pamphlet ended: 'in closing—I remind you that taking authority is in between our hands.'[95] A month later, in September, al-Nabhani was even more confident, writing that the *Umma* recognised that socialism and democracy had failed them, and were looking to Islam for a solution. The trend towards Islam was noticeable, and people 'only trusted Hizb-ut-Tahrir.'[96]

As it turned out, the officers won over by al-Faqir and others were soon ready to undertake a coup attempt in Jordan to remove Hussein and establish the Islamic state. Though the party did not consider Jordan a viable starting point for the establishment of the caliphate, due to its small army and geography, when offered the chance by eager officers the party leadership believed that it had enough support among the public and the military in the region to quickly unite with at least one of its neighbours, likely Iraq or possibly Syria. Arrangements were made for known individuals among supporters and members of the party, such al-Tamimi and Amin Shinnar to remain on stand-by to address the nation over the radio when the coup was completed.[97] The two leading officers of the coup, Col. Atallah Ghasib and First Lt. Abdul Hadi Falah were ready, with Falah in the palace on the night of the event and zero hour set for 25 December 1968.

On the night of the event, al-Nabhani and al-Da'ur were staying in Amman awaiting news. At the royal palace that night, Falah had had a last-minute change of heart and instead of following through with the plan surrendered himself to the king while confessing to have betrayed him. He also gave up the names of the others he knew were involved, who were quickly apprehended. As a result of initial interrogations a total of about eighty arrests were made, including several officers. Instead of receiving a call confirming that the coup had taken place, al-Nabhani and al-Da'ur received a call informing them that the owner of the flat they were staying in, Nimr Ibrahim Abu Taha, had been arrested. They left immediately before any attempt was made to arrest them. Al-Da'ur subsequently decided to turn himself in, in an attempt to save their host from being tortured.[98]

While the central figure of the coup, First Lt. Falah, had given himself up rather than proceed with the coup attempt, a number of the arrested officers also subsequently turned, including Col. Ghasib. In 1969, sixteen people were charged in connection with the coup attempt in a military court, which included seven who were tried in absentia. Among those who had escaped were al-Nabhani himself (who was at the top of the charge list), Arar (who had only left prison about two months earlier), Abdul Halim Zallum and Mahmoud Abu Ubaida, who according to the copy of the court transcript was a member of Fatah and supporter of the *fedayin*.

The nine people who were present and charged included al-Da'ur, al-Faqir, Nabih Umar al-Jaza'iri (who worked at the television station), Yusuf Salim (a driver) and Nimr Ibrahim. From the military, Maj. Abdul Wahab Zallum, Maj. Yusuf al-Zu'bi, Maj. Mahmoud Abu Sawa and First Lt. Salim Hamdan, all from artillery brigades, were also charged. The charges against them were 'participation in a conspiracy which aimed at overthrowing the system of ruling and changing the constitution by violence' and 'membership of an illegal association (Hizb-ut-Tahrir).'

The interrogation committee was led by Dib Badr, the specialist head of investigations into Hizb-ut-Tahrir in the Jordanian secret police, along with military investigators Muhammad Bashir Shishani and Anwar Mustafa. There were also (unsubstantiated) rumours that the committee had a British presence. The court file detailed the prosecution case brought by state prosecutor Muhammad Manku, which outlined how since the end of 1966 the leadership of the illegal party decided to try to infiltrate the army, meeting soldiers to convince them to 'join a military organization which aimed to overthrow the ruling system through armed power at some point in the future', with the most significant culprit in these efforts being al-Nabhani.

Abdul Halim Zallum was also a significant character in the case file, which mentioned how his brother Maj. Abdul Wahab had been a member of the party since 1954. The document also included how the officers were won over, such as when Falah had visited al-Faqir's car showroom intending to purchase a car from him and al-Faqir had begun to discuss the necessity of working to establish Islamic rule and over time convinced him to join the movement. There were also a number of operational details outlined, such as meetings and messages passed between the various accused; and plans to arrest the head of the army and close the airports, before forcing the chief of staff to sign statements in the name of the party announcing the establishment of the caliphate. Eleven witnesses were mentioned as signatories confirming the details, along with a reference to the confessions of those charged. The eleven included nine from the military, the first two being Col. Ghasib and First Lt. Falah, the two operational leaders of the coup. Ghanim Abdu, who had left the party some years earlier, was one of the two civilians mentioned.[99]

The prosecution asked for sentences in line with the constitution, and the death penalty was duly handed out to all of those charged (five of them given the death penalty in absentia), with all others involved and arrested given fifteen-year sentences, the only exceptions being those who had agreed to testify against the others involved in the case. Some of those charged and sentenced to imprisonment had no relation to the case at all, but were members of the party who had been arrested after going on the run from the authorities following the 1967 pamphlet distribution, immediately after the loss of the West Bank. Among them was Abu Sha'lan, a former police officer originally from Jerusalem. The prosecutor, Manku, had told him during investigations that this time the sentences being passed out were 'not for a month or two', but 'this time it's fifteen or twenty years', in an attempt to persuade Abu Sha'lan to sign a statement rejecting the views of the party. He was subsequently sentenced to fifteen years with hard labour as part of the case, despite having had nothing to do with the coup attempt.[100]

Six of the nine in prison who were to be executed were Jordanians, with the other three being of Palestinian origin (namely al-Da'ur, Zallum and Ibrahim), indicating that the party's support was not confined to the Palestinians but extended to Hussein's traditional tribal base. Playing the role of a magnanimous monarch by giving amnesty to arrested senior military officers such as Col. Ghasib helped Hussein to regain some of that base within the army, but with al-Nabhani and central members such as Abdul Halim Zallum evading arrest, the final curtain had not yet come down on this particular struggle.

# 5

# THE LONG WAIT

## (1969–1977)

*What the party wants is the establishment of the authority of Islam through the means of those that support Islam and the party, and not simply taking power through any means. So it doesn't want to take power in the way it was taken by Abdul Karim Qasim, Abdul Salam Arif and the Ba'athists in Iraq, just as it doesn't want to take it in the manner of Husni al-Za'im, al-Hanawi, al-Shishakli and the Ba'athists by name in Syria, or the manner of revolution as done by the Syrian nationalists twice in Lebanon, and the Ba'athists twice in Iraq.*

*Rather, the party wants to take power in a specific way which is: the support for Islam, and support for the party. It totally rejects taking power even if it was practically handed it except through this support. It will never accept anything else, even if it remains [without success] for tens of years.*

Sheikh Taqiudeen al-Nabhani, 1970[1]

While in prison, those convicted lived together in decent conditions and were treated well by the prison authorities. Although conditions throughout the interrogations were harsh, especially for those who were unwilling to co-operate, formal imprisonment had provided relief for them. Hizb-ut-Tahrir members were treated with respect, especially as news spread that the coup was not undertaken at the behest of a foreign embassy or for the sake of material gain, but that the explicit goal was to establish an Islamic state that would implement Sharia law. Abu Sha'lan was a personal friend of the prison governor, and as a result the party members were permitted to meet visitors in his office.[2]

137

Al-Da'ur's presence among the prisoners was welcomed because they loved his easy-going personality and respected his role in the leadership of the party. When they heard that he had been whipped daily during interrogations without breaking, he rose even higher in their estimation. The party members were therefore surprised that as a result of their close interaction over their time in prison it was recognised that while al-Da'ur was undoubtedly an Islamic scholar of some knowledge, having graduated from al-Azhar during the same period as al-Nabhani, he was not particularly well versed in the party's teachings. This was due to his having spent much of the past decade in and out of jail as the most prominent symbol of Hizb-ut-Tahrir in Jordan as a result of his time as a parliamentarian in the 1950s. But despite practical reasons for al-Da'ur's relative weakness in understanding, it further enforced the idea in the minds of the members that there was a wide gap in knowledge and understanding between even leading party members and al-Nabhani. Al-Da'ur confirmed this, telling them that while he and the rest of the senior members were at ground level, they all considered al-Nabhani to be somewhere above them 'in the sky'. This was not limited to just one aspect, but in terms of his patience in relation to food, prayer and thought. Al-Da'ur considered him unique in every aspect, from the personal and spiritual to the intellectual and political.[3]

This type of praise—coming from a man who was older than al-Nabhani, a colleague of his in al-Azhar, the most prominent and arguably the most loved member of the party in Jordan, who was known for his sacrifice to the party cause, as well as being a member of the leadership committee—gave extra weight to feelings among some of the members. It ultimately led to one of those in prison who heard the claims to write to al-Nabhani, commenting that there was a noticeable difference between the capability of the leadership (meaning al-Nabhani) and the rest of the party members, asking why it existed and how it could be overcome.[4]

Al-Nabhani sent a reply in which he vigorously asserted that there was no difference in capability, and that he considered that some of the younger members were in fact better than the leadership in some respects. According to al-Nabhani, the perceived difference was only as a result of the leadership holding certain responsibilities, and that when others took up those responsibilities they would be seen to act on the same level,[5] an answer that many of the members found unconvincing.[6]

While all manner of discussions took place within the prison cells, from party issues and politics to exegesis of the Qur'an and other Islamic sciences, al-Daʻur, al-Faqir and the others sentenced to death waited patiently for their punishment to be carried out. Although those on death row were content with their fate, their families outside were growing more desperate as time passed and sought different ways to put pressure on the king to commute their sentences. After the events of Black September in 1970, which saw the Jordanian army fight armed Palestinian factions that threatened to dethrone the monarchy (once again), with neither the Palestinians nor the Jordanian Bedouin tribes pleased with Hussein, the king was as usual treading a fine line trying to maintain his position.

A delegation came to the palace to ask for the prisoners to be pardoned, and a protest made up of their wives and mothers sought an audience with him. Executing the nine would not have ended the activity of the party in Jordan. Al-Nabhani and others were still alive and at large, and could have had the opposite effect of winning the group more publicity and popularity, something Hussein could do without, given his precarious position between the tribes and the *fedayin*. Although routine preparations had begun for the executions, on the advice of his prime minister, al-Tall, the king issued a general amnesty for all those involved in the case, leading to their release less than three years after their arrest.[7]

On leaving prison, a handful of those convicted were immediately expelled from the party by al-Nabhani, including at least one who had been given the death sentence. One of the reasons given was that some of them were not considered to have taken robust enough stances in front of their interrogators, whereas al-Daʻur and others who were seen to have taken principled stances in difficult circumstances remained.

*The second coup attempt and other Jordanian affairs*

The coup attempt and the trial were not mentioned much in the local or regional media at the time (or thereafter), but the Jordanian regime began to link Hizb-ut-Tahrir's central role after the 1968 attempt with the accusation that the group was trying to take 'material actions' to reach its goals. When the interior ministry released a statement to that effect in October 1969, with the accusation repeated on the radio by the prime minister, the party released an open letter in reply to the king, stating that it followed 'the method of the Prophet' in conveying the message of Islam. It did this to win over the support of the people, as well as of those who were the 'material power who would support this idea' by establishing Islamic rule and defending it. In the same way, the party sought to convey its Islamic message to the people of Jordan and to those who had power in the army and individuals from the armed groups among the *fedayin*. In this way the party did not undertake material actions, but rather sought the support of those people at the centres of power who were capable of bringing about a change of the government.

The pamphlet also mentioned that the party had been offered power in Jordan multiple times previously: such as in 1953 when the young king took power after the assassination of his grandfather; or in 1957 when there was in fact an attempt against King Hussein; or 1961 when the UAR separated; and finally in 1963. Hizb-ut-Tahrir had rejected each offer because it considered that the people had not yet embraced the party and its ideas, with all of these apparent offers occurring before the protests against the Pope's visit in 1964, which convinced al-Nabhani that society was ready for the establishment of an Islamic state. It was only then that it began to seek public support to create this Islamic state.

After this series of claims, it was stated that 'the party will reach power irrespective, with the Will of Allah, despite the bad conditions in the country', continuing that 'the party is not only present in Jordan, rather it is present in an area much wider than people imagine' and that 'most of the army in Jordan, if not all of it, is with the party.' The pamphlet went on to mention the names of various supporters from the East Bank, and then stated, 'this is why the party trusts that it will take power in Jordan, and trusts in the Islam of the sons of this *Umma*, in particular those in the army and the armed forces.'

The most interesting part of the statement was that given the king's position as monarch, as well as his claim that he was descended from the Prophet's family (which according to the majority of scholars was at a minimum a recommended characteristic for any caliph), it was possible that the party could have sought support from him to establish the Islamic state directly, in the same way that the party 'requested the *nusra* from the heads of countries such as Abdul Salam Arif.' However, in the case of King Hussein this was considered infeasible because he and his forefathers (such as his grandfather Abdullah) were 'creations of the British', and finally because he had 'surrendered the West Bank, al-Quds, and the great holy places'. It was due to these considerations that the members of the army who had supported Tahrir knew that he would not agree to any proposal from the party to establish an Islamic state, and this is what 'made those whom the party sought the *nusra* from think of removing the material barriers [in the path of establishing the Islamic state] via the means that you have seen'—in other words, the failed coup attempt.[8]

Apart from embodying the type of limitless self-confidence that al-Nabhani had counselled all the members to exhibit, the open letter was interesting for a number of reasons. As far as practical matters were concerned, the first was the open admission of the party's role in the attempt to overthrow the regime, albeit in the indirect manner of a political party encouraging its supporters to take the necessary steps to install it in power. In addition, it documented the party's proposals to Arif in Iraq, which took place just a couple of years earlier, before his death in 1966. The final point was the almost direct challenge to the position of the king, informing him that his days were numbered and that the party was on the brink of taking power, despite it having been less than a year since the first attempt, after which more than ten senior officers were arrested.

The reason for al-Nabhani's confidence was due to the preparations for a second coup attempt that took place shortly afterwards. Despite the loss of the officers in December 1968, that the party was able to put into place arrangements for such a move is perhaps an indication of the depth of their support, within the army as well as the *fedayin*, as well as the significance of the challenge that King Hussein faced, even after the fall of Arab nationalism as a major threat. Not all the officers who had links with the party had been uncovered after the first attempt, and work had begun to make new arrangements, with backing from individuals in Palestinian militias and officers from the army.

The central officer who was responsible for the arrangements, Maj. Muhammad Touqan, was arrested before he began the process of carrying out the coup. The details regarding the arrangements are not well known and remain scant. The plot was apparently uncovered because Touqan told one of his relatives, who was in charge of one of the militias in Amman, about the plan, who then on the night of the event let it slip to the overall commander of the militias there, one of the founding members of Fatah, Nimr al-Saleh, also known as Abu Saleh. Abu Saleh apparently then informed Yasser Arafat (Abu Ammar) that Hizb-ut-Tahrir was planning to overthrow the king, and gave him the name of the person he knew was involved. It is difficult, if not impossible, to substantiate such a claim, but the only name that was known to the authorities at the time of the arrest was that of Touqan. Under interrogation, Touqan insisted that nobody else was involved, and since there was neither any other evidence at hand to prove otherwise nor could anything be extracted from Touqan, he was kept in jail for a time. There was nothing else the authorities could do given they had no other information nor any other witnesses, and in the end Touqan was released without charge.[9]

Al-Nabhani was staying in Amman with Abdul Halim at the time of Touqan's arrest, which had come as a shock to him when he heard about it the day after it occurred. 'I saw the sun turn black', he said, shaken that this second attempt, in which he had invested great hope and confidence, had also been undermined. He had been certain that the Islamic state was going to be established at his hands, and that he would have the opportunity to lead it as caliph for enough time to strengthen its foundations as he had struggled to do with his own party.[10] But it did not occur as planned or hoped for, despite the efforts and arrangements made, and circumstances in Jordan soon meant that there was little scope for any further activity in the army's ranks, with the country descending into chaotic disarray in the early 1970s.

While the first coup attempt had bolstered the credibility of Tahrir internally and externally as a serious entity working to establish a government, based on its programme, the failure of the second coup attempt led some of question the competency of the party.[11] Others became even more afraid of association with the group, having failed in two successive attempts to remove the regime. Questions were raised internally regarding methodology, with the issue of the justification for asking soldiers to act on behalf of the party raised. This was clearly the result of interaction in jail between the members who had been involved in the *nusra* work, and others arrested who were from the general body of the party and previously unaware of the *nusra* activities. those who had been jailed, but were from the general body of the party, who were kept separate from such activity.

Al-Nabhani stated that there was a difference between the party taking material action and requesting it from those from whom it was seeking *nusra*. The proof given was the words of the Prophet to a group of tribal leaders who pledged in Mecca to 'protect [the Prophet] from that which you protect your women and children', or in other words to fight to protect him. They then offered to fight and kill the enemies of the Prophet in Mecca that very night, to which the Prophet replied that they had not been ordered (by Allah) to do so. Al-Nabhani drew an analogy between that situation and the party's seeking support from the army. He also differentiated between Hizb-ut-Tahrir as a party entity and individual members who were members of the armed forces and might, for example, take part in fighting to defend the people or attack an enemy. When such a member took such an action as part of the army, then he was acting as an individual in that specific role and had nothing to do with the actions of the party per se.

The belief that al-Nabhani had fostered that Tahrir was on the cusp of taking power in 1968 meant that impatience was creeping into the party body after two failed attempts in the subsequent two years. Another response to such questions was published in August 1970, when al-Nabhani stated that the party's goal was to restart the Islamic way of life, and not to take power, so the goal of the party would be met if an Islamic state was established, with the identity of who established it irrelevant. With that said, he reiterated his belief that the party had interacted with society to the point that it was ready for an Islamic state to be established, but that unrepresentative regimes stood in their way. All that remained was to gain the *nusra* for the practical steps to remove the barriers to its establishment. As for when that would occur, it was an issue 'not known to anyone except Allah'—it might be after two years or after ten. Although the party 'was certain about its path and actions', and definite that all that remained was formally being given power by the people, it was an issue that was in the hands of God and so should not be a source of impatience.[12]

Meanwhile, it was during this period that the militarised conflict between the Palestinian armed *fedayin* factions and the Jordanian regime threatened to implode the region, with clashes occurring throughout 1970. The different militias increasingly began to base themselves in urban areas, and also undertook actions that undermined the state, such as the kidnap of foreign citizens from local hotels by the Popular Front for the Liberation of Palestine (PFLP). The disorder reached the point where in June Yasser Arafat claimed that Fatah was in control of Amman.[13] Since the end of 1969, the US had been proposing the Rogers Plan—a ten-point proposal for Israel to return land it had taken in the 1967 war in exchange for Israel's recognition within agreed borders—as a way to resolve the ongoing war of attrition between the Palestinian factions and Israel. Nasser agreed to it, and it was then confirmed by King Hussein in June 1970.

In these circumstances, at the end of the month al-Nabhani issued a statement that was primarily addressed to the *fedayin* factions, with whom the party had previously had numerous contacts. Previous analysis by al-Nabhani suggested that the while the *fedayin* forces included sincere individuals who were seeking the liberation of Palestine, the formal structures that controlled the various militias were under the influence of different foreign governments trying to use them for political ends. In the statement al-Nabhani expressed his belief that the rulers of the region had all betrayed the cause of Palestine and that the armed factions were the last chance remaining for its liberation.

While most mainstream analyses considered the presence of the militias in Amman to have been a threat to King Hussein, al-Nabhani believed that their presence there was in fact used to protect him, and counselled them to rid themselves of their leaders such as Arafat and George Habash, whom he believed were insincere. He also advised them to leave the cities, where they had no business being, and instead wage their fight from the mountains and countryside, thereby removing themselves from being under the authority of others. The statement also called on them to continue patiently in their armed struggle and not to give it up.[14]

Events in Jordan came to a head in September 1970, known as Black September, in reference to the internecine conflict between Jordanian and Palestinian *fedayin* forces at the time. Again the king's position was under threat, with his own driver and cook revealed to be members of the *fedayin*. A military government was appointed under the leadership of al-Tall during a month in which the PFLP hijacked multiple passenger planes and chaos and intra-Arab fighting increased in Amman, with the Syrian and Iraqi armies also involved.

Unable to trust his own military officers, the head of a Pakistani training mission to Jordan (who subsequently became Pakistan's military leader), Zia al-Haq, apparently played a leading role in commanding the army against the Palestinians,[15] with the death toll from the attacks estimated ranging from the low thousands to as high as twenty thousand.[16] An emergency Arab League summit was called in Cairo on 28 September, which was boycotted by Iraq, Syria and others, but attended by the Jordanian and Palestinian factions. Nasser presided over an agreement between King Hussein and Arafat to end the fighting, with Arafat agreeing to remove the militias from the cities and focus their actions on the fronts with Israel in exchange for not being targeting by the Jordanian army. However, Nasser died a few hours after the agreement had been confirmed.

Despite the agreement, the situation remained chaotic due to the multitude of elements that made up the Palestinian resistance, backed by other states,[17] and the conflict between the factions continued into the New Year. There was little that Hizb-ut-Tahrir could do to influence events in and around Jordan, but at the beginning of April 1971 it published an open letter addressed to the major leaders including the president of Egypt, Anwar Sadat, King Hussein, Arafat, al-Tall and the tribal heads in Jordan, 'to try to save what remained of the country and people' in the hope that perhaps they would be inspired to separate themselves from the US and British governments and work sincerely for the interests of the people.

The letter analysed major global events occurring at that time, as well as the regional conflict within the paradigm of the Anglo-American struggle for influence, concluding that the current fighting that had gone on for about a year was a result of a US desire to bring about a Palestinian state in Jordan and British attempts to prevent that from happening. Each of the two sides had influence over the various actors on the ground, in what was in effect a proxy war between the US and the UK. While the analysis basically subsumed any agency of the players on the ground into the plans of the great powers, it ended by giving sincere advice to the parties not to allow themselves any longer to be used as tools in the fight over influence in the region by the two Western states. There was a plea for all sides to immediately cease hostilities; for the *fedayin* to limit their actions to operations within Palestine itself; for the Jordanian army to deploy its forces along the country's borders and ready itself for war against Israel rather than against the Palestinians; and for Egypt to stop its political manoeuvring, particularly concerning Jordan, until God brought about the conditions that would unify the Muslims in preparation for the decisive battle under a single flag.[18] It happened that two days after the release of the letter, King Hussein demanded that the *fedayin* remove their heavy weapons from the capital within two days, which was promptly rejected by one of the militia factions.[19]

The continuing events prevented any opportunity to work within the Jordanian army or the *fedayin* for the party's objectives, and instead it continued to try to address the leading players in the conflict in an attempt to influence the direction of events. At the beginning of June, the party wrote another address, this time directed at the heads of the PLO, who were told that their resistance was being used as a tool to bring about the recognition and legitimisation of Israel. The party had, from the time of the PLO's formation in 1964, considered that it was set up as a vehicle to eventually separate the West Bank from Jordan and make it into an independent Palestinian state; and to separate the Palestinian issue from being an Islamic issue into a purely nationalist one, and therefore an un-Islamic enterprise.[20] The letter stated that Hizb-ut-Tahrir did not believe that a Palestinian state would ever come about in any case, and that the intra-Arab fighting that they were involved in was merely the futile spilling of people's blood.[21] After a series of military operations against the Palestinian groups, most were completely routed from Jordan by the end of June.

At the end of the year, al-Nabhani attempted to send a delegation to speak to the various militia leaders regionally, before going on to deliver a message from the party to the Egyptian government. It was originally intended that the delegation would be composed of two members, Ali Ismadi and Dr Abdul

Qadir, who would also be accompanied by one of the party's supporters, a lawyer from Amman. In the end the lawyer excused himself from the task and Ismadi and Qadir travelled without him. Unable to leave Jordan as a result of previous arrests, Ismadi used his brother's passport to get out of the country before using his own passport to travel between Syria, Lebanon and Egypt.

The intention was to ensure that the party's voice was heard directly by the various players involved, by taking political action which would increase Hizb-ut-Tahrir's profile. The delegation was first to deliver messages to *fedayin* commanders in Beirut and Syria, once again exhorting them to confine their bases and activities to rural areas, given that the conflict and bloodshed they were causing was blackening any call to resistance. However, given the heavily secular, leftist ideology of many of the militia leaders, their actions were not constricted by religious values, and some of them were known for being deliberately unobservant of religious precepts or sanctities. Although the message was well received by the various commanders they met, the delegation left with the impression that the commanders were either insincere or unable to change the direction and strategy they had adopted.

From Beirut, the pair flew to Egypt. Al-Nabhani had planned the programme they were to follow in detail, specifying the hotel to book themselves into, the type of car to hire and the attire that they should adopt. Wearing suits, while being driven in a black Mercedes meant that they were able to enter both the presidential palace and the parliament without being stopped or asked any questions, which was credited either to al-Nabhani's insight into Egyptian habits or poor Egyptian security, or a combination of the two.

At the palace, they were met by Sadat's secretary, Usama al-Baz, who was concerned to know why the unexpected visitors wanted to meet the president. They informed al-Baz that they were from Hizb-ut-Tahrir and had a letter to present to him directly. Al-Baz offered to deliver the letter himself, since Sadat was a busy man, but the delegation insisted on meeting him in person. In the end they left the details of the hotel they were staying at (the Hilton) with al-Baz, on the agreement that he would try to arrange an appointment for them. The pair were then driven to the parliament to try to make a similar arrangement with the prime minister.

After returning to the hotel the secret police stormed their room late that night. After a search turned up the letter that they were to deliver and discuss with Sadat, they were taken to the interior ministry where they were held separately in empty cells. They were then interrogated separately, with questions focused on what they wanted with Sadat. Ismadi tried to intimate that the delegation had more details to discuss with Sadat than were contained in the letter, but claimed that it would not be appropriate to divulge that information to anyone other than the president himself. This ploy only served to draw the interrogations out over three days, until Qadir managed to send a message to Ismadi to put an end to the matter. At the next interrogation Ismadi confirmed that in actual fact the letter had all the details within it and that the delegation had nothing further to add.

Part of the interrogation ended up in a discussion about the party's claim that Sadat was a US agent, a claim that bewildered the interrogators. They said that if the party had claimed that Sadat was an agent of the USSR and under Soviet influence it would have been more understandable to them, given that he received weapons from Soviet Bloc allies and there were Russian experts in the country—such an analysis would have appeared much more plausible. Ismadi countered that this was a superficial analysis—the reality was that the president could remove the Russians from the country at the stroke of a pen—and that this did not indicate Sadat's true leanings. Subsequently, in July 1972, Sadat announced the expulsion of Russian military advisers from Egypt, a year prior to the 1973 Arab-Israeli war, after which he openly shifted towards the US.

The pair were deported to Beirut, leaving without having managed to meet anyone significant in the Egyptian regime. Meanwhile, despite the upheavals and instability in Jordan, preparations were continuing elsewhere.[22]

*Government in waiting*

While the conflict between multiple groups, each with their own sponsors and interests, muddied the situation in Jordan, the party continued to work across a wide range of countries, within the region and beyond. In 1968 Abu Muhammad was sent to Egypt with instructions to prepare support there in anticipation of the establishment of the caliphate elsewhere, al-Nabhani's expectation being that the work in Iraq, Jordan and possibly Syria would bear fruit soon enough. Although Tahrir had been present in Egypt since the 1950s, the harsh security environment that clamped down on the party at the first sign, coupled with the lack of a large, strong body of supporters, meant that there were not many members there. The exception to this was Muhammad Abdul-Qawwi, an al-Azhar graduate who joined in the 1950s and had spent time in jail with Sayyid Qutb, among others (on an unrelated charge), in the early 1960s after the arrests of about fifty party members in 1960.[23]

Abu Muhammad set about trying to win over influential preachers, with the idea that they would support the caliphate from the pulpit if it was established elsewhere. The most prominent figure who was happy to support the general principle at the time was Sheikh Abdul-Hamid Kishk, an enigmatic imam who was one of the most charismatic preachers of his era. Kishk was known for his outspoken criticism of the Arab governments at the time, and although he was boycotted by the mainstream media during Sadat's rule, recordings of his speeches were widely distributed.[24] Sheikh Fikri, an al-Azhari imam at a central mosque in the Dokki district of Cairo, was also convinced.

Abu Muhammad was subsequently arrested at Cairo Airport while returning from Beirut, and was deported in 1969.[25] The party then sent Abdul Halim al-Ramahi to lead activities in Egypt towards the end of 1970. Al-Ramahi had been active in Saudi Arabia and recently deported from there back to Jordan, which he soon also left after being pursued by the authorities for a speech he made after Friday prayers regarding the political situation there.[26]

Meanwhile, Abu Muhammad travelled to Iraq to help lead the party work there. But after a year and a half, he was arrested and tortured for three months, before being deported to Syria in 1971, where he was made responsible for activity in Damascus. One of his classmates from back in Palestine in the early 1950s, Abu Imad, was the overall head of activities there. It had been decided to try to address the masses through speeches in mosques, due to the consideration that Hafiz al-Assad was in a precarious position and potentially susceptible, having become president in 1971 after winning a power struggle with Salah Jadid towards the end of 1970, just a few years after the previous 1966 intra-Ba'athist coup.

After a successful attempt to hold such a public speech in a mosque led to the news spreading in the community, the group soon attracted new supporters, who were suspected of having been planted to spy on the party. In particular, a Palestinian supporter drew attention to himself with the expensive brand of cigarettes he smoked, and the fact that he spoke the *Maghrib* (sunset) prayer aloud in all three standings of the prayer, whereas even children would know that the first two are spoken aloud and the third is silent. The second time the party tried to make such a speech in the mosque after prayers, the individual was quickly arrested and bundled into a car with foreign number plates (an indication that it was used by undercover police). Abu Muhammad was then arrested at the end of a campaign that had seen about twenty-five others taken in before him, and he ended up spending more than five years in jail before being deported in 1978.[27]

Rather than Egypt or Syria, it seems that the leadership's main focus at the time was on Iraq. Zallum had remained there after the Ba'athist coup in 1968 to maintain the party's links to supporters and members in the Iraqi army, and in 1969 he was met by Fayiz Taha, who had been sent to Iraq to help support activity. The latter's passport still had the deportation stamps on its pages, as he'd been arrested multiple times there before being expelled from the country at the end of 1966. After trying to bleach the stamp off, which erased the stamp but also the colour from the page, he turned for help to a friend who worked in a foreign consulate, who in turn placed a paper visa over the page covering it entirely (which could have saved Taha the trouble of bleaching it if he had thought of it first). On Taha's arrival in Baghdad, Zallum informed him that the party had a strong presence in the army, in which it had great hopes, and that he was looking to Taha to help develop and expand the party's membership.

There were fewer than ten study circles in Baghdad then, and the party had lost its presence in Basra and Mosul. Taha's major breakthrough came when he managed to win over three students from the law department at the University of Baghdad: Hussain Abdul Qadir, Faruq Nuri and Sa'd al-Dafrawi. The three had previously been part of the Muslim Brotherhood and then the *salafi* movement in Iraq, but had left before coming into contact with Hizb-ut-Tahrir's ideas. They quickly came to understand the party and its ideas, and as they were young activists with many local contacts among the community they were instrumental in helping Taha expand membership and support.

Despite the existence of Hizb al-Dawa, Hizb-ut-Tahrir was still able to build a good presence among the Shia community. The Islamic awakening (*al-sahwa al-Islamiyya*), which was underway in the early 1970s prior to the Iranian Revolution, meant that the atmosphere was Islamic rather than sectarian, with no discernible Sunni-Shia conflict among the general population, as opposed to some of the scholars, particularly in areas such as Najaf. As a result, the party was winning over many Shia members, especially those who had come from non-practising backgrounds and had no previous information about Shia tenets, which they may have felt conflicted with working for a revival by establishing a caliphate based on the normative Sunni orthodox standard of an elected caliph rather than one who was appointed by divine right.

As party activity expanded, it reached a point where there were more than thirty concentrated study circles in Baghdad, around twenty in Basra, and seven or eight in Mosul. With a substantial party membership and the capacity for more discussions, the local leadership assessed that their presence was beginning to be tangibly felt among Iraqi society. In September 1971, after the arrest of ten to fifteen other activists, Taha was arrested and taken for interrogation by the Iraqi internal security apparatus, known as the General Security Directorate (GSD). Ten to fifteen others were also subsequently arrested.

As the leader, Taha was singled out for special attention; he was held in an underground cell about a metre high and taken out for extended physical beatings. After a few days, as a result of his jaw and numerous teeth having been broken, his face had swollen to such an extent that the guards took him to the prison hospital at the medical university. He remained there for forty days, during which time he helped other patients, given that he was in fact the healthiest prisoner there, with others suffering the effects of all manner of torture, from broken limbs to acid burns.

By the time he returned for further interrogation, the investigators had in their possession a letter that had been sent from the central leadership based in Beirut to Baghdad asking Taha about certain administrative issues, which further exposed his role and the international dimensions of the party. After some time, he was interrogated by the notorious Nadhim Kazar, the head of the GSD under Ahmad Hassan Bakr, who led the government. Kazar apologised for Taha's treatment, stating that there had been misunderstanding resulting in the fact that the party was operating secretly. Having read the party's book, *Mafahim Siyasiyya li Hizb-ut-Tahrir* (Political Understandings of Hizb-ut-Tahrir), Kazar told Taha that he knew that Tahrir did not believe that the Ba'ath party was itself a US or British client, and that they were both against imperialism.

The book had been completed in May 1969 (between the two Jordanian coup attempts), and the point Kazar was referring to stated:

> when the 30 July 1968 coup took place and the Ba'athists came to power, Iraq became an independent country, so when the Ba'athists became connected to Abdul Nasser, and Abdul Nasser is an American agent, Iraq became connected to the American designs and so moved with America through Abdul Nasser.[28]

This was an example given in the first edition to highlight the different ways that the international politics of a state could be analysed (subsequently removed by the fourth edition).[29] Given that Tahrir was an Islamic party and the Ba'athists were an Arab party that respected Islam, Kazar said, if members such as Taha had wanted to operate in Iraq then they could have come to either himself, the prime minister or the interior minister to discuss the matter.

Taha understood from the discussion and the jarringly cordial atmosphere that Kazar was trying to win him over. In the end he replied that if Kazar meant what he had said, he should allow him to leave freely, and that just as Kazar was part of one party, he was a member of another, and so it would not be possible for him to make any type of agreement between the two without consulting the party leadership. The meeting ended in the same vein, with Taha deported from Iraq soon after, leading him to make his way to Lebanon. Less than two years later Kazar was at the head of a failed attempted coup, planned for 30 June 1973, against Bakr and his deputy Saddam. He was interrogated by Hussein personally and executed soon after. During the interrogation Kazar claimed that he had planned the coup in order to save the Ba'ath party from the tribal direction he believed it was being taken in.[30]

That Kazar had read *Mafahim* could indicate two things: that he was a meticulous investigator and read all of the materials confiscated during the arrest campaign and that the book happened to be among them; and/or that the book was being read by people in the military and government as a result of party activity in their circles. Whatever the case may be, Iraq was central to the party at the time. Zallum was based there to arrange winning *nusra* support (with al-Da'ur, the only other member of the leadership committee apart from Zallum and al-Nabhani, being in jail). Al-Nabhani would travel to Iraq as part of their efforts, during which time Zallum would take his place in Lebanon, so that someone from the leadership was running central party affairs. After returning from one visit in 1971, al-Nabhani confided to his son that during his last trip they had taken a pledge of allegiance (*bay'a*) from eighty army officers in one sitting, after eight hours of discussions.[31]

The pamphlet that explained to the party body the process that had led to the adoption of the 'caesarean section' as part of Tahrir's methodology was written in January 1972. In it, al-Nabhani began by stating that the party was concerned by society and the ideas that it carried, and not in seeking power for its own sake. Hizb-ut-Tahrir's activity and place of work was among society. He went on to discuss how the party had come to the final conclusion by 1965 that it was necessary to seek *nusra* to remove the 'material barriers' that were preventing the birth of the Islamic state, and how this work had been— and was being—carried out by a select few in secret. It ended with the words 'it is certain that it will definitely succeed, and trusts in the victory of Allah,'[32] indicating al-Nabhani's confidence of how matters were progressing at the time. During the same period, although al-Nabhani would talk of his frustrations in dealing with the officers in Iraq, he was very hopeful and used to praise them at the same time. At that moment he had great hopes that the caliphate was about to be achieved, and used to say that Allah had given him twenty years to lead the party, and that He would, God Willing, give him leadership of the Islamic state for the next twenty.[33]

Before travelling to Iraq in the first half of 1972, al-Nabhani gathered together a group of senior members in Lebanon and informed them that preparations had reached the stage in Iraq when he believed that they were ready to establish the Islamic state there on his next trip. He gave each of them instructions to carry out on hearing his voice on the radio, including organising delegations to visit the Lebanese Dar al-Fatwa, parliament, president and even the Maronite Patriarch. The attendees left the meeting full of anticipation and hope, and al-Nabhani travelled soon after to Iraq. Believing that they could be arrested if they remained in Beirut, three members—Abu Mahmoud, Ibrahim al-Nabhani and Salim Lutfi—went into hiding in Tripoli, and listened to the radio daily, waiting to hear al-Nabhani's voice on Radio Baghdad.

It never happened and they soon realised something had gone awry. While al-Nabhani was in Iraq, a letter regarding routine party affairs was sent to him from Lebanon through an intermediary and a messenger. He wrote his response, which was given to the messenger to deliver back to Lebanon. At the Baghdad airport, the message was discovered during a routine search, and attracted attention by the way that it had been wrapped up in an attempt to conceal it. The messenger was taken for interrogation, giving up the name of the intermediary who had passed him the message to deliver. The intermediary was then arrested, and under pressure told the interrogators that the message was from al-Nabhani, and gave them the address where he was staying. Al-Nabhani was found at the address and taken for interrogation, along with the Lebanese passport he was travelling on (which, for obvious reasons, did not carry the name Taqiudeen al-Nabhani).

Each of the three was held at a different location. Al-Nabhani admitted to having written the letter, but when asked whether he was in fact Taqiudeen al-Nabhani he simply insisted that his name was in his passport. It was sent to the Lebanese embassy, the reply coming back confirming that the passport was authentic. Al-Nabhani stuck to his story under torture. He shared his cell for periods of four to five days at a time with other supposed prisoners, who would try to befriend him and talk to him about his case to extract information in any unguarded moments. After three months, the authorities decided that the man they were holding was not al-Nabhani and deported him to Lebanon.

Arriving late at night at the flat he used in Beirut, al-Nabhani knocked on the door expecting to find Zallum there. Nobody answered the door, and so he sat on the stairwell for a few hours until the time came for the dawn prayer, at which point Zallum opened the door and found al-Nabhani sitting there. Before leaving for Iraq he had been a sturdy looking sixty-year-old. Al-Nabhani had returned looking emaciated after three months' imprisonment, during which time he had been given one spoonful of food a day. Despite his physical state he was a sight to behold for his son. Seeing him alive after expecting to hear news of his death was the happiest moment that Ibrahim had with his father.[34]

Prior to these events, al-Nabhani was convinced that God was going to grant him victory during his lifetime, but all of the preparations and arrangements for any imminent attempt to be made in Iraq had been disrupted. Despite this, al-Nabhani's conviction only appeared to grow stronger. Having thought that his appointed time of death was surely going to be in the Iraqi interrogation cells, his escape made him believe that he had been saved to achieve his goal.[35] He went back to writing and directing the party soon after his return. Zallum had been running administrative matters in his absence, but little had been done in the way of political analysis or any other type of publication while he was away. Nothing of any weight appears to have been published between the end of April and August 1972.

Once he had recovered the publications resumed, with two new books being completed within a year. The first, *Natharat Siyasiyya li-Hizb-ut-Tahrir* (Political Views of Hizb-ut-Tahrir) was completed on 29 December 1972 and published in January 1973. A short treatise comprising sixty pages in its first edition, it asserted that the clash between states was natural due to the clash of civilisations and interests, beginning with the words 'All of the states [today] are enemies of Islam, because they embrace ways of life [or religions] and principles [or ideologies] which contradict Islam, and their viewpoint regarding life differs with, or rather contradicts, the Islamic viewpoint towards life.'[36] The book continued by giving a historic and contemporary analysis of the international situation, above all encouraging Muslims to understand politics, and ending with the words 'In summary, it is imperative that the *Umma* cultures itself politically, and to increase its knowledge of the roots and branches [of political issues], since it is the *Umma* that undertakes political actions, irrespective [of] whether [they are] the actions of liberation or carrying Islam to the world.'[37]

The second book, titled *al-Tafkir* (Thinking) was completed on 12 March 1973, soon after the first. The book dealt with defining the mind, thinking, different types of thinking, and discussing the rise and decline of Muslim thought. The inspiration for the book had occurred some years earlier, during a visit that al-Nabhani had paid to Ghanim Abdu, during which Abdu's young nephew came in carrying a reading book that contained some pictures of animals. Al-Nabhani pointed to a picture of a rooster and asked the child what it was, a question to which the child replied correctly. He then pointed to a picture of a lion, and again asked what he was pointing at, to which the child replied 'horse'. After that, a discussion began around the reason behind the difference between the answer and the reality, which ultimately resulted in al-Nabhani writing on the subject.[38]

The book began by identifying the ability to think as the unique character-istic that gave human beings superiority over all other creation. After criti-quing other attempts at definitions of the mind and thought (and, specifically, communist views on materialism, including the claim that consciousness is a reflection of the reality on the brain), he concluded that 'intellect, thought, or comprehension is transferring the sensation of the reality via the senses to the brain with the presence of previous information, through which this reality is explained/understood.'[39] One of the examples given by al-Nabhani appears to allude to the visit he made to Abdu:

> 'Let us take also a child of four years old, who neither saw nor heard about lions, nor a pair of scales, nor dogs, nor elephants. If we placed before him a lion, a pair of scales, a dog, and an elephant, or pictures of them, and we then asked him to tell us the name of any one of them and what it is, he would know nothing. He would not also have any intellectual process relating to any of them. If we made him memorize their names in their absence, detached from them and without being linked to them [that is, teach him the words lion, dog etc. without showing him their pictures or explaining what they are], and then we again placed these pictures before him and told him these are their names, meaning the names you memorized are the name of these things—he would not be able to recognize the name of any one of them. But if we gave him the name of each one of them in front of its reality, and linked them together [that is, told him the name of each while showing him its picture], until he memorized the names, each one linked with its reality, then he would know each thing by its name. In other words he knows what that thing is—is it a lion or is it a pair of scales?—and he will not make a mistake. If you tried to cheat him [for example by saying this is a dog while pointing at a picture of a lion], he will not agree with you.'[40]

This is how al-Nabhani defined rational thinking, which he believed was the basis of thought, whereas other forms of thinking, such as scientific thought, were sub-branches of thought and not the basis of thinking. The book criticised both capitalism and communism for adopting scientific thought as the basis for thinking, highlighting its limitations and the possibility for erroneous conclu-sions. It also outlined the long decline of Muslim thought, concluding that in origin it had occurred more than ten centuries earlier, with the call to close the doors of *ijtihad* (juristic reasoning through which new rules are derived from the Islamic sources of the Qur'an and traditions of the Prophet when new realities occur) that became dominant and restricted people to relying on what had previously been written and decided, leading to replication and blindly following rather than dynamism and thinking. Written to try to revive thought among the Muslim *Umma*, and despite admitting that even if millions of such books were written they could not guarantee that revival, al-Nabhani believed that the multitude of events that had occurred in the region during that period created hope that it could yet occur.[41]

The most important part of the book at this particular juncture was that while al-Nabhani had initially considered that it would take twenty-five years to establish the Islamic state, at this time he revised his estimate. Al-Nabhani criticised the idea of delaying the achievement of the goal of re-establishing the Islamic way of life and leaving it to future generations, claiming that while there may have been certain planning issues that span generations, which encompass general ideas, specific goals should be realised by those who sought them—in other words, within the same generation. A decade was sufficient to transform a people, and at most thirty years was required if there was opposition to change from foreign elements.[42] Though al-Nabhani had added five years to his estimate, he was convinced that the goal had to be reached within his generation.

*Tumbling to reassessment*

There were minor internal rumblings in the early 1970s, with some individuals from the party again raising concerns privately that al-Nabhani was too harsh as a leader and stubborn in his opinions, refusing to climb down from any decisions he had taken. One of the members called for a meeting to consider the issue of asking him to resign and to hand the leadership over to Zallum instead, something that was only taken up by two or three others. Nothing came of the issue, and they were duly removed from the party as soon as al-Nabhani received news regarding their machinations.[43]

Around the same period, pamphlets were prepared with the title 'All Praises are due to Allah, who blessed us with the return of the Caliphate', which were sent to and printed in various locations, including Turkey and Egypt, where forty thousand copies were made. This was not in response to or in anticipation of any specific event, but with the general expectation that the caliphate would soon be established, and because members needed to be prepared to announce it to the general public. There were blank spaces left in the pamphlet wherever it mentioned the location where the expected state had been established.[44] The party also sent members to Pakistan in an early attempt to begin the call there as well,[45] the second major Muslim country outside of the Arab world deliberately targeted for party work after Turkey.

The Arab-Israeli war began on 6 October 1973 when a joint Egyptian-Syrian effort launched a surprise offensive against Israel. By the end of the first day, Syrian forces had broken through Israeli defences at the Golan Heights, and the Egyptians met with similar success in Sinai. Although Israeli Prime Minister Golda Meir had been secretly informed of the possible attack in advance by King Hussein, the Israelis were woefully unprepared, and despite hopes that the arrival of reserve troops would reverse their losses, the first counter-attack against Egyptian forces in the Suez on 8 October failed miserably.

On 9 October, after suffering the losses of fifty combat planes and some five hundred tanks, Israeli military leaders began to raise the idea of using nuclear weapons to 'save the people of Israel from these madmen.' Defence Minister Moshe Dayan raised the nuclear option with the prime minister that morning, giving an overall assessment that Israel was quickly approaching the point of 'last resort.'[46] Despite the military gains by the Egyptians, which surprised Sadat, there was no intention to push beyond the Sinai, and they did not continue the offensive into Israel itself; no major action between the two sides occurred between 10 and 13 October. Meanwhile, on the Syrian front, by 10 October the Syrian army had been repelled and forced back from the Golan Heights.

Al-Nabhani issued a pamphlet from Tahrir on 10 October, four days after the war began, while the fighting was in the balance between the two sides. The war was placed within the context of the Rogers Plan. The problem for Sadat, who had stood by the Rogers Plan at the time, was that he had made promises to the Egyptians and Arabs that he would enter into a war with Israel; while in Syria Assad was threatened by the possibility of another coup by the Syrian army ('the norm' according to al-Nabhani).

According to the leaflet, Sadat and Assad needed a war with Israel to resolve their internal problems and remove the barriers to the regional solution proposed by the US in 1970, a plan that they were both working towards—as US agents. In summary, it was 'a war in order to solidify the position of the rulers in Egypt and Syria, and enable them to proceed towards implementation of the solution [in other words, recognition of Israel for return of land] that had been agreed upon.' The pamphlet also suggested that the US and USSR would ultimately get involved to ensure that the Arabs were not defeated in the same manner as 1967, since that would lead to negative repercussions for both Sadat and Assad and upset the status quo.[47]

Both the Arabs and Israelis were rearmed, by the USSR and US respectively, with a massive airlift of weapons to the Israelis on 14 October, shifting the balance decisively in their favour. By the time of a UN Security Council-brokered ceasefire on 22 October, Israeli forces had advanced far into Egyptian and Syrian territory. Although fighting continued beyond the ceasefire, with Israeli forces surrounding the Egyptian Third Army, most of the heavy fighting had concluded by 26 October. After the announcement of the ceasefire on 24 October, al-Nabhani issued another analysis, which stated that without international intervention in the war, the defeat of the Arab forces would have been worse than 1967, which was only averted by US pressure. Along with other points, the analysis concluded that Palestine was just one of the issues concerning the Muslim *Umma*, and that the central issue was that of Islam in society. In closing, al-Nabhani stated: 'for that reason, we see that the way to fight Israel and remove it, along with the liberation of the countries from the influence of all disbelieving nations whoever they may be, would only be achieved through the establishment of the single Islamic state.'[48]

Although there are certainly contentious aspects to al-Nabhani's analysis, the conclusion that Egypt and Syria entered the war with a nod to internal considerations, as well as the intention, to proceed to a peaceful solution with Israel that would result in its recognition, was not unusual, particularly with hindsight. But for the party to have issued this analysis from within the Middle East at the height of the war was possibly unique. Sadat went on to sign the Camp David accords in 1978, after becoming the first Arab leader to visit Israel in 1977, giving it implicit recognition. Meanwhile, as a result of casualties of the fighting, Tahrir had lost the most senior officer it had in the Syrian army, setting back its work to gain support within the Syrian military.[49]

In April 1974, a plan to overthrow Sadat involving a group of junior military officers was uncovered, a plot known as the 'Military Academy attempt'. The basic outline of the plot was that the group would break into the military academy and take command of weapons and vehicles, which would then be used to surround Sadat and other generals while they were holding a meeting at the Socialist Union headquarters. It was led by an Iraqi Palestinian, Saleh Siriyya, who was subsequently executed in 1976, along with Karim al-Anadoli, for their role in leading the attempt.

Over the years the attempt has been linked to both the Muslim Brotherhood and Hizb-ut-Tahrir. But during investigations the prosecutor found no domestic or foreign links to the attempt, which had been undertaken independently under Siriyya's leadership. There have been rumours that Siriyya was formerly linked to Tahrir, with security reports claiming that he was a member of the party in Jordan, while others have claimed he was involved with the party in Iraq. In what can be described as a cocktail of errors, not unusual in the genre of contemporary counter-terrorism literature, Marc Sageman has gone to the extent of claiming that Siriyya formed a group called the Islamic Liberation Organization, after arriving in Egypt from Jordan, having failed to overthrow Hussein during Black September in 1970.[50]

According to his son, Siriyya was never a student or member of Hizb-ut-Tahrir, and the reason for the confusion and rumours was because Siriyya's brother, Yusuf, was married to one of al-Nabhani's nieces, leading to the assumption that they were connected.[51] While in Iraq, Siriyya was involved with al-Badri, but more than a decade after al-Badri had left Hizb-ut-Tahrir. While in Iraq, Siriyya had in fact been a member of the Iraqi Muslim Brotherhood, under the leadership of Abdul Karim Zaydan, though conflict between them led to his leaving the Brotherhood, before being forced to leave Iraq after the abduction, torture and killing of al-Badri in 1969, due to his activity against the Ba'athist regime.[52]

Other members of Siriyya's group in Egypt also confirm that they had nothing to do with any other movement. Although some of their members were from the Muslim Brotherhood initially, around 1971, they split away due to differences in methodology. Siriyya met the main members of the group for the first time at a later date. He agreed with their idea of trying to overthrow the government by force and ended up leading them.[53]

Another reason for the conflation of the Military Academy attempt with Tahrir is that approximately two hundred members of the party had been arrested around the same period on entirely unrelated charges. After al-Ramahi had come to Egypt at the end of 1970, he set about trying to extend the party beyond the handful of Egyptians and Jordanians who were there at the time, while completing his masters at al-Azhar university and before beginning a doctorate in *usul al-fiqh* (principles of jurisprudence), studies that naturally brought him into contact with other Islamic studies students and teachers there. This was after a decade during which the party's growth had been curtailed by the security services, with arrests of members occurring in 1960, 1965 and 1969.[54]

After a time Hizb-ut-Tahrir began to build a membership in the hundreds in some of the major cities, particularly in Asyut in Upper Egypt (which would later become the major stronghold of *al-Jama'a al-Islamiyya*, the Islamic Group, which was responsible for the assassination of Sadat in 1981). The party also managed to win over officers in the army, but none of any influence, and was incapable of deep penetration due to the presence of multiple foreign agencies at work there. Nevertheless, the party had a small presence across Egypt and was beginning to become known in mosques. The activity led to al-Ramahi's surveillance by the Egyptian *aman al-dawla* (state security or secret police), which eventually pursued him back to Jordan where he was arrested by the Jordanian authorities, who held him for a few days before the Egyptian *mukhabarat* (foreign intelligence—the equivalent of the British MI6) arrived to interrogate him.

Meanwhile in Egypt, forty thousand pamphlets that had been printed in anticipation of the establishment of the caliphate were being kept in a mosque storeroom by the imam, Dr Reda Abu Majd, who was a member of the party and a specialist in the Arabic language from al-Azhar University. Although he believed he had sole access to the room, one of the employees at the mosque, suspicious about what was kept inside, entered the room one day and found the pamphlets. He took one to the *aman al-dawla*, who proceeded to follow Abu Majd for the next few days to uncover all his connections, leading to a series of arrests that eventually numbered around two hundred. Although this occurred just after the Military Academy attempt, no link was found between the two events, and eventually those arrested who were linked to Tahrir, including the military officers linked to Abu Majd, were separated from the case against Siriyya's group and released.[55]

The mid-1970s appear to have been a difficult period for the party, with little or no progress being made in terms of winning over society, in part but not solely due to security issues. In Syria and Egypt, the bulk of the party was either in jail or had dispersed as a result of security efforts against them. Work in Iraq was continuing, but had been set back by al-Nabhani's arrest in 1972, and although all the imprisoned members had been released from Jordanian jails in 1972, it does not appear there was any major progress made there. There were also arrests in areas beyond the party's focus, such as in Libya.

In Lebanon, where al-Nabhani was still based, civil war broke out in 1975, which would continue for more than a decade and involve US and Israeli forces over time. The general feeling among the population was that the liberation of Palestine would occur through the armed resistance of the *fedayin*, making the call of the party difficult in an environment where weapons not thoughts were the currency of persuasion.[56] Despite that, the party had influence among scholars of the Sunni and Shia communities, the most prominent being Sheikh Abdul Razzaq Saleh, who was known for his Qur'an recitations on Lebanese radio.[57]

After the two failed attempts in 1969, which had come after such a build-up of internal expectations, a period of slow internal decline began to take place. The long wait for victory was taking its toll on the party members by the early 1970s, with questions raised regarding the party's membership, as well as the lack of appropriate activity taken. As far as membership issues went, there was a feeling among some, dating back years, that not enough attention had been given to developing the personal behaviour of the individuals in the party, and that it was merely assumed that they would take the necessary time and effort in activities such as reading the Qur'an, additional prayers, studying wider Islamic literature and so on.

Despite advice to al-Nabhani regarding this issue, he believed that lapses in the behaviour of a few individuals were normal and that after the establishment of the Islamic state the issue would be resolved.[58] In an internal pamphlet in mid-1971, he made it clear that everyone had shortcomings, but that lapses in behaviour did not indicate a personality problem, whereas if they consistently committed sins or did not fulfil their obligations, that would indicate that they did not have the essential Islamic personality.[59]

A prominent poet, Amin Shinnar, left the party over the issue, believing that the party was too political and not spiritual enough, which is what led to many members and supporters washing their hands of Tahrir after their first taste of pressures such as jail. Shinnar subsequently became an ascetic Sufi and later withdrew from society entirely.[60] Al-Nabhani, however, believed that only those with a strong belief in God would be able to withstand the tests of societal and government pressure, as well as torture and jail, and fully expected a large turnover of members due to the nature of the party's work. In between the two positions, there was concern that some in the party were not sufficiently dedicated to shoulder the heavy burden required in such work, and that members of Tahrir had to be at a high level politically and spiritually, an issue that al-Nabhani agreed with in essence, but never found a way to remedy.

There were also questions and concerns over party activities in the perceived final stage of preparing to take power. Members began asking in early 1971 why certain committees and members were not taking political action, but were instead still discussing cultural and intellectual issues with people, despite the fact that the party was supposed to be taking practical actions and steps.[61] At the same time, some feared that there was a gap between the capabilities of the leadership and the general members,[62] and that a lack of ability was leading to inertia.

As time passed without visible results, questions were asked in 1974 about the reason behind the party's not being able to produce any influential individuals in society, despite having stressed the need to do so for more than the ten years. The reply was that the party was confronted by its opponents from the very beginning of its call, and as soon as it made attempts to connect to society it was subjected to fierce and harsh treatment, which led many to leave or simply give up the necessary actions to win influence in society. The only way to produce such individuals was by constant contact with society through visits, something that the members were not doing enough.[63]

A few months later, a pamphlet was issued that stated it was absolutely imperative for members to take whatever steps necessary to address the masses with the party's ideas, to overcome the barriers the government placed between these ideas and society.[64] Frustrated with the lack of progress, al-Nabhani began to contemplate that he might not be granted his wish of seeing the Islamic state within his lifetime. His face still suffered from the paralysis that afflicted him in the late 1950s, and he had continued to use an electric massager on it. He would massage his face, commenting that the paralysis was deep, deeper than he had first imagined, and in the same way the decline of the Muslim society was deeper than he had thought.[65]

The party leadership realised around the same time that it had to rectify internal issues, and so pamphlets and discussions focused on what made an effective Islamic politician. A pamphlet issued in October 1974, titled *al-Wasat al-Siyassi* (The Political Environment), discussed how to create a political environment that was the province of the people and not simply the rulers. While members had become adept political analysts by this stage, there were still shortcomings in their ability to provide analysis from an Islamic perspective rather than a purely political one.[66]

Another internal pamphlet issued almost a year later in August 1975, entitled *'Amal Haml al-Da'wa* (Actions of the one who carries the call) listed appropriate actions, starting with adherence to Islamic commandments, reading the Qur'an, meeting people, reading and following events.[67] The first two, and particularly the encouragement to read the Qur'an more (identifying members as the people who ought to be among its foremost readers), were an implicit indication that concerns over personality were being addressed. There had been an earlier attempt by al-Nabhani to order all members to carry copies of the Qur'an with them wherever they went, as part of an effort to make them read it more often. Though members agreed with the idea in principle, they argued that such a stipulation infringed on personal worship and was therefore beyond the party's remit. The order was retracted, proving that al-Nabhani was not immovable when it came to having his decisions questioned.[68]

Despite the various set-backs and concerns at the time, al-Nabhani still believed that he might be able to establish the Islamic state, though by now this was more tempered. In Iraq the party had the support of a group of officers based in Baghdad, which led to al-Nabhani making arrangements for an attempt to take power again in 1976. He ordered his son to take his family to Abu Dhabi, where they were to listen to Iraqi radio for news. After a month in Abu Dhabi without word from his father or any significant regional event occurring, Ibrahim travelled back to Beirut to see what progress had been made. On seeing him, al-Nabhani became angry, asking if Ibrahim thought that such arrangements were easily completed, like eating sweets or simply saying 'Be' and it will be. Al-Nabhani told his son to return to Abu Dhabi and not try to contact him again unless he heard from him first. In the end, according to al-Nabhani, the officers involved were transferred away from the capital, and again any arrangements that had been made were postponed indefinitely.[69]

After the failure of this plan, al-Nabhani wrote his final book, *Sur'at al-Badiha* (Quick Intuition), which he began on 11 November 1976, completing it the same day. It is a short piece, which was intended as a remedy to the lack of improvisation, spontaneity and ability to quickly make decisions among the people of the region, because their minds had been colonized by Western thought/culture. Al-Nabhani was likely to have been motivated out of frustration at the missed opportunity in Iraq or possibly as a result of interaction with Syrian officers at the time.[70] Some party members felt that the book was not of a comparable quality to his previous work. With ill health encroaching upon him, rather than publish it as a party book al-Nabhani asked the party members to publish it with their money, as a personal loan, and told them who to go to in the event of his death to settle his debts.[71] Soon after, two internal talks presented at the party's regular monthly circles bore witness to the internal re-evaluation that was taking place.

The first was dated 15 November and was a review of Hizb-ut-Tahrir since its inception. It claimed that soon after the party was formed its members realised that their role was to be the politicians of the *Umma*, but they remained isolated from society and were therefore unable to practise politics at any level. As a result of the obstructions and problems that the party faced in the late 1950s and early 1960s in reaching mass support through interaction with the people, the leadership decided that it would attempt to establish the Islamic state first, which would then naturally lead to the emergence of politicians from within the party membership, as well as society as a whole, as opposed to the situation that society was living under, where civil space for political discussion was denied by the assortment of dictatorships and monarchies in the region.

At this point, some time between the end of 1964 and the beginning of 1965, the leadership secretly began working with a few members to try to bring about the Islamic state without having to rely on the general membership, referring to the attempts to seek *nusra* to establish the state through military coups. This was done to establish the state practically, such that the members would be able to see the reality of practical politics and understand it through its practical manifestations—a nod to the lack of success of the many pamphlets around the late 1950s and early 1960s, in which al-Nabhani repeatedly stressed that it was necessary for the membership to move beyond cultural and intellectual discussions and into the arena of political discussions and affairs.

However, more than ten years passed and the party leadership had been unable to achieve its goals of establishing the Islamic state, after multiple attempts, with the closest being the two attempts in Jordan. At this point, the party 'realised that its members had to become politicians, even if the state was not established, and [the party] needed to be concerned with that', explaining the shift in emphasis as al-Nabhani began to try to develop the internal membership into practical politicians, recognising that he might not manage to establish the state within his lifetime. Hence the publication of *al-Wasat al-Siyassi* in 1974, after trying other means such as asking members to hold weekly discussions about the political events in their area and write about the political solutions they proposed. When this exercise first began, al-Nabhani was unimpressed with the results, claiming that the conclusions were all conceptual or juridical rather than political and practical.[72]

The failure to take power in Jordan in the late 1960s was—perhaps surprisingly—described as a 'good thing', with the reflection on history being that it 'was as though [we] were tumbling to establish the state', appearing to admit that Hizb-ut-Tahrir's attempts to take power had been premature. It perhaps also necessarily implies that the assessment that the Islamic state had been established in 1964 among the people—as evidenced by their 'embracing' of the party during the visit of the Pope at the start of the year—was incorrect.

Given that al-Nabhani and the leadership began to realise around 1974 that their success in establishing the Islamic state had at a minimum been delayed, the party began to take specific action to encourage the political thinking of its members, such as writing political commentaries and so on. Al-Nabhani had recognised that it was imperative to build politicians within the party in the event that he died before the state that he hoped would produce them naturally was established. According to this assessment at the end of 1976, members had become politicians, able to connect their concepts and ideas to practical realities and state-level actions (that is, explain how the future Islamic state ought to resolve problems as they occurred), as well as provide good analysis of events. However, it also admitted that they remained unknown among the general public, a problem which required individual members to undertake practical political actions that showed to society that they were politicians.

The problem was that the members remained intellectuals rather than practical politicians, and leading the masses required that political actions were taken that they could connect to and associate themselves with. All that they saw instead were words, admonitions and 'promises from the sky,' telling people to trust in Allah and request his help, mixing up issues of belief and practical actions that were forced on people. This led the public to believe in the members and their words as a result of their shared religious convictions, but to regard them simply as theoreticians, good people but not leaders. The pamphlet closed with an exhortation:

> "it is imperative for the members to undertake political actions in front of the people until they trusted in them. As for what those actions are, defining and picturing them is difficult. Rather, it is the reality that would dictate that, and it is enough for it to be said that they are political actions, and that it is necessary for this actions [sic.] to be undertaken.[73]

The transcript of the second internal monthly is not dated, but the political events mentioned as taking place at the time (namely, the December reformation of the Japanese government of the Liberal Democratic Party as a result of the Lockheed scandal) indicates that it was either presented in December 1976 or January 1977. It was clearly written as a continuation of the November talk, giving broad outlines of the kind of actions required to make people understand the true meaning of politics (taking care of people's affairs) and how to show them that the party members were politicians capable of undertaking that responsibility.

Although political actions ought to be undertaken by the state, which could practically implement them, it was obligatory for the Tahrir members to undertake them since the government was not doing those actions, instead permitting others to—or in other words the state was failing its responsibility. This was explained through a simple example of taking a neighbour to help him register his children at school, while at the same time pointing out to him that the state should have arranged the issue (likely meaning in terms of the failures of its bureaucratic process or such issues). In doing so, the member would have undertaken a political action (through taking care of his neigh-bour's affairs for him), while at the same time explaining his own viewpoint with respect to the action and criticising the current government, thus win-ning his neighbour's trust and belief in him as a politician.

In essence, this was a push to return the party body to the pre-1964 mental-ity, relying on members to win over leadership of society through practical politics. Perhaps one of the most important points in the talk came after it acknowledged again that while the members had previously remained 'living among their ideas', they were now becoming politicians, though they still remained 'outside of the society.' The transcript then stated:

> 'and though the party [previously] made two attempts in Jordan [referring to the two actual coup attempts, which were both undone at the later stages, as opposed to other more speculative preparations made in Iraq] in order to create a situation that would give the members the chance to be inside the society, during an era when attempts [to take power] came from individuals, and the leaders would win the people, it later became apparent that the people are the root [of the power], and they are the ones who drive the leaders and individuals.'[74]

This realisation, or acknowledgment, is what led the leadership to again focus on its members. It appears that while the aspect of *talab al-nusra* (seeking sup-port) was still considered a part of the method to establish the Islamic state, the idea of doing it by 'caesarean section' was, at a minimum, before its time.

The review was undertaken in light of the failure to achieve the goals of winning mass support for the party and establishing the Islamic state by the mid-1970s, which again indicates a level of self-awareness and capacity for self-criticism, and is seen as proof of the serious and political mentality of the party. While this push for a return to roots was ongoing, al-Nabhani remained in contact with officers in the Syrian army who apparently made many prom-ises throughout 1976 and 1977, but ultimately failed to deliver on them. Although he expected something to take place during Sadat's visit to Assad in November 1977, prior to visiting Israel, al-Nabhani was again left disap-pointed.[75] Illness had confined him to his bed by this time, but he was still asking his son to tune into Radio Syria for any news. Al-Nabhani's health had deteriorated by December and he was taken to hospital, for the first time checking in under his real name, perhaps an acknowledgment that he was on his death-bed. In and out of consciousness, when barely awake he would recite the Qur'an under his breath as others sat at his bedside, before passing away on 11 December 1977.[76]

## The end of an era

The death of al-Nabhani marked the passing away of the founder of the party, its most prominent figure and intellectual. It was announced to the party membership through a short letter of condolence, asking for God to have mercy upon him. At the same time, in acknowledgment of his place among the members and his centrality to the party, the note encouraged them not to lose their energy and determination to continue their work to resume the Islamic way of life.[77] The reaction varied from stoicism to despair, with some who had been attending an administrative meeting in Jordan at the time the letter was delivered reduced to tears,[78] while elsewhere a group of around twelve members in jail took in the news with more fortitude, arranging chairs for a meeting with other prisoners who had come to pay their respects.[79] There was universal shock and sadness, especially as many of the members, particularly those from the older generation, believed that the caliphate was going to be established by al-Nabhani, an indication of the confidence he inspired in others.

The older members of the party certainly viewed al-Nabhani as a unique personality, whether in terms of effort and energy (he reportedly only slept four hours a day) or the fact that they considered him to be a genius in terms of his Islamic and political understanding. At the same time, he was by some accounts a difficult person to debate with, with al-Nabulsi reported to have said after a fruitless day-long debate with al-Nabhani in the early 1950s, 'every time I mentioned an opinion, idea or conviction, I wished that he could say yes to [at least] one of them.' As a result, in the early days of Tahrir senior members such as al-Khayyat would initiate debate with others, and once they were convinced of some principles then al-Nabhani would come to discuss the details.[80]

As suggested by al-Nabulsi's comments, it appears that al-Nabhani was a dominating opponent in debate. As an example, about a year after al-Nabhani's death a lawyer named Abdullah Hamsa from Homs in Syria came to the office for *al-Waʿi* in Beirut (which was the party's unofficial base there), looking for al-Nabhani. The reason was simply that they had previously had an argument in which al-Nabhani made the claim that the Islamic state would be established within twenty-five years (of the establishment of the party), and he wanted to tell al-Nabhani personally that he had been wrong—highlighting both what could be described as an unhealthy obsession and the deep impression that the debate must have had.[81]

It would be easy to consider such self-belief as arrogance, particularly when it manifested itself in a dominating personality and vigorous debates. That al-Nabhani remained self-critical throughout his lifetime, admitting mistakes and shortcomings in party actions and decisions taken, while constantly reviewing the party's progress and its understanding of the reality of society, provides an alternative view to such a claim. On a personal level, all accounts suggest that al-Nabhani was seen as a humble man who would not accept praise or attempts to win favour through it, though he was very forceful to the point of stubbornness when discussing his convictions. But despite the fact that al-Nabhani was clearly firm in his principles and beliefs, he was not entirely immovable, taking decisions such as the retraction of the order for members to carry a copy of the Qur'an with them or his willingness to discuss strategy, though these discussions and differences were within parameters and on principles he had outlined and believed in. It is also apparent that he was quite open to the principle of debate itself, whether with opponents or supporters, often discussing and debating ideas through the night with party members on issues ranging from jurisprudence to political analysis.

His firmness in discussion was also mirrored by strictness in party administration. Al-Nabhani was fully committed to the party cause and to some extent expected at least a comparable commitment and sacrifice from other members, sometimes unrealistically, given the unusual and difficult circumstances he lived under. The turnover of members was expected by al-Nabhani, who believed that the nature of Tahrir's political struggle meant that very few individuals would be able to maintain the necessary effort and willingness to make sacrifices and persist in them consistently. This led to the many suspensions and expulsions of activists due to their shortcomings and inability to withstand the pressures that being a member of an illegal party persecuted by the governments of the region brought.

Expulsions generally occurred due to matters deemed dangerous to the existence of Tahrir, such as betraying the party to the authorities, publicly denouncing it under government pressure, or trying to initiate a change of leadership within the party, whereas suspensions were for lesser issues, such as not fulfilling required activities. For his part, al-Nabhani considered the punishments to be a test, comparable to a shock or a warning to the activist, given to them if he believed they were in fact looking for a way to leave the party in any case, and that if the member was sincere and committed he would force himself on the party irrespective of the suspension and whether he believed it was justified or not.[82] On the other hand, many of the members from his time believed that he could be excessively strict.[83]

In all matters, administrative, political and intellectual, al-Nabhani acted in a self-assured manner. This confidence, coupled with his constant activity and writing, meant that he became the embodiment of his party's ideas, as mentioned by the political scientist Ihsan Samara.[84] Given that the members viewed him in this way, this ultimately led to the fossilisation of the party body, as members began to wait expectantly for him to establish the caliphate. The lack of initiative that al-Nabhani repeatedly identified and complained of may have partially stemmed from the belief in the party and himself that he had imbued in them, along with the strict adherence to party administration that he expected of them. Harsh security conditions during much of his leadership would also have contributed negatively.

Conversely, the establishment of a party such as Hizb-ut-Tahrir during an era when intellectual trends were shifting decisively towards secular nationalism—with a goal that has sometimes been derided as unrealistic and utopian, even with the passing of time, which has witnessed an increase in the religiosity in the region—would not have been possible without a very high level of self-confidence and belief. The obstacles the party faced and the set-backs throughout al-Nabhani's leadership meant that anything less than the full conviction and self-belief that he was capable of achieving the establishment of the caliphate to begin the revival of the Islamic way of life may have led to an early surrender. That same confidence, required to begin and persist with such a programme, was also a contributing factor to an atmosphere that may have constrained internal development, because of the personal confidence he inspired in others.

Another aspect that may have hampered the development of other members was al-Nabhani's centralised style of leadership, which was in part due to the lack of viable communication channels, as well as being forced to operate in secret. The party body was also deprived of many prominent visible practical examples of leadership, given that al-Nabhani and other leading members had gone into hiding by the end of the 1950s. Although the pamphlets and books may have imparted intellectual concepts and political analysis, along with outlines of how the party should work to gain the leadership of the society, al-Nabhani was unable to practically manifest this in front of the general public. The repeated enjoinders in party literature explaining how to take political action, win people's trust and build mass support remained as ink on paper, and in this case al-Nabhani was unable to give any practical guidance.

While the party's decline in the late 1950s and slow start in the 1960s were due to the rise of Nasser and the increasing security crackdown on the party, the vacuum created by the loss of a visible leadership was another blow. This was particularly true in Amman, which was initially a central hub for party membership while al-Nabhani's strong presence was there, and though this continued for a short while after he was forced to leave Jordan to avoid arrest, the party suffered his loss there. At the same time, al-Nabhani literally lived for his ideas. While he asked a lot of others and was sometimes unreasonable in his expectations, he was the most active party member throughout his time as leader. Despite having a death sentence hanging over him, he travelled across the region, meeting other members, prominent individuals and military officers to seek support in achieving the goals of his party.

The security considerations that al-Nabhani lived with meant that at the end of a lifetime of underground political activity, there were approximately twenty people who prayed over him before his burial in the Awza'i graveyard in Beirut, some of whom did not know who the man they were praying over was. According to Fatah member Muhammad Dawud Owda, who knew al-Nabhani in his youth and was one of those at the burial, he died in poverty, an old man who used to wear a ripped jacket living in a small flat on the fifth floor of an apartment block, with only stairs for access, despite his age and illness.[85]

Al-Khayyat stated that all the Arab and Islamic newspapers across the region were prohibited from writing obituaries for him, due to his reputation. When he heard of al-Nabhani's death, some twenty years after he had left the party, he only managed to have it mentioned briefly in one national paper due to his close friendship with the editor.[86]

Given his politics, al-Nabhani has remained a polarising figure not short of critics, with many books, articles and interviews written against his ideas, including during his lifetime, such as by contemporary establishment scholars such as Muhammad Said Ramadan Buti, a prominent supporter of the Assad regime in Syria including during the revolution against Bashar al-Assad, until he was killed in suspicious circumstances in 2013. As far back as 1964, Buti outlined some of the common criticisms, whether accurate or not, against al-Nabhani and Hizb-ut-Tahrir's thought and methods, from political issues such as the legitimacy of the governments of the day or the fact that al-Nabhani envisaged a consultative council that would allow women members to participate (as opposed to Buti's more restrictive stance), to more abstract theological issues.[87]

Despite such criticisms, the breadth, depth and volume of al-Nabhani's writings mean that he can justifiably be accepted as one of the most foremost Islamic political thinkers of the twentieth century. Although others may have made specific contributions that stand out in one area, such as Qutb's exegesis of the Qur'an,[88] the scope and detail of al-Nabhani's work across disciplines such as Islamic jurisprudence (*fiqh*), the principles of jurisprudence (*usul al-fiqh*), political analysis and philosophy are arguably unparalleled in his position as an Islamic scholar and active politician and leader, responsible for founding, developing and administering Hizb-ut-Tahrir.

Samara comments that al-Nabhani was an accomplished politician and analyst, and deserves to be recognised as one of the foremost intellectual and political thinkers of the twentieth century.[89] According to Turki Abdul-Majid al-Samani's doctoral research on al-Nabhani's political and intellectual programme, al-Nabhani was 'a political thinker of the first order of this era' who produced 'a complete political system', and despite his errors and differences with him 'it is possible to say that he founded an intellectual school, and an Islamic movement which supports the Islamic revival project.'[90]

Having laid the intellectual foundation of the party, and continued its development through the turbulence that the region witnessed during his lifetime, by the time of his death the corpus of material he had laid down regarding the aims of the party and the methodology to achieve it was largely settled. But a little more than twenty-five years after first trying to get Hizb-ut-Tahrir officially recognised by the Jordanian government, al-Nabhani's role was at an end.

# 6

# REVIVING THE REVIVALISTS

## (1977–1990)

صارحوها بالذي سـاء . و سـر!          خـدم الأمة أنتم . فـاعـمـلوا

انـا الـعـزلة يـأس . و خـور!          و احـذروا الـعـزلـة . و امشـوا قـدمـا

انـا سـعـي بلا قصد خطر!          و ابـتـغـوا الـغـايـة فـي أعـمـالكـم

*'You are servants of the Umma, so work—Express to her what is wrong, openly and in secret!*

*Beware of isolating yourselves, and march forward-Isolation is only despondency, and weakness!*

*And seek the objective in your actions—proceeding without purpose is nothing but danger!'*

Amin Shinnar, verses 162–5 from *'The Radiance of Belief'*[1]

At the time of al-Nabhani's death no other member of the leadership committee was present. Word was sent to Zallum to return to Beirut, after which condolences were written and sent to the various regional leaders to inform the rest of the Hizb-ut-Tahrir membership. As the reality of al-Nabhani's death began to sink in among members, after the initial shock it began to engender a new sense of responsibility among a few. The realisation that he was in fact not going to lead the party in establishing the caliphate and resuming the Islamic way of life meant that others had to step up to shoulder the burden.

Although al-Nabhani had spent years trying to cajole and encourage each and every member that they represented the party in its entirety, it seems to

171

have taken his absence to bring that point home even to the most active and senior among them. In Jordan, fearing the end of the party in the minds of the members there, regional leader Abu Iyas immediately set about writing pamphlets for distribution, to impress upon the rest that despite the loss of al-Nabhani it was business as usual.[2]

The administrative rules outlined that the position left vacant on the leadership committee had to be filled, after which a leader from among the three would be agreed on. As the head of Tahrir in Jordan, the historic base of the party and central area of its work, Abu Iyas was appointed to the committee to work alongside Zallum and al-Da'ur. In a message that Zallum sent to him, Abu Iyas was also offered the leadership of the party, which he rejected, stating that the only possible candidate was Zallum himself. By this time, al-Da'ur was almost seventy years old, and had spent much of his time in and out of prison, whereas Zallum was in his early fifties and had deputised in place of al-Nabhani to run party affairs when the latter used to travel outside of Lebanon.[3] It appears that Zallum was not only the consensus choice, but to some extent the only choice, given that no-one else had comparable leadership or administrative experience.

There was a change in the leadership philosophy, with Zallum seeking to involve several other senior members, whom he trusted in party affairs, from the beginning.[4] The difference in the two personalities was pronounced: while al-Nabhani had immense confidence in himself and his decisions, Zallum was much more open to participation, in part out of necessity, given the acknowledged gap in ability between the two.[5] Although he may have been the most capable immediate choice, he was not al-Nabhani, something of which he was fully cognizant.

Al-Nabhani had been the founder of the party and the formulator of its ideas, and the difference between him and the rest of the membership in terms of understanding and vision was particularly pronounced in the early days. This was despite the fact that people such as Zallum had been involved in early discussions and participated as much as anyone else. On the other hand, when Zallum became leader, the ideas were developed and settled, and the membership had spent many years studying them, closing the gap that existed between them and the leadership. Zallum was taking over a more experienced, cultured, politically aware and perhaps cynical group, that considered him to be on their level.[6]

The centralised leadership, which was a result of the security conditions, and the lack of Zallum's consistent participation in central party administration, meant that the initial task was to get an understanding of the state of the party. Information had to be gathered from the different regions to assess what the reality was before decisions on how to proceed could be made. Within six months, an assessment had been made; the party membership had largely become listless after years of unfulfilled expectations, having lost focus of the main work and aims that were needed for revival.

A long pamphlet was sent to all the members addressing these points, beginning with another overview of party history, though it was the first such review written since al-Nabhani's leadership. The historical themes were similar to those mentioned at the monthly circles at the end of 1976 and beginning of 1977, but there were more details and additional conclusions. The pamphlet mentioned that the first coup attempt—referring to the end of 1968—made people realise that the party was serious in its efforts to establish the caliphate, leading to it being given more attention by the government and states internally in Jordan and internationally. Through the coup attempt, Tahrir had shown that 'it was not a party of leaflets and words' but 'a party that truly aimed to reach authority in order to establish the caliphate and implement the Islamic laws.' This was also the case for the members, who understood that this meant they were truly a party that was serious about reaching its objectives, increasing their self-confidence and trust in the party. Although the first attempt did not succeed, there was a belief that 'though they may have failed today, tomorrow they would be successful.'[7]

The second attempt confirmed their determination, but at the same time led some people, including members, to criticise the party. Doubts began to creep in regarding organisational capability and the members' ability to manage plans precisely while maintaining secrecy. At that time, they all still felt determined, and they believed that they would keep trying until they were successful. However, repeated failures had led to deeper scepticism, with more analysis and questions, which led to a few 'losing their self-confidence' and 'losing hope that they would reach [power].' And yet they still persevered in their trust and belief that the Islamic state would be established, as their expectations were buoyed up by repeatedly being told that something was going to happen, to the point that 'they were on the edge of their nerves, sometimes for months on end.' During that time 'it became normal to wake up, and before washing for morning prayer they would turn on the radio thinking that the caliphate had been established.'[8]

As this continued, party members waited in expectation and became concerned with following the news at the expense of everything else. This 'made them reduce their efforts in their constant work', which was to interact with people in society, calling them to the ideas of the party. They instead believed that seeking *nusra* support among ruling elites was the only thing that would result in the caliphate being established, and that working among the masses would not produce the same results due to society at that time also having lost hope in everything and being simply resigned to its situation. These circumstances made the members lose energy, to the point that they became 'bored and lazy.'[9]

The pamphlet criticised this understanding, as al-Nabhani had also repeatedly tried to, highlighting that 'establishing the caliphate is not the goal, and rather it is only the method to implement Islam so that people can live an Islamic life' and ultimately 'carry Islam as a message of guidance and light to the rest of the world.' Therefore the internal call to simply concentrate all efforts on seeking support to establish the state was incorrect and lacking in understanding, since the implementation of Islam would 'go against people's material interests,'[10] and so if they did not believe in it with certainty and the understanding that the party had it would be difficult for them. For example, people had to be ready to implement harsh Islamic rulings, such as the death penalty for apostates, and they also had to be prepared to carry Islam to the world through jihad by the state. All of this required them to understand Islam as a complete way of life, and that their ultimate aim in this life was to carry the call to others, rather than material or individual aims.

While it appeared that al-Nabhani had begun to recognise that the party needed to find ways to cultivate an atmosphere that would encourage further development of the personal attributes of its members, the new leadership was more direct in linking the lack of effort in party activity to the lack of closeness to God. The pamphlet said that anyone working for the resumption of the Islamic way of life could never be content with merely doing the minimum required of them, but had to seek to increase their acts of personal worship, given that they should have a better understanding of Islam than others. The themes remained similar, indicating the deep-rootedness of the problems that had in some cases been identified years before. Towards the end the pamphlet also criticised the tendency to simply analyse news without linking it to the party's aims, concluding that 'yes, we are a political party, but based upon Islam, and we want to bring Islam into the reality', meaning that they were carrying a call, and not merely journalists or analysts.[11]

This was the first of several efforts to redress what the new leadership considered was an imbalance between the political and the personal, believing that personal shortcomings in spiritual development had led to a lack of effort and consistency in members' daily work in spreading Tahrir's ideas. This had manifested itself as a party that had some members who were content to act as commentators and spectators, analysing news and giving opinions as to which Great Power was behind the events of the day, rather than acting as Islamic politicians who would deliver their views linked to their beliefs and aims. There is no suggestion that members were irreligious in any sense, but rather that the leadership wanted them to increase their supererogatory acts of worship to build their spiritual fortitude, and draw them closer to God. It was not sufficient to be average; rather, they had to excel in all aspects to be granted victory.

The pamphlet highlighted the challenges that Zallum believed he faced in taking responsibility for leadership of the party, and pointed to a deliberate introspection and self-criticism, as well as a clear concern that there was a need to re-invigorate the party membership. As during the last years under al-Nabhani, the party recognised its responsibility in the failure to achieve its goal, and sought to redress this in accordance with the ideas it carried. Shortly thereafter, the party would undertake two of its most prominent political actions in the region.

### In Libya—Delegation to Muammar Gaddafi

In August 1978, a delegation made up of three members was sent to meet Libyan leader Muammar Gaddafi, on the back of a speech he was reported to have given in Tripoli on 3 July where he in effect denied the validity of referring to Prophetic narrations as an Islamic source of legislation. The party leadership decided to address Gaddafi directly rather than through the medium of a statement, as a political action to try to impose Hizb-ut-Tahrir on the discussion. The party was known to the Libyan regime, with a number of Libyan members sentenced to life imprisonment in 1977.

The first members of Tahrir arrived in Libya during the late 1950s, with many Arabs arriving in the 1960s after the discovery of oil in the same period. Some had arrived to teach there, among them Ahmed Bakr, who was a university lecturer from 1959 before leaving at the beginning of the 1960s. The most high-profile member to come to Libya at the time was Sultani, who initially went to Benghazi where he taught as a secondary school teacher, while also becoming known for his Qur'an recitation and Friday sermons. These early arrivals were not concerned with building the party body in Libya, as it was not one of the countries targeted for work by al-Nabhani, and their activities were limited to spreading their ideas rather than promoting Hizb-ut-Tahrir itself. Despite the lack of attention to growing the membership base, by the mid 1960s a number of people had become attracted to Sultani's ideas and coalesced around him, the first group of Libyans including Hussain al-Darrad and Hasan al-Kurdi.[12]

As a result of the efforts of this initial group of locals, other small groups of Libyans began studying with the party around the country, including Muhammad Muhathab Haffaf and Muhammad Ali Yahya Muammar, who studied with another member from outside of Libya, Azmi Atiyya, in the west of the country. However, the name of the party remained largely unknown among the general public, apart from among the personal contacts of these few individuals.

Then in 1969 a bloodless coup by a group of Arab nationalist officers removed King Idris and turned Libya into a republic. It was headed by twenty-seven-year-old Muammar Gaddafi, a captain in the army who became the chairman of the Revolutionary Command Council that took over the country. Sultani was expelled from Libya soon after,[13] his political ideas and viewpoints being well known in Benghazi where the Libyan Military Academy that Gaddafi and other officers graduated from was located. A few months later, Atiyya was also deported, leaving behind a handful of Libyan members such as al-Kurdi and Haffaf, who were sufficiently developed to continue carrying the call independently.[14]

In the early 1970s members of Gaddafi's council toured the country, giving speeches to build public opinion in their favour, having come to power through a coup rather than popular support. They would sometimes visit universities, where Gaddafi, Sadik Nayhum, Umar al-Muhayshi, Bashir Hawadi and others from the government would give speeches promoting socialism and Arab nationalism. There were several arguments at meetings and on university campuses between them and Tahrir members, such as the stir caused as a result of Haffaf getting into a debate with al-Muhayshi and Hawadi during a public meeting entitled 'The Seminar of Revolutionary Thought', which took place in May 1970.[15]

Two years later, on 7 May 1972, there was a televised exchange between Gaddafi and a student called Salih Muhammad al-Farisi which took place during a speech given at the medical college in the University of Benghazi. During the speech Gaddafi praised Arab nationalism and the Arab nation using the word *Umma* to mean the Arab peoples, when al-Farisi interrupted him loudly criticising Gaddafi's views on nationalism and asserting that Islam viewed the *Umma* as a people bound together by their belief rather than ethnicity or race.[16]

Shocked by the intervention, live on television, Gaddafi retorted that the student must be a mentally ill member of the Muslim Brotherhood. In actual fact, al-Farisi was a student with Hizb-ut-Tahrir at the time, though the party was not generally known, unlike the Brotherhood. After two or three days of interrogation and torture, al-Farisi appeared on television to renounce what he had said. (Al-Farisi left Libya the same year and continued his studies in the UK, from where he left to join the anti-Soviet resistance in Afghanistan in the early 1980s as the first Arab doctor to arrive there. He was eventually killed there towards the end of 1989.)[17]

The decision to deal with the party came as part of the clampdown on all political opposition that was launched a year later. On 16 April 1973 Gaddafi gave a speech in the city of Zuwara where he launched what he called the 'cultural revolution'. He announced a five-point plan, which included the abolition of the constitution and existing laws ('all existing laws must be repealed and replaced by revolutionary enactments'), and the banning of political groups, claiming that whoever belonged to a political party had betrayed the revolution (under the second point that 'all feeble minds must be weeded out of society by taking appropriate measures toward perverts and deviationists.')[18] Many 'feeble-minded' people including students, university professors and professionals were taken into custody as Gaddafi sought to purge the country of any opposition, particularly Islamic groups such as Hizb-ut-Tahrir and the Muslim Brotherhood (who were present in greater numbers).

Hizb-ut-Tahrir members were specifically targeted, with the authorities having carefully noted anyone who spoke against them while touring the country over the previous two years. The arrests of sixty-one members were ordered soon after Gaddafi's Zuwara speech, among them five Palestinians. This, in effect, decapitated the party in the country, with those remaining at liberty too inexperienced to continue any form of activity. Those arrested spent a year in military prison, the first eight months of which included frequent interrogation and torture, a common practice being to surround the prisoners and beat them as they were made to walk between the guards.[19]

After a year they were transferred to a civilian prison, before being taken to court a few months later, with the judge ruling that there had been no legal justification for their arrest and ordering their release, which occurred in three groups. The authorities then ordered their re-arrest almost immediately, leading to some of those who had been released as part of the third group being arrested again on the way back to their homes. Though the order to re-arrest all of those released was general, in the end only twenty-two were taken back, and the five Palestinians were deported. Others were placed under enforced residency, with a curfew to return to their houses by 6 pm, having to sign in at the police station every week.[20]

In April 1975 there were student demonstrations in Tripoli and Benghazi against the Gaddafi regime. The response was to send in government troops and to arrest and jail a number of the protestors. Members of the Revolutionary Council turned against Gaddafi, with a failed coup attempt later in the year involving Hawadi. A year after the first set of student demonstrations, there were clashes in universities between supporters and opponents of the regime, with government troops again being sent onto campuses to arrest opposition protestors. A year later, in April 1977, a number of student leaders were rearrested and two were hanged publicly in one of many such events that Gaddafi presided over in person.[21]

That year a special court was formed to rule against opposition members. Known as the 'Security of the Revolution', it was headed by a general and had no right of appeal. In February the court handed down sentences to about forty Tahrir members originally arrested, ranging from five to fifteen years, based on testimonies extracted under torture. However, despite the fact that theoretically there was no right of appeal, the sentences were all increased shortly afterwards, apparently at the behest of Gaddafi—those who had received five years were given fifteen, and those who had received fifteen years sentenced to life.[22]

When the three members of Tahrir approached the Libyan embassy in Kuwait to request a meeting with Gaddafi, the party was known. When the ambassador asked why they wanted to meet Gaddafi, the party members replied that they had heard that Gaddafi had given a speech rejecting the *Sunna* and because they did not believe that it was appropriate for an Arab leader to make such a claim they wanted to discuss the issue with Gaddafi directly. His well-documented vanity resulted in a personal invitation from Gaddafi, with the ambassador stating that his leader was a supporter of intellectuals and discussions[23] (an ironic conceit that would persist throughout his lifetime and sometimes indulged by others; for example, when the London School of Economics invited him to give a speech via video-link in December 2010).

In 1978, the delegation was invited to Tripoli towards the end of Ramadan (the Muslim month of fasting), which fell across August and the beginning of

September that year. The three members were Faruq Habayib, Fawzi Nasir and Mahmoud Khalidi, two teachers and an engineer. Habayib was the head of the delegation, Khalidi was a Sharia graduate and expert in Islamic law, and Nasir's role was to take full notes during the meeting. They prepared their personal affairs before leaving, in consideration of the fact that Gaddafi was known to be ruthless and unstable, along with the fact that numerous members of the party were serving long sentences in Libya.[24]

When they arrived in Tripoli, they were told that the government had arranged accommodation for them in one of the main hotels used to host visitors. They refused, explaining that the delegation had come for a specific purpose and were not there as guests at the expense of the government. After the officials failed to convince them, the delegation went into the city to find their own accommodation, accompanied by a Libyan official, Nuri al-Mudi.

Once they were booked into an alternative hotel and their location and contact details were known to al-Mudi, they settled in to wait for an appointment. They were offered a tour of the city, which they turned down, saying that they wanted to be ready if they were called to the meeting (having been told to come to Libya for the appointment from a certain date without being given a specific time, in keeping with Gaddafi's inconsistent nature).

Al-Mudi was clearly the government handler, and kept asking questions such as who was the head of the delegation (Habayib), what were their positions in the party (normal party members, who did not hold any administrative positions at that time), and what was the reason for their visit (to discuss the issue of belief in the Prophetic *Sunna* with Gaddafi). After repeatedly receiving the same answers, al-Mudi eventually commented on the unusual nature of their visit, since normally delegations to Gaddafi came to ask for either financial or material help. No-one else had come to discuss anything like their issue before.[25]

On the evening of 30 August the delegation was called to meet Gaddafi. That night was also the twenty-seventh night of Ramadan, during which a substantial number of Muslims spend the evening in congregational prayers due to a belief in its additional significance as the night during which the Qur'an was first revealed. No press conferences had been arranged for the delegation prior to the appointment, as would occur when Gaddafi received favoured political emissaries, such as the PFLP leader George Habash. The three were roughly searched and taken to a room where Gaddafi was sitting, before beginning a debate that lasted for four hours. Throughout the meeting, Gaddafi kept an eye on a silent television screen behind the delegates, to watch for any possible security breaches, likely wary of a delegation that claimed not to want anything from him and would not accept having its expenses paid.[26]

Habayib began their discussion by talking about the history of Libya in the context of the fight against colonialism and the 'train of Jihad' of the past. Over the next four hours the discussion moved between the two sides, with the delegation insisting that the Qur'an had established laws and compelled all Muslims to follow the example of the Prophet, quoting verses such as 'And whatsoever the Messenger gives you, take it, and whatsoever he forbids you, abstain (from it).'[27] Gaddafi rejected their argument, so Habayib challenged him that although the Qur'an mandates prayer it does not mention how to pray, with the method of prayer defined by Prophetic practice.

The delegation also insisted that the discussion was not simply theological, but was also political because Muslims had to live according to the Qur'an and *Sunna*, and it was imperative for any ruler to implement Islam. Gaddafi retorted that Mustafa Kamal Atatürk—the former president of the Turkish republic who had abolished the Ottoman caliphate and established the Turkish republic in its place in 1924—had praised the idea of the separation of religion and state. Habayib responded that Kemal was an agent of the English, while carefully avoiding any direct accusation against Gaddafi.

They also argued over Gaddafi's claim that politics was all about lying and cheating and therefore had nothing to do with Islamic morals, Habayib countering that political understanding and political morals were two different issues. Habayib also tried to discuss Arab nationalism, claiming that Arab intellectuals had taken their ideas from orientalists and simply imported a foreign ideology into their works. Gaddafi generally did not respond positively or give up his positions, his only concession being that they were unable to implement the Qur'an and *Sunna* in its entirety at that time, so it made sense to start with the Qur'an first.

There was no political discussion regarding Libya or Gaddafi directly in the meeting, with the delegation having decided to stick to the remit that they had been sent with. Given that they did not receive any indication that Gaddafi was willing to consider changing his views and that he instead insisted on his rejection of the *Sunna* as a whole, they did not bother to try to win him over for *nusra* support. After the discussion concluded, the delegation left and made preparations to return to Kuwait.

By coincidence, they were staying in the same hotel as Imam Musa al-Sadr, who was also there to meet Gaddafi. Al-Sadr was a leading Lebanese Shia scholar and very influential in Lebanon at that time. He had pushed for recognition of the Alawi branch of Shi'ism to be accepted by the mainstream Twelver Shia branch as fellow Muslims and a subset of the Twelvers (which occurred in 1973 after four years of discussions, other Shia having considered the Alawis to be heretics outside the fold of Islam until then).[28] While waiting in the hotel lobby in preparation to leave the country, they noticed a number of regime officials who had come looking for 'the religious people'.

Al-Sadr subsequently disappeared, last seen on 31 August, though the Libyan regime consistently denied they had anything to do with his disappearance. It has since transpired that, according to Abdullah al-Senussi, a regime intelligence official, Gaddafi ordered al-Sadr to be killed in front of him after a fist fight between the two of them, because al-Sadr refused to take money to further inflame the ongoing Lebanese civil war.[29]

On the plane back to Kuwait Nasir set about writing a complete report of the meeting, which the delegation sent to the party leadership on arrival. On 9 September the party issued a 7,000-word pamphlet that detailed the reasons behind sending the delegation to meet Gaddafi, the discussion that ensued and a concluding address from the party leadership that went beyond the points that the delegation had raised. In justifying the decision to send the delegation, the document stated that the action came under the rubric of holding rulers to account and was a political rather than an intellectual issue. The discussion was 'on one of the sources from the Islamic sources' for 'the sake of implementation', which 'the party does in all the countries [where] it is based', which included Libya, that belonged 'to all Muslims in the same way that Mecca, Medina, Cairo, Amman and Jerusalem' did. Since Gaddafi had rejected one of the sources of Islamic legislation that was agreed upon in normative Islam, it was 'fundamental' rather than being 'a trivial issue that does not befit a political party working to establish the Khilafah.'[30]

The main substance of the pamphlet then explained the normative Islamic view, following the example of the Prophet, with multiple verses from the Qur'an that explicitly mentioned the obligation to do so, finishing by stating that whoever rejected it in its entirety as a source had committed an act of clear unbelief. It then asserted that there was a growing Islamic consciousness among the Muslims at the time who had withdrawn 'their trust in all the ideas presented to them by the disbelieving West', including the ideas of 'patriotism, capitalism, socialism and communism', while also having 'lost all confidence in political parties and blocks presented to them whether Ba'athist, Arab nationalist, Communist, socialist or Nasserite.' It ended with a call to Gaddafi to leave behind his 'greenness' (in reference to the *Green Book* he had published in 1975 outlining his 'political philosophy') and to 'hand over to us the authority so as to declare the establishment of the caliphate and appoint a caliph to whom we will pledge to hear and obey, on the Book of Allah and the *Sunna* of His Messenger.'[31]

The document was printed and widely distributed by the party, with the hope that it would raise Tahrir's profile among Muslims generally and those in political circles specifically. Because the pamphlet ended with a call for the establishment of the caliphate, it has been claimed that the delegation had been sent to Gaddafi with that purpose. In fact, the delegation's sole purpose was to hold Gaddafi's rejection of the *Sunna* to account, and the discussion was limited to that, although the pamphlet produced afterwards included such calling for the caliphate as a political statement.

The conflict between the two sides had not reached its conclusion, with Gaddafi's intelligence services targeting opposition activists abroad. In 1980 two Libyan dissidents were assassinated in London by two assailants who were acting on instructions from the Gaddafi regime. Moussa Koussa, who had close ties with British and US intelligence services, as one of the key players in Libya's intelligence apparatus before the fall of the Gaddafi regime in 2011,[32] was ambassador to the UK at the time and stated that the regime had decided to kill them both and that he approved of the decision.[33] The first man killed was Muhammad Mustafa Ramadan, who used to work for the BBC World Service. He was shot outside Regent's Park mosque after Friday prayers on 11 April. Later that year, Libyan lawyer Mahmud Abu Salem Nafa was killed in West Kensington.

Although unknown to many (including perhaps the Libyan regime), it was claimed that Ramadan was a member of Tahrir, and party members in Europe released a statement four days after his assassination, which situated the event as part of Gaddafi's war against Islamic opposition within and outside of the country.[34] It appears that Ramadan had come to the regime's attention after he sent a number of open letters to Gaddafi, which were delivered to him through personal contacts, the last dated 17 February 1977, in which he focused on the state of the Islamic nation and what was required for its revival. He rejected the idea of 'socialist Islam', stating that the religion revealed by God was called Islam and was complete; therefore what was needed was to work to ensure that Muslims understood it correctly. In the letter, he also suggested the establishment of an international radio station, to be called 'The Voice of Islam', which would help overcome the barriers that had been placed between Muslims and the correct understanding of Islam by 'the crusader and Zionist powers.' Ramadan had sent the letter a few months before the public hanging of students in Benghazi, and made a decision thereafter not to send any more letters, believing Gaddafi was beyond hope and reason. Two Libyans, Hasan al-Masri and Najib al-Qasimi, were convicted of the murders and sentenced to life imprisonment in September of the same year.[35]

There were also a number of arrests of Tahrir activists in Libya that year. As Palestinians and Jordanians continued to come to Libya during the 1970s, some of those associated with the party had begun their activities again. One of the members was involved in a car accident, which led to the involvement of the police, who found a party book in the car, along with a list of names of other members. As a result, all of those on the lists were arrested and interrogated. They spent two years in jail before, on 7 April 1983, some of them were publicly hanged by regime supporters in the schools and colleges where they had worked, in front of their families and students, on the direct orders of Gaddafi.

Among them was Nassir Sirris, a Palestinian Jordanian who was brought out to be executed in front of a crowd that included his wife and children, shouting that they were being killed for the sake of Islam, and that any talk of weapons being found was false.[36] Some the prisoners had been in jail since 1973, such as Haffaf and al-Kurdi, and were also hanged in the courtyard of the Engineering College at the University of Tripoli. Eye witnesses said that, not satisfied with hanging their victims, throughout the hanging and afterwards, the regime supporters continued beating the lifeless bodies.[37]

According to a Hizb-ut-Tahrir pamphlet released two months after the executions, thirteen members were killed, ten by public execution and three as a result of torture while being interrogated in Tripoli. The pamphlet also explained that the motivation behind Gaddafi's actions was a result of the publication of the discussions that took place regarding the *Sunna* in 1978, which accused him of unbelief.[38] It appears that, although plausible, the accusation was based on deduction rather than any clear indication that this was the case. The reality is that numerous party members had been imprisoned after the publication of the talks, and Gaddafi could have taken his revenge immediately if he had wanted to. It is possible that the continued existence of Tahrir's activity in Libya, after and despite the long sentences handed down in April 1977, played at least an equal role in hardening Gaddafi's already harsh stance towards it.

Throughout the 1980s, the treatment of prisoners worsened across the board, with a number dying from torture. The Haffaf family was blacklisted, with Haffaf's father and brother also jailed for a period without cause. Anyone with the name was forbidden from travelling, even if they were from far removed branches of the family. Other prisoners' families were also treated similarly, with the house of one demolished followed by the exiling of the family from their town. This reached the point that when the father died, his body was disinterred and the family informed that it was not permitted to bury him.[39]

Taking into account the history from the mid-1960s until the mid-1980s, Libya expert Ronald Bruce St John's description of the group being a 'remarkably persistent organization' rings true.[40] But the executions in 1983 ended any meaningful activity in Libya by Tahrir, with the party having been violently uprooted twice before it had a chance to spread. Despite their enmity towards Gaddafi, after US planes bombed Tripoli on 15 April 1986 the party issued a declaration the same day that the attacks were not aimed simply at Gaddafi, but were against Libya, and therefore were an issue for all Muslims worldwide. The pamphlet went on to explain how the Islamic obligation on the Muslims was to repel aggression against any part of their lands, and that this required them to remove their rulers and unite under the single banner of the caliphate.[41]

The last members of Tahrir to be released from prison in Libya were freed in 2003, thirty years after their arrests. As a result of the overthrow of Gaddafi in 2011, more details regarding his regime's treatment of opposition have become publicly available. The most notorious event was the 1996 Abu Salim massacre, during which up to 1,200 inmates were killed, according to Libyan human rights groups.[42] During the US-led war on terror, which began after 9/11, the Gaddafi regime announced that it would end its chemical weapons programme in 2004 and began working closely with British and US intelligence agencies, with documents indicating that rendition of opposition figures to Libya was aided in at least one case by the CIA, and that British intelligence traced phone numbers for Libyan intelligence.[43]

While declining to comment on the authenticity of the documents, CIA spokesperson Jennifer Youngblood stated that 'it can't come as a surprise that the Central Intelligence Agency works with foreign governments to help protect our country from terrorism and other deadly threats.'[44] Turning against its former ally in possibly one of the more easily decided volte-faces made necessary by the Arab revolutions that began at the end of 2010, Western militaries helped bring down the Gaddafi regime after a popular uprising began in Benghazi. Gaddafi was executed in October 2011, soon after being pulled from a drain pipe where he had been hiding. On 7 April 2012 a commemoration for those killed thirty years earlier was held at the University of Tripoli, with the courtyard where they were executed renamed after 'The Martyr Muhammad Muhathab Haffaf'.[45]

## Khomeini and the Islamic Revolution

In the same period as the delegation to Gaddafi, the Iranian revolution was in full swing, with strikes and demonstrations against Shah Reza Pahlavi paralysing the country. A deeply unpopular figure, he had been returned to power on the back of a coup orchestrated by the CIA and British intelligence in 1953 against the then prime minister Muhammad Mosaddegh, despite Mosaddegh enjoying '95 to 98 percent' support of the Iranian people, according to Henry Grady, the US Ambassador to Iran.[46] In the quarter of a century that followed, the Shah continued as a stalwart ally of the West, while repressing the local population through the SAVAK, a domestic intelligence agency formed under the guidance of US and Israeli intelligence officers in 1957. Widespread demonstrations against the Shah's regime began in October 1977, erupting due to a mix of the increasingly oppressive nature of the regime, dissatisfaction with the Westernisation and liberalisation of society, and anger rising from economic problems that peaked in the same period.

The most prominent leader of the opposition was religious scholar Ayatollah Ruhollah Khomeini, one of the six Grand Ayatollahs who headed the Twelver Shia sect. Khomeini had been living in exile since 1964, after being imprisoned in Iran due to continued criticism of the regime and its links to the West. Most of his time in exile was spent in Najaf, Iraq, before being expelled by Saddam in 1978, which led him eventually to go to France, where he decamped to a village near Paris in October of the same year. The choice of destination was not random. Khomeini's special representative abroad, Ebrahim Yazdi (a key member of the opposition Freedom Movement of Iran, who had been based mainly in the US since 1960) suggested the location because it gave them the opportunity to access Western media.[47] It also gave Muslims in Europe the opportunity to approach the ayatollah, including his followers, general well wishers, and a delegation sent by Tahrir on the orders of its leadership.

Hizb-ut-Tahrir had been present in Germany since the late 1950s. Members travelled there to study or work, with Dr Taufiq Mustafa and Qadri al-Nabulsi among the earliest arrivals. Many Arab and Middle Eastern citizens staying in the region for either study or work were therefore potential recruits for the party. Members had been present in neighbouring countries such as Austria since the 1960s. Among those who studied with Mustafa in Hamburg was Muhammad Beheshti, who worked as an imam at the Islamic Center of Hamburg between 1965 and 1970. He spent three years studying with Tahrir during that time, but left without being offered membership due to differences with the party leadership.[48] Beheshti was part of the opposition to the Pahlavi regime. He continued to agitate against the regime after his return to Iran in 1970, and was to play a key role during the revolution. He had a part to play in the delegations from Tahrir to Khomeini in Iran in 1980.

In 1978 Mustafa headed to meet Khomeini at his temporary residence in the village of Neauphle-le-Château, 25 miles from Paris. Mustafa was accompanied by Fathi Abdullah, who had been an officer of the Arab Legion in the early 1950s, and Dr Muhammad Jaber, a Lebanese member of the party with a Shia background. The meeting took place in late October or early November, and after sitting in a tent that had been set up in the gardens to accommodate them, waiting journalists were invited in to speak to Khomeini himself. The discussion went through a translator, despite the fact that Khomeini must have been reasonably fluent in Arabic as a result of his Islamic studies and years in Najaf. This was likely due to the formality of the meeting, with Khomeini's responses written down in their entirety by one of his associates.[49]

The delegation presented Khomeini with a number of party books, including a copy of the proposed constitution of the Islamic state, and a small booklet about the contradictions between democracy and Islam. Delivering the constitution was an obvious choice given that Khomeini was seen as a likely leader in waiting, while the booklet on democracy was chosen due to Khomeini's adoption of the word as part of his discourse in opposition, talking about how his vision was for an Islamic and democratic Iran.[50]

After introductions, during which Khomeini indicated that he had heard of the party previously (likely during his stay in Najaf, as well as perhaps from Beheshti), Mustafa first explained the general concepts of Tahrir, its vision that the Muslim *Umma* was a single whole, and that the party did not differentiate between schools of thought. His main focus was to impress upon Khomeini that if he came to power in Iran, he should establish a state that would be for all Muslims, rather than a sectarian Shia state or a nationalist Iranian state. While he could freely adopt the *Ja'fari* school of jurisprudence in the state (which was the basis of Twelver jurisprudence), relations within the state and those between the state and other states in the international community should be based on Islam rather than sectarian or nationalist interests. He added that if Khomeini implemented such a vision, instead of seeking to establish a second Islamic state elsewhere, Tahrir would work to join other Muslim countries to Iran under a single leadership. Jaber recalled that Khomeini stared at them with his piercing eyes, and simply replied, 'God willing, as long as we are all working for Islam, then it is good.'[51]

The second part of the discussion was led by Abdullah, during which he concentrated on Tahrir's view on the contradictions between Islam and democracy, and the conflict between the Sharia as the source of legislation, and legislation being decided freely by the people. Khomeini replied to this in more detail, stating that when he used words such as democracy and republic, he meant that people had the right to elect their leaders and not that they had the right to legislate. (This is a common explanation often given by proponents of 'Islamic democracy', including mainstream scholars such as Yusuf al-Qaradawi.)[52] Abdullah retorted that as long as the terms had specific meanings in Western terminology, they should not be used, since they would confuse people about what was intended. (Later, when deciding on the name for the new Iranian state after the revolution, Khomeini opposed the inclusion of the word 'democracy' in the title of the 'Islamic Republic of Iran', stating that it would be known as 'The Islamic Republic, not one word less, not one word more.')[53]

When Khomeini was asked whether he and those in opposition with him had adopted any specific programme to implement if they took power, he firmly denied anything was in place and indicated that a council would be set up to discuss and decide upon, the constitution and its articles. At this Abdullah presented Khomeini with a copy of the draft constitution and the Islamic evidences it was based upon prepared by Tahrir, suggesting that it could be adopted during any interim period before the council had reached its own conclusions as to what it would adopt. With that, the meeting ended with mutual good wishes exchanged between the two sides.[54]

Two months later, towards the end of December, events had progressed to the point that it was becoming apparent that the Shah's days were numbered. The US administration of President Jimmy Carter, the Shah's most prominent backer, was also beginning to fray internally over its approach to the opposition, with differences over the regime's longevity and what approach should be taken towards it having begun to emerge between the US State Department and the CIA some months earlier.[55] By December, Khomeini and US officials were exchanging letters through the US embassy in France, with the US concerned over the fate of oil supplies from the potential new regime. The letters were translated by Yazdi, who would also translate the replies back, including Khomeini assuring the US that he was not interested in cutting off its oil, but would seek to invest the revenues in developing Iran's industry and agriculture[56] (one of numerous assurances Yazdi gave US officials, including that Iran would not turn towards the USSR or seek to foment revolution across the region).[57]

Given the developing situation, the local leadership of Hizb-ut-Tahrir based in Europe decided to send another delegation to meet Khomeini, to see if he had considered anything they had discussed with him during their first meeting. Jaber led the new delegation, along with two other members, one of Tunisian origin and the other from Palestine. On arrival at Khomeini's base near Paris it was clear that getting any type of meeting with the ever busier leader in waiting was going to be a struggle, something that one of his administrators tried to impress upon them. The delegation insisted that they meet the man, the three of them having travelled from Germany, making any subsequent journey to return at a more suitable time cumbersome.

Eventually, they were given a ten-minute slot between meetings, during which Khomeini came to see them, greeting Jaber more warmly than the first time, apparently more comfortable and confident in his surroundings by then. The conversation was more direct on this occasion, with the delegation asking Khomeini, given it appeared he would be in power soon, whether he had considered what he would do in that position. Once again, Khomeini's reply was non-committal, telling them that he had not had much time to discuss the issue since their last meeting, but that the council would be created to formulate the constitution within the next month. Thinking this would be the last meeting between them, he concluded by praising their sincerity, and informed them he would follow their affairs in the future.

On their way out of the meeting, the delegation passed through the tent of journalists, where they ended up in a discussion with a US reporter who questioned them over how they could talk to Khomeini about the caliphate given that he was a Shia imam. The Tunisian member explained that Hizb-ut-Tahrir did not differentiate between Muslims, and that they had told Khomeini, this time and before, that if he ruled Muslims according to Islam, with justice and Islamic proofs on his side, as well as establishing relations with non-Muslim nations on an Islamic basis, then the party would call all Muslims to follow him. On the other hand, if Khomeini did not fulfil these conditions, they would neither support him nor call others to.[58] This was not an unusual position, with individuals and Islamic movements backing Khomeini and the revolution in its early days, due to the universal Islamic rhetoric used.[59]

Jaber took a delegation to meet Khomeini in France one final time at the end of January 1979. The Shah had left Iran two weeks earlier on 16 January, leaving behind a government led by Prime Minister Shapour Bakhtiar. On their arrival they were surprised to find that preparations were being made for Khomeini to leave that night to return to Iran. The delegation spent two hours talking to Imam Mahmudi, who was responsible for his appointments, and though he went back and forth numerous times to try to arrange a meeting, the response was that Khomeini was not available. Jaber impressed on Mahmudi that at the very least they wanted the opportunity to give Khomeini their best wishes before he left for Iran, and managed to secure a short five-minute talk. They took their final chance to ask about the constitutional committee again (to which Khomeini replied that it had been formed) and that any future state he established had to be for all Muslims, rather than a sectarian or national entity. The brevity and circumstances of the meeting meant that nothing more was mentioned than the vague responses of the previous discussions, with regards exchanged between the two groups before Khomeini left them to prepare for his triumphant return to Tehran.[60]

The Iranians were waiting expectantly for their revolutionary leader to return to the country after more than a decade in exile, a matter complicated by the position of the military, whose top officers were loyal to the Shah. By this time US officials were in regular contact with Yazdi, including formal meetings with the embassy's political counsellor, Warren Zimmerman, and informal phone calls with State Department Desk Officer Henry Precht. An American academic, Professor Cottam, had also visited Tehran and introduced the embassy there to Beheshti, the most senior cleric known to US officials at the time.[61] Gen. Robert Huyser, deputy commander in chief of US European Command at the time, was sent by Carter to Iran to stabilise the situation—or to destabilise the Shah's government, depending on whose perspective is taken. According to National Security Council (NSC) staff member Gary Sick, Carter's National Security Advisor Zbigniew Brzezinski stressed to Huyser that he should make sure that the military option (to carry out a coup attempt against any possible Khomeini-led government) remained open.[62] However, after Khomeini returned to Iran on 1 February, he soon set up an alternative government to the one led by Bakhtiar as a direct challenge to Bakhtiar's authority.

The Iranian army declared its neutrality on 11 February, a move that led to the fall of the government. Bakhtiar subsequently said that the 'Americans played such a disgusting role'[63] in the uprising, claiming that Huyser had been behind the army's decision to remain neutral. (Meanwhile, however, Brzezinski was trying to arrange a military coup to end the conflict up until the last minute).[64] Although the US administration had been fully behind the Shah, as realism set in official and unofficial contacts were ongoing between the two sides, which had led to a feeling on the US side that they could do business with Khomeini (particularly if it meant keeping out communist influence, perhaps as part of Brzezinski's arc of Islam to combat the 'arc of crisis', a label he used to describe regional instability on which the USSR was looking to capitalise).[65] One of the most prominent meetings was the visit to Tehran and Paris by the former US attorney general Ramsey Clark, and Richard Falk, the chair of a small American committee opposed to American intervention in Iran, which led to their praising the Iranian revolution, with Falk writing in mid-February in *The New York Times* that Carter and Brzezinski had 'until very recently' associated Khomeini with 'religious fanaticism,'[66] implying that this was no longer the case.

At the end of March there was a referendum in Iran, which offered the chance to either support or reject the idea of abolishing the monarchy and establishing an Islamic republic in the country, with 99.3 per cent supporting abolition,[67] leading Khomeini to declare the establishment of the Islamic Republic of Iran on 1 April. In the same period, Zallum sent a delegation to Qom, the seat of Shia religious learning in Iran, where Khomeini and other senior clerics were based. The head of this group was al-Da'ur, still one of Hizb-ut-Tahrir's leadership committee and the most senior member to meet with Khomeini. The rest of the group was made up of four others: Abu Mahmoud and Abdul Rahman Hudruj from Lebanon, and Abu Rami Muhammad Nafi and one other member from Kuwait. The delegation had arranged its meeting through the Iranian embassy, and therefore there was no need for negotiations with any gatekeepers in this case. According to Hudruj, the group went in the hope that it would be able to convince the leaders of the revolution to establish their vision of the Islamic state, and if not then at least win support from other influential figures in Iran.[68]

Once again the delegation brought several books with them, and once again the constitution was one of them. At the meeting with Khomeini, al-Da'ur spoke for about five minutes, before Khomeini then gave a long fifteen-minute reply in Farsi. He then instructed the translator to take them to another room and explain what he had said to them. In other words, rather than a discussion between the two sides, the delegation was given a short speech before being ushered away. They left feeling that they had been treated inappropriately, and were unhappy with the meeting. The most prominent part of the translated speech was that Khomeini considered their delegation to have been the one group that had come to give him advice purely for the sake of Allah, normally something that would be considered praise, but in this case it was difficult to see it as anything more than a polite brush-off.[69]

The delegation then set about arranging meetings with the major figures in Qom. Beheshti met with them and aided the delegation, in making contacts, one of the most prominent being Ayatollah Muhammad Kazem Shariatmadari, with whom they debated the compatibility of Islam with democracy. They were generally optimistic after completing their mission, feeling that they had successfully entered the Iranian political environment and imparted their opinions effectively among key leaders and decision makers, though they were clearly unimpressed with Khomeini himself. Other than one meeting, during which one of the Shia clerics stated that they did not take any jurisprudence from outside of their own sect, the delegation felt that its ideas would be considered by those who were charged with formulating the new proposed constitution.[70]

In the meantime, the provisional government headed by Mehdi Bazargan proposed a draft constitution on 18 June, which apart from proposing a president instead of the Shah was not substantially different from the 1906 constitution. The draft also accorded no special role to the clerics in the new state. Khomeini was prepared to submit the draft to a national referendum, but this was opposed by other revolutionaries, with the demands to submit the draft to a constituent assembly being made most vehemently by the leftist elements and Shariatmadari.[71] An Assembly of Experts made up of seventy-three members, mainly clerics and Islamic Republic Party members, convened on 18 August to consider the draft constitution. The constitution was redrafted to establish the basis for clerical domination of the state and to vest ultimate authority in Khomeini as the Leader of the Revolution.[72]

By October, it was becoming clear to Bazargan and others in the government that the draft constitution was going to institutionalise a dominating role for the clerics in the state. A number of cabinet members, including Bazargan, tried persuading Khomeini to dissolve the Assembly of Experts, but failed.[73] A different type of criticism emerged from outside the country—with Tahrir members making unsuccessful attempts to obtain copies of the draft from numerous different Iranian embassies. In the end a translation was printed in Lebanese newspaper *Al-Safir* across three issues between 21 and 23 October, which was confirmed as accurate by the Iranian embassy in Beirut. On 30 October, Hizb-ut-Tahrir issued a refutation of the proposed

Iranian constitution, which began by stating the actions and recommendations that they had made to Khomeini and those around him through the party's various delegations, particularly with regards to the Iranian government's relations with the US and USSR, ending with the complaint that 'more than four months have passed since our last meeting, and you have done nothing, and the situation remains as it was.'[74]

The majority of the rest of the document of about 10,000 words was a point-by-point critique of the proposed constitution, starting with the first article, which stated that Iran was an Islamic republic, while the system of a republic was a democratic rather than Islamic form of rule. Numerous other criticisms followed, with the claim that the constitution was basically a copy of Western-inspired Arab constitutions rather than one derived from Islamic belief. Attention was paid to the claim that the Ja'fari school of thought was mentioned explicitly in the text, meaning that 'it is not an Islamic state for all Muslims', and that it was clear that the state proposed was a national state like any other in existence, this particular one for the people of Iran.[75] The document also deemed that the oath that was to be taken by elected representatives was un-Islamic.

Although the copy Hizb-ut-Tahrir criticised was different from the final version decided on by the time the Assembly of Experts had finished its deliberations on 15 November, the substance was at least similar if not identical.[76] The constitution was adopted after a referendum at the beginning of December, with official results again claiming a very high 99.5 per cent acceptance, though the turnout was approximately five million lower (approximately 25 per cent) than the twenty million who participated in the referendum to abolish the monarchy and establish an Islamic republic.[77]

Members of the delegations to Khomeini were surprised by the draft constitution, particularly by the sectarian and nationalist nature that they believed it institutionalised in multiple articles.[78] However, while it appears that those who were sent to meet Khomeini were hopeful of positive results, Zallum himself did not share their optimism. Although he had ordered the delegations to hold the discussions with Khomeini and those around him, Zallum did not believe that there was much likelihood that the ayatollahs would agree to establish a caliphate, but it was the party's Islamic duty to try to hold them to account.

The reasons for Zallum's pessimism were two-fold: in the first place he was of the opinion that throughout history many Shia clerics had been opponents rather than supporters of the caliphs, and his own discussions in Najaf with leading Shia scholars in the late 1950s over al-Nabhani's booklet *al-Khilafah* (The Caliphate) would only have convinced him further of that view. Secondly, Zallum believed that the US had supported the Iranian revolution and backed Khomeini after the Shah's rule became untenable.[79]

This position was made clear after a group of Iranian students stormed the US embassy in Tehran on 4 November, in response to the Shah going to the US for medical treatment in October. The intrigues around the event are too many to be explored in any depth here, but the occupation of the embassy, initially planned to be a short two- to three-day operation, ended up lasting more than a year and led to Carter's defeat in the 1980 presidential election. At the same time, Khomeini also used it to strengthen his own position, which resulted in the resignations of Bazargan and Yazdi, whom the US considered moderates. Tahrir's analysis was that Iran and the US had planned the embassy takeover to strengthen Khomeini's position (with protests against Khomeini from opposition ranks growing at the time) and help Carter get re-elected.[80] While the first did occur, the second most certainly didn't.

The party's analysis was based on the open support that Khomeini gave to the hostage takers, support that the analysis considered implausible unless he had a prior agreement with the US to act so brazenly, given that the occupation was well outside of acceptable international norms. This was as well as the occupation and hostage-taking being un-Islamic, because the Prophet guaranteed ambassadors the full protection of the state. (Although there have since been other similar conspiracy theories around the events of the embassy takeover, they have tended to suggest that the events were manipulated by Carter's opponents in the CIA, with the objective of getting Ronald Reagan and George Bush into the White House.)[81]

Irrespective of the accuracy of Hizb-ut-Tahrir's analysis, the party was by then entirely convinced that the US had directed the revolution. Despite his distrust of Khomeini, Zallum sent a final delegation to Iran at the beginning of 1980 to try to meet other revolutionary leaders and clerics in Tehran and present them with the party's criticism of the Iranian constitution, while proposing its own alternative. This time Abu Mahmoud led the delegation, which included Hudruj and Sherif al-Husseini, and which spent approximately two months in Iran during this final trip.

The delegation received a mixed reception, the best response from one cleric being an acceptance of the criticism and a promise to work for reform, which in the end could be considered as perhaps nothing more than the same rhetoric that the previous four delegations had all heard. The delegation arranged for the translation of the proposed alternative constitution into Farsi and printed 25,000 copies, which were distributed during Friday prayers in Tehran and other towns, with a written message from Beheshti guaranteeing them security in the face of any problems from local authorities. As previously, he was their main supporter in Iran at the time, and provided indirect backing for the delegation as a result of his respect and previous affiliation to Tahrir.[82]

After two months, the delegation left Iran and there were no further attempts at contacting the revolutionary leadership. On 28 June 1980, as part of the mainly Marxist violent opposition to the Islamic republic, a bomb blast at the headquarters of the Islamic Republican Party killed Beheshti along with seventy-three other party members, including numerous cabinet ministers.[83]

Having taken an active interest in the Iranian revolution, interaction with Khomeini and the revolutionaries convinced Zallum and the leadership that there would be no Islamic state established in Iran as they envisaged it from their understanding of the religion. The disillusionment took a while longer to sink in for others, including movements such as the Jama'at and Muslim Brotherhood in Egypt, who were first supportive of the revolution as 'a death-blow to the era of shahs, the Atatürks, and the Bhuttos'[84] and went as far as omitting discussion regarding the Shia elements of the Iranian constitution when addressing it in their articles, symptomatic of their uncritical approach to the revolution's means and goals.[85] Over time they were initially apologetic, then defensive, as a result of the various excesses committed against the opposition in Iran and the onset of the Gulf War, before becoming preoccupied with affairs closer to home.

Although Tahrir had historically recruited many members from the Shia community, particularly in Lebanon and Iraq in the 1950s, the Iranian revolution was identified by several members of Shia background as the main reason behind the drop in such recruitment. Many Shia who were with the party or attracted by its ideas believed that their goal of establishing an Islamic state had been reached. The establishment of the Islamic Republic of Iran is sometimes identified by Hizb-ut-Tahrir members as the root cause behind the inflammation of sectarianism in the region, explaining why even today Shia remain hesitant to work with the party, despite the loss of the initial Islamic shine to the Iranian state.

Another reason for this hesitancy is that a Twelver Shia (a member of the majority Shia sect in contemporary times, which is dominant in Iran) could not in any practical sense remain a Twelver as a member of Tahrir. This is because some of the fundamental understandings that members are obliged to adopt contradict central Twelver tenets, specifically their belief in the infallibility of their imams and that Imam Ali's claim on the caliphate immediately after the death of the Prophet was founded on revelation.[86] Although members of a Shia background, such as Jaber, have claimed that they do not have to relinquish 'core Shia beliefs'[87] to join Tahrir, they can only mean Shia in the original sense of the word, used to refer to the followers of Ali and encompassing all those who believe that Ali was a more capable or correct candidate for the caliphate than those who came before him. Such an opinion, which is the root all Shia belief (which then divides into different sects that hold different positions on numerous issues, ranging from the preference of Ali as caliph to believing that Ali was in fact a divine figure), would not in essence be incompatible with membership of the party, as opposed to the Twelver doctrine, which contradicts the party on multiple counts.

A good example of the beliefs of Shia members of Hizb-ut-Tahrir would be those held by Sameh Atif al-Zain, who was close to al-Nabhani until leaving the party at the end of the 1950s and whose non-sectarian attitude is well known. Like the current members from Shia backgrounds, the belief that Muslim and Islamic unity is more important than other any issue was front and foremost. The confrontation over the caliphate among the first generation after the Prophet is considered to have been a political difference between Muslims that might naturally occur, and the caliphates of the first three caliphs before Ali (namely Abu Bakr, Umar and Uthman) were valid.[88] Furthermore, as party members must reject the infallibility of anyone other than the Prophets, the Shia members of the party are in reality indistinguishable from those of a Sunni background in terms of core beliefs. These are limited to what is commonly referred to in Islamic scholarship as the *arkan al-iman* (pillars of belief)—namely the belief in God, the Day of Judgement, angels, the revealed books, all the messengers of God and that God has knowledge of all affairs.[89]

Thus, al-Nabhani limited the party's adopted beliefs to the undisputed central tenets of Islamic theology, which form a part of Hizb-ut-Tahrir's idea of revival, believing that the sectarian disputes that dominated Islamic discourse for centuries stand in the way of unity based on Islam. As expressed by Jaber, the party aimed 'to promote a common Islamic identity on the global stage' and he considered that it had 'a vision and plan to eventually eliminate these schisms and sectarian divisions among the Muslims.'[90] In the party's eyes, what it considered to be the sectarian and nationalist state that emerged after the Iranian revolution was a major cause in exacerbating rather than healing such splits.

*Between Arab pressure and global expansion*

The delegations to Libya and Iran early in Zallum's leadership were intended as prominent political actions that would impose the party on the political environment. Despite the internal lethargy noted after the death of al-Nabhani, the leadership continued addressing political events as they occurred through commentary and pamphlets. The other major event in the region was the set of secret negotiations between Sadat and Israeli Prime Minister Menachem Begin, which were facilitated by the US government and resulted in the signing of the Camp David Accords on 17 September 1978. The initial agreement signed included a framework for negotiations to establish an independent authority in the West Bank and Gaza Strip and to implement UN Security Council Resolution 242, which called for Israeli withdrawal from lands occupied in 1967 and recognition of the sovereignty of both sides. The Egypt-Israel peace treaty was signed soon after in March 1979 and included the return of the Sinai Peninsula to Egypt, mutual recognition between the two countries, and normalisation of relations. The agreement was considered a betrayal of the Arab and Islamic causes and inflamed opposition against Sadat, particularly within the army. He was killed by Lt Khalid Islambouli on 6 October 1981.

Hizb-ut-Tahrir issued a response to the initial Camp David negotiations in October 1978, stating that any peace treaty with Israel was unacceptable, and that any agreement on 1967 borders was against Islam, because it was forbidden to surrender occupied land. The only Islamic solution was to liberate the whole of Palestine through the removal of the Israeli entity, and therefore it was incumbent on the whole of the Muslim *Umma* to reject the accords and anything stemming from them.[91] In response to a fatwa issued by the Sheikh of al-Azhar on 10 May 1979, which justified the Egyptian peace treaty with Israel based on the precedent that the Prophet had made peace with those who fought against him from Mecca, an event referred to in Muslim sources as the Treaty of Hudaybiya, the party issued a detailed refutation that mentioned numerous reasons why the analogy was false, including that the Hudaybiya treaty was time-limited and did not involve the permanent surrender of occupied land.[92] After Sadat was killed in 1981, the party released a statement that celebrated his death (the pamphlet's title can be translated as 'And the traitor came across his reward'), while stating that to resolve the issue correctly required the establishment of the Islamic state in place of the regime left behind.[93]

Despite the active commentary by the leadership of the party on affairs as they took place, there appears to have been little if any direct involvement in Egypt. The assassination of Sadat has been claimed by Islamic Jihad and the Islamic Group, two of the militant Islamic movements who opposed Sadat and his successor Hosni Mubarak throughout the 1970s until the turn of the century. Two of the principal figures in Islamic Jihad at the time were Ayman al-Zawahiri and Aboud al-Zumur, the first a medical doctor (who went onto become Osama bin Laden's righthand man and successor as leader of al-Qaeda) and the second a military colonel and hero of the 1973 war who was the chief strategist of the movement.

The group was trying to organise a plan that would remove the top leaders of the government while taking over strategic buildings, such as army head-quarters and the state radio and television building, from where a broadcast would be made to encourage a popular uprising to support the coup attempt. One of their group was arrested in February 1981 while transporting weapons and maps, which led to a widespread crackdown on all opposition. Sadat ordered the arrests of 1,500 people in September including Marxists, journalists and intellectuals with no political leanings, as well as members of the Islamic opposition. Though the leadership of Islamic Jihad was mostly decapitated, one of the surviving cells independently decided to carry out an assassination attempt during a military parade. The attempt succeeded, but given it was an opportunistic attack it simply resulted in the replacement of Sadat with his vice-president Mubarak, and a further crackdown which led to the arrests of thousands more.[94]

The only speculative connection of these events with Tahrir was through Muhammad Salem Rahhal, a Palestinian Jordanian who was studying at al-Azhar at the beginning of the 1970s and was active among Islamic Jihad and Islamic Group members in an effort to unite them under a single umbrella. It is commonly claimed that Rahhal was originally a member of Hizb-ut-Tahrir, though this has remained unsubstantiated and is often just conjecture based on Rahhal's goal of establishing the caliphate, a typical example being the case of Muntasir al-Zayyat's retelling of his personal experiences with the Islamic Group at the time.[95]

This speculation is largely based around the claim that members of Rahhal's extended family—the most common name mentioned being Abdul Fattah Rahhal—were either influenced by or members of Hizb-ut-Tahrir.[96] This type of conflation is common, and as mentioned previously the party had been connected with the 1974 coup attempt undertaken by Saleh Siriyya, an erroneous link made based on speculation about Siriyya's background and family links (and one that al-Zayyat also makes).[97] That the leadership in Egypt and Jordan knew nothing of Muhammad Rahhal means that it is likely that at most he was influenced by some of their ideas regarding the necessity of establishing an Islamic caliphate, as was the case with many other activists in the region at the time.

There was a noticeable response from Hizb-ut-Tahrir to Israel's bombing of Iraqi nuclear facilities on 7 June 1981, with an open letter to Saddam stating that it 'would have been honorable to retaliate likewise.' The letter accused Hussein of being insincere towards the Arabs, since their honour throughout history had been derived from their implementation of Islam, whereas he simply uttered empty slogans without meaning.[98] Also noteworthy was the party's position of neutrality during the Iran-Iraq War, counselling that it was the responsibility of all the leaders in the region to seek peace between Muslims rather than looking to inflame matters, while criticising King Hussein for a proposal he made on television on 28 January 1982 to create an Arab army to fight on the side of Iraq against Iran.[99]

In response to the Israeli invasion of Southern Lebanon in June 1982, the party issued a statement that began 'we apologize to our Lord, as we did not wish to write a leaflet or write a single letter, since the circumstances are not one of writing nor issuing leaflets, but of fighting and killing', and wrote of their hope that the caliphate should have been established by now that might have led the military in repelling the enemy, while adding 'but the establishment of the caliphate has been delayed, for a reason unknown other than to Allah.' The pamphlet ended with a call to the military to put pressure on the leaders to fight against the Israeli aggression, claiming that they had the material capability to do so, whereas the people were living under the 'fire and steel' of the rulers, a reference to the oppressive nature of dictatorial regimes at the time.[100]

These and similar pamphlets since the change of leadership all indicated that the party was still active centrally, though the issue of internal stagnation still concerned them, with two leaflets issued internally within days of each other towards the end of 1980. They both identified the continuing problem—referred to as the 'big mistake'—of thinking that all party efforts had to be centred on seeking material *nusra* support to establish the Islamic state, and that some had reached the conclusion that there was no use in undertaking any other type of activity at all. Some practical solutions were given, with a noticeable focus on encouraging becoming closer to God, through extra nightly prayers, fasting, charity, congregational prayers in mosques and reading the Qur'an.[101] There appeared to be certain similarities with the period of stagnation that al-Nabhani complained about at the beginning of the 1960s, and although the causes and remedy in this case contained differences, the act of acknowledging internal shortcomings coupled with the leadership's persistent attempts at treatment were common to both eras.

Hizb-ut-Tahrir's thirtieth anniversary of its official existence was in 1983, and questions were raised about the issue of the party being successful within thirty years, as was written in *al-Tafkir*. The leadership's response was that this was an example of incorrect *ijtihad* (reasoning), rather than something derived explicitly from a textual evidence, and that many of the Prophets had faced even life-long struggles. Therefore, although al-Nabhani had initially believed that they would be successful within twenty-five years, which he then extended to thirty, this was simply a misjudgement.[102] The response also mentioned that one of the reasons for the delay in victory was the harshness shown to the party by the authorities and those who supported them internationally, with Zallum using the metaphor that each time they saw the water boiling (in other words, society looking for change) they would place chunks of ice in the cup to cool it back down again.[103] The main issue was not to lose hope, as the victory would come at its appointed time, and to become more active rather than despondent.

Despite worries about continuing inactivity, subsequent events involving Tahrir between 1982 and 1984 indicated that either the prognosis was overly pessimistic, or was perhaps confined to a segment of the body. There was sufficient activity in the Middle East to lead to numerous arrests across the region, including in Jordan, Tunisia, Egypt and Iraq, as well as Libya where there were public executions in 1983. The pressure on members in Jordan continued throughout the 1980s, where numerous arrests took place in 1982, 1984, 1987 and 1988. The most prominent prisoner was leadership member Abu Iyas, who was arrested in 1982 and remained imprisoned without charge for six years. Others were arrested multiple times and as punishment were prevented from travelling abroad to study; some, who were not prevented from leaving, emigrated as a result of the pressure.[104]

In 1983, there were reports of the arrest of sixty activists in Egypt, while in Tunisia thirty-four were arrested, including twenty-three from various branches of the military.[105] With the widespread clampdown on Islamic political opposition after the assassination of Sadat, the resulting treatment of prisoners and continued arrests and harassment of other members eventually led to a low-scale conflict between the Mubarak regime and the Islamic Jihad and

Islamic Group movements during the 1980s and 1990s. The idea of taking up arms against the ruler began to take root in Egypt, and spread abroad as people such as Zawahiri left Egypt to escape persecution by the authorities. This constricted party activity in Egypt, due to Hizb-ut-Tahrir's belief that the role of the group was intellectual and that the method of re-establishing the caliphate was dependent on changing people's convictions rather than taking up weapons against the state.

Numerous discussions between Tahrir members and members of these other movements took place in Egypt and other countries such as Saudi Arabia.[106] In response, the party issued a pamphlet that explained its viewpoint that removing the *munkar* (clear wrongdoing) by hand was restricted to those who had the capability and authority to do so. (For example, it was not permitted for any individual other than one from the government to carry out punishments.) If someone had the capability to do so, then it would be obligatory for them to make the necessary change; and if the wrongdoing was done by the ruler then 'it is obligatory for all Muslims to hold him to account'. However, it was prohibited to rebel against the ruler 'except in the circumstance where he does not rule by what Allah has revealed', in which case 'the obligation to rebel against him with weapons is conditional upon the capability to remove him, and to remove the rule of disbelief by material power.'[107]

The last point caused internal questions and accusations that Zallum was changing the party methodology—various groups such as Islamic Jihad and Islamic Group claimed that they were preparing to make themselves capable of fighting against the regime. Was their approach correct? And how was this understanding compatible with the party's belief in intellectual and political struggle alone? In response, the party leadership issued a clarification in which the leadership stated that it was 'pleased by the questions and accounting', believing that it showed 'the critical minds of the members and adherence to the culture.' It then went on to make clear that the party's opinion was that the correct method of preparing material strength to remove un-Islamic systems and replace them with the Islamic system was through seeking the *nusra* support, following the example of the Prophet, and that the party would never arm itself or train its members for such a purpose given that its work was intellectual and political.[108] (In addition, the party differentiated between changing an un-Islamic system to an Islamic one, which required an intellectual revolution in society to demand such a change, and correcting any deviation within an already existing Islamic system.) The intra-Islamic debates were largely academic. A combination of the heightened security situation, coupled with the rising heat in the conflict with the Egyptian government, made it very difficult for any inroads to be made in society there during the 1980s.

The situation was calmer in Tunisia, where there were no beginnings of an armed insurrection against the regime. The first Tunisian member of Hizb-ut-Tahrir was a teacher, called Fadil Eshtara, who returned to Tunisia in 1974 after a period in Germany, where he had come across and joined the party. His first recruit was a fellow teacher Muhammad Hajaji, and along with two others the first private circle began in Tunis.

There was no formal organization or connection between Tunisia and the central leadership until 1978, when Mustafa travelled from Germany and appointed the first local committee made up of Hajaji, Muhammad Jarbi and three other Tunisian members.[109] Air Force Capt. Muhammad Ali al-Boazizi appears to have been the central member of the military involved, having come across the party while at college in Greece between 1975 and 1980.[110] As a result, the ideas of the party began to spread among a few officers in the military, but it seems that this was a natural progression rather than because of any specific intent, with Tunisia not considered as a viable location to establish the Islamic state due to its size and location.

There was a substantial growth in circles and membership during the late 1970s and early 1980s, but there was no public activity. Most discussions centred on intellectual issues rather than political events, with the Tunisian branch not coming into direct confrontation with the government of Habib Bourguiba. In June 1983, the security service found the names of five hundred members after a detailed investigation that had been initiated after a letter about party administration was accidentally posted into a letterbox next to the one that was being used by Muhammad Jarbi. Jarbi was arrested, and investigations into the five hundred individuals named in the letter, which included many of them being questioned, resulted in the arrest of thirty-four people, including twenty-three from various branches of the military, who were taken to court on 25 August 1983.[111]

The charges brought against those in the military were for belonging to a political party, while the civilians were charged with encouraging soldiers to join a political party, both illegal according to Tunisian law. Capt. al-Boazizi informed the court that his confession had been extracted under torture,[112] a matter backed up by Hajaji, who stated that some of those interrogated were electrocuted during questioning.[113] The defence claimed that the accused were studying Islam due to their concern over the affairs of Muslims, and when asked whether the books they were studying were political the response was that they comprised Islamic thoughts, and Islam did not differentiate between religious and worldly affairs.[114] During the court case, government sources were reported as stating that there was no proof that the group was seeking power in Tunisia, and that its activity was purely intellectual.[115] The civilians in the case were all given two-year sentences, and those from the military between five and eight years. Teachers such as Hajaji were prevented from working in government schools, with official notices issued to them after their convictions informing them of the decision.[116]

While Tunisia was not central to Tahrir's work at the time, setbacks in Iraq were more critical. There had been a number of arrests in 1979, including some Palestinian Jordanians, but they were granted amnesty at the end of the year. Due to constant pursuit by the authorities there, coupled with the onset of the Iran-Iraq war, there was little scope for increasing membership among the general public due to these circumstances and the fact that most men aged eighteen to forty-five had been drafted into the military. The party made great efforts between 1980 and 1983 to win over influential tribal leaders and the military, which apparently met with great success. However, one of those involved, a military doctor called Zahir Abdullah, contacted Saddam to inform him directly about the party's activities, leading to the arrest of approximately two hundred people in June 1983.[117]

In 1984, the regime executed sixty party members. Names mentioned included Ahmad al-Banna, along with his two brothers Hasan and Najm, Abdul Qadir al-Suweidi, and Muhammad Shafiq al-Badri, the brother of Abdul Aziz, who was killed in 1969. A number of officers were also among those executed. Muhammad Ubaid had also been arrested and expected to be executed as well, but according to his own recollection he was spared due to a combination of al-Badri's claiming that he was not connected to the rest of the group and the personal intervention of one of his friends, Talal Faisal, who was also an associate of Saddam.[118]

Similar to the harsh blow Hizb-ut-Tahrir was dealt in Libya, the numerous executions in Iraq uprooted the party and limited its activity there; the few individuals who remained were managed through party members in Kuwait. In Tunisia, a second set of arrests in 1986 took place in a number of cities, including Tunis and Susa. After Ben 'Ali took over the presidency through a bloodless coup on 7 November 1987, there was a political amnesty, which led to the release of political prisoners including the Hizb-ut-Tahrir members who were still in jail. However, their ease was short lived as arrests in 1989 led to the first court case involving Islamic opposition to Ben 'Ali's government in March 1990.

228 Hizb-ut-Tahrir members were accused of distributing pamphlets in mosques, and in the summer of 1991 another case was brought involving eighty members (as well as further cases in 1994 and 1996).[119] With the increased political oppression of Ben 'Ali's opponents, and in particular the Islamic opposition, even without arrests many were forced to report regularly to their local police stations. People such as Hajaji had to sign in daily, and at inconvenient times, which made it impossible for them to secure work. For Hajaji, this went on for seven years, with many others including other members of Hizb-ut-Tahrir under the same restrictions. People commonly spent between two and ten years under administrative monitoring, having to report to the police, in some cases, up to twelve times a day, including at night.[120]

By 1990, it had been decided to try to re-establish the party structure in Iraq. The various members gathered together, but their work was mainly focused on maintaining the existing membership, while avoiding conflict with the regime. However, a number of members were being monitored by the intelligence services, which led to more than twenty-five arrests at the end of 1990. Nine of those arrested were given death sentences, with the remaining sixteen receiving various sentences, up to life imprisonment. The party attempted to send delegations to Iraqi embassies in different countries, including Jordan, to petition the authorities on their behalf, but they were unsuccessful, and the nine death sentences were carried out.[121]

Meanwhile, in Jordan, for the first time the party opened a central press office in 1989, in an attempt to take advantage of the more open political environment during the first general elections held since 1967, which took place on 8 November 1989. In 1990, the party was able to print and distribute its books and pamphlets without punishment, as well as hold talks and press conferences.

Despite the fraught relations with the Iraqi regime, during a press conference held on 14 August 1990, a week after the arrival of the first US troops in Saudi Arabia as part of Operation Desert Shield to eject Iraqi forces from Kuwait (which they had entered on 2 August), the party's first ever spokesman, Abu al-Rashta, stated that Hizb-ut-Tahrir 'supports every unification in Muslim lands, but it does not support any of the standing ruling systems in the Islamic lands as they do not rule by Islam.'[122] In other words, they were not against uniting Iraq with Kuwait, but they were against both the Iraqi and Kuwaiti regimes in principle. The statement made clear that they were also against the foreign troops arriving in the Gulf, as well as any government fighting alongside them, and blamed 'government scholars' for legitimising the decisions of the Saudi Arabian regime.

The press conference was held soon after the party leadership published a pamphlet that ridiculed the claim that the US was seeking to uphold international law as its justification for preparing to fight in Kuwait, highlighting the US's hypocrisy in ignoring international law during its invasions of Lebanon, Panama and Grenada, and bombing of Libya.[123] Instead, US interests were explained in terms of its desire for hegemony—politically, economically and militarily—over the Gulf region,[124] summed up in the simple idea that it was all about the oil.[125] Just as the military assault began at the beginning of 1991, the party issued a pamphlet that explained the obligation to resist the US attack, opining that the aim of Operation Desert Storm was fundamentally neither to protect Saudi Arabia nor return the al-Sabah family to its position of ruling Kuwait, but rather simply to protect US interests in the region.[126]

The space for open political expression in Jordan was short lived, with arrests beginning once again in 1991. But as the fortunes of Hizb-ut-Tahrir seemed to wax and wane in the Middle East, signs were emerging that the party was spreading globally, a result of a combination of political refugees taking their ideas to new shores and a new generation of young students carrying the party call outside of the Middle East, just as the first generation had carried it throughout the region, beyond the East and West Banks.

# 7

# A GLOBAL PARTY

## (1990–2012)

أنت حي يا أخي...رغم الصعاب
ان في بردیك اعصار السباب
فليفض نحو الأماني العذاب

*'You are alive my brother...despite the difficulties*
*In your heart lies the wind of youth*
*So head towards the sweet hopes'*

Amin Shinnar, from *'The Birth of a Poet'*[1]

During part of the later period of al-Nabhani's leadership, which was characterised by the expectancy that the caliphate was on the verge of being established, members were actively encouraged not to move outside of the countries that Hizb-ut-Tahrir was concentrating on. As time passed without the expected victory, some became frustrated by the informal restrictions placed on them, which ultimately had a de-motivating effect. Zallum made a conscious decision not to advise against or block anyone's travel plans or personal and professional development.[2] As a new, younger generation of activists emerged either from the families of previous activists or from fresh recruitment, more travelled abroad for studies and work, carrying the party ideas with them.

Although such travel had occurred during the time of al-Nabhani as well, he had been unconcerned with trying to connect administratively with all those living outside of the areas of the work to establish the Islamic state, which was restricted to countries such as Syria, Iraq, Jordan, Lebanon and Egypt, with Turkey the sole non-Arab nation considered as a viable location to re-establish the caliphate. For example, when informed in 1975 that a member who had travelled to Australia and managed to win over about thirty-five others to the party call wanted to be connected to the party leadership administratively, al-Nabhani declined and suggested that they be left to work on their own, completely independently.[3]

However, as people began to travel further afield while still carrying the party call, the party leadership under Zallum began to connect with the growing numbers of members around the world. If a country was not considered a viable place to re-establish the caliphate—such as non-Muslim countries in Europe, the Americas, Africa or Australia, or due to their size and location such as the Arab Gulf states—then they were not expected to engage in a political struggle to try to change the system there, but instead were supposed to carry the creedal call to Islam in a manner appropriate to societal circumstances in that location.

With this new approach, Hizb-ut-Tahrir began to grow without specific instruction from the leadership, as members began using their own initiative to a greater extent. Although Zallum deliberately sent a few members to specific key Muslim countries to try to build the party structure there during the 1980s, namely Turkey and Pakistan, the seeds of growth were planted elsewhere without the leadership's knowledge until the fruits became apparent years later. From Muslim countries such as Uzbekistan and Indonesia to Western countries such as the US and the UK, the party was beginning to truly spread globally, through a combination of students, professionals and political refugees who carried the party call with them.

Party activities began in the US and the UK during the 1980s, with Middle Eastern immigrants such as Palestinian Jordanian Iyad Hilal playing central roles in establishing the group in areas on both the west and east coasts of America,[4] while Abu Muhammad was the first member to establish a party structure in London after arriving there in the mid-1980s.[5] However, while Hizb-ut-Tahrir in America remained low key for several reasons— including the demographics of the Muslim community and its geographical disparity, along with the seemingly conservative mentality of the members, who were accustomed to working in secretive conditions as a result of the security situation in the Middle East—in the UK the party spread more quickly among the more densely populated Muslim community and was more open in its activities.

This was largely due to the efforts of the initial members won over, who included a diverse array of characters, among them immigrant Pakistanis and Muslim converts. The Lebanese Omar Bakri Muhammad provided a very visual media front for the party, actively courting publicity and viewed by some as comical. In 1996 he left Hizb-ut-Tahrir and instead became leader of his own group, Al-Muhajiroun. According to Muhammad this was due to his disagreement over the role of Tahrir in the West, with Muhammad believing that it was necessary to try to establish the caliphate in the UK, as opposed to the party's methodology, which specified a few Middle Eastern countries, Turkey and subsequently Pakistan as suitable.[6] As a result of interaction with Asian immigrant communities in North America and the UK, Tahrir subsequently gained footholds in Pakistan and Bangladesh from the early 1990s.

The party spread to Uzbekistan as the result of Palestinian student Abu Talha travelling to Tashkent in the early 1980s. The first indigenous Uzbek to be won over was a young man called Rahmatullah, who became convinced after reading the party books. A popular, friendly figure with a strong attachment to his religion, Rahmatullah won over many other locals to the party. It is claimed that he ended up coming under government surveillance after an Islamic conference during which an Egyptian participant, Fahmi Huwaidi, publicly exposed the relationship between the two, Abu Talha already a known Tahrir activist.[7]

In the late 1980s Rahmatullah was killed in a car accident, which his family believed was a government-orchestrated event. As a result, contact between the central leadership and party members in Uzbekistan ended. At this point, although individual members remained, the focus turned to spreading ideas more than building the party structure. This changed at the start of the 1990s, when more students from the Middle East arrived and reconnected local members to the party through contacts in Turkey.[8]

In a similar vein, the establishment of the Indonesian branch of Hizb-ut-Tahrir resulted from the efforts of Indonesian Islamic scholar Abdullah Bin Nuh and a young Lebanese member, Abdulrahman al-Baghdadi. Bin Nuh was a popular lecturer, who by the end of the 1970s had become disillusioned with the existing Islamic movements in Indonesia. He became acquainted with the ideas of Hizb-ut-Tahrir through his interaction with members of the party in Sydney, Australia (some of whom had migrated there in the 1960s from the Middle East to avoid persecution), during visits he made while his son was studying there.[9] Al-Baghdadi travelled to Indonesia at Bin Nuh's invitation, using Bin Nuh's Al-Ghazali Islamic boarding school in Bogor city as a base for activities to disseminate party ideas.

The initial interaction was mainly with Muslim students at the Bogor Institute of Agriculture mosque, called Al-Ghifari, before spreading to other universities, particularly in Java. Through the LDK (Lembaga Dakwah Kampus—an Islamic circle that had existed in virtually all universities in Indonesia since the 1980s), the party endeavoured to disseminate its thoughts.[10] At the same time, the party name itself was kept hidden for security reasons under the dictatorial regime of President Suharto, due to fear of state repression. Nevertheless, its key ideas, such as the necessity of resuming the Islamic way of life through the comprehensive implementation of Islam and the establishment of the caliphate, were widely disseminated. A local leadership committee led by Bin Nuh was established by the mid-1980s, and the first recruits were formally inducted by 1988.[11] Even by this stage, very few people on university campuses were aware of the existence of Hizb-ut-Tahrir in Indonesia, something that would remain largely the case until after Suharto's reign had ended in 1998.[12]

*Heartland problems, hinterland success*

By the 1990s, Tahrir had spread across several countries beyond the Middle East, including in Central Asia, the Far East, and several non-Muslim-majority countries in North America and Europe. There was central direction to try to bring the party out into the open as much as possible, which, coupled with the geographical spread of its members, began to transform Hizb-ut-Tahrir into a truly global party. This emphasis came after a meeting of around twenty senior members during the annual *hajj* pilgrimage to Mecca, during which discussions revolved around a complete review of the party, its methodology, its history, current status and the state of the Muslim *Umma* at large. This led to a written review of more than seventeen pages entitled *ia'datu al-nathar* (Another Look) in 1985, which went beyond the first efforts in 1978.[13]

The review again identified that the party had over time concentrated its activities on seeking support to establish the caliphate, and that it was necessary to increase other actions that had been left behind. In particular, it was decided that seeking support should deliberately target those who could help protect the party call, even if they could not materially establish the Islamic state. This was imperative because the party had to reinvigorate its efforts to interact with society and win mass support, a very big task in the heavily securitised regimes that dominated the Middle East. While societies in the Middle East had largely lost belief that they could change their rulers, and that the rulers' authority ultimately rested on their acquiescence, the members had to find ways to address the public, build their confidence and win them over.[14]

It stressed the necessity of finding ways of addressing people in the same way that they used to through public talks and seminars in the 1950s, before the security clampdown on practically all areas of the party's work. Although the security situation had not improved, the party had to find alternative ways to contact the public directly. It also identified key areas for discussion that had to be addressed, beginning with a concentration on Islamic *aqida* (belief), building it among the masses in a way that influenced people such that their relationship with God and following His commandments would become their driving motivation.[15]

It was with this central direction and focus that events such as the opening of a media office in Jordan took place. Zallum believed that breaking what he perceived to be a media silence around the party and its activities was crucial to building public opinion about it. Although conditions in Jordan had deteriorated again, with arrests at the end of 1991, that the party was making clear attempts to operate openly appears to have convinced many members, in the Middle East and beyond, at least in terms of understanding that they were expected to win over the public, even if specific circumstances forced to operate in the shadows.

Although members were arrested in Jordan over their outspoken opposition to the Gulf War, they continued operating in a more open manner. One of the senior members, Yusuf al-Sabatin, began visiting the heads of tribes with delegations to convey the party's ideas to them. Historically, the Jordanian monarchy had relied on the Bedouin tribes for support, so it was likely these visits provoked the response that ultimately became known as the Mut'a military college case. The accusation levelled against those involved was that they had attempted to collect weapons to assassinate the king. The case received a lot of media attention, which was unusual because several campaigns of arrests against party members in Jordan in the past decade had not received any coverage. Party members believed that the reason for the increased attention was to try to link Hizb-ut-Tahrir to violence, thereby discrediting it in the eyes of the public. Those involved received initial sentences ranging from life imprisonment to death, but by 1995 on appeal the case was thrown out when it came to light that confessions had been forced from the accused under torture. The scandal led to the resignations of a number of a senior judges. If the intention had been to use the case to try to paint the party as a terrorist group it seemed to have backfired.[16]

During the same period of the mid-1990s, there were a series of arrests of party members in Saudi Arabia. Although the Gulf region was generally peripheral to the aims of the leadership, because it had never been considered a suitable location to re-establish the Islamic state, economic migration meant that party members had been going to Saudi Arabia since the early 1960s, and likely to the United Arab Emirates (UAE) around the same period or even earlier, given that the first members were in Kuwait in the early 1950s. It appears that Tahrir members were generally not paid any attention unless they drew it to themselves through their activities and discussions. Arrests led to deportation rather than court cases and jail sentences. For example, a number of arrests followed a campaign in around 1986 in Abu Dhabi, when 5,000 letters were sent explaining party ideas to anyone who had a local tribal name. More than a hundred letters were received by members of the intelligence services, who spent the next year trying to find the source of the letters, arresting and interrogating known party members until they arrived at the one responsible. After confessing, he was deported in 1988.[17]

Around 1989 the situation changed, with the emergence of local Saudi members of Tahrir such as Dr Muhammad al-Mas'ari, a Saudi rights activist who joined the party during his studies in Europe. With the Gulf War occurring soon after, the Saudi regime became much more wary of internal Islamic opposition as a result of its agreement to host US troops in the fight against Saddam, which was at least partially responsible for the emergence of Osama bin Laden and al-Qaeda.[18] This issue of accepting military help from a non-Muslim nation against other Muslims went against religious principles commonly taught in Saudi schools,[19] and created a problem for the monarchy, which based its legitimacy on the religious backing of the clergy.

In May 1993 the Committee for the Defense of Legitimate Rights (CDLR) was established in Riyadh, led by a group of six prominent scholars and lawyers. Al-Mas'ari was appointed as the spokesman for the committee, which accused the Saudi regime of not implementing Sharia. The regime disbanded the group less than two weeks after its establishment, with its leaders dismissed from their professional positions and al-Mas'ari arrested.[20] As a result of his arrest and interrogations, the intelligence services realised that Saudi citizens were now involved in Hizb-ut-Tahrir, and not simply Arab workers from other countries in the region who could be easily deported. Among those identified were Dr Muhammad Said Turki (who joined the party from Austria), Dr Abdul Rahim Qari, Dr Fu'ad Dahlawi (who was the head of the electrical engineering department in the University of Abdul Aziz in Jeddah) and Dr Muhammad Safadi (who worked the education department in King Saud University in Riyadh).

As a result of these discoveries, a number of arrests took place in the mid-1990s. There was no media coverage at all, which was not unusual given the propensity of the regime at the time to minimise any evidence of political opposition. Due to regime worries about the discontent that had simmered in some quarters since the Gulf War, according to those interrogated the intelligence services were using Egyptian interrogators, whose techniques included torture during the investigations, a departure from the relatively good treatment detainees had received prior to the 1990s. In 1995, a group of eight Tahrir members, which included Saudis such as Turki, were taken to court in the first formal case involving the party. Refused lawyers in court, the judge relied on an edict issued by the leading government scholar of the time, Bin Baz, which stated that Hizb-ut-Tahrir was not a legal party. They were eventually sentenced to two-and-a-half years in jail, after which those from outside the country were deported. During their time in prison, there was a further campaign of arrests of around fifteen other members of the party.[21]

While progress in the Middle East was limited, there were some steps forward in two key non-Arab countries, Turkey and Pakistan. By the mid-1990s, changes were under way in the party's approach in Turkey, which had previously relied on Arab students to carry the bulk of responsibilities and activity. This made it easy for the Turkish security establishment to monitor and control Hizb-ut-Tahrir, with any clampdown leading to the expulsion of non-Turkish members, which decapitated the local structure. Therefore there was a greater emphasis on recruiting local members, with a programme to translate more materials into Turkish undertaken in the mid-1990s to facilitate the process.[22]

At the same time, the leadership was receiving reports from Pakistan in 1996 of a large growth in membership, the result of Pakistani members of Tahrir recruited mainly in North America and the UK returning home. Further investigation by the leadership found that the reports had been exaggerated, but it was felt that there were the beginnings of a structure being built across Pakistan that could be expanded with effort.[23] The call to a caliphate there had earlier gained an influential figure in Dr Israr Ahmad, the leader of another Islamic party called Tanzeem-i-Islami, who had met and talked with Tahrir members in North America. Influenced by core Hizb-ut-Tahrir concepts, in the early 1990s he announced the establishment of the Tahreek-e-Khilafat movement from the Karachi Press Club, and began promoting the idea of Pakistan as a potential starting point for a caliphate.[24]

In Uzbekistan, the building of the party body began in earnest after seventeen local activists became members and were placed into official positions of responsibility, marking the first formal structure of Tahrir in Uzbekistan.[25] After years under communist rule, the collapse of the USSR opened an opportunity for other groups and ideas to spread their ideas among society publicly. According to activists who spent time in Uzbekistan, Uzbek society was open to an ideological call based on Islamic principles due to their love of learning and teaching ideas, a continuation of the custom of some Uzbeks of learning Arabic and Islam literally underground in large basements during the era of Soviet oppression. Local members at this time were known to be very active, with various accounts of people working simply to earn enough to survive while using the rest of their time for discussion and debate.[26] By the mid-1990s, there was unprecedented growth in party membership, similar to the early spread of Tahrir in Transjordan between 1953 and 1955.

In the same vein, similar to the spread of the party across the Middle East carried initially through the Palestinian diaspora decades earlier, the party spread from Uzbekistan across the Central Asian region through its Uzbek membership, and the ethnic Uzbeks who resided in neighbouring countries such as Tajikistan and Kyrgyzstan—particularly through the Fergana Valley—and Kazakhstan.[27] There was also a wider regional effect, with south China and Russia also witnessing Tahrir activity as a result. An example of how this spread was achieved is Ukraine, where two Uzbeks—known as 'Muhammadain', meaning literally the two Muhammads—were sent to Crimea to start the party there in 1995. Within a year, large numbers began studying with the party, including senior religious figures, leading to a spread among the indigenous Muslim population.[28] The extent of the growth, according to estimates from law enforcement sources, varies between 7,000 and 10,000 members by 2008,[29] a large number especially considering that Muslims in Ukraine numbered around 400,000.

The spread of Tahrir in Uzbekistan and around the region in the 1990s was an unprecedented event in party history in terms of the scale of uptake and recruitment. While there had been an initial spread in the Middle East up until 1955, much of it was through the Palestinian communities in the region, and local growth and leadership was not achieved. To give a comprehensive explanation for the difference in success would require a separate analysis, but there are a number of reasons that can be briefly summarised. Party growth in the early 1950s was stunted by a combination of three major factors. The most important was the rise of Nasser and pan-Arabism; the other two were the internal disruptions that led to the loss of Syria and to some extent Iraq, and the increasing harshness of the various security apparatuses against party activists. In Central Asia, rather than the emergence of an alternative such as pan-Arabism, the collapse of the USSR removed communism as an alternative ideology, leaving behind a vacuum in ideas that Islamic activists, previously suppressed under communist rule, now exploited.

Additionally, the party's ideas were fully developed by the time of the death of al-Nabhani, having settled into a corpus of accepted (adopted) material that was eagerly picked up by religiously inclined Uzbeks and others who were eager to expand their knowledge of their religion after years of Soviet oppression. Taking advantage of the confusion in the years after the collapse of the USSR, these factors meant that by the time the security services of the regional governments made serious attempts to clamp down on party activity, specifically within Uzbekistan, the regional branch was already firmly embedded.

As for the issue of leadership problems, while they affected initial growth in the early 1950s, due to the young state of the party, the growth in areas beyond the Middle East under Zallum's leadership took place largely without central direction. This meant that the growth would be to some degree insulated and protected from any disruptions in the central leadership, as long as the party administration was not fatally disputed. In fact, the growth on the periphery of Tahrir's activity took place during a time of internal rupture, with an event in 1997 that internal sources believe was the largest existential threat that the party ever faced, due to an attempt to remove the Zallum leadership, which almost caused the party to split in two.

The internal division climaxed in 1997, though the origins of the differences appear to have been longstanding. Former members have speculated that they in fact dated back to the appointment of Zallum as leader in 1977, claiming that the position was coveted by Abu Rami Muhammad Nafi, who was based in Kuwait at the time.[30] Nafi had initially been a member of the political committee appointed by Zallum to produce party analysis, before being removed and subsequently made responsible for local administration in Jordan, later becoming the leadership's representative to Jordan in the mid-1990s.

Zallum sent Fawzi Nasir as a delegate to investigate reports that members in Jordan were openly discussing how to change the party leadership in their circles. After a number of meetings indicated that Nafi was at the root of the dissent, he apparently admitted to Nasir that he was unhappy with the state of the party, and he did indeed want a change of leadership, believing that he owed no allegiance to Zallum because he had taken his oath to join the party under al-Nabhani. He was not alone in his opinion, with the head of the Jordanian administration also in agreement. As a result, Zallum expelled Nafi and a number of other senior members such as Adham Awwad and Ibrahim Jarrad in the middle of 1997.[31]

In October 1997 the expelled group published a pamphlet that decried what they believed to be the declined state of the party, along with criticism of weak political analysis and complaints over the adoption of a book written in 1996 that was intended to motivate party activists by linking the tasks and obstacles facing Tahrir in the contemporary era with stories of the struggles of previous Prophets in the Qur'an.[32] The leaflet announced that Zallum was hereby expelled from his position as leader of the party, along with the author of the book, Abu Iyas, Zallum's brother Abdul Halim, and Muhammad Sabri, who was the second member of the political committee established by Zallum that had included Nafi.[33]

The audacious move came as a complete surprise to the party leadership and other senior members in Jordan who were not connected to Nafi's faction. Having been in control of the whole of the party apparatus in Jordan, Nafi and his allies initially took half to three quarters of the party body there with them.[34] As a result of personal contacts with members in Europe, the pamphlet found its way to Denmark and England, where debate and discussion also ensued, though there is no evidence that the group emerged as a significant faction anywhere other than in Jordan, even at its peak.

Ultimately the leadership challenge failed, with more than half of those who had originally sided with Nafi returning to the party under Zallum's leadership as the circumstances of the affair became clearer over time. A number of factors undermined the attempt, even though those leading it had prepared the ground for discontent among activists for a number of years, particularly in Amman, the first and most obvious being that the attempt came as a reaction to the expulsion of Nafi and his colleagues. This also meant that the motives of those who had challenged Zallum were open to question, particularly as some of the complaints they had raised, such as weakness in political analysis, could easily be explained away as Nafi's bitterness at his removal from the political committee. In addition, the faction claimed that the party spokesman, al-Rashta, was one of their leaders, something which al-Rashta, who was in prison throughout these events, angrily denied.[35]

All of this meant that after initially threatening the integrity of the party in Jordan, the Nafi faction quickly faded. It is commonly referred to as the *Nakithin* faction by Hizb-ut-Tahrir members, literally meaning those who violated their oaths—a reference to the belief that they had betrayed their oath to obey the party leadership by rebelling without valid cause. The death of Nafi within a year of the attempted leadership challenge caused further fragmentation; and over time it appears that the faction has had a negligible presence, with no activity of note. According to members of Tahrir in Amman, ten to twenty people are still affiliated with the remains of the Nafi faction, though the original leaders are either dead or actually now opposed to them, such as Awwad.[36] A handful of others are possibly dispersed throughout Europe, but this is difficult to ascertain because they have no public presence.

Although al-Nabhani had faced a challenge from within his own leadership a few years after the establishment of the party, leading to the complete loss of the party membership in Syria, which was under al-Masri's control at the time, there was no suggestion that al-Masri and Dawud Hamdan attempted to wrest control from al-Nabhani. Other later challenges to al-Nabhani's position were small isolated incidents. In Zallum's case, the Nafi faction was a direct challenge to his leadership and, according to senior members, an existential threat to the party. But it was mainly localised and in the end the majority of the party members in Jordan remained with him.

Whereas the party was in effect encapsulated by and wholly reliant on al-Nabhani for its ideological output and direction at the time of the initial leadership conflict, Zallum was not indispensable as party leader. In one way, this worked to Hizb-ut-Tahrir's benefit, with the upheaval in Jordan having a negligible effect on the party's work elsewhere, which continued independently as normal. Ironically, Zallum had agreed a year earlier to resign from his position and hand over to a younger member, once a suitable candidate had been found and agreed on (Zallum was more than seventy years old by 1996), an issue that was known to members of the leadership such as Nafi, which may have inadvertently encouraged the leadership challenge.[37] As a result of the events, Zallum would remain as leader of the party until he was almost eighty, before resigning in 2003, perhaps wary of setting a precedent by resigning soon after the internal conflict.

As the internal problems subsided in Jordan, al-Rashta was released from jail in 1998, and the local leadership there decided to hold a celebration as a challenge to the authorities. 500 invitations to an event to mark al-Rashta's release were sent to prominent and influential figures. Attendance was good, marking the continued presence of the party in Amman, which also served as a confidence-building measure for local activists. Impressed by his loyalty, Zallum had hoped that al-Rashta would leave Jordan and join him in

Lebanon to avoid the regular imprisonment he suffered from in Amman and take advantage of the relative political freedom in Beirut. This had to be delayed for a year because al-Rashta was arrested soon after his release, it is believed in response to the very public party celebrations. On his release for the second time that year, he left the country without fanfare or any trouble from the authorities.[38]

Despite, or perhaps in some cases because of, the internal issues that the leadership was dealing with between 1996 and 1998, a number of significant new publications were written, covering varied topics. Among them was a book that Zallum wrote to address Islamic views regarding contemporary scientific issues, such as cloning and human organ transplant (concluding that cloning animals and plants was permitted, while human cloning was forbidden due to loss of lineage, among other reasons; while organ transplant was permitted from live donors if the organ was not essential to their own well-being).[39]

In light of the stock market crashes as a result of the Asian financial crisis in 1997, the party published a short booklet explaining the reasons for the crisis, along with its view on the Islamic ruling on stock markets. It contained some prescient sections (in the light of the subsequent 2008 financial crisis), stating that 'another shock in the major stock markets in the West could reveal the frailty of its cobweb, expose the defects of the Capitalist economic system, and reveal that its shine is pure deception.' Capitalism was accused of being 'based on the lowest motives of man' with 'material values as their only concern' and in reality 'a small group of capitalists dominate the overwhelming majority who work hard and live in constant anxiety.'

Despite the party's belief in 1997 that a full-blown economic crisis that could bring down the entire capitalist system was imminent, it also noted that 'it would be wrong to wait for a major economic setback in the Western stock markets for the Muslims to realise that they had been duped by the capitalist thoughts and the stock markets and that they really are nothing but cobwebs', and that it was 'imperative to outline their reality now, to expose their corruption and explain that Islam forbids these thoughts and practices', which formed the justification for the topic being addressed at the time.[40]

Other significant literature included a series of books outlining what the party believed was an ongoing US campaign against Islam, a theme that it believed was being promoted by the US after the collapse of the USSR confirmed the failure of communism and left Islam as the sole ideology that was preventing the adoption of secular capitalism in the Muslim world. Two books focused on ideological concepts that the West was promoting internationally and particularly in the Middle East in this campaign against Islam, including democracy, pluralism, human rights and free-market policies, which all in effect promoted the fundamental idea of the separation of religion from life's affairs, in other words secularism. 'Pillars' used for the campaign such as the international media and the local rulers were also identified.[41]

While the first book identified the Western ideas being promoted, the second, published soon after, identified slogans that were being used to try to 'create a new religion for the Muslims', which would be 'based upon the creed of separating religion from life.' This was due to the belief that the US viewed Islam as the remaining ideological competitor to capitalism, quoting scholars such as Bernard Lewis and Francis Fukuyama, who identified the 'threat' of Islam to Western values. For example, Fukuyama wrote in 1992 that:

> It is true that Islam constitutes a systematic and coherent ideology, just like liberalism and communism, with its own code of morality and doctrine of political and social justice. The appeal of Islam is potentially universal, reaching out to all men as men, and not just to members of a particular ethnic or national group. And Islam has indeed defeated liberal democracy in many parts of the Islamic world, posing a grave threat to liberal practices even in countries where it has not achieved political power directly.[42]

The first slogan identified and criticised in the book was the use of the term 'terrorism' and the push from the G7 and US for new terrorism legislation, which Tahrir characterised as seeking 'the right to arrest and kidnap any person America considers guilty of any terrorist act and implement any punishment they deem appropriate.' This analysis came a few years before the war on terror. (Although the existence of a complex rendition programme has become more well known in the post-9/11 era, the CIA programme initially began in 1995[43] and was involved in renditions of Egyptians to the regime of Mubarak in the 1990s; for example, a case referred to as the 'Returnees from Albania', involving numerous accused who were arrested and returned from Albania to Egypt,[44] some of whom were subsequently executed by the Egyptian government.)

The book also criticised the political use of the term and its legislation, stating that 'the anti-terrorism laws adopted by the United States are one of the strategic weapons it uses to tighten its grip on the world', which is why Islamic movements in particular were being designated as 'terrorist' as a pretext to act against them in US interests. In respect of this issue, Muslims were advised that since they were 'a direct target of the so-called policy of anti-terrorism' it was incumbent on them to 'expose the reality of this law to Islamic and global public opinion.' In a similar vein, the use of the paradigm of 'compromise' and 'fundamentalism' was also criticised later in the book, with other sections also addressing the call for 'globalization' as being a method to open third-world markets to Western goods and services.[45]

The most critical publication was a third book published in early 1998, written in the light of the growing militarisation of the Gulf in preparation for increased hostilities against Iraq. It stated that the US was 'the biggest terrorist nation on the earth', which sought to impose its own decisions on the rest of the world through the use of arms. The theme of the book was the need to expel the US military from the Middle East region, an argument that chimed with public opinion, but was resisted with the complicity of the various regimes backed by the West. As was common in Hizb-ut-Tahrir literature throughout the period, it tried to convey that Muslim society had the capability and capacity to affect the decisions of its rulers, but this was dependent on applying pressure through different means with consistency until it either changed the behaviour of the rulers or removed them.[46]

The US was not alone in being criticised for its perceived war against Islam, with Europe in particular blamed for the killings of Muslims across the Balkans that began during the break-up of the former Yugoslavia at the beginning of the 1990s. During the NATO bombing of the Federal Republic of Yugoslavia in 1999 to drive Serbian forces out of Kosovo, a leaflet entitled *Western Nations Slaughter the Muslims in the Balkans* was issued, which claimed that the states involved were only doing so in their own interests rather than for humanitarian reasons, which were only promoted and referred to in a Machiavellian manner. In this case the interest was identified as reducing Russian influence in the region by weakening its allies.

There was also reference to the Bosnian conflict, which took place between 1992 and 1995, referring to leaked memos purported to have been from British Prime Minister John Major to his foreign secretary, Douglas Hurd, in which it was stated that it was imperative not to allow an Islamic state to be formed in Europe, that there should be no training or arming of Bosnian Muslims, that it was necessary to monitor Muslims in the West in case of radicalisation, and that Bosnia could not be allowed to become an independent state. This was framed by Tahrir as part of a narrative that as long as Muslims left their issues to other states to resolve rather than establishing a universal Islamic state that would seek to protect and uphold Muslim values and life internationally, they would ultimately remain at the mercy of the whims of other powers to deal with their issues as they pleased, whether in Palestine, Iraq or Kosovo.[47]

The issue of the leaked memo is one of the most prominent stories linked to the Bosnian conflict. According to Stjepan Mesić, the last president of Yugoslavia, the Russians had informed Serbian leader Slobodan Milošević that Bosnia could be divided along Serb-Croat lines, while the UK and France had intimated the same policy to Franjo Tudjman. As an example, in a secret meeting with Croatian leadership during the war, Tudjman, who would subsequently become the first president of Croatia, produced the memo between Major and Hurd, which included a section saying that all public statements should indicate support for the continued existence of Bosnia-Herzegovina, but that the real policy was that it should be 'partitioned between Croatia and Serbia, and the Muslims cease to be a factor in the region.' When the Croatians raised the memo with the British ambassador, they were informed that the memo was a forgery.

After the war, Mesić visited London for diplomatic meetings and raised the issue with an unnamed senior official, who confirmed that the memo was 'certainly a forgery', then added, 'but that was the policy', confirming its contents as true even if the memo itself was falsified.[48] Former US president Bill Clinton mentioned in his autobiography that one of the factors behind Europe's failure to resolve the conflict in the Balkans at the time was that 'some European leaders were not eager to have a Muslim state in the heart of the Balkans, fearing it might become a base for exporting extremism, a result that their neglect made more, not less, likely.'[49]

At the same time, the conduct of UN peacekeeping forces during the conflicts in the Balkans was also seen as less than exemplary, with atrocities varying from accusations that they were running prostitution rings in Bosnia (there were also accusations that sex-trafficking was taking place in Kosovo); that Canadian troops were involved in beatings and rape as well as the sexual abuse of a handicapped girl;[50] to the failure of Dutch troops to prevent the Srebrenica genocide, during which more than 8,000 Muslim civilians were killed (causing the entire Dutch government to resign).[51] Although there are certainly counter-arguments that can be made (particularly if one unquestioningly accepts the 'Blair Doctrine' of claiming humanitarian intervention as justification),[52] all of the aforementioned events and statements provided plenty of evidence to build a narrative of double standards and hypocrisy when the intervention in Kosovo took place.

The 'clash of civilizations' narrative, with which much of the literature of Hizb-ut-Tahrir can be identified, was introduced into popular discourse in the US and Western Europe during the 1990s, as debate ensued around Samuel Huntington's book *The Clash of Civilizations*, developed from an article he published in 1993. The book was a response to Fukuyama's thesis in *The End of History and the Last Man*, which proclaimed that the values of liberal democracy were destined to dominate the world, since it was a 'common evolutionary pattern for *all* human societies—in short, something like a Universal History of mankind in the direction of liberal democracy.'[53]

Although Fukuyama had identified the potential universality of Islam earlier, he did not believe that it was relevant in the contemporary era as a potentially universal model, since according to his theory Muslim society was a few stages behind the evolutionary cycle of the West. Huntington did not accept the inevitable victory of liberal democracy, and detailed the potential for clashes between differing civilizations, including the claimed universal values of the West and those of Islam, and identified that the absence of an Islamic core state represented a problem for Muslim and non-Muslim societies alike.[54] While groups such as Hizb-ut-Tahrir, which represented and proclaimed Islam as an alternative universal model, were largely unknown in the Western public sphere at the time, the events of 9/11 would bring the movement into media and government spotlights.

*Reaction to the war on terror*

The attacks against the World Trade Center in New York and the Pentagon in Virginia using civilian airliners resulted in almost 3,000 deaths in the immediate aftermath. Although they came after a decade that saw other attacks targeting US civilians, such as the US embassy bombings in Kenya and Tanzania in 1998, and less than a decade after a previous attack against the World Trade Center in 1993, which led to 7 casualties, the physical impact of the attacks (removing the Twin Towers from the New York skyline), the number of people killed, the use of civilian airliners as weapons, and the images that this created all made 9/11 an iconic moment for the US population.

The finger of accusation was pointed straight at al-Qaeda and bin Laden, who at the time was based in Afghanistan, which was under the administration of the Taliban. While bin Laden denied his involvement, the US administration dismissed this and set about building domestic and international support for a global, open-ended war on terror. In particular, pressure was applied to Middle Eastern governments, along with Pakistan, to publicly support the US-led campaign, and provide full co-operation across a range of intelligence and military matters.

Declassified documents showed that within two or three days a list of demands was given to Pakistan's president Pervez Musharraf, including provisions that basically entailed an almost complete surrender of sovereignty, such as blanket flight and landing rights to conduct any and all military and intelligence operations, all of which were agreed to, putting in place a vital element of support for the future war against Afghanistan. Arab governments, with Saudi Arabia and Egypt specifically targeted, were asked for similar unconditional support, with the Egyptian foreign and interior ministries recorded as being 'ready to help.' Support was also sought from states in Central Asia and the Caucasus region, which, as became clear, included Uzbekistan.[55]

Meanwhile, President George Bush gave a speech on 16 September in which he stated that 'people have declared war on America' and announced that the leaders of Pakistan, India and Saudi Arabia had pledged their full support. He also continued to prepare the public for the beginning of a long campaign, stating that 'this crusade, this war on terrorism is going to take a while.' The enemy motivation was framed in simple terms: 'They can't stand freedom; they hate what America stands for', and therefore it was going to be 'a long campaign, a determined campaign—a campaign that will use the resources of the United States to win.'[56] And so began the 9/11 mythology that held that the attack on the Twin Towers was the initial act of war, and in doing so dismissed the litany of possible grievances that drove the perpetrators to such acts.

Whether Bush's language was sloppy or deliberate, the use of the phrase 'crusade' passed largely unnoticed in the US, while ringing alarm bells in Europe, where there was belief that the potential for a clash of civilizations 'sowing fresh winds of hatred and mistrust' between Christians and Muslims had to be avoided.[57] (An unconcerned Bush continued using the phrase, such as when commending Canadian troops for helping take part in the 'incredibly important crusade to defend freedom' in Afghanistan.)[58] The war on terror started off in danger of appearing a lot like a 'war on Islam', with Muslim countries and citizens targeted, the clash of values highlighted as the reason behind the conflict, and a reference to a centuries-long series of conflicts between Islam and Christendom.

Hizb-ut-Tahrir issued a pamphlet a week after the attacks, which questioned the official account of the event itself and the motivations behind the US response. It noted that neither bin Laden nor the Taliban admitted having had anything to do with the event, and in fact had rejected any involvement. In fact, the pamphlet added, both al-Qaeda and the Taliban had been well infiltrated by the CIA and so if they had had anything to do with it, it would be impossible that US intelligence did not know about the plot in advance, particularly given the number of people required to carry out the attacks and the time and preparation that would have been necessary to successfully implement it. Finally, it stated that the attacks themselves contradicted the rules of Islam, which dictated that non-combatants such as old men, women and children should not be attacked, even on a battlefield, let alone using civilian aircraft full of innocent victims to fly into buildings, which themselves had innocent civilians working or residing there. In conclusion, 'all of these types of enmity are prohibited by Islam, and are not the actions of Muslims.'[59]

On the political front the pamphlet placed the US response in the context of the plan for the 'New World Order' announced by George Bush, Sr, in the early 1990s. The collapse of the USSR meant that a new paradigm had emerged along with a new international world order, with the US left as the unrivalled sole superpower without a counter-balance. The new alliance against terrorism was being formed to increase US control over the world, specifically in Islamic countries and other countries that might threaten US influence, such as China. The demand either to stand with the US or with the terrorists was rejected outright, with the US considered to be in no position to ask such a question, given that its own actions had shown that it had no values and acted as a terrorist entity itself (a reference to US foreign policy, primarily with regards to the Middle East). The pamphlet ended with a declaration that Islam forbade any alliance with the US for all the aforementioned reasons, and encouraged the peoples of the region to stand against their agent rulers who submitted to such an alliance.[60]

In sum, the party rejected both sides, equating US foreign policy to the terrorism meted out on 11 September; while the attacks against civilians were not justified, neither was the promised retaliation. Though the pamphlet did not go as far as to explicitly suggest that the US government was behind the act, it suggested that the intelligence agencies must have been aware of the plans, and that in the aftermath the US government cynically took advantage of events to further its own geo-political interests and secure its position as the leading power internationally. It also picked up on the use of the term 'crusade', which it believed was another indication that the war on terror was simply a cover for a war on Islam.

Two days after the beginning of the attack on Afghanistan on 7 October 2001 by the US-led coalition, the party released another pamphlet, which stated that the aggression was in revenge for 9/11, and restated that it was a crusade and war against Islam under the guise of the war on terrorism. It also announced that the war against Afghanistan was a declaration of war against all the Muslims, since the Muslim *Umma* was a single entity without any differentiation between Kabul, Damascus, Baghdad or Cairo, quoting that in the constitution of the first Islamic state in Medina, the Prophet had written that the Muslim community was one, and that they had to support each other and not support others against themselves.[61]

While Muslim populations remained largely unheard across the world, their leaders facilitated the US campaign, leading to a swift resolution as far as conventional warfare in the war in Afghanistan was concerned. After the initial air war, with ground support from the Northern Alliance, which led to the expulsion of the Taliban from Kabul and other major cities, and the capture of a range of individuals either in or linked to Afghanistan at the time, Bush's State of the Union address on 29 January 2002 celebrated the fact that 'terrorists who once occupied Afghanistan now occupy cells at Guantanamo Bay.' At the same time, he stated that 'what we have found in Afghanistan confirms that, far from ending there, our war against terror is only beginning.'[62] The speech was famous for the term 'axis of evil', identified as Iraq, Iran and North Korea, and could be seen as part of the preparations to justify the invasion of Iraq that would be undertaken by the US military, along with their British allies, in the face of international condemnation a year later in 2003.

A day after the invasion of Iraq on 19 March 2003, Hizb-ut-Tahrir issued a statement that Bush's declaration of war on Iraq was a declaration of war against the whole of the Muslim *Umma*, in the same vein as what was issued in response to the Afghanistan invasion. It further stressed that the regimes in the region were supporting the US in their belief that in exchange the US would help them maintain their positions and defend them from the wrath of their own people (with the Iraqi invasion inflaming opinion at the time). The motive was identified as the intention to extend US hegemony and influence in the region, while returning to the old style of military imperialism that was common between the eighteenth and mid-twentieth centuries. It ended with the consistent call to establish the caliphate and give the pledge of allegiance to a caliph who would rule them by Islam, with the understanding that this was the only protection for Muslims (based on the Prophetic narration that states that 'Only the Imam is a shield, you fight from behind him and you are protected by him').[63]

The war provided an opportunity for Hizb-ut-Tahrir to operate publicly in Iraq, a chance they took to state that any co-operation with occupying forces, contentment with occupation or lack of effort to work for its removal was forbidden according to Islam.[64] (As sectarian attacks started soon after, the party issued pamphlets warning against such killings, stating that it was not permitted for Muslims to kill fellow Muslims, and that whenever the US occupied a country, the occupying forces purposely inflamed sectarianism to weaken resistance through infighting.)[65]

The invasion of Iraq had occurred soon after a change of leadership in the party. Earlier in 2003 Zallum resigned from his position, and four candidates put themselves forward to take his place. Soon after his resignation Zallum fell ill and was transferred to a hospital in Beirut. Al-Rashta was appointed as the new leader after winning an internal election, which was relayed to Zallum, who favoured al-Rashta as the most capable person to lead the party.[66] Zallum died on 29 April 2003 aged almost eighty, and once again attempts to have an obituary printed in papers failed (with the Jordanian dailies al-Rai, al-dustur and al-arab al-yawm declining to do so, which resulted in the accusation that they were unable to print a word without the permission of the government).[67] Zallum's death meant that all of the members of the leadership committee from the time of al-Nabhani were dead, al-Da'ur having died two years earlier in 2001 aged over ninety, after spending his last ten years bed-ridden.[68]

Under Zallum's leadership, the party had refocused its members on the core activity of trying to build mass support for its ideas. After inheriting a developed and settled corpus of party material, but also a membership body that had not been able to consistently penetrate society, Zallum had managed to lead some of the most prominent political acts undertaken by sending delegations to Libya and Iran. Facing early setbacks, with the mass execution of members in Iraq and Libya, as well as extensive arrests in Tunisia, Egypt and elsewhere, the party spread internationally on its members' initiative. This spread was a result of Zallum's hands-off approach, rather than direct intervention.

The looser approach to administration may also have contributed to the enormity of the challenges he faced to his leadership, allowing internal dissent to spread in a way that would have been unimaginable under al-Nabhani's strict control. Zallum had involved several others in the party leadership, as opposed to al-Nabhani's more controlling style, and as a result the handover of leadership close to his death was an organised affair, with the numerous leadership candidates indicating the emergence of multiple capable figures under his stewardship as a result of his consultative style.

While al-Nabhani was convinced he would establish the caliphate, Zallum was much more circumspect and had no conviction that he would become the caliph at any point.[69] At the same time, the party's situation when he died highlighted the progress made during his leadership in terms of raising the public profile of the group and building an international membership, and the state of the party in an age of globalised communications. However, it may be argued that these achievements in themselves have little to do directly with the original goal of the party, and that despite the passage of time Zallum was unable to properly address some of the fundamental deficiencies identified shortly prior to al-Nabhani's death.

According to a publication linked to the party, memorials were held for Zallum in Beirut and Amman for people to pass on their condolences. Given that his family remained intact in Hebron, unlike that of al-Nabhani, which had been expelled from Ijzim, a large gathering was held in his hometown, with members and others from surrounding areas coming to present speeches and read poetry in his remembrance. At the same time, members from Sudan, Kuwait, Egypt, Indonesia and Europe passed on their respects through mobile phone messages.[70]

Zallum had been greatly concerned with trying to break what he considered to be the media silence surrounding the party, and imposing it on the political environment, with one of the major themes throughout his period the attempt to make society in the Middle East recognise that the authority to select and remove its rulers ultimately lay in its hands. It was perhaps fitting that his leadership was succeeded by former media spokesman al-Rashta, who subsequently established a central media office, along with media spokesmen and—women across the countries in which Tahrir operated. In another break from the past, he had been an engineer by profession, the first leader who was not a graduate from al-Azhar University, but rather a product of the party enculturation process itself, one of a number of leading members who emerged under Zallum's more collaborative leadership and who have published a number of works on Islam and politics.[71]

*To Western eyes*

By 2003, the party was being mentioned more often in the media, with greater Western attention on Islamic groups in the wake of 9/11, at the start of a period where there was a greater securitisation of anyone espousing Islamic politics. According to Kirstine Sinclair, writing about Hizb-ut-Tahrir in Denmark, although before 9/11 the group 'got positive media coverage in Denmark based on what was perceived to be a social profile of activities... this changed overnight after 11 September 2001.' While they were previously noted for 'achieving remarkable results in terms of engaging former gang members in socially burdened areas of Copenhagen in their work and activities... [s]uddenly, after 11 September 2001, Hizb-ut-Tahrir was perceived as a local Danish variant of al-Qaeda.'[72] In 2002, Fadi Abdelatif, Hizb-ut-Tahrir's spokesman in Denmark was given a sixty-day suspended sentence after being found guilty of distributing racist propaganda, with the court rejecting his argument that he was merely quoting from the Qur'an.[73]

In Germany the party as a whole was prohibited from public activity, on charges of spreading anti-Semitic propaganda, the only official ban in a Western European country. The accusations were summed up in the comments made by German interior minister Otto Schily in January 2003, when he stated that the group was 'spreading hate and violence' and was calling for the killing of Jews, an accusation rejected by the party's representative in Germany, Shaker Assem, who replied that 'we, the members of Hizb-ut-Tahrir, are not anti-Semitic... we do not call to kill Jews'; rather, the party call was 'addressed to the Muslim people to defend themselves against the Zionist aggression in Palestine', and claiming that 'they have the right to do so.'[74]

There was also media attention in the UK, some of it in line with the suspicions levelled against the group elsewhere in Europe, but also from a human interest perspective after a case that involved the arrest of more than one hundred people in Egypt linked to Hizb-ut-Tahrir, which included Russians, a Japanese student, Palestinians and four British nationals. Three of the British nationals were charged as part of a case eventually brought against twenty-six of those arrested, with the initial charges—promoting the goals of Hizb-ut-Tahrir through speech and writing, possessing and distributing printed literature that 'promoted Hizb-ut-Tahrir's message' and possessing a printer used for 'propagating' the group's ideology[75]—reduced to a single charge of membership of an illegal group; they were ultimately sentenced to five years' imprisonment.[76] The case was covered by local and international media, including a front-page piece in *The Times*, after it was found that one of the British nationals involved had been tortured during interrogation.[77] (These allegations would subsequently pale into insignificance when stories of the treatment of British nationals detained at Guantanamo Bay emerged.)

The British branch of Hizb-ut-Tahrir also waged a high-profile campaign using the short slogan 'Who Killed Farhad Usmanov?',[78] referring to a member of Hizb-ut-Tahrir in Uzbekistan and the son of a prominent imam in Tashkent who was tortured and killed while detained by Uzbek security forces in 1999.[79] The Uzbek regime had begun a crackdown against Islamic opposition generally and Hizb-ut-Tahrir specifically after a bomb attempt against

Uzbek president Islam Karimov in Tashkent in 1999, which the regime blamed on the opposition. Most analysts did not take the accusation seriously, with the general belief that the sophistication of the attack indicated that it was either the work of the regime or sponsored by a foreign state.[80]

There were numerous other cases raised by the party in Uzbekistan, such as that of Qayyum Jan, a blind and diabetic member who was tortured to death in prison soon after being sentenced to sixteen years for his membership and activities.[81] By the beginning of 2000, the local branch released a statement claiming that more than 4,000 members had been arrested, with a call to human rights organisations to 'ask Karimov... why he arrested 4000 who have done nothing wrong' and asking if in fact 'these organizations are only for the human rights of non-Muslims.'[82]

Hizb-ut-Tahrir in the UK undertook public demonstrations and marches as part of their campaign to try to highlight the situation in Uzbekistan, while at the same time using the issue as proof that the US's global war on terror was in fact aimed at Islam. During a march to the Uzbekistan embassy in London, a party member stated that the demonstration was 'to show that what America calls her war against terror is really a war against Islam and the Muslims', adding that they believed 'the rulers in the Islamic world are corrupt and tyrannical and they are the unscrupulous allies in America's war against terrorism.'[83]

Uzbekistan (along with Egypt) was considered to be an extremely important ally of the US post-9/11, with Bush linking al-Qaeda to the Egyptian Islamic Jihad and the Islamic Movement of Uzbekistan. In reality, according to Karimov's spokesman, Rustam Jumaev, the two countries had already been co-operating 'two or three years' before then, with Secretary of Defense Donald Rumsfeld stating that US interest in Uzbekistan had preceded 9/11.

The two sides signed agreements that gave the US permission to use Uzbek airspace, and military and civilian infrastructure, as well as a 'Strategic Partnership Agreement.' The US got to use military bases in Uzbekistan for the air campaign against Afghanistan, while the Uzbek government received over US $200 million in aid in 2002 alone, with almost US $80 million for 'law enforcement and security', as well as the opportunity for Karimov to participate as a valued ally on the world stage alongside high-ranking US officials such as Secretary of State Colin Powell and Rumsfeld,[84] with being hosted by Bush in March 2002 the apex,[85] giving legitimacy to a regime that according to Human Rights Watch was boiling prisoners alive in jail during the same year.[86]

As a result of the increased attention on the region following the Western occupation of Afghanistan, coupled with Hizb-ut-Tahrir's growing profile and substantial membership across Central Asia—in Uzbekistan, Kazakhstan, Kyrgyzstan, Tajikistan, Turkmenistan and slightly further afield in Russia, Ukraine and Xinjiang—there was more interest in the group generally and with respect to Central Asia specifically. One of the earliest commentaries on the party post-9/11 was journalist Ahmed Rashid's book *Jihad: The Rise of Militant Islam in Central Asia*, in which he claimed that the group was formed in Saudi Arabia and according to un-named leaders of the group was based on the 'revivalist Wahhabi movement'[87] and virulently anti-Shia, common themes for other analysts looking to link the party to al-Qaeda ideology.

Writing for the Conflict Studies Research Centre in the United Kingdom Michael Fredholm also followed the same theme, stating that the party was as 'simplistic and single-minded as in all other Wahhabi groups', and because Hizb-ut-Tahrir was 'a strong threat to Uzbek rule' Karimov retained 'the full support of the international community in his fight against the Islamic opposition.'[88] Meanwhile, in the US Ariel Cohen of the conservative think-tank the Heritage Foundation also chimed that '[a]t its inception, Hizb likely had strong connections to Saudi Wahhabism' and that 'experts have speculated that Iran, Saudi Arabia, and the Taliban regime in Afghanistan have been involved' in sponsoring the group. He concluded his report by stating that 'Hizb may launch terrorist attacks against U.S. targets and allies, operating either alone or in cooperation with other global terrorist groups such as al-Qaeda' and that the US and its allies 'must do everything possible to avoid' the group establishing its envisaged Islamic state.[89]

These were dominant themes in initial reports on Hizb-ut-Tahrir, based more on inaccurate speculation than any evidence (for example, the claim of links to Saudi Arabia and the accusation of anti-Shia sectarianism, which ran counter to the party's history and ideology). There were some dissenting voices, such as Jean-François Mayer, who wrote that the party was the 'perfect candidate for being seen as a new threat' since there were 'no experts on it; and [it] has a radical discourse',[90] and often enumerated similar grievances against Western foreign policy as al-Qaeda. Mayer criticised Cohen as being completely unfamiliar with Tahrir, relying on conjecture while ignoring the only in-depth study on the party in English at the time (Suha Taji-Farouki's *A Fundamental Quest*).[91] He also criticised claims that Hizb-ut-Tahrir was the 'next al-Qaeda', believing that '[m]ost Hizb-ut-Tahrir members will continue with their non-violent methods', with the more general observation that 'it is remarkable to see how many Islamic militants around the world, despite ferocious repression or harassment, have often shown considerable restraint in their reactions, notwithstanding the widely-publicized cases of those who choose the path of violence.'[92]

A report published by the International Crisis Group in 2003 held similar views, stating that '[h]istorically, the party's record provides no evidence of it being involved in terrorist activity against civilians, or in military actions against U.S. or Western interests', although 'there is good evidence of its involvement in a series of failed coups and attempts to overthrow governments in the Middle East.'[93] It warned: 'Lumping them together with violent groups such as alQaeda merely undermines the campaign against terrorism and gives ammunition to those radicals who claim that the West is acting against free speech and Islam in general' and advised governments against the temptation to ban the group.[94] The report concluded that Hizb-ut-Tahrir had 'gained popularity because it offered an alternative to a sometimes grim reality' and that the 'utopia of a Caliphate may be unachievable, but the idea of a just order, in a state with open borders, and a fair economy, has attracted thousands of supporters', meaning that the party's 'ideology will not be beaten by force alone' and so 'real reforms across the board are needed to undermine its support.'[95]

However, the dominant voice in the debate was provided by Zeyno Baran, the director for International Security and Energy Programs at the Nixon Center, when she organised a conference in Ankara, Turkey, entitled 'The Challenge of Hizb-ut-Tahrir: Deciphering and Combating Radical Islamist Ideology', which involved more than twenty participants. The conference was part of 'second-track American efforts to engage with the Uzbekistani leadership to come up with better strategies to combat HT [Hizb-ut-Tahrir]'s hold in Central Asia' and that she had 'enjoyed the cooperation of the Uzbekistani government' in her efforts. She also wrote that 'Foreign Minister Sadik Safaev and Presidential Advisor Zukhriddin Khusnidinov were among several others who expressed great interest in trilateral cooperation between Washington, Ankara and Tashkent', which was what led the Nixon Center to organise the conference.[96]

The US administration was heavily involved in helping, with Baran acknowledging the 'tremendous intellectual and personal support' given to her by Matthew Bryza, the deputy assistant secretary of state for Europe and Eurasia at the time. The conference was held over two days in February 2004, with contributions that often contained unsubstantiated assertions, such as Nanyan Technological University professor Rohan Gunaratna's claim that Abu Musab al-Zarqawi (the head of al-Qaeda in Iraq at the time, who was commonly accused of attacking Shia targets there) was a member of Tahrir.[97]

Michael Whine, director of the Group Relations Division of the Board of Deputies of British Jews, offered a more considered view that 'there is no evidence that HT is involved in or encourages terrorism in western Europe or that it is moving towards terrorism', and that there 'have been no reports that members have joined or become involved in al-Qaeda or the global jihad movement.' He also mentioned that members 'are not thought to have joined the Taliban, nor is it believed that any are being held by the United States at Guantanamo Bay.'[98] However, in Baran's executive summary she wrote her personal conclusion that 'Hizb-ut-Tahrir does not itself engage in terrorist acts, but it also does not repudiate the use of violence to reach its end goal' and that the most dangerous threat it posed was 'the impact of its ideology in shaping the outlook of the international Muslim community.' Her final message warned against leaving the party to operate freely, stating that it was 'part of the conveyor belt that produces terrorists.'[99]

Baran went on to write a series of articles and monographs in which she continued to promote her theory that Hizb-ut-Tahrir was a 'conveyor belt to terrorism' that needed to be banned in the West, and that Central Asian and Middle Eastern allies such as Uzbekistan needed to be supported against the group. In other words, although she claimed there was a need to engage in a 'war of ideas', it seems she envisaged the opponents in any such war as hooded, gagged and subjected to an unanswered stream of propaganda.[100] She also appeared in congressional hearings to give the same message, as well as travelling to London to take part in debates in Downing Street over the issue of radicalisation.[101]

In response to Baran's claims, the British branch of Hizb-ut-Tahrir wrote a letter to her in which they rejected her theory as lacking any evidence, and wryly observed that '[w]ere the production of terrorists our goal, we would find it hard to compete with American foreign policy, which Muslims perceive in the same way that Americans perceive the brutal tactics of the English during the War of Independence.'[102]

Ultimately, the US government's attempts to maintain publicly strong ties with the Uzbek regime despite its oppression of opposition failed, as a result of the Andizhan massacre on 13 April 2005. Witnesses reported that troops killed hundreds during a crackdown on crowds demonstrating in the eastern city. With the US administration already facing mounting criticism due to renditions, Guantanamo Bay and evidence of indiscriminate killings and torture in Iraq and Afghanistan, maintaining openly close relations with Karimov was becoming untenable, despite the politically motivated cover Baran provided, as well as support for the Uzbek regime from Israel, due to the openly close ties between the two countries (which was unusual for a Muslim country).[103]

As a result of stronger than normal US criticism of the bloodshed and systematic human rights violations, Uzbekistan expelled US forces from a key air base. According to a report by the Council of Europe the US government had previously rendered kidnapped individuals to Uzbekistan for interrogation (its record of torture was likely to have been considered a positive factor rather than an impediment, along with other destinations, including Egypt, Jordan, Morocco and Pakistan),[104] so it is unlikely that the Bush administration had a sudden moral awakening. Accordingly, relations were reconciled after a suitably long enough period for public outcry to subside, despite there being no improvement in the regime's behaviour—to the dismay of human rights organisations.[105]

Baran's core ideas about a 'conveyor belt to terrorism' have subsequently become standard government fare on both sides of the Atlantic, and form much of the thinking around 'counter-extremism' despite having no academic basis. They were adopted in the UK after the bombings carried out by four young British Muslims on 7 July 2005, which targeted civilians on public transport in London. Video statements prepared in advance by the perpetrators linked the bombings to the ongoing Western military presence in Afghanistan and Iraq, with Mohammad Sidique Khan copying al-Qaeda's ideology of reciprocity, saying to the Western audience 'your democratically elected governments continuously perpetuate atrocities against my people all over the world',[106] while Shehzad Tanweer said that attacks would continue 'until you pull your forces out of Afghanistan and Iraq.'[107]

British involvement in Iraq was deeply unpopular among large sections of the public who considered the war to have been illegal. By then, American government reports were stating that '[w]orldwide anger and discontent are directed at America's tarnished credibility and ways the U.S. pursues its goals'[108] and Prime Minister Tony Blair admitted that 'the majority view of a large part of western opinion, certainly in Europe' was that:

> the policy of America since 9/11 has been a gross overreaction; George Bush is as much if not more of a threat to world peace as Osama bin Laden; and what is happening in Iraq, Afghanistan or anywhere else in the Middle East, is an entirely understandable consequence of US/UK imperialism or worse, of just plain stupidity.

According to Blair, this was all incorrect and there was an alternative narrative to the claim that foreign policy grievances lay behind the hatred towards the US and the UK among Muslims worldwide. This alternative 'Blair narrative' was that 'extremist' ideology was the driving factor, a clash between the 'we' who believed in 'democracy, liberty and human rights administered by secular courts' versus those who followed an ideology that was born and exported around the world from 'offshoots of the Muslim brotherhood, supported by Wahhabi extremists and taught in some of the Madrassas of the Middle East and Asia.'[109] The idea that 'religious extremism' or what Blair thought was composed of 'their attitude to America... their concept of governance... their positions on women and other faiths'[110] led to terrorism was akin to the 'conveyor belt' theory that Baran espoused.

Soon after the July 2005 attacks Blair announced his intention to ban Hizb-ut-Tahrir, among other groups, and attempted to pass new legislation that would make 'glorifying terrorism' illegal (which would have made it easier to proscribe Hizb-ut-Tahrir). The legislation failed to pass through the House of Lords. Meanwhile, Foreign Office officials noted in a leaked memo that the group was active in the Middle East and Central Asia and that there was 'no apparent case to proscribe [Hizb-ut-Tahrir] because its activities abroad include involvement in terrorism' and that it was 'not entirely clear whether they would be caught under a future criterion of "justifying or condoning violence"' since '[m]uch of their literature explicitly rejects the use of violence.'[111]

By the end of the year, Blair shelved the proposed ban after discussions with counter-terrorism officials and legal advisors. The decision was considered a personal blow, coming a month after he had assured Musharraf that the ban would go ahead (Musharraf had urged Blair that outlawing the group had to be a priority for the UK, a step he had taken in 2003 as a result of increased Hizb-ut-Tahrir activity in Pakistan).[112] The whole affair was an embarrassment for the British Labour Party, but a few years later the party had the consolation that the Conservatives under David Cameron also pledged to ban the group before coming into power and had to make an equally if not more embarrassing climbdown after realising that they had no legal basis to do so.[113]

Although neither the US nor British governments were able to proscribe Tahrir as a terrorist organisation, the 'conveyor belt' theory or 'Blair narrative' that ideas such as a belief in the contemporary applicability of Sharia law, the concept of belonging to a single international Muslim community, the legitimacy of resisting armed attack and occupation through the use of force, and aspiring to live under an Islamic caliphate would lead people to commit acts of terrorism[114] is the staple diet of the lucrative counter-terrorism industry spawned both sides of the Atlantic—rather than, for example, because they may know of friends, family members or co-religionists who have been killed, tortured or rendered by US or British troops, and that they perceive the West to be supporting the dictatorial regimes over them.

There is scant empirical evidence for such claims. Often suggestions by journalists and others that people such as al-Zarqawi, Khalid Sheikh Muhammad and similar figures were members of Hizb-ut-Tahrir appear purely conjectural and lack evidence, and are denied by internal sources.

Additionally, despite decades of being driven underground by the various state security apparatuses in the Muslim world, and having had many members jailed, tortured and executed, the party methodology and ideology remained largely consistent. In any case, despite the continued push from the counter-terrorism industry and its political backers, restricted government papers in the UK concluded that they 'do not believe that it is accurate to regard radicalisation in this country as a linear "conveyor belt" moving from grievance, through radicalisation, to violence,' and that the 'thesis seems to both misread the radicalisation process and to give undue weight to ideological factors.'[115] Despite being discredited, the idea of a 'conveyor belt to terrorism' informs almost all of the debate in media and within government regarding security and terrorism, with the idea that 'extremism' may lead to 'violent extremism' an accepted 'truth'.

US and British attempts to ban Tahrir can be linked to attempts to aid their allies in the war on terror against the domestic opposition that the party represented, primarily in Uzbekistan and Pakistan. At the same time, these Western regimes also believed that the narrative espoused by groups such as Hizb-ut-Tahrir was hurting their image across Muslim countries. As early as 2004 US government sources identified that 'the perception of intimate U.S. support of tyrannies in the Muslim World is perhaps the critical vulnerability in American strategy'[116] to win the so-called battle for 'hearts and minds'. It was stated that, contrary to the Bush mantra, 'Muslims do not "hate our freedom", but rather, they hate our policies' with the 'overwhelming majority voic[ing] their objections to what they see as one-sided support in favor of Israel and against Palestinian rights, and the longstanding, even increasing support for what Muslims collectively see as tyrannies, most notably Egypt, Saudi Arabia, Jordan, Pakistan, and the Gulf states.'[117] This and similar advice did not chime with the political prerogative of the day according to the Bush-Blair alliance, while the Baran-Blair narratives did.

*The opening of the political space*

Conversely, while efforts were underway to ban Hizb-ut-Tahrir in Western countries, it was recognised as a legal party in 2006 by Lebanese Interior Minister Ahmad Fatfat. The decision came as a result of the spread of the party within Lebanon, leading to more activity including public distribution of party materials.

The Syrian military, which was present in Lebanon between 1976 and 2005, and Syrian intelligence, were particularly active and cautious, and party activists were often arrested during the period. Arrested activists were regularly brought before judges on charges of distributing party literature, something that was considered strange in what was viewed as one of the region's more permissive political environments. Although dozens of cases had been brought to court since 2000, the military police who brought the cases admitted that the party had no military apparatus or activities, and judges often threw the cases out because nothing illegal had taken place, with the materials being distributed openly and containing political ideas and views.[118]

In July 2004, Hizb-ut-Tahrir led a demonstration against the visit of interim Iraqi prime minister Ayad Allawi, during which the party called for Allawi to be expelled along with the US ambassador. This was the first public demonstration Tahrir had held in the Middle East for more than four decades and it attracted wide media attention. Lebanese television channel LBC aired a report on the party on 28 July that included interviews recorded with Uthman Bakhach, the party spokesman and head of the central media office in Beirut, and Ahmad al-Qasas, the spokesman for the Lebanese branch. The next day both men were arrested by the intelligence services, joining another two members who had been arrested within the previous ten days. Tahrir issued a statement in which it claimed that the arrests indicated that Lebanon was a 'police state' where people were forcibly prevented from speaking, with 'proofs and evidences' met with 'steel and fire.' It closed by stating that Tahrir would not alter its methodology of calling the people to Islam even if met by arrests and prison.[119]

The arrests were followed by a campaign in the media asking questions over why the arrests had taken place. Even Bakhach's interrogators admitted that they knew that Tahrir's work was limited to leaflet distribution, and the arrest was linked to the fact that they had moved to collective mass action, which had raised their media profile and was moving them into mainstream political discussion.[120] The party also linked the arrests to the fact that they were protesting against US foreign policy, with signs posted on streets protesting over the arrest of members asking, 'For how long will the decision to arrest the sincere sons of the Muslims remain in the hands of the American embassy?'[121]

In 2005 a new Lebanese government formed and Fatfat was appointed as the interior minister. In August Tahrir made another application to be recognised as a political party and lobbied political leaders and officials for their support.[122] According to Bakhach, after another series of arrests of party activists in May 2006, Fatfat made enquiries into why the arrests had taken place and was told that it was because the movement was calling for an Islamic state. When he protested that this was no reason to arrest them, he was told the party had not been issued a permit.[123] Within a few days Fatfat issued the necessary permit for Hizb-ut-Tahrir along with ten other political parties, dismissing objections as counter to the principles of democracy that he believed in and refused to apply selectively or hypocritically.[124]

Fatfat's decision was controversial locally and caused enough consternation internationally for him to address it during an official visit to the US.[125] A year later he stated that he was 'proud of the issue of this party' because he was a democrat and despite 'very fundamental political differences' with Hizb-ut-Tahrir, it 'had not carried out any action which would prohibit it from being granted a permit according to Lebanese law.' As far as the issue of extremism was concerned, he stated that the only thing they could be accused of was 'intellectual extremism' and that there was not a single case of the party using violence.[126]

This was an important milestone under al-Rashta's leadership, with the rising prominence of the central media office, the emergence of Tahrir activists and supporters in public demonstrations, more serious media coverage and official recognition of the party all heralding successes in trying to enter the public political medium in the Muslim world. In September 2006 a speech was read out after Friday prayers and distributed in cities across more than twenty countries, telling the Muslims that the time was opportune to establish the caliphate and encouraging them to work with Hizb-ut-Tahrir for its return.

The speech was delivered in Lebanon, Jordan, Iraq, Sudan, Turkey, Kazakhstan, Kyrgyzstan, Tajikistan, Yemen, Indonesia, Malaysia, Bangladesh, Pakistan, and even in Uzbekistan where members decided to pre-record the speech and play it on a stereo in front of the congregation—a decision they had taken on their own initiative, despite a request from the party leadership not to read the speech because of the security situation. It was also printed and distributed in Palestine, Syria, Egypt, Tunisia, Algeria, Morocco, Kuwait, Afghanistan, India and the UAE. There was some local media coverage, as well as limited international coverage, which focused on specific countries and arrests carried out in the aftermath;[127] most reports did not connect the disparate acts together. According to one calculation, around 400 to 500 people were arrested as a result of the call (including in Lebanon again, despite the legal permit). Some of those arrested were released the same day, others remained in jail for a period, and some received prison sentences, with the majority of the arrests taking place in Jordan, Turkey and Uzbekistan.[128]

The geographic spread of the actions highlights the number of Muslim countries where the party was active by 2006, and its capacity for coordinated activity. The following year, in August 2007 during the month of Rajab, according to the Islamic *hijri* calendar (matching the month that the speeches were made in 2006), a conference attended by around 100,000 Indonesian Muslims resulted in much greater international attention.

The attendance indicates the growth of the party in Indonesia since moving into public view, after the end of the Suharto regime in 1998. The first conference that Tahrir held in Indonesia took place on 28 May 2000, when the party name was not only introduced to the Indonesian public, but also to many of those who had been studying its ideas and thoughts, since al-Baghdadi and Bin Nuh had been careful to keep the identity of the group secret during the time of the dictatorship.[129] Seven years on, the scale of the conference, which was held in the Gelora Bung Karno sports stadium, the largest in the country, raised the party's international profile. The majority of the attendees were women, with female chapters of the party growing and becoming more visible, particularly in non-Arab countries.[130]

Subsequently, international conferences in Muslim countries have become regular occurrences, notably including an economics conference held in the Sudanese capital Khartoum in January 2009, an international 'ulama' (scholars) conference in Indonesia in 2009, and an international media conference in Beirut in July 2010. This was in addition to conferences the party regularly held in countries where it was able to operate publicly such as Yemen, England, Australia, Denmark, Ukraine and elsewhere, with attendance normally in the thousands. While it was still facing a harsh security environment across most of the Middle East, the Arab uprisings that had begun at the end of 2010 in Tunisia changed the political landscape of the region.

The popular uprisings against a number of Middle Eastern regimes closely allied to the West began after Tunisian street vendor Mohamed Bouazizi set himself alight on 17 December 2010 to protest against his treatment by government officials. This was the catalyst for street protests that eventually led to Ben 'Ali fleeing the country to Saudi Arabia on 14 January 2011. As with most other Islamic opposition, Tahrir activists had been forced to operate underground for the previous two decades because of government pressure, often being forced to sign in at police stations daily—even several times a day—and having to seek permission to leave their city of residence. Since about 2005, the party had returned to organised activity, leading to more than ten court cases against activists between 2006 and 2010, where they were tried according to the law prohibiting associations, leading to jail terms of between six months and two years.[131]

After the revolution began, the party released and distributed a pamphlet on 3 January 2011 that criticised the regime for its history of harsh behaviour, claiming that it had 'thrown Islam behind its back and jumped into the arms of Western imperialists' and that the solution for good governance and economic policy was to implement Islamic Sharia in its entirety.[132] There was an attempt to arrest the members involved in the distribution, but several went into hiding and fewer than ten were detained.[133] On Friday 14 January, thousands of people in the capital Tunis descended on the interior ministry, a symbol of the regime's repression, in protest against the government. At the same time Tahrir members outside of the city organised and led a march of a few hundred people into Tunis.[134] Ben 'Ali dissolved parliament and declared a state of emergency, before fleeing the country and eventually landing in Saudi Arabia after President Nicolas Sarkozy—proving to have been something of a fair-weather friend—refused him permission to land in France.[135]

With the breaching of the barrier of fear that seemed to have enveloped the Middle East for decades, the fall of Ben 'Ali encouraged protesters elsewhere. The Mubarak regime in Egypt was the next to face pressure, with protests beginning on 25 January 2011, millions harbouring bitterness against the brutality of the police state. The occupation of Tahrir Square in Cairo for more than two weeks eventually led to Mubarak's resignation, at the cost of almost 1,000 lives.[136] Hizb-ut-Tahrir in Egypt publicly announced its support for the revolution before other Islamic opposition movements, but with limited numbers of supporters in the country it played no significant role in the protests.

After the removal of Mubarak, a party delegation met the leader of the Supreme Council of the Armed Forces (SCAF), the military council that had taken over administration of the country, presenting him with Hizb-ut-Tahrir's view of Islam and advising the SCAF to establish an Islamic state.[137] Another delegation also met representatives from al-Azhar University after it had issued a document endorsing a modern national democratic state (the document was entitled *wathiqa al-Azhar*).[138] Most strikingly, after Tahrir's central media office released a video statement criticising the SCAF towards the end of 2011, the council issued a response from its Facebook page rejecting the advice on the basis that the group was Palestinian and had no right to interfere in domestic Egyptian matters. This in turn led to a response from the local branch's media office stating that the party was not a Palestinian group, but was an international party working for the unity of the Muslim *Umma*, with the back and forth playing out across social media and beyond.[139] Since the military's removal of the elected president, Mohamed Morsi, Tahrir has reduced its public profile in Egypt, but remains active.

In Libya, revolts against Gaddafi required foreign military support to succeed, with former allies the UK, France and the US deciding to support the uprisings, which were mainly based in Benghazi at the start. Hizb-ut-Tahrir had no presence on the ground in Libya as a result of the imprisonment and execution of its members in the early 1980s, and support was limited to congratulating the Libyans for removing the regime. In Yemen, where protests eventually succeeded in forcing Ali Abdullah Saleh from his position as president, while the rest of the regime remained intact, the party held numerous conferences and gatherings to promote its agenda of establishing a caliphate.

In Syria, where demonstrations against the regime of Bashar al-Assad began with localised demonstrations on 15 March 2011, it appears that Hizb-ut-Tahrir has had a significant influence. The party was historically hampered by campaigns of arrests against activists, the most notable being between the end of 1999 and the beginning of 2000, which began with the arrest of more than sixty activists in Homs.[140] A party statement claimed that more than 800 people including women were subsequently arrested by the secret police, with deaths occurring during the arrests and in interrogation[141] (confirmed by news reports, which stated that more than 500 members had been arrested).[142]

However, the party had enough presence during the period of the protests, which spread across the region, to distribute pamphlets in Syria at the start of the uprisings, with one release on 26 March that encouraged the people to voice their discontent, and for the army to remove the regime, referring to the arrest and torture of children from the city of Daraa the previous month for writing anti-regime slogans on walls.[143] As a result, Syrian news profiled the group on 28 March, quoting Syrian security sources as saying that Tahrir had a major role in instigating the initial protests.[144]

As the opposition protests developed into armed resistance as a defence against the harsh crackdown by the Syrian regime, the influence of Tahrir on the political views of the popular resistance became more visible, with opposition brigade spokesmen openly declaring that in the eventuality of coming to power they hoped to establish a state based on 'what is written in the books of Hizb-ut-Tahrir, who have presented a complete and comprehensive political program and constitution.'[145] The declaration of the ISIS caliphate (almost universally rejected as invalid including by Tahrir)[146] has further confused the situation on the ground in the region, but it is clear that, as in the past, laying claim to the caliphate has once again become a legitimising mechanism for some.

The causes, analysis and implications of the uprisings are all topics beyond the scope of what is written here, but it is evident that there was no clear detailed vision of what the populations of the region wanted, other than removal of the regimes in place. As such, it was a rejection of the US-sponsored status quo in the region. But although the heads of the regimes were removed, the post-colonial structure remained in place, with analysts positing that Western interests remain protected through the building of new alliances or sponsorship of counter-revolutions.[147] The main beneficiaries of the elections in the immediate aftermath of the uprisings in Tunisia, Egypt and Libya were the Muslim Brotherhood and their affiliated parties, using their vast grassroots network of activists to mobilise public support behind Islamic slogans. This was not to last, as the revolutions did not fully uproot the previous power structures, which have subsequently reasserted themselves. Hizb-ut-Tahrir, on the other hand, has remained largely on the fringes throughout, not having comparable numbers of supporters or the belief in pragmatism to participate in elections under what remained in their view a secular state system.

The most important result of the uprisings for Tahrir was that the 'barrier of fear' was initially diminished, and the people of the region believed that they had the right to openly hold their governments to account and were willing to attempt to do so. This resulted in the opening of the political space, something that Tahrir attempted to take advantage of, having been granted an official permit in Tunisia[148] and opening media offices in Tunisia and Egypt. Members, such as party spokesperson Reda Belhaj, regularly appear on Tunisian and Arab television, and Hizb-ut-Tahrir Egypt presented a weekly television show on satellite television before the media clampdown presided over by Gen. Abdel Fattah el-Sisi. Conferences were also held in Egypt and Tunisia, with Tunisia hosting an international women's conference on 10 March 2012, which was attended by female Tahrir delegates from several countries and reported on by al-Jazeera. A conference in Egypt in July 2012 garnered a lot of attention in the local press, such as a ten-page pull-out published in *Al-Wathiqa* newspaper explaining the party's manifesto and methodology.[149]

Other countries in the region were not immune to the winds of change, but some remained more closed to Tahrir than others. In particular, the Jordanian government continued to try to enforce a media embargo on the party by pressuring various satellite channels not to interview Hizb-ut-Tahrir members. The Arab Post satellite channel was closed down and its owner, Dr Ali al-Dala'in, was prevented from leaving the country the day after the station broadcast a one-hour programme with a party spokesman.[150]

Across the border in the West Bank and Gaza, Tahrir's growing presence in its birthplace was highlighted by an attendance numbering in the tens of thousands at an outdoor conference in Hebron on 17 June 2012. Commemorating the abolition of the caliphate, the conference was well covered by local media, and a number of Arab satellite channels ran reports on it. The following day a march was held in Gaza, after a campaign to distribute tens of thousands of pamphlets, among other activities, to promote the party call.[151] Although generally tolerated by the Fatah and Hamas administrations, the party's activities have sometimes been curtailed and its members arrested. Despite this, the large attendances at events under al-Rashta's leadership, such as a 10,000-strong rally in al-Bireh, north of Jerusalem, and similar gatherings in 2006 in Hebron and Ramallah, under the slogan 'The caliphate is the rising force', highlighted its growing presence in Palestine.[152]

Further afield, the party remained banned in Turkey and sometimes pursued by the authorities; for example, in 2009 200 activists were arrested two days before a scheduled conference.[153] Despite the setbacks, it appears that the group is now well enough established among the local population to continue its activities irrespective, holding conferences in support of the Syrian revolution simultaneously in seventeen cities across Turkey on 16 September 2012, with video recordings showing hundreds of attendees at the Istanbul conference.[154] Elsewhere, in Pakistan numerous members have regularly been pursued and arrested by the government. The profile of the party was raised after the arrest in May 2011 of a brigadier accused of having links to the group, became a major media story.[155] The case concluded in August 2012 after a military court convicted Brig. Ali Khan, Maj. Sohail Akbar, Maj. Jawad Baseer, Maj. Inayat Aziz and Maj. Iftikhar for having links with Hizb-ut-Tahrir and sentenced them to terms ranging from five years to eighteen months.[156]

In conclusion, the international spread of the group has been impressive. By 2009 it claimed to operate in over forty Muslim countries in conditions varying from being banned and facing security crackdowns, as in Bangladesh, to the more permissive atmosphere of Indonesia. In the areas where the party is banned, it restricts its activities to personal contact to convince individuals to study with the party while using public events such as the Friday prayer to distribute its literature to the masses as circumstances permit. In arenas where Tahrir is able to operate publicly, activities may also extend to hosting public talks and conferences, using avenues from mosques to universities to propagate their call for a return to a caliphate on a public level, while continuing with personal contact for more detailed discussion. In all cases, the party does not aim at mass membership, but rather mass support for its ideas, as its members are expected to gain the leadership and trust of the society through their political and ideological stances, with membership to the party theoretically based on adherence to its core literature and ideology.

Hizb-ut-Tahrir carries out its public activities with the aim of undermining the confidence of the people in the political regimes that rule over them, while building a critical mass of support for its political programme, such that its envisaged call for the return to an Islamic system of governance will build momentum, leading figures of political and military influence in the country to throw their weight behind the group.

In doing so, Tahrir has continued to promote the caliphate as the only vehicle for true liberation from the forces of colonialism, and a comprehensive solution to the issues facing not only the Arabs or Muslims, but the whole of mankind, after the failure of Communism and the proclaimed self destruction of global capitalism.

As the party continues its work across dozens of countries in varying conditions, its message and methodology have remained fundamentally consistent since its inception in the early 1950s. The opening of the political space in the Middle East as a result of protests and uprisings, along with the fact that we are now living in a globalised world with unprecedented access to all forms of conventional and alternative media, mean that while the history of Tahrir may have remained untold for decades, its future need not be.

# CONCLUSION

## 'A REMARKABLY PERSISTENT ORGANIZATION'

*[Effective movements] do not occur when affluence prevails, and natural rights are secured, propensity is ensured, and people are selected to hold important positions based on their competence...*

*...the success of the collective movement is measured by its ability to instigate resentment amongst the masses and to exhort their resentment each time the regime undermines or manipulates the ideology according to its own whims and interests*[1]

Taqiudeen al-Nabhani

Irrespective of opinions regarding Hizb-ut-Tahrir and its ideology, and whatever its future holds, as an international political party in an era of nation states it will hold a place in history as a rare entity.

Emerging out of the rupture of the *Nakba*, al-Nabhani established Hizb-ut-Tahrir, a political anomaly in the era in that it sought to reverse the events of 1924 and the abolition of the caliphate—the nadir of a decline he argued began centuries earlier—at a time when other anti-colonial, nationalist and pan-Arabist movements were mainly concerned with ideas of regional unity to reverse the events of the 1948 war.

While other movements primarily strove for liberation from colonial military occupation, the goal of Hizb-ut-Tahrir—the Liberation Party—was to free the region from the shackles of post-colonialism. In its view, liberation would only be achieved when the minds of the Muslims were freed from the worldviews imposed on them by colonialists, disposing of nationalism, materialism, secularism and capitalism and returning to viewing life, politics and international relations through Islam.

From its inception the party aimed at the ambitious task of what it termed as the resumption of the Islamic way of life and carrying the call of Islam to the world through the establishment of a unified Islamic state, which would replace what it considered to be artificial, fragmented countries in the region, created out of the fall of the Ottoman state. From its beginnings, Tahrir adopted a methodology that it had derived from its understanding of the life of the Prophet and of the Prophetic path to establishing the first Islamic state in Medina, relying on an intellectual revival that would win mass support for the radical challenge of changing the systems in place.

Through various wars, coups, counter-coups and revolutions, from the Cold War to the war on terror, the party has maintained its stance, despite the various pressures on it and potential openings that lay ahead of it if it changed its position. As noted by Mayer, 'there is an uncompromising dimension in its ideology.'[2]

This ideological certitude can be summed up in Hizb-ut-Tahrir's response to the events of 9/11, when it condemned the attacks as un-Islamic within the context of explaining the US plan to exploit the attacks and further its foreign policy agenda to extend its control over the 'Greater Middle East' and use the issue of 'terrorism' as a political weapon against those it believed threatened US interests. As such, it is difficult to accuse the party of simply saying something for media consumption, a charge often levelled at other politicians of any stripe.

At the same time, the confidence in its understanding of Islam and lack of willingness to compromise did not seem to prevent the party's leaders from honest self-reflection and appraisal throughout its history. Originally intended as a party to win over mass support for the call for an Islamic state, which would create a popular demand for its political goals, it stumbled in its first steps as it moved from being an intellectual movement to a fully fledged political party in the late 1950s. While to some extent it was a victim of circumstance, with harsh repression forcing the party leadership underground and making interaction with the wider society a difficult proposition, the leadership also blamed itself for failing to make the necessary and correct efforts to achieve the required results.

Since announcing that the party had entered the 'interaction phase' in 1960, Hizb-ut-Tahrir has largely been deprived of any opportunity to freely interact with society. Driven underground throughout core Muslim countries in the Middle East for approximately half a century, it was difficult for the party to spread its ideas, and even more difficult to increase its membership in its main areas of work. Partly as a consequence, it spread internationally, with members taking its call with them wherever they travelled for work, study or refuge.

As a result, the group now operates in more than forty countries internationally. Circumstances vary between locations, from the party operating successfully in the public arena in Indonesia, to the wide spread of the party across the Fergana Valley in Central Asia, despite repressive conditions in the countries there. Its willingness to openly challenge the political status quo has often chimed with the public—something articulated by one religious leader in Tajikistan generally opposed to Tahrir who said, 'You might not like them, but you can't deny they are the only people telling the truth about Tajikistan.'[3]

Despite the obstacles faced, particularly in the Middle East, Tahrir emerged after the Arab uprising of 2011 with a party body operating openly in Egypt, Tunisia, Lebanon, Sudan, Yemen and Syria. It is now recognised as a legal political party in a number of Arab countries, and while barriers still exist in other areas central to its work, such as Turkey and Jordan, the party is able to hold large public events and appears to have enough support to withstand any government campaign of arrests.

Hizb-ut-Tahrir has clearly not yet won mass support across the Muslim world, and by its own measurement of success it falls well short. It can point to the fact that when the party was established it was unique as a political party in adopting the call for the re-establishment of the caliphate as an explicit objective, at a time when Islam was seen as cultural rather than political. Sixty years after Tahrir's establishment, the caliphate is at a minimum a recognised part of the political discourse in Muslim countries. There have been numerous claimants to the caliphate, ranging from fringe individuals to the claim made by ISIS in 2014, highlighting its continued meaning and competition over its legitimising power. At the same time, the demand for Islamic politics is mainstream, and even secular politicians have to cloak their discourse in Islamic terms to win support. The persistence and consistency of Tahrir, its influence on other individuals, movements and intellectual strands have all contributed to this change.

Alternatively, when compared to other major trends and movements in the Middle East, its numbers appear small and its name relatively unknown. Its unwillingness to compromise with the authorities has never permitted it the space afforded to some other movements in periods of their history; its open political discourse has led to its repression; and its methodology stopped it from taking up arms in an attempt to bring about change or from serving as a grassroots social services movement to win support. This has negatively impacted on its size, not only in terms of membership but also in terms of support.

At the same time, this has meant that it has held onto its intellectual foundations and ideology largely unchanged, with a membership that understands, adopts and promotes the same beliefs and ideas whether in Jakarta, Tashkent, Islamabad, Cairo or Tunis, lending it an ideological consistency not found in other movements.

Its adherence to 'ideology' long after the debates of the Cold War era ended will seem anachronistic to many observers, who have seen other Islamic organisations seemingly making more headway by adopting a more pragmatic line. What Tahrir would argue is a dilution of principle, others argue is adapting to the harsh reality of today's politics. On the other hand, Tahrir has consistently argued that its goal is not to reach power itself, but to establish the Islamic system, something it believes has not yet been achieved, despite the electoral successes of Islamic parties and the claims of ISIS originating from Mosul.

On several issues, Tahrir seems to have been ahead of the curve in the Muslim world. The call for Muslim governments to implement Islam and the call for a unified Islamic state are no longer anomalies. In political analysis, many of its claims that were ridiculed at the time have become more mainstream, such as the US using Nasser to reduce British influence in the region and the prediction that Jordan would surrender the West Bank (which played out in 1967). Likewise, the party's opinion that the aim of the 1973 war was to ultimately reach a peace accord with Israel and that the PLO was set up to reduce the question of Palestine to a national issue have been vindicated to a great extent.

From its inception, Hizb-ut-Tahrir has believed that the authority to decide the political system belongs to the people as a whole, along with the right to appoint who runs it on their behalf. Its attempts to overthrow the regimes in the Middle East were born out of the belief that the people wanted the establishment of the Islamic state, that authority had been stolen from them and they did not realise that it was in fact their right, and therefore the way to return that right to them was to remove the regimes that had in any case been artificially imposed on them.

Despite stating clearly in its literature and internal documents that it seeks to build mass support for the party's ideas, on which the caliphate will be established, Hizb-ut-Tahrir has been characterised as a 'top-down' revolutionary movement. Although that opinion may be inaccurate, it is not altogether surprising when it is taken into consideration that, according to the party leadership, the problem that afflicted the party between 1975 and 1985 was that many of its members had given up thinking that interacting with society was possible or useful, and that the only way to achieve the Islamic state was through seeking the material support that would bring it into being.

After the uprisings that began in 2011 across the Middle East, which have shown the masses that they do indeed have the potential to hold authority in their hands, Tahrir could possibly now have its first opportunity to truly interact in the Middle East in a manner envisaged by its founders.

Despite the tumultuous situation in the contemporary Middle East, the opening of the political space because of the Arab uprisings is unlikely to be reversed for an extended period of time, whatever efforts are made. The fact that social media and modern communications have changed the way people absorb news and information means that Hizb-ut-Tahrir has the opportunity to present its ideas and arguments to a wide audience in the Middle East for the first time in decades. Given the apparent failure of the Muslim Brotherhood to work 'within the system' in Egypt, and disillusionment over the attitude of armed groups in Syria and Iraq, such as ISIS, there may even be the possibility that alternative visions will find a receptive audience, however unlikely that may appear during a time of instability and conflict.

Whatever the case, as a political party that has established itself across the Middle East and beyond, Hizb-ut-Tahrir's successes will be judged by its ability mobilise to the masses based on its understanding of Islam and politics.

# APPENDIX I

## CONSTITUTION

The following is a translation of the first seventeen articles of the original draft constitution (which contains eighty-nine articles) for the Islamic state, which was printed as part of the second edition of the book *Nitham al-Islam* (The System of Islam) published in 1953.[1] This is no longer the adopted constitution of the party. The most recent version, which totals 191 articles, can be found in the book *Muqadimma al-Dustur*.

*General Rules*

Article 1: The Islamic belief is the basis of the state, the constitution and the rest of the laws.

Article 2: Islam is the *din* (religion) that Allah revealed to our leader Muhammad, peace be upon him, that organises the relationship between man and his Creator—the *'aqa'id* (beliefs) and *'ibadat* (personal worship); the relationship with himself—manners, food, clothing; and with others—transactions and punishments.

Article 3:

a. The Holy Qur'an, and what is authenticated from the Prophetic narrations (words, actions and confirmations), the consensus of the companions and *qiyas* (analogy) are the detailed evidence for Sharia rules.

b. The opinion of a companion in the issues of *ijtihad* (juristic deduction) is not a Sharia evidence, rather it is like the opinions of the leading scholar and the *mujtahidin* (those who practise *ijtihad*) and is considered to be a Sharia verdict which can be adopted.

c. *Ijtihad* is a collective obligation, and every Muslim has the right to *ijtihad* so long as they fulfil its conditions.

d. The caliph adopts specific Sharia laws in transactions and punishments, and if he adopts a law in those issues it is obligatory to obey him, and his order is implemented externally and internally.

e. The caliph should not adopt any Sharia rule in *'ibadat* (personal worship) other than *zakat* (tax upon wealth), or in ideas that are linked to the Islamic *'aqida*.

Article 4: The state looks at all those who carry the Islamic citizenship from the angle of their shared humanity.

Article 5: Sharia law is implemented upon all those who hold citizenship of the Islamic State, whether Muslims or not, in the following manner:

a. The Sharia law is implemented in its entirety, without exception, on all Muslims.

b. Non-Muslims are allowed to follow their own beliefs and worship.

c. In matters of food and clothing the non-Muslims are treated according to their religions within the limits allowed by the general system.

d. Personal affairs such as marriage and divorce among non-Muslims are settled in accordance with their religions, but between non-Muslims and Muslims they are settled according to the rules of Islam.

e. All the remaining Sharia rules, such as: the application of transactions, punishments and the systems of ruling, economics and others are implemented upon everyone, Muslim and non-Muslim alike.

Article 6: The Islamic *Umma* is one, and *Umma* is the group of people collected upon a single belief from which a system emanates.

Article 7:

a. Islamic citizenship is loyalty to the Islamic State, and the Islamic system.

b. All citizens of the Islamic state are entitled to enjoy the divine rights and duties.

Article 8: The Arabic language is the single language of Islam, and it is the single language used by the Islamic state.

Article 9: Every individual is innocent until proven guilty, and no-one shall be punished without a court sentence. Torture is absolutely forbidden and whoever inflicts torture on anyone shall be punished.

Article 10: Things are permitted in origin, as long as there is no evidence of prohibition, dislike, obligation, or recommendation.

Article 11: All Muslims carry the responsibilities of Islam, and therefore there is no clergy in Islam. The state must prohibit anything that indicates the existence of clergy.

Article 12: Carrying the invitation to Islam is the primary action of the state.

*The Ruling System*

Article 13: The ruling system is founded upon four principles:

1. Sovereignty belongs to the Sharia.
2. Authority belongs to the *Umma*.
3. The appointment of one caliph is an obligation upon all Muslims.
4. Only the caliph has the right to adopt the Sharia laws and thus he passes the constitution and the various canons.

Article 14: The rule is centralised, and administration is de-centralised.

Article 15: The institutions of the state are established upon seven pillars:

a. The caliph
b. The executive body (the assistants)
c. The governors
d. The judges
e. The army
f. The administrative system
g. The *Shura* (consultative) council.

Article 16: Those who represent the views of the people to the caliph are the *Shura* council.

Article 17: Whoever carries Islamic citizenship, and is adult and sane, has the right to be a member of the *Shura* council, and to elect its members, irrespective of whether they are Muslim or non-Muslim, male or female.

# APPENDIX II

## LITERATURE

*A. Titles of adopted books of Hizb-ut-Tahrir*

*al-Amwal fi Dawla al-Khilafa* (The Funds in the Caliphate)
*al-Dawla al-Islamiyya* (The Islamic State)
*al-Nitham al-Hukm fi-l-Islam* (The Ruling System in Islam)
*al-Nitham al-ijtimaʿi fi-l-Islam* (The Social System in Islam)
*al-Nitham al-Iqtisadi fi-l-Islam* (The Economic System in Islam)
*al-Nitham al-Islami* (The System of Islam)
*al-Shakhsiyya al-Islamiyyah 1–3* (The Islamic Personality, volumes 1–3)
*al-Takattul al-Hizbi* (The Party formation)
*Mafahim Hizb-ut-Tahrir* (Concepts of Hizb-ut-Tahrir),
*Mafahim Siyasiyyah li Hizb-ut-Tahrir* (Political Concepts of Hizb-ut-Tahrir)
*Muqaddima al-Dustur* (Introduction to the Constitution)
*Nasharat u-Sayr* (The Progress Booklets)
*Natharat Siyasiyya li Hizb-ut-Tahrir* (Political Views of Hizb-ut-Tahrir)
(Any book that contains the words 'from the leaflets of Hizb-ut-Tahrir' is also
considered to be an adopted book.)

*B. Titles of non-adopted books published by Hizb-ut-Tahrir*

*Ahkam al-Salah* (Rules of Prayer)
*Ahkam ul-Bayyinat* (Rules of Prosecution Evidences)
*al-Fikr al-Islami* (The Islamic Thought)
*al-Nitham al-Uqubat* (Penal Code)
*al-Siyasa al-Iqtisadiyyah al-Muthla* (The Politics of Economic Policy)

*al-Tafkir* (Thinking)
*Kayfa Hudimat al-Khilafa* (How the Caliphate was Destroyed)
*Naqd al-Ishtirakiyya al-Marxiyya* (Refutation of Marxist Socialism)
*Sur'a al-Badiha* (Presence of Mind/Quick intuition)

# APPENDIX III

## ILLUSTRATIONS

*People and events*

### Al-Nabhani and scholarly influences

Sheikh Yusuf al-Nabhani
1849–1932

Sheikh Muhammad al-Khidr
Hussain 1876–1958

Sheikh Taqiudeen al-Nabhani
1911–77

### Leadership Committee 1955–77

Sheikh Ahmad al-Da'ur
1909–2001

Sheikh Taqiudeen al-Nabhani
(after going into hiding)

Sheikh Abdul Qadeem
Zallum 1924–2003

## Prominent early members who subsequently left Hizb-ut-Tahrir

Sheikh Abdul Aziz al-Badri
1932–69

Sheikh Asad al-Bayoud
al-Tamimi 1925–98

Sheikh Abdul Aziz al-Khayyat
1924–2011

## Victims among Hizb-ut-Tahrir members

Muhammad Mustafa Ramadan, assassinated by the Gaddafi regime, shot outside London's Regent's Park mosque after Friday prayers on 11 April 1980 by two Libyan agents.

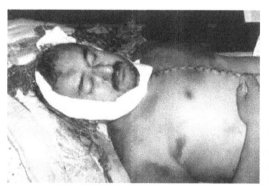

A picture of the body of Farhad Usmanov (showing signs of torture), returned to his family after being held by the Karimov regime in Uzbekistan (1999).

## Contemporary Hizb-ut-Tahrir events

A crowd of 100,000 attended the Hizb-ut-Tahrir Khilafah Conference, Jakarta, Gelora Bung Karno stadium, on 12 August 2007.

Advertisements in Khartoum for Hizb-ut-Tahrir's international economics conference held on 3 January 2009.

Thousands attending an international *'ulama'* (scholars) conference on 21 July 2009 in Istora Senayan, Jakarta.

Tens of thousands attend the Khilafah conference held by Hizb-ut-Tahrir Palestine in Ramallah on 17 June 2012.

Selected pictures of sources

On 6 July 1932 *Al-Karmil* newspaper, Haifa, published an article celebrating the achievement of Taqiudeen al-Nabhani on graduating from Dar al-Ulum university in Egypt (the full article is printed in the far left column under the title *al-Ustadh al-Nabhani*).

The front and contents pages of the 1951 sixth issue of *al-Wa'i al-Jadid* (The New Awareness). The final article entitled *al-Nitham al-Islami* (The Islamic System) was written by al-Nabhani, but was redacted from the contents, presumably for security reasons.

258

A copy of the front page of the 1952, first edition of *al-Dawla al-Islamiyya* (The Islamic State) written by al-Nabhani.

Copies of newspapers covering the case of Hizb-ut-Tahrir members arrested in Tunisia.

The upper paper is the 26 August 1983 edition of the Tunisian daily *Watha'iq*.

The lower paper is the 29 August 1983 edition of the Lebanese weekly *An-Nahar Arab and International*.

A picture printed in the 5 October 2004 edition of *al-Nahar* showing a sign in Tripoli regarding the arrest of Hizb-ut-Tahrir member Wasim Sha'rani in Lebanon linked to planned protests requesting the expulsion of the US ambassador and Iraqi prime minister Ayad Allawi from Lebanon. The sign asks, 'For how long will the decision to arrest the sincere sons of the Muslims remain in the hands of the American embassy?'

A copy of the third page of a Lebanese court judgment of 29 December 2005, from the Criminal Court, Beirut (Case number 2005/14846), which found the two defendants Muhammad al-Tayish and Sharif al-Hallaq innocent of any crime, given they were distributing the leaflets publicly and openly promoting Hizb-ut-Tahrir materials, which contained political views and opinions that called on others to adopt them.

A copy of the front page of a twelve-page special supplement on Hizb-ut-Tahrir printed in the Egyptian newspaper *Al-Wathiqa* on 6 July 2012.

# NOTES

## INTRODUCTION

1. Amin Shinnar, *Al-Mash'al Al-Khalid*, Al-Bira: Matba' al-Sharq, 1957.
2. Shahab Jaffary, 'Hizbut Tahrir Complicates Military's Terrorism Calculus', *Pakistan Today*, http://bit.ly/SYBVo6.
3. Equivalent to 3 Mar. 1924.
4. Commonly known as Saladin in Western Europe, he was a Kurdish Muslim who in the twelfth century united disparate Muslim forces across Egypt and Syria and led them in several successful campaigns against the Crusaders, including the Battle of Hittin, which was marked as a turning point in the conflict between Muslim and Crusader forces.
5. Qutuz was a Mamluk leader in the thirteenth century who led successful campaigns against the Mongols in the region of modern-day Syria, including the Battle of Ain Jalut in 1260, recognised as the turning point in the military fortunes of the Mongols.
6. Referred to as Sultan Mehmet the Conqueror, he conquered Constantinople and brought an end to the Byzantine Empire in 1453 while still in his early 20s.
7. For a detailed discussion regarding the meaning of the consensus in normative Islamic scholarship on the obligation of the Muslim community to elect a single ruler to govern them according to Islamic law (with the system usually termed the caliphate and the ruler as the caliph), see the introduction of my previous book, Reza Pankhurst, *The Inevitable Caliphate?*, London: Hurst & Co., 2013.
8. Hizb-ut-Tahrir, *Waqa'i Nida Hizb Ut-Tahrir Illa Al-Umma Al-Islamiyya*, n.d., p. 27. The complete text of the address is from pp. 11–27.
9. Our Correspondent, 'Call to Revive Khilafat', *The News International*, 3 Sept. 2005.
10. 'Hizb Stresses Need for Khilafah', *The Nation*, 3 Sept. 2005.
11. The call was distributed in locations in India, Afghanistan, UAE, Saudi Arabia, Kuwait, Syria, Egypt, Palestine, Tunisia, Morocco, and Algeria; and was read out

in Malaysia, Bangladesh, Pakistan, Kazakhstan, Kyrgyzstan, Uzbekistan, Tajikistan, Yemen, Jordan, Iraq, Lebanon, Sudan and Turkey.

12. Hizb-ut-Tahrir collected and printed copies of media reaction from seventeen of the countries where the call was delivered, as part of a 309-page report describing the activities undertaken and any responses from the political medium; Hizb-ut-Tahrir, *Waqa'i*.

13. Muhammad Muhsin Radi, 'Hizb Ut-Tahrir: Thiqafatahu Wa Minhajahu Fi Iqama Dawla Al-Khilafa Al-Islamiyya', The Islamic University, 2006, p. 100.

14. Lucy Williamson, 'Stadium Crowd Pushed for Islamist Dream', BBC News, http://bbc.in/QNUYBG.

15. Hizb ut-Tahrir, *Hizb Ut-Tahrir*, 2nd edn., 2010, p. 23.

16. Ibid., pp. 35–6.

17. WorldPublicOpinion.org, 'Muslim Public Opinion on US Policy, Attacks on Civilians and Al-Qaeda', The Center for International and Security Studies at Maryland, 2007, p. 15.

18. Ian Cobain, 'Islamist Group Challenges Berlin's Five-Year Ban in European Court', *The Guardian*, 24 June 2008.

19. Ariel Cohen, 'Hizb Ut Tahrir: An Emerging Threat to US Interests in Central Asia', *Heritage Foundation Backgrounder*, 1656 (2003).

20. Michael Fredholm, 'Uzbekistan & the Threat from Islamic Extremism', Camberley: Conflict Studies Research Centre, 2003.

21. Zeyno Baran, *The Challenge of Hizb Ut-Tahrir*, Ankara, Turkey: Nixon Center, 2004.

22. The Heritage Foundation is an influential conservative think-tank based in Washington, DC, the Conflict Studies Research Centre was part of the UK Defense Academy in 2003 and the Nixon Center is another Washington-based public policy think-tank.

23. Malik Asad, 'Hizbut Tahrir Made Three Attempts to Penetrate Army', *Dawn*, 29 Oct. 2012.

24. Jamie Doward and Gaby Hinsliff, 'PM Shelves Islamic Group Ban', *The Guardian*, 24 Dec. 2006.

25. Martin Bright, 'Losing the Plot', *New Statesman*, 30 Jan. 2006.

26. Kamran Yousaf, 'Army chief in London: UK urged to act against HuT, Baloch separatists', *The Express Tribune*, 15 Jan. 2015

27. Zeyno Baran, *Hizb Ut-Tahrir Islam's Political Insurgency*, Washington, DC: The Nixon Center, 2004.

28. Rohan Gunaratna, 'Links with Islamist Groups: Ideology and Operations', in *The Challenge of Hizb ut-Tahrir*, ed. Zeyno Baran, Ankara, Turkey: Nixon Center, 2004. Shiv Malik, 'For Allah and the Caliphate', *New Statesman*, 13 Sept. 2004.

29. Jean-François Mayer, 'Hizb Ut-Tahrir—the Next Al-Qaida, Really?', *PSIO Occasional Paper*, 2004: p. 11.

30. Emmanuel Karagiannis, 'Hizb Ut-Tahrir Al-Islami: Evaluating the Threat Posed by a Radical Islamic Group That Remains Nonviolent', *Terrorism and Political Violence* 18, no. 2, 2006: p. 316.

31. Suha Taji-Farouki, *A Fundamental Quest: Hizb Al-Tahrir and the Search for the Islamic Caliphate*, London: Grey Seal Limited, 1996.

32. Well-researched academic work in Arabic on Hizb ut-Tahrir. Radi. Turki Abdul-Majid al-Samani, *Taqiudeen Al-Nabhani Wa Mashru'ihi Al-Fikri Wa-L-Siyasi*, Baghdad: University of Baghdad, 2012.

33. Auni al-Ubaidi, *Hizb Ut-Tahrir Al-Islami*, Amman: Dar al-liwa li-l-Sahafa wa-l-Nashr, 1993.

34. Ali Ismadi, interview by author, Jordan, 25 June 2012.

35. Emmanuel Karagiannis, 'Political Islam in Central Asia: Hizb Ut-Tahrir Al-Islami', *Europe-Asia Studies* 58, no. 2 (2006): p. 265.

36. Fredholm, p. 13.

37. ''Itiqalat Fi Hizb Ut-Tahrir Al-Islami Fi Suriya', Syria News, http://www.syria-news.com/readnews.php?sy_seq=151.

38. Owen Bowcott, 'Egypt Pressed over 'Torture' of Britons', *The Guardian*, 21 Sept. 2002.

39. Annahar—Beirut, 'Ahmad Fatfat: Hasan Nasrullah Kan Yahmi 'Fath Al-Islam' Fi-L-Barid', *Annahar*, 6 Oct. 2007.

40. Annahar—Beirut, 'Ahmad Fatfat: La Mani' Min Al-Tarkhis Li 'Hizb Ut-Tahrir' Wa in Kunna Nakhtalif Ma'ahu Fi-L-Rai' '*Annahar*, 25 June 2006.

41. HTTunisia, 'Masira Hizb Ut-Tahrir Tunis Yawm 14 Janafi 2011', http://www.youtube.com/watch?v=6ZkyWAFAb-w.

42. 'Mulhaq Khas 'an Hizb Ut-Tahrir', *Al-Wathiqa*, 6 July 2012.

43. This is based on part of one of the narrations attributed to the Prophet Muhammad where he is reported to have said:

    There will be Prophethood for as long as Allah wills it to be, then He will remove it when He wills, then there will be caliphate on the Prophetic method and it will be for as long as Allah wills, then He will remove it when He wills, then there will be biting kingship for as long as Allah Wills, then He will remove it when He wills, then there will be oppressive kingship for as long as Allah wills, then he will remove it when He wills, and then there will be caliphate (once again) upon the Prophetic method.

    This is found in: Ahmad bin Hanbal, *Musnad Al-Imam Ahmad Bin Hanbal* (Beirut: Muassisa al-Risala, 1999), vol. 30, p. 355, narration 18406.

44. Muslim Aziz, 'Nitham Bashar Yatahim Hizb Ut-Tahrir Bi-Ish'al a-Thawra', http://www.youtube.com/watch?v=_y3CNtWnIUw

45. Dalia Shams, 'Al-Natiq Al-Siyasi Li-Liwa Amru Bin Al-As', *Al-Shuruq*, 22 Nov. 2012.

46. Jamal Harwood, 26 July 2010.

47. Al-Jazeera, 'Al-Islamiyun—Hizb Ut-Tahrir', Qatar, 2009.

48. Emmanuel Karagiannis, *Political Islam in Central Asia*, London: Routledge, 2009.

49. Claudia Nef, 'Promoting the Caliphate on Campus: Debates and Advocacies of Hizbut Tahrir Student Activists in Indonesia', in *Demystifying the Caliphate*, eds Madawi al-Rasheed, Carool Kersten and Marat Shterin, London: Hurst & Co., 2013.

## 1.  TAQIUDEEN AL-NABHANI (1911–48)

1. 'Al-Ustadh Al-Nabhani', *Al-Karmil*, 6 July 1932.

2. Efrat Ben-Ze'ev, 'The Palestinian Village of Ijzim During the 1948 War: Forming an Anthropological History through Villagers Accounts and Army Documents', http://www.palestineremembered.com/Haifa/Ijzim/Story21109.html.

3. Qur'an: Chapter 17, Verse 1.

4. Abul Husain, 'Asakir-ud-Din Muslim', *Sahih Muslim*, Beirut: Dar al-Fikr, 1998, vol. 5, p. 87, narration 415.

5. Hanbal, vol. 5, p. 18, narration 21646.

6. Mohsin Muhammad Salih, *Al-Tayyar Al-Islami Fi Filistin Wa Atharahu Fi Haraka Al-Jihad 1917–48*, Kuwait: Maktaba al-Falah, 1989, pp. 45–7, 50, 73.

7. Walid Khalidi, *All That Remains: The Palestinian Villages Occupied and Depopulated by Israel in 1948*, Washington, DC: Institute for Palestine Studies, 1992, p. 164.

8. For example, Ihsan Samara in *Mafhum Al-'Adala Al-Ijtima'iyya Fi Al-Fikr Al-Islami Al-Mu'asir* (Jerusalem: Al-Risala, 1987, p. 140) claims 1909, influencing most subsequent accounts, such as Taji-Farouki (p. 9): 1909; al-Ubaidi (p. 45): 1909 or 1910; and Hisham Ulaywan in *Al-Sheikh Taqiudeen Al-Nabahani* (Beirut: Center of Civilisation for the Development of Islamic Thought, 2009, p. 15): 1914.

9. Ibrahim al-Nabhani, interview by author, Sweden, 12 May 2012.

10. Samara, p. 140.

11. al-Nabhani, interview.

12. Marwan Murshid Rashid Ubaid, interview by author, Jordan, 19 June 2012.

13. al-Nabhani, interview.

14. Adil Manna, *A'lam Filastin Fi Awakhir Al-'Ahd Al-'Uthmani (1800–1918)*, Beirut: Institute for Palestine Studies, 1990, pp. 349–52.

15. al-Nabhani, interview.

16. Abdul Razzaq al-Baytar, *Hilyutu Al-Bashar Fi Tarikh Al-Qarn Al-Thalithi Al-'Ashr*, Beirut: Dar Sadir, 1993, vol. 3, p. 1612. al-Ubaidi, pp. 37–8.

17. B. Abu-Manneh, 'Sultan Abdulhamid and Shaikh Abulhuda Al-Sayyadi', *Middle Eastern Studies in Intelligence* 15, no. 2 (1979): p. 138.

18. Al-Ubaidi, p. 38.

19. Yusuf al-Nabhani, *Kitab Al-Ahadith Al-Arba'in Fi Wujub Ta'a Amir Al-Mu'minin*, Beirut: Al-Matba' al-Ababiya, 1894.

20. Yusuf al-Nabhani, *Jami' Karamat Al-Awliya*, Gujrat: Markaz-e-Ahl-e-Sunnat Barkat-e-Raza, 2001.

21. Yusuf al-Nabhani, *Kitab Al-Ahadith Al-Arba'in Fi Fadl Al-Jihad Wa-L-Mujahidin*, Beirut: Dar al-Basha'ir al-Islamiyya, 1970.

22. Yusuf al-Nabhani, *Al-Majmu'a Al-Nabhaniyya Fi-L-Mada'ih Al-Nabawiyya*, Beirut: Dar al-Kutub al-'ilmiyya, 1996.

23. The poem was entitled *al-Ra'iya al-Sughra*.

24. Al-Ubaidi, p. 40.

25. In books of *usul al-fiqh*—the basis or foundations of jurisprudence—*ijtihad* is normally defined as the comprehensive exertion of a jurist (through the application of certain defined principles) to derive an Islamic ruling by the method of extraction from the Islamic sources. See, for example, Abdul Allah bin Yusuf al-Juda'i, *Tayseer 'Ilm Usul Al-Fiqh*, Beirut: Mu'assa al-Rayyan, 2006, p. 341.

26. Yusuf al-Nabhani, *Kitab Al-Ahadith Al-Arba'in Fi Fadl Al-Jihad Wa-L-Mujahidin*.

27. Al-Ubaidi, p. 44.

28. In origin, the Arabic word *salaf* means predecessors. In an Islamic context, it is meant to refer to the first generation of Muslims, who are considered the exemplars for Muslim practices. When the term was adopted by reformists, it was to claim that they were returning to the original pristine Islamic practice of the *salaf*, which was necessary due to the erosion of correct practice and introduction of innovative practices and beliefs into normative orthodoxy, which have occurred in the centuries since then, up to present time.

29. Hala Fattah, '"Wahhabi" Influences, Salafi Responses', *Journal of Islamic Studies* 14, no. 2 (2003).

30. al-Ubaidi, p. 44.

31. Mahmud Shukri al-Alusi, *Kitab Ghayat Al-Amani Fi-L-Radd Al-Nabhani*, published privately by Abdul Aziz al-Jamih and Muhammad Abdullah al-Jamih, http://ia600304.us.archive.org/21/items/sewsdsewsd/garn1.pdf

32. Al-Ubaidi, p. 46.

33. Abdul-Hadi Abu Mahmoud, interview by author, Lebanon, 4 July 2012.

34. Al-Nabhani, interview.

35. Hizb ut-Tahrir, 'Jawab Su'al 6–5–1970', 1970.

36. Yusuf al-Nabhani, *Jami' Karamat Al-Awliya*, p. 14.

37. Taqiudeen al-Nabhani, *Al-Shakhsiyya Al-Islamiyya—Al-Juz Al-Awwal*, 6th edn., Beirut: Dar al-Umma, 2003, p. 295.

38. The Shafi', Hanafi, Hanbali and Maliki schools of thought, named after their founders, are considered the most authoritative sources of Islamic legal opinion within normative Sunni tradition.

39. For a more detailed discussion of the debates around the abolition of the caliphate in the early 1920s, refer to the second chapter ('The Caliphate between Rejection, Reform and Revival') in Reza Pankhurst, *The Inevitable Caliphate?*, London: Hurst & Co., 2013.

40. al-Nabhani, interview.

41. Samara, p. 141.

42. 'al-Ustadh; al-Nabhani'.

43. al-Waie, 'Buzugh Nur Min Al-Masjid Al-Aqsa', no. 234–5 (2006): p. 12; al-Ubaidi, p. 47. Sheikh Fathi Salim, 'Special Interview with Sheikh Fathi Salim', http://goo.gl/UF4Il

44. Great Britain. Colonial, O. and W. S. Shaw (1930). Report of the Commission on the Palestine disturbances of August, 1929. [S.l.], H.M.S.O.

45. For details of global reaction to the abolition of the caliphate, refer to Mona F. Hassan, 'Loss of Caliphate: The Trauma and Aftermath of 1258 and 1924', Princeton University, 2009.

46. 'Extracts from the Pioneer Mail Dated March 14, 1924', in *The Caliphate Question: deposition of Caliph Abdul Mejid by the Angora Assembly IOR/L/PS/10/1111*, London: India Office, British Library, 1924, pp. 298–301.

47. Tarek al-Bishry, 'Al-Malik Wa-L-Khilafa Al-Islamiyya', *Al-Katib* 13, no. 142 (1973): p. 46.

48. Rashid Rida, 'Inqilab Al-Deeni Al-Siyasi Fee Al-Jumhuriyya Al-Turkiyya', *al-Manar* 25, no. 4 (1924).

49. Rashid Rida, 'Al-Khilafa Wa-L-Mu'tamar Al-Islami', *al-Manar* 25, no. 5 (1924).

50. Further details regarding the conferences held post-1924 can be found in Martin S. Kramer and Merkaz Dayan, *Islam Assembled: The Advent of the Muslim Congresses*, New York: Columbia University Press, 1985.

51. Ali Abdul-Raziq, 'Al-Islam Wa Usul Al-Hukm', in *Al-Islam Wa Usul Al-Hukm— Darasa Wa Watha'iq*, ed. Muhammad 'Amara, Beirut: *Al-Mua'sasa al-Arabiyya li-l-darasat wa-l-nashr*, 1972.

52. Muhammad 'Amara, *Ma'raka Al-Islam Wa Usul Al-Hukm*, Cairo: Dar al-Sharook, 1997, p. 171.

53. Muhammad al-Khidr Hussein, 'Naqd Kitab Al-Islam Wa Usul Al-Hukm (1925)', in *Ma'raka Al-Islam Wa Usul Al-Hukm*, ed. Muhammad 'Amara, Cairo: Dar al-Sharook, 1997.

54. Other critiques of Raziq's work include: Muhammad Bakhit Al-Mutee'i, *Haqiqa Al-Islam Wa Usul Al-Hukm*, Cairo: Al-Matba'a al-Salifiyya, 1925; Muhammad Al-Tahir ibn 'Ashur, *Naqd 'Ilmy Li Kitab Al-Islam Wa Usul Al-Hukm*, Cairo: Maktaba al-Salafiyya, 1925.

55. Muhammad 'Amara, 'Taha Hussein Wa-L-Khilafa Al-Islamiyya', *Al-Ahram*, 15 Nov. 2011.

56. Taha Hussein, *Fi-L-Shi'ir Al-Jahili*, Susa: Dar al-Ma'arif, 1997.

57. Joseph Glicksberg, 'The 1926 Uproar over Taha Husayn's On Pre-Islamic Poetry:

Islamist-Secularist Debate and the Subversion of Secular Identity in Monarchical Egypt', Philadelphia: American Political Science Association, 2003, p. 2.

58. *Muhammad al-Khidr Hussein, Naqd Kitab Fi-L-Shi'ir Al-Jahili*, Cairo: Al-Maktaba al-Azhariyya li-l-turath, n.d.

59. Majid al-Samani, *Taqiudeen Al-Nabhani Wa Mashru'ihi Al-Fikri Wa-L-Siyasi*, Baghdad: University of Baghdad, 2012, p. 66.

60. Taha Hussein, *Hafiz Wa Shawky*, Cairo: Maktaba al-Khanji, 1933.

61. al-Nabhani, interview.

62. Samara, pp. 141–2.

63. Ziyad Ahmed Salama, interview by author, Jordan, 21 June 2012.

64. Al-Ubaidi, p. 83.

65. Samara, p. 144.

66. Al-Waie, p. 12.

67. Mustafa al-Ja'bari, interview conducted by Dr Badar, Palestine, 23 Aug. 2012.

68. Samara, p. 143.

69. al-Nabhani, interview.

70. Ibid.

71. Samara, p. 144.

72. al-Nabhani, interview.

73. Muhammad Muhammad Hasan al-Shurrab, *Izz Al-Din Al-Qassam: Sheikh Al-Mujahidin Fi Filistin*, Damascus: Dar al-Qalam, 2000, p. 118.

74. Beverley Milton-Edwards, *Islamic Politics in Palestine*, London: Tauris Academic Studies, 1999, pp. 12–13.

75. Al-Shurrab, p. 355.

76. Taqiudeen al-Nabhani, *Inqath Filistin*, Damascus: Ibn Zaydun, 1950, p. 58.

77. al-Nabhani, interview.

78. A British Foreign Office report in 1920 mentioned that the British recruiter for the Arab army, C.D. Bruntun, worked with al-Husseini, who was 'at the time being described as very pro-English', despite officially being a fugitive from British justice at the time, having been accused of complicity in the Easter riots. Cited in Sahar Huneidi, *A Broken Trust: Sir Herbert Samuel, Zionism and the Palestinians*, London: I.B. Tauris, 2001, p. 35.

79. Salih, p. 278.

80. Milton-Edwards, p. 12.

81. Sheikh Taleb Awadallah, 'The Beloveds of Allah—Emergence of Light from Al-Aqsa Mosque—Launch of Hizb Ut-Tahrir's March', 2006, p. 68.

82. Salih, p. 444.

83. Faisal al-Shabul, 'Muthakarrat (Interview with Abdul-Aziz Al-Khayyat)', *Al-Wasat*, 10–16 July 1995, p. 33.

84. Ulaywan, p. 75.

85. Al-Shabul, p. 33.

86. Al-Hiwar, 'Memoirs with Munir Shafiq', http://goo.gl/ZL9HL.
87. Rashid Khalidi, *The Iron Cage: The Story of the Palestinian Struggle for Statehood*, Oxford: Oneworld Publications, 2006, p. 108.
88. Taqiudeen al-Nabhani, *Inqath Filistin*, p. 139.
89. al-Nabhani, interview.

## 2. THE BIRTH OF HIZB-UT-TAHRIR (1948–1953)

1. Taqiudeen al-Nabhani, *Nitham al-Islam*, 2nd edn., Jerusalem, 1953, p. 32.
2. Taqiudeen al-Nabhani, *al-Takattul al-Hizbi*, 4th edn., 2001, p. 24.
3. Ibrahim al-Nabhani, interview by author, Sweden, 12 May 2012.
4. Ziyad Ahmed Salama, *Faqir Min Bilad al-Sham*, Amman: Dar al-Salam, 2007, p. 76. Alhough Samara claims that al-Nabhani resigned to run for election in April 1950, as does Taji-Farouki (likely based on Samara's claim), al-Nabhani's address to a conference in Alexandria, Egypt, in August 1950 introduced him as a member of the appeals court in Jerusalem. This indicates that Samara was in fact mistaken, and the elections that al-Nabhani resigned to take part in were those of 1951 and not 1950, as mentioned by al-Nabhani's close associate at the time, Sheikh Abdul Aziz al-Khayyat.
5. Samara, pp. 143–4; al-Nabhani, interview.
6. Ilan Pappé and St Antony's College, *Britain and the Arab-Israeli Conflict 1948–51*, Basingstoke: Macmillan, in association with St Antony's College, Oxford, 1988, pp. ix.
7. Ibid., p. 11.
8. Avi Shlaim, 'Israel and the Arab Coalition in 1948', in *The War for Palestine: Rewriting the History of 1948*, eds Eugene L. Rogan and Avi Shlaim, Cambridge: Cambridge University Press, 2001, p. 81.
9. al-Nabhani, *al-Takattul*, p. 24. The full sentence in the book reads, 'Vitality usually streams into the *Ummah* when severe shocks in the society produce a common feeling.'
10. Abdullah al-Tall, *Karitha Filistin*, 2nd edn., Alexandria: Dar al-Huda, 1990, p. 460.
11. Douglas Little, 'Cold War and Covert Action: The United States and Syria, 1945–1958', *Middle East Journal* 44, no. 1 (1990): pp. 55–6.
12. Betty S. Anderson, *Nationalist Voices in Jordan: The Street and the State*, Austin, TX: University of Texas Press and Chesham: Combined Academic [distributor], 2005, p. 136.
13. al-Tall, p. 591.
14. Samara, p. 145.
15. al-Nabhani, interview; Samara, p. 145; Sheikh Taleb Awadallah, 'The Beloveds of Allah—Emergence of Light from Al-Aqsa Mosque—Launch of Hizb Ut-Tahrir's March', 2006, p. 83.

16. Taji-Farouki, pp. 3–4.
17. Salama, interview.
18. Hizb-ut-Tahrir, 'Muthakirra Hizb Al-Tahrir Li Ra'is Wa 'Ada Majlis Al-'Ayan Wa-L-Nawab Fi-L-Urdan', 1960.
19. al-Shabul, p. 33.
20. Taqiudeen al-Nabhani, *Inqath Filistin*, p. 3.
21. Ibid., p. 4.
22. Ibid., p. 12.
23. Ibid., p. 14. Al-Nabhani mentions that he made this point clear in a previous book, *Nitham al-mujtama'* (The System of Society). Unfortunately, I was unable to find any further information regarding this book.
24. Ibid., p. 18.
25. Ibid., p. 58.
26. Ibid., p. 66.
27. Ibid., pp. 91–5.
28. Ibid., p. 139.
29. Ibid., pp. 144–5.
30. Ibid., p. 164.
31. Ibid., p. 169.
32. Ibid., p. 178.
33. Ibid., p. 187.
34. Ibid., p. 190.
35. Salama, interview.
36. Taqiudeen al-Nabhani, 'Risala Al-Arab', Alexandria, 1950.
37. Taqiudeen al-Nabhani, 'Al-Nitham Al-Islami', *Al-Wa'i al-jadid* 1, no. 6, 1951.
38. al-Ubaidi, p. 53.
39. *Risala al-Arab* is mentioned as one of the books of Hizb-ut-Tahrir in the introductions of the following first editions printed in 1953, among others, including *al-Nitham al-Islami*; Taqiudeen al-Nabhani, *Al-Shakhsiyya Al-Islamiyya*, 1st edn., Amman: Al-Maktaba al-'Amma, 1952; Taqiudeen al-Nabhani, *Al-Dawla Al-Islamiyya*, 1st edn., Damascus: al-Manar, 1952. By the second edition of books, printed in 1953, it was no longer mentioned, e.g. al-Nabhani, *al-Nitham al-Islami*; Taqiudeen al-Nabhani, *Nitham Al-Iqtisad*, 2nd edn., Jerusalem, 1953.
40. al-Nabhani, interview.
41. Samara, p. 145.
42. Sabri Aruri, interview by author, Jordan, 19 June 2012.
43. Salama, *Faqir*, pp. 8–12.
44. al-Shabul, p. 30.
45. Salama, *Faqir*, p. 65.
46. al-Shabul, p. 33.

47. Ibid., p. 32.
48. Salama, *Faqir*, p. 69.
49. al-Shabul, p. 32, 34.
50. Salama, *Faqir*, p. 90.
51. al-Shabul, p. 33.
52. Ibid.
53. al-Nabhani, *al-Takattul*, p. 7.
54. Salama, *Faqir*, p. 79.
55. al-Hiwar, 'Memoirs with Ibrahim Ghosha', http://goo.gl/0tZTK.
56. Sadiq Amin, *al-Da'wa al-Islamiyya: Farida Shara'iyya Wa Darura Bashariyya*, Amman: Dar al-Tawzi' wa-l-nashr al-islamiyya, n.d., p. 100.
57. al-Ubaidi, pp. 108–9.
58. Radi, p. 52.
59. Abdul-Halim al-Ramahi, interview by author, Jordan, 18 June 2012.
60. Taji-Farouki, p. 6.
61. Dawud Hamdan, 'Hasan Al-Banna Muslih Al-'Asr', *al-Wa'i al-jadid* 1, no. 6 (1951): p. 14.
62. For more discussion on the legacy of Hasan al-Banna between Sayyid Qutb and the current Muslim Brotherhood, refer to Chapter 3 of Reza Pankhurst, *The Inevitable Caliphate?*, London: Hurst & Co., 2013.
63. Hamdan, p. 16.
64. al-Ramahi, interview.
65. al-Shabul, p. 34.
66. al-Ubaidi, p. 7.
67. Salama, *Faqir*, p. 82.
68. al-Ubaidi, p. 79.
69. 'Secret Memo 13 August 1952', in *FO/816/177*, London: Foreign Office, National Archives, 1952.
70. Radi, p. 47.
71. Hasan Muhammad Ali Hudruj, interview by author, Lebanon, 27 June 2012; Yaqub Abu Rumaila, interview conducted by Dr Badar, Palestine, 16 Aug. 2012.
72. Radi, p. 46.
73. Salama, *Faqir*, p. 87.
74. al-Nabhani, interview.
75. Aruri, interview.
76. al-Ja'bari, interview.
77. Rumaila, interview.
78. Awadallah, p. 38.
79. Rumaila, interview.
80. Qadri Dawud al-Nabulsi, interview by author, Jordan, 25 June 2012.
81. Hudruj, interview.

82. Abdul Halim Zallum, interview by author, Jordan, 21 June 2012.
83. al-Nabulsi, interview.
84. Aruri, interview.
85. Abu Mahmoud, interview.
86. al-Nabhani, *Al-Shakhsiyya Al-Islamiyya*, pp. 2–5.
87. Ibid., pp. 7–10.
88. al-Ubaidi, p. 12.
89. al-Ramahi, interview.
90. al-Nabhani, *Al-Dawla*, p. 6.
91. Al-Nabhani, *Nitham Al-Islam*, pp. 7–8.
92. Ahmad al-Faqir, interview by author, Jordan, 20 and 25 June 2012.
93. Salim.
94. al-Nabhani.
95. al-Nabhani, *Nitham Al-Islam*, p. 76.
96. Hizb-ut-Tahrir, 'Bayan Min Hizb Ut-Tahrir Al-Muqaddam Li-L-Hukuma Al-'Ordaniyya 1/6/1953', 1953.
97. Amnon Cohen, 'Political Parties in the West Bank under the Hashemite Regime', in *Palestinan Arab Politics*, ed. Moshe Ma'oz, Jerusalem: Jerusalem Academic Press, 1975, p. 28.
98. al-Waie, p. 15.
99. Samara, p. 147.
100. al-Waie, p. 15.
101. Salama, *Faqir*, pp. 82–3.
102. Ibid., p. 83.
103. Hizb-ut-Tahrir, 'Bayan 1/6/1953'.
104. al-Ubaidi, p. 8.
105. Taji-Farouki, p. 8.
106. The three initial books studied by anyone in *halaqa* are *al-Nitham al-Islami* (The System of Islam), *Mafahim Hizb ut-Tahrir* (Concepts of Hizb ut-Tahrir) and *al-Takattul al-Hizbi* (The Party Formation)
107. Awadallah, p. 44.
108. al-Faqir, interview.
109. Ibid.
110. Al-Jazeera, 'The Palestinian Revolution According to the View of Muhammad Dawud Owda, 24 July 1999', http://goo.gl/1pLk3
111. al-Nabulsi, interview.
112. Salama, *Faqir*, p. 85.
113. al-Samani, p. 117.
114. Abu Mahmoud, interview.
115. Dr Falah Abdullah al-Madaris, *Hizb Ut-Tahrir Fi Kuwait*, Kuwait: Dar al-Qurtas, 2007, p. 50.

116. Radi, p. 61.
117. Muhammad al-Aleisi, *Abdul Aziz Al-Badri—Al-'Alim Al-Mujahid Al-Shahid*, Amman: Dar al-Bayareq, 2001, pp. 61–7.
118. Radi, p. 61.

## 3. TRYING TO ENTER SOCIETY (1954–1959)

1. Shinnar, p. 7.
2. Dawud Hamdan, *Usus Al-Nahda*, Beirut: Dar al-Kasshaf, 1953.
3. One of al-Nabhani's sons had a brief sojourn with the Ba'ath party that he put down to teenage rebellion, which had the effect of upsetting his father when he found out. He soon left the Ba'athists, and joined Hizb-ut-Tahrir some years later, unbeknown to his father. The son took pride in the fact that he had become convinced about Hizb-ut-Tahrir independently of his father, and recounted how he had decided to join after reading the 1963 book *Naqd al-Ishtirakiyya al-Marxiyya* (Refutation of Marxist socialism), which he believed was written by Ghanim Abdu, whose name was on the cover. Ironically, as with most other books published by Hizb-ut-Tahrir under names other than al-Nabhani's, the book was in fact written by al-Nabhani himself and attributed to Abdu to promote him as a public figure.
4. Ibrahim al-Nabhani, interview by author, Sweden, 12 May 2012.
5. Amnon Cohen, *Political Parties in the West Bank under Jordanian Regime 1949–1967*, London: Cornell University Press, 1982, p. 215.
6. Cohen, 'Political Parties in the West Bank under the Hashemite Regime', p. 40.
7. al-Jazeera.
8. Quoted in al-Ubaidi, p. 66.
9. al-Hiwar, 'Shafiq'.
10. al-Hiwar, 'Ghosha'.
11. al-Hiwar, 'Shafiq'.
12. Abu Muhammad, interview by author, UK, 4 April 2012; Zallum, interview.
13. US Embassy (Amman) to State Department, 27 Nov. 1954, NA 785.00/11–2754. Referenced in Shmuel Bar, *The Muslim Brotherhood in Jordan*, Tel Aviv: Moshe Dayan Center for Middle Eastern and African Studies, 1998.
14. D.M. Summerhayes, 'Annual Political Review for Jordan 1954', in *FO/371/115635*, London: Foreign Office, National Archives, 1955.
15. 'Secret Memo 13 August 1952', in FO/816/177, London: Foreign Office, National Archives, 1952.
16. 'From Amman to Foreign Office 31 December 1957', in *FO/371/134008*, London: Foreign Office, National Archives, 1957.
17. John Bagot Glubb, *A Soldier with the Arabs*, London: Hodder and Stoughton, 1957, pp. 349–50.

18. Nasif Abdul Latif al-Khatib, interview by author, Lebanon, 3 July 2012.
19. Clinton Bailey, *Jordan's Palestinian Challenge, 1948–1983: A Political History*, Boulder, CO and London: Westview, 1984, p. 8.
20. Al-Hiwar, 'Ghosha'.
21. Abu Muhammad, interview.
22. Cohen, *Political Parties*, p. 211.
23. Abu Mahmoud, interview.
24. Al-Hiwar, 'Shafiq'.
25. al-Nabulsi, interview.
26. Ibid.
27. Fawzi Musa Muhammad Nasir, interview by author, Kuwait, 16–17 June 2012.
28. Aruri, interview.
29. al-Nabhani, *al-Takattul*, pp. 30–1.
30. Hudruj, interview.
31. Faruq Habayib, interview by author, Kuwait, 15 June 2012.
32. Taji-Farouki, p. 10.
33. al-Nabhani, *al-Takattul*, p. 36.
34. Hizb-ut-Tahrir, *Nuqta al-Intilaq Li Hizb Ut-Tahrir*, 1954, p. 1.
35. Ibid., pp. 1–4.
36. Ibid.
37. Ibid., pp. 4–7.
38. Ibid., pp. 9–10.
39. al-Ubaidi, p. 22.
40. al-Nabulsi, interview.
41. 'Secret Memo 13 August 1952', in FO/816/177, London: Foreign Office, National Archives, 1952.
42. Hizb-ut-Tahrir, *Nuqta al-Intilaq*, p. 15.
43. al-Ubaidi, pp. 71–2.
44. Salama, *Faqir*, p. 87.
45. al-Ubaidi, p. 73.
46. Glubb, pp. 350, 354–5.
47. Sheikh Taleb Awadallah, 'The Beloveds of Allah—Emergence of Light from Al-Aqsa Mosque—Launch of Hizb Ut-Tahrir's March', 2006, p. 69.
48. Abu Iyas, interview by author, Jordan, 24 June 2012.
49. Habayib, interview.
50. Aruri, interview; Awadallah, p. 212.
51. Zallum, interview.
52. Abu Muhammad, interview.
53. Zallum, interview.
54. al-Nabulsi, interview.
55. Taji-Farouki, p. 11.

56. John Calvert, *Sayyid Qutb and the Origins of Radical Islamism*, London: Hurst & Co., 2010, p. 187.
57. al-Nabulsi, interview.
58. Radi, p. 62.
59. Rafiq al-Dik, interview by author, Lebanon, 29 June 2012.
60. al-Khatib, interview.
61. al-Nabhani, interview.
62. Radi, p. 72.
63. al-Ubaidi, pp. 61.
64. Salama, *Faqir*, p. 84.
65. Cohen, *Political Parties*, p. 213.
66. Salama, *Faqir*, p. 84.
67. Abu Muhammad, interview.
68. Thomas R. Dye and L. Harmon Zeigler, *The Irony of Democracy: An Uncommon Introduction to American Politics*, Millennial edn., Fort Worth: Harcourt Brace College Publishers, 2000.
69. Hizb-ut-Tahrir, 'Naqd al-Qanun al-Madani', 1955.
70. Ibid.
71. Hizb ut-Tahrir, 'Bayan Fi Majlis Al-Nawwab', 1955.
72. Cohen, *Political Parties*, p. 224.
73. John Foster Dulles, 'Speech Made before the Council on Foreign Relations, New York, N. Y., on Aug. 26 (Press Release 517)', ed. US State Department, Office of Public Communications, 1955.
74. Aruri, interview.
75. Abu Mu'tasim, interview by author, Kuwait, 16 June 2012.
76. al-Ubaidi, pp. 67–9.
77. Cohen, *Political Parties*, pp. 187–9.
78. Ali al-Tantawi, 'Nasiha', *Al-Muslimum* 2, no. 26 (1955).
79. B. Kemal Yesilbursa, *The Baghdad Pact: Anglo-American Defence Policies in the Middle East, 1950–1959*, London: Frank Cass, 2005, p. 140.
80. Beverley Milton-Edwards and Peter Hinchcliffe, *Jordan: A Hashemite Legacy*, 2nd edn., London: Routledge, 2009, p. 35.
81. al-Hiwar, 'Memoirs with Munir Shafiq'.
82. Hamdan was expelled from the party in 1956 due to a leadership conflict with al-Nabhani, as is addressed in the subsequent section.
83. Salama, *Faqir*, pp. 87–8.
84. al-Nabulsi, interview.
85. Salama, *Faqir*, p. 94.
86. al-Ubaidi, p. 86.
87. 'From Amman to Foreign Office 20 March 1957', in *FO/371/127878*, London: Foreign Office, National Archives, 1957.

88. al-Faqir, interview.

89. Cohen, *Political Parties*, p. 147.

90. Lawrence Tal, 'Britain and the Jordan Crisis of 1958', *Middle Eastern Studies* 31, no. 1 (1995): p. 50.

91. Cohen, *Political Parties*, p. 186.

92. Uriel Dann, *King Hussein and the Challenge of Arab Radicalism: Jordan, 1955–1967*, New York and Oxford: Oxford University Press, 1989, p. 17.

93. Ibid., p. 40.

94. 'From Amman to Foreign Office 26 February 1958', in *FO/371/134008*, London: Foreign Office, National Archives, 1958.

95. Eugene L. Rogan, *The Arabs: A History*, New York: Basic Books, 2009, pp. 303–4.

96. Taji-Farouki, p. 14.

97. Abu Iyas, interview.

98. See, for example, Ricky-Dale Calhoun, 'The Musketeer's Cloak: Strategic Deception During the Suez Crisis of 1956', *Studies in Intelligence* 51, no. 2 (2007); Miles Copeland, *The Game Player: Confessions of the CIA's Original Political Operative*, London: Aurum, 1989, pp. 153–5.

99. Abu Sha'lan, interview by author, Jordan, 23 June 2012.

100. al-Ubaidi, pp. 84–5.

101. Zallum, interview; Habayib, interview; al-Ubaidi, p. 70.

102. Ibid., pp. 70–1.

103. al-Madaris, p. 50.

104. al-Nabulsi, interview.

105. Salama, *Faqir*, p. 94.

106. al-Nabulsi, interview.

107. Yusuf al-Ba'darani, 'Al-Wad' Fi Suriyya', 1964.

108. Salama, *Faqir*, p. 89.

109. Nadir al-Tamimi, interview by author, Jordan, 24 June 2012.

110. Awadallah, p. 59.

111. Ali Kawrani al-Alami, 'Illa Talib Al-'Ilm', 2010, p. 223; Talib Aziz, 'Baqir Al-Sadr's Quest for the Marja'iya', in *The Most Learned of the Shi'a: The Institution of the Marja'i Taqlid*, ed. Linda S. Walbridge, New York and Oxford: Oxford University Press, 2001, p. 141.

112. Jamal Sankari, *Fadlallah: The Making of a Radical Shi'ite Leader*, London: Saqi, 2005, p. 85.

113. Hizb-ut-Tahrir, *al-Khilafa*, n.d.

114. al-Khatib, interview.

115. Fayiz Taha, interview by author, Lebanon, 27 and 29 June 2012.

116. Shinnar; Ziyad Ahmed Salama, 'Farhun La Yantahi', Amman: unpublished work, 2011, p. 257.

117. Abu Mu'tasim, interview.

118. Hizb-ut-Tahrir, *Dukhul al-Mujtama'*, 1958, p. 1.

119. Abu Mahmoud, interview.

120. Rogan, pp. 306–8.

121. Tal, p. 41.

122. 'From Amman to Foreign Office 31 December 1957'.

123. Salama, *Faqir*, pp. 89–92.

124. Ibid., p. 29.

125. Habayib, interview; al-Badri's biographer, Muhammad al-Aleisi, believes that he left Tahrir in 1956, but multiple internal sources reported him participating in their activities across the region as a member at the time, and other close contemporaries have provided details of the timing and circumstances of the end of his membership in 1958.

126. al-Aleisi, pp. 69–72.

127. Ibid., pp. 197–205.

128. Jack O'Connell and Vernon Loeb, *King's Counsel: A Memoir of War, Espionage, and Diplomacy in the Middle East*, 1st edn., New York and London: W.W. Norton, 2011, p. 7.

129. Bar, pp. 42–9.

130. Abu Muhammad, interview.

131. Nasir, interview; Zallum, interview; Abu Muhammad, interview.

132. Hizb-ut-Tahrir, *Nuqta al-Intilaq*, pp. 2–8.

133. Ibid., pp. 9–12.

134. al-Dik, interview.

135. al-Nabhani, *al-Takattul*, p. 52.

136. Taji-Farouki, p. 22.

137. Zallum, interview.

138. Abu Mahmoud, interview.

139. Hizb-ut-Tahrir, 'Jawab Su'al 8–5–1970', 1970.

140. Bar, p. 15.

141. US Embassy (Amman) to State Department, 5 February 1955, NA 785.00/2–555; US Embassy (Amman) to State Department, 9 Dec. 1958, NA 785.00/12–958; referenced in ibid., p. 20.

142. Taha, interview.

143. Abu Mahmoud, interview; al-Nabhani, interview.

## 4. ESTABLISHING THE CALIPHATE (1960–1968)

1. Shinnar, p. 95.

2. Abu Mahmoud, interview.

3. al-Ja'bari, interview.

4. Taji-Farouki, p. 22.
5. Falih Abdul Jabbar, *The Shi'ite Movement in Iraq*, London: Saqi, 2003, p. 125.
6. Radi, pp. 61–2.
7. Hizb-ut-Tahrir, 'al-Khitab', 1961.
8. Hizb-ut-Tahrir, 'Jawab Su'al 26–5–62', 1962.
9. Ibid.
10. Hizb-ut-Tahrir, 'Untitled Internal Leaflet 27–1–72', 1972.
11. Hizb-ut-Tahrir, 'Khutut 'Arida 'an Qiyam Al-Hizb Bi-L-'Amal Al-Juz'iyya', 1961.
12. Hizb-ut-Tahrir, 'Jawab Su'al 20–6–69', 1969.
13. Hizb-ut-Tahrir, 'Untitled Internal Leaflet', 1960.
14. Hizb-ut-Tahrir, 'Muthakirra'.
15. Mustafa Zahran and Mahmud Tarshubi, *Hizb Ut-Tahrir—Ya'ud Li-L-Hayat Ma'a-L-Thawrat Al-'Arabiyya*, Cairo: Markaz al-Din wa-l-siyasa li-l-dirasa, 2012, p. 26.
16. Uthman Salhiyya, 'Murafi'a Uthman Salhiyya Amam Mahkama Aman-Al-Dawla Fi Dimasqh', 1960.
17. Interview, Abu Iyas.
18. Hizb-ut-Tahrir, 'Untitled Internal Leaflet 27–1–72'.
19. Hizb-ut-Tahrir, 'Khutut''.
20. Hizb-ut-Tahrir, 'Muqtatafat Siyasiyya', 1961.
21. Hizb-ut-Tahrir, 'Munaqasha Bayn Ithnayn Min Al-Shabab', 1961.
22. Hizb-ut-Tahrir, 'al-Khitab'.
23. Abu Muhammad, interview; Abu Mahmoud, interview.
24. Taqiudeen al-Nabhani, *al-Shakhsiyya al-Islamiyya: al-Juz al-Thani*, 3rd edn., Beirut: Dar al-Umma, 1994, pp. 59–101.
25. Hizbut-Tahrir, *Muqadimma al-Dustor*, 1963.
26. Muhammad Muhammad Ismael, *al-Fikr al-Islami*, 1958.
27. Ahmad al-Da'ur, *al-Ahkam al-Bayyinat*, 1965.
28. Ali Raghib, *al-Ahkam al-Salah*, 1958.
29. Abdul Rahman al-Maliki, *Nitham al-'Uqubat*, 1965.
30. Ghanim Abdu, *Naqd Al-Ishtirakiyya Al-Marksiyya*, 1963.
31. al-Ramahi, interview; Abu Mahmoud; Abdul-Rahim Faris, interview by author, Jordan, 23 June 2012.
32. Samara, p. 151.
33. Hizb-ut-Tahrir, 'Bayan Min Hizb Ut-Tahrir', 1962.
34. Hizb-ut-Tahrir, 'Al-Zu'ama Muslimin Lubnan Yu'adun Al-Jizya Li-L-Hukam Al-Nasara', (1961).
35. Yusuf al-Ba'darani, interview by author, Lebanon, 29 June 2012.
36. Marion Farouk-Sluglett and Peter Sluglett, *Iraq since 1958: From Revolution to Dictatorship*, [Rev. edn.], London: I.B. Tauris, 2001, p. 327. For more details on US involvement with the Ba'ath party read Chapter 3, 'Gun for Hire', in Said K. Aburish, *Saddam Hussein: The Politics of Revenge*, London: Bloomsbury, 2000;

and Harry August Rositzke, *The CIA's Secret Operations: Espionage, Counterespionage, and Covert Action*, New York: Reader's Digest Press, distributed by Crowell, 1977.

37. Radi, p. 64.
38. Hizb-ut-Tahrir, 'Hamla Al-Baba Al-Salabiyya Min 'Ajl Tadwin Al-Quds', 1962.
39. Hizb-ut-Tahrir, 'Khitab Ila-L-Umma Hawl Tadwil Al-Quds', 1963.
40. Ismadi, interview.
41. Cohen, *Political Parties*, p. 212.
42. Hizb-ut-Tahrir, 'Untitled Internal Leaflet 27–1–72'.
43. Hizb-ut-Tahrir, 'Kitab Maftuh Min Hizb Ut-Tahrir Ila-L-Malik Hussein', 1969.
44. Abu Iyas, interview.
45. al-Ba'darani, interview.
46. Yusuf al-Ba'darani, 'Al-Bayan Al-Intikhabiyya', (1964).
47. al-Ba'darani, interview.
48. Yusuf al-Ba'darani, 'Al-Wad' Fi Suriyya', 1964.
49. Zallum, interview.
50. Radi, p. 64.
51. al-Waie, p. 34.
52. Ibrahim Usman, personal communication with author, 25 July 2012.
53. Hizb-ut-Tahrir, 'Untitled Internal Leaflet 27–1–72'.
54. Abu Mahmoud, interview.
55. Hizb-ut-Tahrir, 'Nida' Harr Min Ila-L-Muslimin Min Hizb Ut-Tahrir', Khartoum, 1965.
56. Usman, interview; al-Ba'darani, interview.
57. al-Waie, p. 33.
58. Zallum, interview.
59. Rusen Cakir, 'The Rise and Fall of Turkish Hizb Ut-Tahrir', in *The Challenge of Hizb ut-Tahrir*, ed. Zeyno Baran, Ankara, Turkey: Nixon Center, 2004.
60. al-Waie, pp. 33–5.
61. Hizb-ut-Tahrir, 'Kitab Maftuh Min Hizb Ut-Tahrir Ila-L-Ra'is Al-Wuzara' Suleyman Demirel', 1967.
62. Cakir.
63. Radi, p. 64.
64. Abu Mahmoud, interview; Zallum, interview; al-Nabhani, interview.
65. Radi, p. 64.
66. AP, 'Abdel-Rahman Aref, 91, Former Iraqi President, Is Dead', *The New York Times*, 25 Aug. 2007.
67. Abu Mahmoud, interview.
68. Zallum, interview; Taha, interview.
69. Hizb-ut-Tahrir, 'Al-Ahkam 'Ama', 1966.
70. Raymond A. Hinnebusch, *Syria: Revolution from Above*, London: Routledge, 2001, pp. 44–50.

71. Hizb-ut-Tahrir, 'Ila Mata Tadhil Ahkam Al-Kufr Tutabak Ala-L-Muslimin', 1966.
72. Hizb-ut-Tahrir, 'Al-Ta'liq Al-Siyasi 13–7–1966', 1966.
73. al-Tamimi, interview.
74. Dann, p. 146.
75. Ibid., pp. 150–1.
76. Hizb-ut-Tahrir, 'Al-Ta'liq Al-Siyasi 13–7–1966'.
77. al-Khatib, interview.
78. Taha, interview.
79. al-Faqir, interview.
80. Dann, p. 154.
81. Hizb-ut-Tahrir, 'Al-Ta'liq Al-Siyasi 23–11–1966', 1966.
82. al-Ubaidi, p. 72.
83. al-Faqir, interview.
84. Dann, pp. 162–3.
85. Hizb-ut-Tahrir, 'Bayan Suqut Al-Aqsa', 1967.
86. Hizb-ut-Tahrir, 'Al-Malik Hussain Yanjaz Fi London', 1967.
87. Zallum, interview. Taha, interview.
88. Shahada Arar, 'Murafi'a Shahada Arar 7–2–1968', 1968. Taha, interview.
89. Qur'an, Chapter 33, Verse 23.
90. al-Faqir, interview.
91. Hizb-ut-Tahrir, 'Jawab Su'al 8–5–70', 1970.
92. Hizb-ut-Tahrir, 'Qadiyatuna Laysa Istilam Al-Hukm', 1968.
93. Zallum, interview.
94. Hizb-ut-Tahrir, 'Jawab Su'al 5–8–68', 1968.
95. Hizb-ut-Tahrir, 'Marhala Al-Tafa'ul', 1968.
96. Hizb-ut-Tahrir, 'Al-Tariq Al-Siyasi Huwa Tariq Al-Hizb Fi Haml Al-Da'wa', 1968.
97. Salama, 'Farhun', p. 257; al-Tamimi, interview.
98. al-Faqir, interview; Zallum, interview.
99. *Military Court Case Number 069/390*, undated copy of transcript, 1969.
100. Sha'lan, interview.

## 5. THE LONG WAIT (1969–1977)

1. Hizb-ut-Tahrir, 'Jawab Su'al 7–8–70', 1970.
2. Sha'lan, interview.
3. Faris, interview; al-Faqir, interview.
4. Faris, interview.
5. Hizb-ut-Tahrir, 'Jawab Su'al 7–5–71', 1971.
6. Faris, interview. Abu Iyas, interview.
7. Sha'lan, interview; al-Faqir, interview; Faris, interview.
8. Hizb-ut-Tahrir, 'Kitab Maftuh'.
9. Zallum, interview; al-Nabhani, interview.

10. Zallum, interview.
11. Hizb-ut-Tahrir, 'Kitab Ila-L-Shabab', 1978.
12. Hizb-ut-Tahrir, 'Jawab Su'al 7–8–70'.
13. Miriam Joyce, *Anglo-American Support for Jordan: The Career of King Hussein*, New York: Palgrave Macmillan, 2008, p. 46.
14. Hizb-ut-Tahrir, 'Bayan Min Hizb Ut-Tahrir 28–6–1970', 1970.
15. Tariq Ali, *The Clash of Fundamentalisms: Crusades, Jihads and Modernity*, London: Verso, 2002, p. 189.
16. Joyce, p. 60.
17. Patrick Seale, *Abu Nidal: A Gun for Hire*, New York: Random House, 1992, p. 67.
18. Hizb-ut-Tahrir, 'Khitab Min Hizb Ut-Tahrir 4–4–1971', 1971.
19. Joyce, p. 74.
20. Hizb-ut-Tahrir, 'Hukm Al-Amal Ma'a Al-Hayia Al-Tahrir Al-Felistiniyya', 1964.
21. Hizb-ut-Tahrir, 'Khitab Min Hizb Ut-Tahrir 3–6–1971', 1971.
22. Ismadi, interview.
23. Zahran and Tarshubi, p. 26.
24. John L. Esposito, *The Oxford Dictionary of Islam*, Oxford: Oxford University Press, 2003.
25. Abu Muhammad, interview.
26. al-Ramahi, interview.
27. Abu Muhammad, interview.
28. Hizb-ut-Tahrir, *Mafahim Siyasiyya Li-Hizb Ut-Tahrir*, 1st edn., 1969, p. 20.
29. Hizb-ut-Tahrir, *Mafahim Siyasiyya Li-Hizb Ut-Tahrir*, 4th edn., 2005, p. 23.
30. Bilal Al-Wais, 'Dabit Mutaqa'id Yarwi Tafasil Mu'amara Nadhim Kazar', Shabika al-'Ilam al-'Iraqiyya fi-l-Denmark, http://bit.ly/13Q1wIl
31. Zallum, interview; Taha, interview; al-Nabhani, interview.
32. Hizb-ut-Tahrir, 'Untitled Internal Leaflet 27–1–72'.
33. Abu Mahmoud, interview.
34. al-Nabhani, interview; Abu Mahmoud, interview. The details of this account are taken from those directly related to and involved with al-Nabhani, who heard it from the primary source. This conflicts with other accounts of his imprisonment and torture, such as that found in Radi (pp. 34–5), which appear to contain numerous inaccuracies (such as that the torture caused the paralysis in his face, which was in fact a condition al-Nabhani had suffered from since 1957, as mentioned in Chapter 4).
35. al-Nabhani, interview.
36. Hizb-ut-Tahrir, *Natharat Siyasiyya Li-Hizb Ut-Tahrir*, 1973, p. 1.
37. Ibid., p. 60.
38. al-Ubaidi, pp. 101–2.
39. Taqiudeen al-Nabhani, *al-Tafkir*, 1973, p. 26.
40. Ibid., pp. 18–9.

41. Ibid., pp. 174–5.
42. Ibid., pp. 104.
43. Ismadi, interview.
44. al-Khatib, interview; al-Ramahi, interview.
45. al-Nabhani, interview.
46. Avner Cohen, 'The Last Nuclear Moment', *The New York Times*, 6 Oct. 2003.
47. Hizb-ut-Tahrir, 'Al-Ta'liq Al-Siyasi 10–10–1973', 1973.
48. Hizb-ut-Tahrir 'Al-Ta'liq Al-Siyasi 23–10–1973', 1973.
49. al-Nabhani, interview.
50. Marc Sageman, *Understanding Terror Networks*, Philadelphia: University of Pennsylvania Press, 2004, pp. 27–8.
51. Amru Abdul Mun'im, 'Ibn Salih Siriyya Qa'id Amaliyya Al-Finiyya Al-Askariyya Li 'Muhit' (2/2)', http://www.masress.com/moheet/69572, last accessed 12 Apr. 2016.
52. Hizb-ut-Tahrir, 'Ibn Salih Siriyya Qa'id Amaliyya Al-Finiyya Al-Askariyya Li 'Muhit' (1/2)', http://www.masress.com/moheet/72784, last accessed 12 Apr. 2016.
53. Muhammad Al-Sayyid Salim, 'Al-Haqiqa Fima Nushira 'an Qadiyya Al-Finiyya Al-Askariyya', Al Maqreze Center for Historical Studies, http://www.almaqreze. net/ar/news.php?readmore=260
54. Zahran and Tarshubi, p. 26
55. al-Ramahi, interview.
56. Abu Muhammad Ahmad and Abu Bilal, interview by author, Lebanon, 1 July 2012.
57. Taha, interview.
58. Abu Iyas, interview; al-Nabulsi, interview.
59. Hizb-ut-Tahrir, 'Untitled Internal Leaflet 2–6–71', 1971.
60. Salama, 'Farhun', p. 258.
61. Hizb-ut-Tahrir, 'Jawab Su'al 23–4–71', 1971.
62. Hizb-ut-Tahrir, 'Jawab Su'al 7–5–71', 1971.
63. Hizb-ut-Tahrir, 'Jawab Su'al 18–1–74', 1974.
64. Hizb-ut-Tahrir, 'Tarh Al-Fikra Ala-L-Jamahir', 1974.
65. Abu Mahmoud, interview.
66. Hizb-ut-Tahrir, 'Al-Wasat Al-Siyassi', 1974.
67. Hizb-ut-Tahrir, ''Amal Haml Al-Da'wa', 1975.
68. Faris, interview.
69. al-Nabhani, interview.
70. Taqiudeen al-Nabhani, *Sur'at Al-Badiha*, 1976.
71. Faris, interview.
72. Taha, interview.
73. Hizb-ut-Tahrir, 'Al-Kalima Al-Shariyya', 1976.

74. Hizb-ut-Tahrir, 'Al-Kalima Al-Shariyya', 1977.

75. Abu Mahmoud, interview.

76. al-Nabhani, interview; Hizb ut-Tahrir, 'Condolences', 1977. The common claim that al-Nabhani died on 20 June 1977 is plainly inaccurate, as shown by the date of the condolence message sent by the party after his death, as well as multiple witness statements, including the fact that he was alive at the time of Sadat's visit to Damascus and then Tel Aviv in Nov. 1977. The reason this is normally given as the date is due to the error existing in the two main sources regarding al-Nabhani's life in Arabic and English, respectively, al-Ubaidi and Taji-Farouki.

77. Hizb-ut-Tahrir, 'Condolences'.

78. Abu Iyas, interview.

79. Ismadi, interview.

80. al-Ubaidi, p. 17.

81. Abu Mahmoud, interview.

82. Taha, interview.

83. This was stated independently by several of those interviewed.

84. Samara, p. 149.

85. Al-Jazeera.

86. al-Ubaidi, p. 8.

87. Muhammad Said Ramadan al-Buti, 'Das Khatir La Majal Li-L-Sukut 'Anhu', *Hadaratu al-Islam* 4, no. 4 (1963).

88. Sayyid Qutb, *Fi Dhilal Al-Qur'an*, Cairo: Dar al-Shuruk, 2004.

89. Samara, pp. 148–9.

90. al-Samani, p. 660.

## 6.  REVIVING THE REVIVALISTS (1977–1990)

1. Shinnar, p. 95.

2. Ahmad and Abu Bilal, interview; Abu Iyas, interview.

3. Abu Iyas, interview; Abu Mahmoud, interview.

4. Abu Mahmoud, interview.

5. Zallum, interview; Nasir, interview; Ismadi, interview.

6. Taha, interview; Muhammad al-Ansari, interview by author, Kuwait, 15 June 2012; Nasir, interview.

7. Hizb-ut-Tahrir, 'Kitab Ila-L-Shabab'.

8. Ibid.

9. Ibid.

10. Ibid.

11. Ibid.

12. Abu Yusuf, interview by author, Tunisia, 13 Aug. 2012.

13. Zahran and Tarshubi, p. 79.

14. Abu Yusuf, interview.

15. Fathi al-Fadili, 'Shahid Al-Mabadi... Ibn Al-Watan: Muhammad Muhathab Haffaf', http://www.fathifadhli.com/aws7.htm

16. Fathi al-Fadili, 'Al-Shahid Salih Muhammad Al-Farisi', http://www.fathifadhli.com/art5.htm

17. Ibid.

18. Ronald Bruce St John, *Historical Dictionary of Libya*, 4th edn., Lanham, MD and Oxford: Scarecrow Press, 2006, p. 204.

19. Abu Yusuf, interview.

20. Ibid.

21. Sijjil, 'April Victims of the Gaddafi Regime', Tripod, http://sijill.tripod.com/victims/. Fawzi Abdelhamid, 'Hujum Al-Gaddafi Ala-L-Jami'a', http://www.libyawatanona.com/adab/forfia/fo30108a.htm.

22. Abu Yusuf, interview.

23. Habayib, interview.

24. Nasir, interview.

25. Habayib, interview; Nasir, interview.

26. Habayib, interview.

27. Translation of the meaning of the Qur'an, Chapter 59 Verse 7.

28. Martin Kramer, 'Syria's Alawis and Shi'ism', in *Shi'ism, Resistance and Revolution*, ed. Martin Kramer, London: Mansell, 1987.

29. Said al-Gharib, 'Al-Sanussi: Al-Gaddafi Ta'araka Bi-L-Aydi Ma'a Al-Sadr Wa Amara Bi Qatlihi', *Al-Ahram*, 12 Sept. 2012.

30. Hizb-ut-Tahrir, 'Muthakira Min Hizb Ut Tahrir Muqadamma Illa-L-Aqid Al-Gaddafi', 1978.

31. Ibid.

32. Ian Cobain and Martin Chulov, 'Libyan Papers Show UK Worked with Gaddafi in Rendition Operation', *The Guardian*, 4 Sept. 2011.

33. Duncan Gardham, 'Libya: MI5 Believed Moussa Koussa Was Involved in Assassinations', *The Telegraph*, 5 Apr. 2011.

34. Members of Hizb-ut-Tahrir in Europe, 'Statement Dated 15 April 1980', 1980.

35. Fathi al-Fadili, 'Shahid Al-Kalima... Wa-L-Fikra... Al-Ustadh Muhammad Mustafa Ramadan', http://www.fathifadhli.com/aws4.htm; 'Al-Rasa'il Allati Hakamat 'Ala Muhammad Mustafa Ramadan Bi-L-Tasfiyya Al-Jasadiyya', Arab News, http://bit.ly/Xn7PfB.

36. Umm Ma'mun, interview by author, Jordan, 23 June 2012.

37. Al-Fadili, 'Shahid Al-Mabadi'.

38. Hizb-ut-Tahrir, 'Iqdam Al-Mujrim 'Adu Allah Al-Gaddafi 'Ala I'dam Ba'd Shabab Hizb Ut-Tahrir', 1983. The names of those executed were Nasir Sirris, Ali Ahmad Iwad Allah, Badi' Hasan Badr, Nimr Salim Isa, Abdullah Hamuda, Abdullah al-Maslati, Hasan al-Kurdi, Muhammad Haffaf, Salih al-Nawal, and al-Nawal's nephew (unnamed). Those named as having been killed during interrogation were Majid al-Dawaik, Muhammad Buyumi and al-Faquri.

39. Abu Yusuf, interview.
40. St John, p. 124.
41. Hizb-ut-Tahrir, 'Hatha Balaghun Li-L-Nas', 1986.
42. Evan Hill, 'Libya Survivor Describes 1996 Prison Massacre', Al-Jazeera English, http://www.aljazeera.com/indepth/features/2011/09/20119223521462487.html.
43. Cobain and Chulov, 'Libyan Papers'.
44. Rod Nordland, 'Files Note Close C.I.A. Ties to Qaddafi Spy Unit', *The New York Times*, 2 Sept. 2011.
45. 'Jamia Trabulus Tuhyi Dhikr Al-Sabi' Min April', Al-Watan al-Libiyya, http://bit.ly/UZG4HI
46. Stephen Kinzer, *Overthrow: America's Century of Regime Change from Hawaii to Iraq*, New York: Times Books/Henry Holt, 2006, pp. 123–4.
47. M. Reza Ghods and Thomas W. Foster, 'Conversation with a Revolutionary', *Middle East Studies Association Bulletin* 36, no. 1, 2002: p. 28.
48. al-Khatib, interview.
49. Dr Muhammad Jaber, interview by author, Lebanon, 5 July 2012.
50. Shaul Bakhash, *The Reign of the Ayatollahs: Iran and the Islamic Revolution*, New York: Basic Books, 1984, p. 72.
51. Jaber, interview.
52. For example, see Yusuf al-Qaradawi, *Min Fiqh Al-Dawla Fi-L-Islam*, Cairo: Dar al-Sharouq, 1997.
53. Forough Jahanbakhsh, *Islam, Democracy and Religious Modernism in Iran, 1953–2000*, Leiden and Boston: Brill, 2001, p. 135.
54. Jaber, interview.
55. Henry Precht, 'The Iranian Revolution: An Oral History with Henry Precht, Then State Department Desk Officer', *Middle East Journal* 58, no. 1, 2004: p. 19; Gary Sick, *All Fall Down: America's Tragic Encounter with Iran*, New York: Random House, 1985, p. 121.
56. Jaber Ahmad, 'Asrar Al-Thawra Al-Iraniyya Bayn Ma Huwa Mu'lan Wa Ma Huwa Khafi', Al-Hewar al-Mutamadin, http://www.ahewar.org/debat/show.art.asp?aid=129579.
57. Sick, pp. 143–4.
58. Jaber, interview.
59. Lawrence Wright, *The Looming Tower: Al-Qaeda and the Road to 9/11*, New York: Knopf, 2006, p. 47. Rudi Matthee, 'Egyptian Reactions to the Iranian Revolution', in *Shi'ism and Social Protest*, ed. Juan R.I. Cole and Nikki R. Keddie, New Haven and London: Yale University Press, 1986.
60. Jaber, interview.
61. Precht, p. 21.
62. Sick, p. 142.

63. Shahpur Bakhtiar and Fred Halliday, 'Shahpur Bakhtiar: "The Americans Played a Disgusting Role"', *MERIP Reports*, no. 104 (1982): p. 13.

64. Precht, p. 25.

65. Peter Dale Scott, *The Road to 9/11: Wealth, Empire, and the Future of America* (Berkeley, CA and London: University of California Press, 2007), p. 67.

66. Richard Falk, 'Trusting Khomeini', *The New York Times*, 16 Feb. 1979, p. 27.

67. Dieter Nohlen, Florian Grotz, and Christof Hartmann, *Elections in Asia and the Pacific: A Data Handbook*, Oxford: Oxford University Press, 2001, vol. 1, p. 72.

68. Abdul-Rahman Hudruj, interview by author, Lebanon, 27 June 2012; Abu Mahmoud, interview.

69. Hudruj, interview; Abu Mahmoud, interview.

70. Hudruj, interview; Abu Mahmoud, interview.

71. Helen Chapin Metz and Library of Congress, Federal Research Division, *Iran: A Country Study*, 4th edn., Area Handbook Series (Washington, DC: The Division). For sale by the Supt. of Docs, US GPO, 1989, p. 54.

72. Glenn E. Curtis, Eric J. Hooglund, and Library of Congress. Federal Research Division, *Iran: A Country Study*, 5th edn. (Washington, DC: Library of Congress, Federal Research Division, 2008), p. 56.

73. Helen Chapin Metz and Library of Congress, *Iran: A Country Study*, pp. 54–5.

74. Hizb-ut-Tahrir, 'Nas Naqd Al-Dustur Al-Mashro' Al-Irani', 1979.

75. Ibid.

76. Rouhollah K. Ramazani, 'Constitution of the Islamic Republic of Iran', *Middle East Journal* 34, no. 2 (1980).

77. Nohlen, Grotz, and Hartmann, p. 72.

78. Jaber, interview. Hudruj, interview.

79. Zallum, interview.

80. Hizb-ut-Tahrir, 'Untitled Political Analysis 22–11–1979', 1979.

81. Finian Cunningham, 'The 1979 Iranian US Embassy Siege and Hostage Crisis. Was It a Covert CIA Operation?', Global Research, http://www.globalresearch.ca/the-1979-iranian-us-embassy-siege-and-hostage-crisis-was-it-a-covert-cia-operation/30291

82. Abu Mahmoud, interview; Hudruj, interview.

83. Glenn E. Curtis, Eric J. Hooglund, and Library of Congress, *Iran: A Country Study*, p. 63.

84. Matthee, p. 257.

85. Ibid., p. 260.

86. These key tenets are refuted in the Hizb-ut-Tahrir literature that all party members adhere to; the most detailed discussions can be found in al-Nabhani, *al-Shakhsiyya al-Islamiyya: al-Juz al-Thani*.

87. Mahan Abedin, 'Islamic Movement: Hizbut Tahrir's New Drive in the Levant—an Interview with Dr Mohammed Jaber', Religioscope, http://religion.info/english/interviews/article_474.shtml.

88. al-Khatib, interview; Jaber, interview; Hudruj, interview.

89. Abdullah bin Salih al-Qusayyir, *Bayan Arkan Al-Iman*, Riyadh: Maktaba al-Malik Fahd al-Wataniyya, 2003, p. 9.

90. Abedin.

91. Hizb-ut-Tahrir, 'Nida Min Hizb Ut-Tahrir Ila-L-Umma', 1978.

92. Hizb-ut-Tahrir, 'Bayan Min Hizb Ut-Tahrir 13–5–1979', 1979.

93. Hizb-ut-Tahrir, 'Wa Nal Al-Kha'in Jaza'ahu', 1981.

94. Mohamed Sid-Ahmed, 'Egypt: The Islamic Issue', *Foreign Policy*, no. 69, 1987: p. 25; Wright, pp. 48–50.

95. Muntasir Zayyat, *al-Jama'at al-Islamiyya: al-Ru'ya Min al-Dakhil*, Cairo: Dar al-Masr al-Mahrusa, 2005, p. 119.

96. Hazem al-Amin, 'Bakura 'Al-Jihad Al-'Alami'', Kalamon, http://www.kalamon.org/articles-details-12#axzz2P91SOp4A; Usama al-Esa, 'Filistini Arada Ightiyal Al-Sadat Wa Isqat Nithamihi Antaha Ma'tuha', Elaph Publishing Limited, http://www.kalamon.org/articles-details-12#axzz2P91SOp4A.

97. Zayyat, p. 96.

98. Hizb-ut-Tahrir, 'Al-Kitab Ila Saddam Hussein', 1981.

99. Hizb-ut-Tahrir, 'Bayan Min Hizb Ut-Tahrir 30–1–1982', 1982.

100. Hizb-ut-Tahrir, 'Bayan Min Hizb Ut-Tahrir Ila Al-Umma Al-Islamiyya 1–7–1982', 1982.

101. Hizb-ut-Tahrir, 'Tanshit Al-Shabab', 1980; Hizb-ut-Tahrir, 'Uslub Al-Kasb Al-Umma', 1980.

102. Hizb-ut-Tahrir, 'Jawab Su'al 14–10–83', 1983.

103. Zallum, interview.

104. Abu Iyas, interview; Ubaid, interview; Ahmad Abu Quddum Abu Usama, interview by author, Jordan, 24 June 2012.

105. An-Nahar, 'Iktishaf Hizb Ut-Tahrir Yuqarrib Al-Haraka Al-Islamiyya Mina-L-Sulta', *An-Nahar Arab and International*, 29 Aug. 1983.

106. Uthman Bakhach, interview by author, Lebanon, 30 June 2012.

107. Hizb-ut-Tahrir, 'Inkar Al-Munkar Fard', 1989.

108. Hizb-ut-Tahrir, 'Kitab Ila-L-Shabab Hawl Al-Nashra Inkar Al-Munkar Fard', 1989.

109. Muhammad Hajaji, interview by author, Tunisia, 12 Aug. 2012.

110. Watha'iq, 'A'da Hizb Ut-Tahrir Al-Islami Amam Al-Mahkama', *Watha'iq*, 26 Aug. 1983.

111. Hajaji, interview.

112. Watha'iq.

113. Hajaji, interview.

114. Watha'iq, interview.

115. An-Nahar, interview.

116. Al-Hadi al-Sariti, 'Notice from Minister for National Education 4 October 1983', Tunis, 1983.

117. Radi, p. 70.
118. Ibid.
119. Tawfik Al Madini, 'Tasa'ud Hizb Ut-Tahrir Fi Tunis', Nawaa, http://bit.ly/skmUXz.
120. Hajaji, interview; Usama al-Majeri, interview by author, Tunisia, 14 Aug. 2012
121. Radi, p. 84.
122. Research Department, 'Hizb Ut-Tahrir', *Al-Juthur*, Feb. 1991.
123. Hizb-ut-Tahrir, 'Hatha Balaghun Li-L-Nas, Wa Li-Yuntheru Bihi', 1990.
124. Hizb-ut-Tahrir, 'Bayan Sahafi', 1990.
125. Joseph S. Nye, Jr, 'Why the Gulf War Served the National Interest', *The Atlantic Monthly* 268, no. 1 (1991).
126. Hizb-ut-Tahrir, 'Al-Islam Yufrid Muqatila Amrika', 1991.

7. A GLOBAL PARTY (1990–2012)

1. Shinnar, p. 30.
2. Zallum, interview.
3. Faris, interview.
4. Madeleine Gruen, 'Hizb-Ut-Tahrir's Activities in the United States', The Jamestown Foundations, http://www.jamestown.org/single/?no_chache=1&tx_ttnews%5Btt_news%5D=4377.
5. Abu Muhammad, interview.
6. Mahan Abedin, 'Al-Muhajiroun in the UK: An Interview with Sheikh Omar Bakri Mohammed', The Jamestown Foundation, http://www.jamestown.org/single/?no_cache=1&tx_ttnews%5Btt_news%5D=290.
7. Ubaid, interview.
8. Ubaid, interview.
9. Greg Fealy, 'Hizb Ut Tahrir in Indonesia: Seeking a "Total" Islamic Identity', in *Islam and Political Violence: Muslim Diaspora and Radicalism in the West*, eds Shahram Akbarzadeh and Fethi Mansouri, London and New York: Tauris Academic Studies, 2007, pp. 154–5.
10. Muhammad Ismail Yusanto, personal communication with author, 21 July 2012.
11. Fealy, p. 155.
12. Yusanto, interview.
13. Hizb-ut-Tahrir, 'Kitab Ila-L-Shabab'.
14. Hizb-ut-Tahrir, 'Ia'datu Al-Nathar', 1985.
15. Ibid.
16. Ibrahim Ghurayaba, 'Maqtal Al-Diplomasi Al-Amriki Fi Amman Wa Siyaq Al-Unf Fi-L-Urdan', Al-Jazeera, http://www.aljazeera.net/opinions/pages/dd91a489-c9cc-4d99-9fe8-479d3eb5bd83; Abu Hamada, interview by author, Jordan, 24 June 2012.
17. Al-Khatib, interview.

18. Reza Pankhurst, 'The Caliphate, and the Changing Strategy of the Public Statements of Al-Qaeda's Leaders', *Political Theology* 11, no. 4, 2010.

19. See, for example, *Risala Nawaqid al-Islam* (Nullifiers of the Islamic Belief) by Imam Muhammad Abdul Wahhab, in which the eighth nullifier listed is helping the idol worshippers against Muslims.

20. Leslie Cockburn and Andrew Cockburn, 'Royal Mess', *The New Yorker*, 28 Nov. 1994.

21. Bakhach, interview.

22. Ubaid, interview; Ahmad and Abu Bilal, interview.

23. al-Ramahi, interview.

24. Reza Pankhurst, *The Inevitable Caliphate?*, London: Hurst & Co., 2013, pp. 171–2.

25. Abu Mahmoud, interview.

26. Ibid.; Ubaid, interview; Karagiannis, *Political Islam*, p. 62.

27. Karagiannis, *Political Islam*, pp. 60–70.

28. Ubaid, interview.

29. Zeyneb Temnenko, 'Islam and Hizb Ut-Tahrir's Activities in Crimea, Ukraine', *Centro Argentino de Estudios Internacionales*, 2009: p. 5.

30. Faris, interview; Yusuf as-Sabatin, 'Muthakarat Yusuf Al-Sabatin', http://www.alokab.com/forums/index.php?showtopic=23784&st=20

31. Nasir, interview; Zallum, interview; Abu Iyas, interview.

32. Mahmoud Abdul Latif Iwaida, *Haml Al-Da'wa Wajibat Wa Sifat*, Hizb-ut-Tahrir, 1996.

33. Abu Rami Faction, 'Bayan Ila Shabab Hizb Ut-Tahrir', 1997.

34. Faris, interview.

35. Usama, interview.

36. Abu Iyas, interview; Faris, interview.

37. Nasir, interview.

38. Usama, interview.

39. Abdul Qadeem Zallum, *Hukm Al-Shar Fi-L-Istinsakh*, 1997.

40. Hizb-ut-Tahrir, *Hazzat Al-Aswaq Al-Maliyya: Asbabuha Wa Hukm Al-Shar Fi Hathihi Asbab*, 1997, p. 4.

41. Hizb-ut-Tahrir, *Al-Hamla Al-Amrikiyya Li-L-Qada Ala-L-Islam*, 1996.

42. Francis Fukuyama, *The End of History and the Last Man*, New York: The Free Press, 1992, p. 45.

43. Frontline World, 'Rendition Timeline', PBS, http://www.pbs.org/frontlineworld/stories/rendition701/timeline/timeline_1.html

44. Shaul Shay, *Islamic Terror and the Balkans*, New Brunswick, NJ and London: Transaction Publishers, 2006, p. 101.

45. Hizb-ut-Tahrir, *Mefahim Khatira Li-Darb Al-Islam*, 1998.

46. Hizb-ut-Tahrir, 'Amrika Dawla Irhabiyya Yajib Tarduha Kuliyyan Min Jami' Al-'Alim Al-Islami', 1998.

47. Hizb-ut-Tahrir, 'Duwal Al-Gharb Yuthbahu Al-Muslimin Fi-L-Bulqan', 1999.

48. For full details refer to Branka Magas and Ivo Zanic, *The War in Croatia and Bosnia-Herzegovina, 1991–1995*, London: Frank Cass, 2001.

49. Bill Clinton, *My Life*, London: Arrow Books, 2005, p. 466.

50. Michael J. Jordan, 'Sex Charges Haunt UN Forces', *The Christian Science Monitor*, http://www.csmonitor.com/2004/1126/p06s02-wogi.html.

51. Paul Vallely, 'The Big Question: Why Are Dutch Soldiers Being Sued for the Massacre at Srebrenica?', *The Independent*, 19 June 2008.

52. John Sloboda and Chris Abbott, 'The "Blair Doctrine" and After: Five Years of Humanitarian Intervention', OpenDemocracy, http://www.opendemocracy.net/ globalization-institutions_government/article_1857.jsp.

53. Fukuyama, p. 48.

54. Samuel P. Huntington, *The Clash of Civilisations and the Remaking of a World Order*, New York: Simon & Schuster, 2003, p. 135.

55. Numerous documents can be accessed from the National Security Archives, in particular: National Security Archive, 'Secret U.S. Message to Mullah Omar: "Every Pillar of the Taliban Regime Will Be Destroyed"', National Security Archive, http://www.gwu.edu/~nsarchiv/NSAEBB/NSAEBB358a/index.htm#7;

56. George Bush, 'Remarks by the President Upon Arrival', The White House, http:// georgewbush-whitehouse.archives.gov/news/releases/2001/09/20010916–2.html.

57. Michael J. Jordan, 'Europe Cringes at Bush 'Crusade' against Terrorists', *The Christian Science Monitor*, http://www.csmonitor.com/2001/0919/p12s2-woeu. html.

58. George Bush, 'President Rallies the Troops in Alaska', The White House, http:// georgewbush-whitehouse.archives.gov/news/releases/2002/02/20020216–1.html, last accessed 12 Apr. 2016.

59. Hizb ut-Tahrir, 'Al-Tahaluf Ma' Amrika Jarima Kubra Yuharimuha Al-Islam', 2001.

60. Ibid.

61. Hizb-ut-Tahrir, 'Bayan Min Hizb Ut-Tahrir', 2001.

62. George Bush, 'Text of President Bush's 2002 State of the Union Address', *The Washington Post*, http://www.washingtonpost.com/wp-srv/onpolitics/tran-scripts/sou012902.htm.

63. Hizb-ut-Tahrir, 'Nida Min Hizb Ut-Tahrir', 2003.

64. Hizb-ut-Tahrir Iraq, 'Hizb Ut-Tahrir Fi-L-Iraq Yastasrikh Ahl Al-Iraq', 2003.

65. Hizb-ut-Tahrir, 'Nida Min Hizb Ut-Tahrir', 2004.

66. Zallum, interview; Nasir, interview.

67. Hizb-ut-Tahrir, 'Yan'i Hizb Ut-Tahrir Li-L-Umma Al-Islamiyya Amiruhu', 2003. Hizb-ut-Tahrir Jordan, 'Bayan Min Hizb Ut-Tahrir', 2003.

68. Hizb-ut-Tahrir, 'Yan'i Al-Sheikh Al-Fadil Ahmad al-Da'ur', 2001.

69. Zallum, interview.

70. al-Waie, p. 19.

71. Alhough not formally trained at any Islamic centre of learning, Abu al-Rashta has published work on Islamic issues such as exegesis of the Qur'an and the principles of Islamic jurisprudence, which indicate a level of competency and familiarity with theology; see, for example, Ata' bin Khalil, *Taysir Al-Wasul Ila-L-Usul*, Beirut: Dar al-Umma, 2000.

72. Kirstine Sinclair, 'The Caliphate as Homeland: Hizb Ut-Tahrir in Denmark and Britain', University of Southern Denmark, 2010, p. 178.

73. 'Background: The Guardian and Dilpazier Aslam', *The Guardian*, http://www.guardian.co.uk/media/2005/jul/22/theguardian.pressandpublishing1.

74. Sophie Lambroschini, 'Germany: Court Appeal by Hizb Ut-Tahrir Highlights Balancing Act between Actions, Intentions', Radio Free Europe, http://www.rferl.org/content/article/1055527.html.

75. BBC News, 'Trial of Britons in Egypt Delayed', BBC News, http://news.bbc.co.uk/1/hi/uk/2693257.stm.

76. BBC News, 'Freed UK Three Return to Families', BBC News, http://news.bbc.co.uk/1/hi/uk/4763056.stm.

77. Stephen Farrell, 'Confession Signature Code Reveals Briton's Torture in Cairo Prison', *The Times*, 18 Nov. 2002.

78. 'Who Killed Farhad Usmanov?', Arab News, http://www.arabnews.com/node/222162.

79. Acacia Shields, 'Creating Enemies of the State: Religious Persecution in Uzbekistan', New York: Human Rights Watch, 2004, p. 229.

80. Craig Murray, *Murder in Samarkand: A British Ambassador's Defiance of Tyranny in the War on Terror*, Edinburgh: Mainstream, 2006, p. 330; Ubaid, interview.

81. Hizb-ut-Tahrir Uzbekistan, 'Shahid Jadid Taht Al-Ta'thib', 1999.

82. Hizb-ut-Tahrir, 'Illa-L-Munathamat Huquq Al-Insan', 2000.

83. BBC News, 'Protesters Highlight "War against Muslims"', BBC News, http://news.bbc.co.uk/1/hi/uk/2139955.stm.

84. John C.K. Daly *et al.*, 'Anatomy of a Crisis: U.S.-Uzbekistan Relations, 2001–2005', Washington, DC: Central Asia-Caucasus Institute & Silk Road Studies Program, 2006, pp. 72–6.

85. Marc Perelman, 'Uzbek Unrest Shines Light on Leader's Ties to Jewry', *The Jewish Daily Forward*, http://forward.com/articles/3544/uzbek-unrest-shines-light-on-leaderes-ties-to-je/.

86. Shields, p. 273.

87. Ahmed Rashid, *Jihad: The Rise of Militant Islam in Central Asia*, London: Yale University Press, 2002, p. 116.

88. Fredholm, pp. 14–5.

89. Cohen, 'Hizb Ut Tahrir: An Emerging Threat to US Interests in Central Asia', pp. 9–11.

90. Mayer, p. 11.

91. Taji-Farouki.

92. Mayer, p. 24.

93. ICG, 'Radical Islam in Central Asia: Responding to Hizb Ut-Tahrir', in *Asia Report*, Brussels: International Crisis Group, 2003.

94. Ibid.

95. Ibid.

96. Baran, *Hizb Ut-Tahrir Islam's Political Insurgency*, pp. 105–6.

97. Gunaratna, p. 124.

98. Michael Whine, 'Hizb Ut-Tahrir in Open Societies', in *The Challenge of Hizb ut-Tahrir*, ed. Zeyno Baran, Ankara, Turkey: Nixon Center, 2004, p. 107.

99. Zeyno Baran, 'Executive Summary', in *The Challenge of Hizb ut-Tahrir*, ed. Zeyno Baran, Ankara, Turkey: Nixon Center, 2004.

100. For example, Baran, *Political Insurgency*; Zeyno Baran, 'Fighting the War of Ideas', *Foreign Affairs*, no. 84 (2005).

101. Ian Cobain and Nick Fielding, 'Banned Islamists Spawn Front Organisations', *The Guardian*, 13 Dec. 2006.

102. Hizb-ut-Tahrir Britain, 'Media Information Pack', 2010.

103. Perelman.

104. AP, 'Report Cites Europe's Role in C.I.A. Renditions', *The New York Times*, 7 June 2006.

105. Reuters, 'Uzbekistan Torture Ignored by the West, Say Human Rights Group', *The Guardian*, 13 Dec. 2011.

106. BBC News, 'London Bomber: Text in Full', BBC News, http://news.bbc.co.uk/1/hi/uk/4206800.stm.

107. BBC News, 'Video of 7 July Bomber Released', BBC News, http://news.bbc.co.uk/1/hi/5154714.stm.

108. Defense Science Board, 'Strategic Communication', Washington, DC: Department of Defense, 2004, p. 14.

109. 'Tony Blair's Speech to the Foreign Policy Centre', *The Guardian*, 21 Mar. 2006.

110. Ibid.

111. Bright.

112. Doward and Hinsliff.

113. Shiv Malik, 'Watchdog Recommends Tory U-Turn on Banning Hizb Ut-Tahrir', *The Guardian*, 18 July 2011.

114. Vikram Dodd, 'Anti-Terror Code "Would Alienate Most Muslims"', *The Guardian*, 17 Feb. 2009.

115. Andrew Gilligan, 'Hizb Ut Tahrir Is Not a Gateway to Terrorism, Claims Whitehall Report', *The Telegraph*, 25 July 2010.

116. Defense Science Board, p. 36.

117. Ibid., p. 40.

118. For example, the judge in *Criminal Court, Beirut: Case Number 2005/14846*,

29 Dec. 2005, found the two defendants, Muhammad al-Tayish and Sharif al-Hallaq, innocent of any crime, given they were distributing the leaflets publicly and openly promoting Hizb-ut-Tahrir materials, which contained political views and opinions that called on others to adopt them.

119. Hizb-ut-Tahrir Lebanon, 'Bayan Min Hizb Ut-Tahrir', 2004.

120. Bakhach, interview.

121. Basim al-Bakur, 'Hizb Ut-Tahrir Yahlim Bi-Istirja' 'Dawla Al-Khilafa' Al-Islamiyya', *Al-Nahar*, 5 Oct. 2004.

122. David Schenker, 'One Year after the Cedar Revolution', The Washington Institute, http://bit.ly/RmsTzF.

123. Bakhach, interview.

124. Annahar—Beirut, 'Ahmad Fatfat: La Mani' Min Al-Tarkhis Li 'Hizb Ut-Tahrir' Wa in Kunna Nakhtalif Ma'ahu Fi-L-Rai'.

125. Ibid.

126. Annahar—Beirut, 'Ahmad Fatfat: Hasan Nasrullah'.

127. Hizb-ut-Tahrir collected and printed copies of the media reaction from seventeen of the countries where the call was delivered as part of a 309-page report describing the activities undertaken and any responses; Hizb-ut-Tahrir, *Waqa'i Nida Hizb Ut-Tahrir Illa Al-Umma Al-Islamiyya*.

128. Radi, p. 100.

129. Yusanto, interview.

130. Williamson.

131. al-Majeri, interview.

132. Hizb-ut-Tahrir Tunis, 'Bayan Min Hizb Ut-Tahrir', 2011.

133. al-Majeri, interview.

134. HT Tunisia.

135. BBC News, 'Tunisia: President Zine Al-Abidine Ben Ali Forced Out', BBC News, http://www.bbc.co.uk/news/world-africa-12195025.

136. AP, 'At Least 846 Killed in Egypt's Revolution', Egypt Independent, http://www.egyptindependent.com/news/least-846-killed-egypt%E2%80%99s-revolution.

137. Mona Madkur, 'Hizb Ut-Tahrir: Hizb Jadid Taht Ta'sis Yas'a Li-Iqama Al-Khilafa Wa Yatabir Misr Wilaya', *Al-Sharq al-Awsat*, 17 Mar. 2012.

138. Zahran and Tarshubi, p. 38.

139. Hizb-ut-Tahrir Egypt, 'Illa Majlis Al-Askari Fi Misr: Hizb Ut-Tahrir Laysa Hizban Philistiniyyan Wa Innama Huwa Hizbun 'Alamiyyun Ya'mal Li-Tawhid Al-Umma Fi-L-Dawla Al-Khilafa', 2011.

140. Hizb-ut-Tahrir, 'I'tiqalat Fi Suriyya Bi-Sabab Al-Rai', 1999.

141. Hizb-ut-Tahrir Syria, 'Untitled Leaflet 13–1–2000', 2000.

142. ''Itiqalat', Syria News.

143. ''Itiqalat', 'Sajjilu Li-Anfusikum Makruma Al-Khilafa Al-Rashida', 2011.

144. Aziz, 'Nitham Bashar'.
145. Shams.
146. For example, Abdel Kafi al-Samad, 'Lebanon's Islamists view declaration of caliphate as heresy', http://english.al-akhbar.com/content/lebanon%E2%80%99s-islamists-view-declaration-caliphate-heresy
147. For example, Joseph Massad, 'The 'Arab Spring' and Other American Seasons', http://www.aljazeera.com/indepth/opinion/2012/08/201282972539153865.html.
148. AFP, 'Tunisia Legalises Second Hardline Islamist Group Hizb Al-Tahrir', Ahram Online, http://english.ahram.org.eg/NewsContent/2/8/48066/World/Region/Tunisia-legalises-second-hardline-Islamist-group-H.aspx.
149. 'Mulhaq Khas'. Al-Wathiqa.
150. Pheladelphia News, 'Qarar Yamna' Al-Na'ib Al-Sabiq Ali Al-Dala'in Min Al-Safar Kharij Al-Balad', Pheladelphia News, http://bit.ly/13XqGWx.
151. 'Hizb Ut-Tahrir Fi Gaza Yuwaji Risalatahu Li-L-Tha'irin 'Abr Masira Jamahiriyya', http://www.masress.com/misrelgdida/92956.
152. Jonathan Spyer, 'Hizb Ut-Tahrir: A Rising Force in Palestinian Territories', Global Politician, http://www.globalpolitician.com/default.asp?23871-palestine/
153. MRS/MMN, 'Turkey Arrests 200 Hizb Ut-Tahrir Suspects', Press TV, http://edition.presstv.ir/detail/101535.html.
154. 'Kalima Al-Muhandis Hisham Al-Baba Fi Istanbul Fi Mu'tamar Turkiyya 16–9–2012', Media Office of Hizb ut-Tahrir Syria, http://www.tahrir-syria.info/index.php/video/172-istanbul-9-2012.html.
155. Declan Walsh, 'Pakistan Army Officer Held over Suspected Hizb Ut-Tahrir Links', The Guardian, 21 June 2011.
156. Asad.

CONCLUSION: 'A REMARKABLY PERSISTENT ORGANIZATION'

1. Taqiudeen al-Nabhani, Al-Takattul Al-Hizbi, p. 27.
2. Mayer, p. 13.
3. ICG, p. 26.

APPENDIX I: CONSTITUTION

1. This is the first English translation of any part of the original 1953 draft constitution. The most recent version, which totals 191 articles, can be found in the book Muqadimma al-Dustur.

# SELECT BIBLIOGRAPHY

**Archival Work**

India Office, British Library and Foreign Office Archives, Kew Gardens in London.

**Academic and Journal Articles, Reports and Theses**

*Arabic*

al-Bishry, Tarek, 'Al-Malik Wa-L-Khilafa Al-Islamiyya', *Al-Katib* 13, no. 142 (1973): 44–72.

al-Buti, Muhammad Said Ramadan, 'Das Khatir La Majal Li-L-Sukut 'Anhu', *Hadaratu al-Islam* 4, no. 4 (1963): 398–408.

al-Nabhani, Taqiudeen, 'Al-Nitham Al-Islami', *Al-Wa'i al-jadid* 1, no. 6 (1951): 75–86.

al-Tantawi, Ali, 'Nasiha', *Al-Muslimum* 2, no. 26 (1955): 125–30.

Hamdan, Dawud, Hasan Al-Banna Muslih Al-'Asr', *Al-Wa'i al-jadid* 1, no. 6 (1951): 12–16.

Radi, Muhammad Muhsin, 'Hizb Ut-Tahrir: Thiqafatahu Wa Minhajahu Fi Iqama Dawla Al-Khilafa Al-Islamiyya', The Islamic University, 2006.

Rida, Rashid, 'Al-Khilafa Wa-L-Mu'tamar Al-Islami', *al-Manar* 25, no. 5 (1924): 367–74.

—— 'Inqilab Al-Deeni Al-Siyasi Fee Al-Jumhuriyya Al-Turkiyya', *al-Manar* 25, no. 4 (1924): 273–300.

*English*

Abu-Manneh, B., 'Sultan Abdulhamid and Shaikh Abulhuda Al-Sayyadi', *Middle Eastern Studies in Intelligence* 15, no. 2 (1979): 131–53.

Bakhtiar, Shahpur, and Fred Halliday, 'Shahpur Bakhtiar: "The Americans Played a Disgusting Role"', *MERIP Reports*, no. 104 (1982): 11–14.

Baran, Zeyno, *The Challenge of Hizb Ut-Tahrir*, Ankara, Turkey: Nixon Center, 2004.

—— 'Executive Summary', in *The Challenge of Hizb ut-Tahrir*, ed. Zeyno Baran, Ankara, Turkey: Nixon Center, 2004.

——— 'Fighting the War of Ideas', *Foreign Affairs*, no. 84 (2005): 11.

——— *Hizb Ut-Tahrir Islam's Political Insurgency*, Washington, DC: The Nixon Center, 2004.

Cakir, Rusen, 'The Rise and Fall of Turkish Hizb Ut-Tahrir', in *The Challenge of Hizb ut-Tahrir*, ed. Zeyno Baran, 37–9, Ankara, Turkey: Nixon Center, 2004.

Calhoun, Ricky-Dale, 'The Musketeer's Cloak: Strategic Deception During the Suez Crisis of 1956', *Studies in Intelligence* 51, no. 2 (2007): 47–58.

Cohen, Ariel, 'Hizb Ut Tahrir: An Emerging Threat to US Interests in Central Asia', *Heritage Foundation Backgrounder* 1656 (2003): 12.

Daly, John C.K., Kurt H. Meppen, Vladimir Socor, and S. Frederick Starr, 'Anatomy of a Crisis: U.S.-Uzbekistan Relations, 2001–2005', Washington, DC: Central Asia-Caucasus Institute & Silk Road Studies Program, 2006.

Defense Science Board, 'Strategic Communication', Washington, DC: Department of Defense, 2004.

Dulles, John Foster, 'Speech Made before the Council on Foreign Relations, New York, N. Y., on Aug. 26 (Press Release 517)', ed. US State Department: Office of Public Communications, 1955.

Fattah, Hala, '"Wahhabi" Influences, Salafi Responses', *Journal of Islamic Studies* 14, no. 2 (2003): 127–48.

Fredholm, Michael, 'Uzbekistan & the Threat from Islamic Extremism', Camberley: Conflict Studies Research Centre, 2003.

Ghods, M. Reza, and Thomas W. Foster, 'Conversation with a Revolutionary', *Middle East Studies Association Bulletin* 36, no. 1 (2002): 27–32.

Glicksberg, Joseph, 'The 1926 Uproar over Taha Husayn's On Pre-Islamic Poetry: Islamist-Secularist Debate and the Subversion of Secular Identity in Monarchical Egypt', Philadelphia: American Political Science Association, 2003.

Gunaratna, Rohan, 'Links with Islamist Groups: Ideology and Operations', in *The Challenge of Hizb ut-Tahrir*, ed. Zeyno Baran, 124–6, Ankara, Turkey: Nixon Center, 2004.

ICG, 'Radical Islam in Central Asia: Responding to Hizb Ut-Tahrir', in *Asia Report*, Brussels: International Crisis Group, 2003.

Joseph S. Nye, Jr, 'Why the Gulf War Served the National Interest', *The Atlantic Monthly* 268, no. 1 (1991): 56–64.

Karagiannis, Emmanuel, 'Hizb Ut-Tahrir Al-Islami: Evaluating the Threat Posed by a Radical Islamic Group That Remains Nonviolent', *Terrorism and Political Violence* 18, no. 2 (2006): 315–34.

——— 'Political Islam in Central Asia: Hizb Ut-Tahrir Al-Islami', *Europe-Asia Studies* 58, no. 2 (2006): 261–80.

Little, Douglas, 'Cold War and Covert Action: The United States and Syria, 1945–1958', *Middle East Journal* 44, no. 1 (1990): 51–75.

Mayer, Jean-François, 'Hizb Ut-Tahrir—the Next Al-Qaida, Really?', *PSIO Occasional Paper* (2004): 1–24.

Pankhurst, Reza, 'The Caliphate, and the Changing Strategy of the Public Statements of Al-Qaeda's Leaders', *Political Theology* 11, no. 4 (2010): 530–52.

Precht, Henry, 'The Iranian Revolution: An Oral History with Henry Precht, Then State Department Desk Officer', *Middle East Journal* 58, no. 1 (2004): 9–31.

Ramazani, Rouhollah K., 'Constitution of the Islamic Republic of Iran', *Middle East Journal* 34, no. 2 (1980): 181–204.

Shields, Acacia, 'Creating Enemies of the State: Religious Persecution in Uzbekistan', New York: Human Rights Watch, 2004.

Sid-Ahmed, Mohamed, 'Egypt: The Islamic Issue', *Foreign Policy*, no. 69 (1987): 22–39.

Sinclair, Kirstine, 'The Caliphate as Homeland: Hizb Ut-Tahrir in Denmark and Britain', University of Southern Denmark, 2010.

Tal, Lawrence, 'Britain and the Jordan Crisis of 1958', *Middle Eastern Studies* 31, no. 1 (1995): 39–57.

Temnenko, Zeyneb, 'Islam and Hizb Ut-Tahrir's Activities in Crimea, Ukraine', *Centro Argentino de Estudios Internacionales* (2009).

Whine, Michael, 'Hizb Ut-Tahrir in Open Societies', in *The Challenge of Hizb ut-Tahrir*, ed. Zeyno Baran, 99–109, Ankara, Turkey: Nixon Center, 2004.

WorldPublicOpinion.org. 'Muslim Public Opinion on US Policy, Attacks on Civilians and Al-Qaeda', The Center for International and Security Studies at Maryland, 2007.

## Books and Book Sections

*Arabic*

'Amara, Muhammad, *Ma'raka Al-Islam Wa Usul Al-Hukm*, Cairo: Dar al-Sharook, 1997.

—— 'Taha Hussein Wa-L-Khilafa Al-Islamiyya', *Al-Ahram*, 15 November 2011.

'Ashur, Muhammad Al-Tahir ibn, *Naqd 'Ilmy Li Kitab Al-Islam Wa Usul Al-Hukm*, Cairo: Maktaba al-Salafiyya, 1925.

Abdu, Ghanim, *Naqd Al-Ishtirakiyya Al-Marksiyya*, 1963.

Abdul-Raziq, Ali, '*Al-Islam Wa Usul Al-Hukm*', in *Al-Islam Wa Usul Al-Hukm— Darasa Wa Watha'iq*, ed. Muhammad 'Amara, Beirut: *Al-Mua'sasa al-Arabiyya li-l-darasat wa-l-nashr*, 1972.

al-Alami, Ali Kawrani 'Illa Talib Al-'Ilm', 2010, http://www.alameli.net/downbooks/taleb%20alam.pdf

al-Aleisi, Muhammad, *Abdul Aziz Al-Badri—Al-'Alim Al-Mujahid Al-Shahid*. Amman: Dar al-Bayareq, 2001.

al-Alusi, Mahmud Shukri, *Kitab Ghayat Al-Amani Fi-L-Radd Al-Nabhani*, published privately by Abdul Aziz al-Jamih and Muhammad Abdullah al-Jamih.

al-Baytar, Abdul Razzaq, *Hilyutu Al-Bashar Fi Tarikh Al-Qarn Al-Thalithi Al-'Ashr*, Beirut: Dar Sadir, 1993.

al-Da'ur, Ahmad, *Al-Ahkam Al-Bayyinat*, 1965.

al-Juda'i, Abdul Allah bin Yusuf, *Tayseer 'Ilm Usul Al-Fiqh*, Beirut: Mu'assa al-Rayyan, 2006.

al-Madaris, Dr Falah Abdullah, *Hizb Ut-Tahrir Fi Kuwait*, Kuwait: Dar al-Qurtas, 2007.

al-Maliki, Abdul Rahman, *Nitham Al-'Uqubat*, 1965.

Al-Mutee'i, Muhammad Bakhit, *Haqiqa Al-Islam Wa Usul Al-Hukm*, Cairo: Al-Matba'a al-Salifiyya, 1925.

al-Nabhani, Taqiudeen, *Al-Dawla Al-Islamiyya*, 1st edn., Damascus: al-Manar, 1952.

—— *Al-Shakhsiyya Al-Islamiyya*, 1st edn., Amman: Al-Maktaba al-'Amma, 1952.

—— *Al-Nitham Al-Iqtisad*, 2nd edn., Jerusalem 1953.

—— *Al-Nitham Al-Islami*, 2nd edn., Jerusalem 1953.

—— *Al-Shakhsiyya Al-Islamiyya—Al-Juz Al-Awwal*. 6th edn., Beirut: Dar al-Umma, 2003.

—— *Al-Shakhsiyya Al-Islamiyya: Al-Juz Al-Thani*, 3rd edn., Beirut: Dar al-Umma, 1994.

—— *Al-Tafkir*, 1973.

—— *Al-Takattul Al-Hizbi*, 4th edn., 2001.

—— *Inqath Filistin*, Damascus: Ibn Zaydun, 1950.

—— 'Risala Al-Arab', 1950

—— *Sur'at Al-Badiha*, 1976.

al-Nabhani, Yusuf, *Al-Majmu'a Al-Nabhaniyya Fi-L-Mada'ih Al-Nabawiyya*, Beirut: Dar al-Kutub al-'ilmiyya, 1996.

—— *Jami' Karamat Al-Awliya*, Gujrat: Markaz-e-Ahl-e-Sunnat Barkat-e-Raza, 2001.

—— *Kitab Al-Ahadith Al-Arba'in Fi Fadl Al-Jihad Wa-L-Mujahidin*, Beirut: Dar al-Basha'ir al-Islamiyya, 1970.

—— *Kitab Al-Ahadith Al-Arba'in Fi Wujub Ta'a Amir Al-Mu'minin*, Beirut: Al-Matba' al-Ababiya, 1894.

al-Qaradawi, Yusuf, *Min Fiqh Al-Dawla Fi-L-Islam*, Cairo: Dar al-Sharouq, 1997.

al-Qusayyir, Abdullah bin Salih, *Bayan Arkan Al-Iman*, Riyadh: Maktaba al-Malik Fahd al-Wataniyya, 2003.

al-Samani, Turki Abdul-Majid, *Taqiudeen Al-Nabhani Wa Mashru'ihi Al-Fikri Wa-L-Siyasi*, Baghdad: University of Baghdad, 2012.

al-Shurrab, Muhammad Muhammad Hasan, *Izz Al-Din Al-Qassam: Sheikh Al-Mujahidin Fi Filistin*, Damascus: Dar al-Qalam, 2000.

al-Tall, Abdullah, *Karitha Filistin*. 2nd edn., Alexandria: Dar al-Huda, 1990.

al-Ubaidi, Auni, *Hizb Ut-Tahrir Al-Islami*, Amman: Dar al-liwa li-l-Sahafa wa-l-Nashr, 1993.

Amin, Sadiq, *Al-Da'wa Al-Islamiyya: Farida Shara'iyya Wa Darura Bashariyya*, Amman: Dar al-Tawzi' wa-l-nashr al-islamiyya, n.d.

Hamdan, Dawud, *Usus Al-Nahda*, Beirut: Dar al-Kasshaf, 1953.

Hanbal, Ahmad bin, *Musnad Al-Imam Ahmad Bin Hanbal*, Beirut: Muassisa al-Risala, 1999.

Hizb-ut-Tahrir, *Al-Hamla Al-Amrikiyya Li-L-Qada Ala-L-Islam*, 1996.

—— 'Bayan 1/6/1953.'

—— *Dukhul Al-Mujtama'*, 1958.

—— *Hazzat Al-Aswaq Al-Maliyya: Asbabuha Wa Hukm Al-Shar Fi Hathihi Asbab*, 1997.

—— *Hizb Ut-Tahrir*, 2nd edn., 2010.

—— 'Khutut 'Arida 'an Qiyam Al-Hizb Bi-L-'Amal Al-Juz'iyya', 1961.

—— *Mafahim Siyasiyya Li-Hizb Ut-Tahrir*, 1st edn., 1969.

—— *Mafahim Siyasiyya Li-Hizb Ut-Tahrir*, 4th edn., 2005.

—— *Mefahim Khatira Li-Darb Al-Islam*, 1998.

—— 'Munaqasha Bayn Ithnayn Min Al-Shabab', 1961.

—— *Muqadimma Al-Dustor*, 1963.

—— 'Muthakirra Hizb Al-Tahrir Li Ra'is Wa 'Ada Majlis Al-'Ayan Wa-LNawab Fi-L-Urdan', 1960.

—— 'Muqtatafat Siyasiyya', 1961.

—— *Natharat Siyasiyya Li-Hizb Ut-Tahrir*, 1973.

—— *Nuqta Al-Intilaq Li Hizb Ut-Tahrir*, 1954.

—— *Waqa'i Nida Hizb Ut-Tahrir Illa Al-Umma Al-Islamiyya*, n.d.

Hussein, Muhammad al-Khidr, *Naqd Kitab Fi-L-Shi'ir Al-Jahili*. Cairo: Al-Maktaba al-Azhariyya li-l-turath, n.d.

—— 'Naqd Kitab Al-Islam Wa Usul Al-Hukm (1925)', in *Ma'raka Al-Islam Wa Usul Al-Hukm*, ed. Muhammad 'Amara, Cairo: Dar al-Sharook, 1997.

Hussein, Taha, *Fi-L-Shi'ir Al-Jahili*, Susa: Dar al-Ma'arif, 1997.

—— *Hafiz Wa Shawky*, Cairo: Maktaba al-Khanji, 1933.

Ismael, Muhammad Muhammad, *Al-Fikr Al-Islami*, 1958.

Iwaida, Mahmoud Abdul Latif, *Haml Al-Da'wa Wajibat Wa Sifat*, Hizb-ut-Tahrir, 1996.

Khalil, Ata' bin, *Taysir Al-Wasul Ila-L-Usul*, Beirut: Dar al-Umma, 2000.

Manna, Adil, *A'lam Filastin Fi Awakhir Al-'Ahd Al-'Uthmani (1800–1918)*, Beirut: Institute for Palestine Studies, 1990.

Muslim, Abul Husain 'Asakir-ud-Din, *Sahih Muslim*, Beirut: Dar al-Fikr, 1998.

Qutb, Sayyid, *Fi Dhilal Al-Qur'an*, Cairo: Dar al-Shuruk, 2004.

Raghib, Ali, *Al-Ahkam Al-Salah*, 1958.

Salama, Ziyad Ahmed, *Faqir Min Bilad Al-Sham*, Amman: Dar al-Salam, 2007.

—— 'Farhun La Yantahi', unpublished manuscript, 2011.

Salih, Mohsin Muhammad, *Al-Tayyar Al-Islami Fi Filistin Wa Atharahu Fi Haraka Al-Jihad 1917–48*, Kuwait: Maktaba al-Falah, 1989.

Samara, Ihsan, *Mafhum Al-'Adala Al-Ijtima'iyya Fi Al-Fikr Al-Islami Al-Mu'asir*, Jerusalem: Al-Risala, 1987.

Shinnar, Amin, *Al-Mash'al Al-Khalid*, Al-Bira: Matba' al-Sharq, 1957.

Ulaywan, Hisham, *Al-Sheikh Taqiudeen Al-Nabahani*, Beirut: Center of Civilisation for the Development of Islamic Thought, 2009.

Zahran, Mustafa, and Mahmud Tarshubi, *Hizb Ut-Tahrir—Ya'ud Li-L-Hayat Ma'a-L-Thawrat Al-'Arabiyya*, Cairo: Markaz al-Din wa-l-siyasa li-l-dirasa, 2012.

Zallum, Abdul Qadeem, *Hukm Al-Shar Fi-L-Istinsakh*, 1997.

Zayyat, Muntasir, *Al-Jama'at Al-Islamiyya: Al-Ru'ya Min Al-Dakhil*, Cairo: Dar Al-Masr al-Mahrusa, 2005.

*English*

Aburish, Said K., *Saddam Hussein: The Politics of Revenge*, London: Bloomsbury, 2000.

Ali, Tariq, *The Clash of Fundamentalisms: Crusades, Jihads and Modernity*, London: Verso, 2002.

Anderson, Betty S., *Nationalist Voices in Jordan: The Street and the State*, Austin, TX: University of Texas Press; Chesham: Combined Academic [distributor], 2005.

Aziz, Talib, 'Baqir Al-Sadr's Quest for the Marja'iya', in *The Most Learned of the Shi'a: The Institution of the Marja'i Taqlid*, ed. Linda S. Walbridge, New York and Oxford: Oxford University Press, 2001.

Bailey, Clinton, *Jordan's Palestinian Challenge, 1948–1983: A Political History*, Boulder, CO and London: Westview, 1984.

Bakhash, Shaul, *The Reign of the Ayatollahs: Iran and the Islamic Revolution*, New York: Basic Books, 1984.

Bar, Shmuel, *The Muslim Brotherhood in Jordan*, Tel Aviv: Moshe Dayan Center for Middle Eastern and African Studies, 1998.

Calvert, John, *Sayyid Qutb and the Origins of Radical Islamism*, London: Hurst & Co., 2010.

Clinton, Bill, *My Life*, London: Arrow Books, 2005.

Cohen, Amnon, *Political Parties in the West Bank under the Jordanian Regime 1949–1967*, London: Cornell University Press, 1982.

——— 'Political Parties in the West Bank under the Hashemite Regime', in *Palestinan Arab Politics*, ed. Moshe Ma'oz, 21–50, Jerusalem: Jerusalem Academic Press, 1975.

Copeland, Miles, *The Game Player: Confessions of the CIA'S Original Political Operative*, London: Aurum, 1989.

Curtis, Glenn E., Eric J. Hooglund, and Library of Congress, Federal Research Division, *Iran: A Country Study*. 5th edn., Area Handbook Series, Washington, DC: Library of Congress, Federal Research Division, 2008.

Dann, Uriel, *King Hussein and the Challenge of Arab Radicalism: Jordan, 1955–1967*, New York and Oxford: Oxford University Press, 1989.

Dye, Thomas R., and L. Harmon Zeigler, *The Irony of Democracy: An Uncommon Introduction to American Politics*, Millennial edn., Fort Worth: Harcourt Brace College Publishers, 2000.

Esposito, John L., *The Oxford Dictionary of Islam*, Oxford: Oxford University Press, 2003.

Farouk-Sluglett, Marion, and Peter Sluglett, *Iraq since 1958: From Revolution to Dictatorship*, [Rev. edn.] London: I.B. Tauris, 2001.

Fealy, Greg, 'Hizb Ut Tahrir in Indonesia: Seeking a "Total" Islamic Identity', in *Islam and Political Violence: Muslim Diaspora and Radicalism in the West*, eds Shahram Akbarzadeh and Fethi Mansouri, 151–64, London and New York: Tauris Academic Studies, 2007.

Fukuyama, Francis, *The End of History and the Last Man*, New York: The Free Press, 1992.

Glubb, John Bagot, *A Soldier with the Arabs*, London: Hodder and Stoughton, 1957.

Hassan, Mona F., 'Loss of Caliphate: The Trauma and Aftermath of 1258 and 1924', Princeton University, 2009.

Hinnebusch, Raymond A., *Syria: Revolution from Above*, London: Routledge, 2001.

Huneidi, Sahar, *A Broken Trust: Sir Herbert Samuel, Zionism and the Palestinians*, London: I.B. Tauris, 2001.

Huntington, Samuel P., *The Clash of Civilisations and the Remaking of a World Order*, New York: Simon & Schuster, 2003.

Jabbar, Falih Abdul, *The Shi'ite Movement in Iraq*, London: Saqi, 2003.

Jahanbakhsh, Forough, *Islam, Democracy and Religious Modernism in Iran, 1953–2000*, Leiden and Boston: Brill, 2001.

Joyce, Miriam, *Anglo-American Support for Jordan: The Career of King Hussein*, New York: Palgrave Macmillan, 2008.

Karagiannis, Emmanuel, *Political Islam in Central Asia*, London: Routledge, 2009.

Khalidi, Rashid, *The Iron Cage: The Story of the Palestinian Struggle for Statehood*, Oxford: Oneworld Publications, 2006.

Khalidi, Walid, *All That Remains: The Palestinian Villages Occupied and Depopulated by Israel in 1948*, Washington, DC: Institute for Palestine Studies, 1992.

Kinzer, Stephen, *Overthrow: America's Century of Regime Change from Hawaii to Iraq*, New York: Times Books/Henry Holt, 2006.

Kramer, Martin, 'Syria's Alawis and Shi'ism', in *Shi'ism, Resistance and Revolution*, ed. Martin Kramer, 237–54, London: Mansell, 1987.

Kramer, Martin S., and Merkaz Dayan, *Islam Assembled: The Advent of the Muslim Congresses*, New York: Columbia University Press, 1985.

Magas, Branka, and Ivo Zanic, *The War in Croatia and Bosnia-Herzegovina, 1991–1995*, London: Frank Cass, 2001.

Matthee, Rudi, 'Egyptian Reactions to the Iranian Revolution', in *Shi'ism and Social Protest*, eds Juan R. I. Cole and Nikki R. Keddie, 247–74, New Haven and London: Yale University Press, 1986.

Metz, Helen Chapin, and Library of Congress, Federal Research Division, *Iran: A Country Study*. 4th edn., Area Handbook Series, Washington, DC: The Division: For sale by the Supt. of Docs, US GPO, 1989.

Milton-Edwards, Beverley, *Islamic Politics in Palestine*, London: Tauris Academic Studies, 1999.

Milton-Edwards, Beverley, and Peter Hinchcliffe, *Jordan: A Hashemite Legacy*, 2nd edn., London: Routledge, 2009.

Murray, Craig, *Murder in Samarkand: A British Ambassador's Defiance of Tyranny in the War on Terror*, Edinburgh: Mainstream, 2006.

Nef, Claudia, 'Promoting the Caliphate on Campus: Debates and Advocacies of Hizbut Tahrir Student Activists in Indonesia', in *Demystifying the Caliphate*, eds Madawi al-Rasheed, Carool Kersten and Marat Shterin, 185–206, London: Hurst & Co., 2013.

Nohlen, Dieter, Florian Grotz, and Christof Hartmann, *Elections in Asia and the Pacific: A Data Handbook*, Oxford: Oxford University Press, 2001.

O'Connell, Jack, and Vernon Loeb, *King's Counsel: A Memoir of War, Espionage, and Diplomacy in the Middle East*, 1st edn., New York and London: W.W. Norton, 2011.

Pankhurst, Reza, *The Inevitable Caliphate?*, London: Hurst & Co., 2013.

Pappé, Ilan, and St Antony's College, *Britain and the Arab-Israeli Conflict 1948–51*, Basingstoke: Macmillan, in association with St Antony's College, Oxford, 1988.

Rashid, Ahmed, *Jihad: The Rise of Militant Islam in Central Asia*, London: Yale University Press, 2002.

Rogan, Eugene L., *The Arabs: A History*, New York: Basic Books, 2009.

Rositzke, Harry August, *The CIA'S Secret Operations: Espionage, Counterespionage, and Covert Action*, New York: Reader's Digest Press, distributed by Crowell, 1977.

Sageman, Marc, *Understanding Terror Networks*, Philadelphia: University of Pennsylvania Press, 2004.

Sankari, Jamal, *Fadlallah: The Making of a Radical Shi'ite Leader*, London: Saqi, 2005.

Scott, Peter Dale, *The Road to 9/11: Wealth, Empire, and the Future of America*, Berkeley, CA and London: University of California Press, 2007.

Seale, Patrick, *Abu Nidal: A Gun for Hire*, New York: Random House, 1992.

Shay, Shaul, *Islamic Terror and the Balkans*. New Brunswick, NJ and London: Transaction Publishers, 2006.

Shlaim, Avi, 'Israel and the Arab Coalition in 1948', in *The War for Palestine: Rewriting the History of 1948*, eds Eugene L. Rogan and Avi Shlaim, 79–103, Cambridge: Cambridge University Press, 2001.

Sick, Gary, *All Fall Down: America's Tragic Encounter with Iran*, New York: Random House, 1985.

St John, Ronald Bruce, *Historical Dictionary of Libya*, 4th edn., Lanham, MD and Oxford: Scarecrow Press, 2006.

Taji-Farouki, Suha, *A Fundamental Quest: Hizb Al-Tahrir and the Search for the Islamic Caliphate*, London: Grey Seal Limited, 1996.

Wright, Lawrence, *The Looming Tower: Al-Qaeda and the Road to 9/11*, New York: Knopf, 2006.

Yesilbursa, B. Kemal, *The Baghdad Pact: Anglo-American Defence Policies in the Middle East, 1950–1959*, London: Frank Cass, 2005.

## News Articles (Print and Web)

*Arabic*

Abdelhamid, Fawzi, 'Hujum Al-Gaddafi Ala-L-Jami'a', http://www.libya-watanona.com/adab/forfia/fo30108a.htm, last accessed on 17 March 2013.

Abedin, Mahan, 'Al-Muhajiroun in the UK: An Interview with Sheikh Omar Bakri Mohammed', The Jamestown Foundation, http://www.jamestown.org/single/?no_cache=1&tx_ttnews%5Btt_news%5D=290, last accessed on 12 April 2013.

——— 'Islamic Movement: Hizbut Tahrir's New Drive in the Levant—an Interview with Dr. Mohammed Jaber', Religioscope, http://religion.info/english/interviews/article_474.shtml, last accessed on 30 March 2013.

Ahmad, Jaber, 'Asrar Al-Thawra Al-Iraniyya Bayn Ma Huwa Mu'lan Wa Ma Huwa Khafi', Al-Hewar al-Mutamadin, http://www.ahewar.org/debat/show.art.asp?aid=129579, last accessed on 17 March 2013.

al-Amin, Hazem, 'Bakura "Al-Jihad Al-'Alami"', Kalamon, http://www.kalamon.org/articles-details-12#axzz2P91SOp4A, last accessed on 1 April 2013.

al-Bakur, Basim, 'Hizb Ut-Tahrir Yahlim Bi-Istirja' "Dawla Al-Khilafa" Al-Islamiyya', *Al-Nahar*, 5 October 2004.

al-Esa, Usama, 'Filistini Arada Ightiyal Al-Sadat Wa Isqat Nithamihi Antaha Ma'tuha', Elaph Publishing Limited, http://www.kalamon.org/articles-details-12#axzz2P91SOp4A, last accessed on 1 April 2013.

al-Fadili, Fathi, 'Al-Shahid Salih Muhammad Al-Farisi', http://www.fathifadhli.com/art5.htm, last accessed on 17 March 2013.

——— 'Shahid Al-Kalima... Wa-L-Fikra... Al-Ustadh Muhammad Mustafa Ramadan', http://www.fathifadhli.com/aws4.htm, last accessed on 17 March 2013.

——— 'Shahid Al-Mabadi... Ibn Al-Watan: Muhammad Muhathab Haffaf', http://www.fathifadhli.com/aws7.htm, last accessed on 17 March 2013.

al-Gharib, Said, 'Al-Sanussi: Al-Gaddafi Ta'araka Bi-L-Aydi Ma'a Al-Sadr Wa Amara Bi Qatlihi', *Al-Ahram*, 12 September 2012.

al-Hiwar, 'Memoirs with Ibrahim Ghosha', http://goo.gl/0tZTK, last accessed on 12 April 2016.

al-Hiwar, 'Memoirs with Munir Shafiq', http://goo.gl/ZL9HL, last accessed on 12 April 2016.

al-Jazeera, 'The Palestinian Revolution According to the View of Muhammad Dawud Owda, 24 July 1999', http://goo.gl/1pLk3, last accessed on 1 April 2013.

'Al-Rasa'il Allati Hakamat, 'Ala Muhammad Mustafa Ramadan Bi-L-Tasfiyya Al-Jasadiyya', Arab News, http://bit.ly/Xn7PfB, last accessed on 17 March 2013.

al-Shabul, Faisal, 'Muthakarrat (Interview with Abdul-Aziz Al-Khayyat)', *Al-Wasat*, 10–16 July 1995, 30–35.

'Al-Ustadh Al-Nabhani', *Al-Karmil*, 6 July 1932.

al-Waie, 'Buzugh Nur Min Al-Masjid Al-Aqsa', no. 234–5, 2006.

Al-Wais, Bilal, 'Dabit Mutaqa'id Yarwi Tafasil Mu'amara Nadhim Kazar', Shabika al-'Ilam al-'Iraqiyya fi-l-Denmark, http://bit.ly/13Q1wIl, last accessed on 11 March 2013.

An-Nahar, 'Iktishaf Hizb Ut-Tahrir Yuqarrib Al-Haraka Al-Islamiyya Mina-L-Sulta', *An-Nahar Arab and International*, 29 August 1983.

Annahar—Beirut, 'Ahmad Fatfat: Hasan Nasrullah Kan Yahmi "Fath Al-Islam" Fi-L-Barid', *Annahar*, 6 October 2007.

—— 'Ahmad Fatfat: La Mani' Min Al-Tarkhis Li "Hizb Ut-Tahrir" Wa in Kunna Nakhtalif Ma'ahu Fi L Rai', *Annahar*, 25 June 2006.

Ghurayaba, Ibrahim, 'Maqtal Al-Diplomasi Al-Amriki Fi Amman Wa Siyaq Al-Unf Fi-L-Urdan', Al Jazeera, http://www.aljazeera.net/opinions/pages/dd91a489-c9cc-4d99–9fe8–479d3eb5bd83, last accessed on 3 April 2013.

''Itiqalat Fi Hizb Ut-Tahrir Al-Islami Fi Suriya', Syria News, http://www.syria-news.com/readnews.php?sy_seq=151, last accessed on 22 December 2012.

'Jamia Trabulus Tuhyi Dhikr Al-Sabi' Min April', Al-Watan al-Libiyya, http://bit.ly/UZG4HI, last accessed on 27 November 2012.

Madini, Tawfik Al, 'Tasa'ud Hizb Ut-Tahrir Fi Tunis', Nawaa, http://bit.ly/skmUXz, last accessed on 1 April 2013.

Madkur, Mona, 'Hizb Ut-Tahrir: Hizb Jadid Taht Ta'sis Yas'a Li-Iqama Al-Khilafa Wa Yatabir Misr Wilaya', *Al-Sharq al-Awsat*, 17 March 2012.

'Mulhaq Khas 'an Hizb Ut-Tahrir', *Al-Wathiqa*, 6 July 2012.

Mun'im, Amru Abdul, 'Ibn Salih Siriyya Qa'id Amaliyya Al-Finiyya Al-Askariyya Li "Muhit" (1/2)', http://www.masress.com/moheet/72784, last accessed on 10 March 2013.

—— 'Ibn Salih Siriyya Qa'id Amaliyya Al-Finiyya Al-Askariyya Li "Muhit" (2/2)', http://www.masress.com/moheet/69572, last accessed on 10 March 2013.

Pheladelphia News, 'Qarar Yamna' Al-Na'ib Al-Sabiq Ali Al-Dala'in Min Al-Safar Kharij Al-Balad', Pheladelphia News, http://bit.ly/13XqGWx, last accessed on 22 April 2013.

Research Department, 'Hizb Ut-Tahrir', *Al-Juthur*, February 1991, 76–81.

Salim, Muhammad Al-Sayyid, 'Al-Haqiqa Fima Nushira 'an Qadiyya Al-Finiyya Al-Askariyya', Al Maqreze Center for Historical Studies, http://www.almaqreze.net/ar/news.php?readmore=260, last accessed on 14 March 2013.

Shams, Dalia, 'Al-Natiq Al-Siyasi Li-Liwa Amru Bin Al-As', *Al-Shuruq*, 22 November 2012.

Watha'iq, 'A'da Hizb Ut-Tahrir Al-Islami Amam Al-Mahkama', *Watha'iq*, 26 August 1983.

*English*

AFP, 'Tunisia Legalises Second Hardline Islamist Group Hizb Al-Tahrir', Ahram Online, http://english.ahram.org.eg/NewsContent/2/8/48066/World/Region/Tunisia-legalises-second-hardline-Islamist-group-H.aspx, last accessed on 22 April 2013.

AP, 'Abdel-Rahman Aref, 91, Former Iraqi President, Is Dead', *The New York Times*, 25 August 2007.

——— 'At Least 846 Killed in Egypt's Revolution', Egypt Independent, http://www.egyptindependent.com/news/least-846-killed-egypt%E2%80%99s-revolution, last accessed on 20 April 2013.

——— 'Report Cites Europe's Role in C.I.A. Renditions', *The New York Times*, 7 June 2006.

Arab News, 'Who Killed Farhad Usmanov?' Arab News, http://www.arabnews.com/node/222162, last accessed on 20 April 2013.

Asad, Malik, 'Hizbut Tahrir Made Three Attempts to Penetrate Army', *Dawn*, 29 October 2012.

BBC News, 'Freed UK Three Return to Families', BBC News, http://news.bbc.co.uk/1/hi/uk/4763056.stm, last accessed on 20 April 2013.

——— 'London Bomber: Text in Full', BBC News, http://news.bbc.co.uk/1/hi/uk/4206800.stm, last accessed on 20 April 2013.

——— 'Protesters Highlight "War against Muslims"', BBC News, http://news.bbc.co.uk/1/hi/uk/2139955.stm, last accessed on 20 April 2013.

——— 'Trial of Britons in Egypt Delayed', BBC News, http://news.bbc.co.uk/1/hi/uk/2693257.stm, last accessed on 20 April 2013.

——— 'Tunisia: President Zine Al-Abidine Ben Ali Forced Out', BBC News, http://www.bbc.co.uk/news/world-africa-12195025, last accessed on 20 April 2013.

——— 'Video of 7 July Bomber Released', BBC News, http://news.bbc.co.uk/1/hi/5154714.stm, last accessed on 20 April 2013.

Ben-Ze'ev, Efrat, 'The Palestinian Village of Ijzim During the 1948 War: Forming an Anthropological History through Villagers Accounts and Army Documents', http://www.palestineremembered.com/Haifa/Ijzim/Story21109.html, last accessed on 6 January 2013.

Bowcott, Owen, 'Egypt Pressed over "Torture" of Britons', *The Guardian*, 21 September 2002, http://www.guardian.co.uk/uk/2002/sep/21/world.owenbowcott, last accessed on 6 January 2013.

Bright, Martin, 'Losing the Plot', *New Statesman*, 30 January 2006, http://www.newstatesman.com/node/195463?, last accessed on 10 January 2010.

Bush, George W., 'President Rallies the Troops in Alaska', The White House, http://georgewbush-whitehouse.archives.gov/news/releases/2002/02/20020216–1.html, last accessed on 4 April 2013.

——— 'Remarks by the President Upon Arrival', The White House, http://georgew-bush-whitehouse.archives.gov/news/releases/2001/09/20010916–2.html, last accessed on 4 April 2013.

——— 'Text of President Bush's 2002 State of the Union Address', *The Washington Post*, http://www.washingtonpost.com/wp-srv/onpolitics/transcripts/sou012902.htm, last accessed on 20 April 2013.

Cobain, Ian, 'Islamist Group Challenges Berlin's Five-Year Ban in European Court', *The Guardian*, 24 June 2008, http://www.guardian.co.uk/world/2008/jun/24/islam.religion, last accessed on 25 March 2013.

Cobain, Ian, and Martin Chulov. 'Libyan Papers Show UK Worked with Gaddafi in Rendition Operation', *The Guardian*, 4 September 2011, http://www.guardian.co.uk/world/2011/sep/04/libyan-papers-show-uk-rendition, last accessed on 20 November 2012.

Cobain, Ian, and Nick Fielding, 'Banned Islamists Spawn Front Organisations', *The Guardian*, 13 December 2006, http://www.guardian.co.uk/uk/2006/jul/22/terrorism.world, last accessed on 20 November 2012.

Cockburn, Leslie, and Andrew Cockburn, 'Royal Mess', *The New Yorker*, 28 November 1994, 54.

Cohen, Avner, 'The Last Nuclear Moment', *The New York Times*, 6 October 2003, http://www.nytimes.com/2003/10/06/opinion/the-last-nuclear-moment.html, last accessed on 14 March 2013.

Cunningham, Finian, 'The 1979 Iranian US Embassy Siege and Hostage Crisis. Was It a Covert CIA Operation?' Global Research, http://www.globalresearch.ca/the-1979-iranian-us-embassy-siege-and-hostage-crisis-was-it-a-covert-cia-operation/30291, last accessed on 28 March 2013.

Dodd, Vikram, 'Anti-Terror Code "Would Alienate Most Muslims"', *The Guardian*, 17 February 2009, http://www.guardian.co.uk/politics/2009/feb/17/counterterrorism-strategy-muslims, last accessed on 2 April 2013.

Doward, Jamie, and Gaby Hinsliff, 'PM Shelves Islamic Group Ban', *The Guardian*, 24 December 2006, http://www.guardian.co.uk/world/2006/dec/24/religion.uk, last accessed on 15 April 2013.

Falk, Richard, 'Trusting Khomeini', *The New York Times*, 16 February 1979.

Farrell, Stephen, 'Confession Signature Code Reveals Briton's Torture in Cairo Prison', *The Times*, 18 November 2002, p. 1.

Frontline World, 'Rendition Timeline', PBS, http://www.pbs.org/frontlineworld/stories/rendition701/timeline/timeline_1.html, last accessed on 18 April 2013.

Gardham, Duncan, 'Libya: MI5 Believed Moussa Koussa Was Involved in Assassinations', *The Telegraph*, 5 April 2011, http://www.telegraph.co.uk/news/worldnews/africaandindianocean/libya/8430344/Libya-MI5-believed-Moussa-Koussa-was-involved-in-assassinations.html, last accessed on 10 March 2013.

Gilligan, Andrew, 'Hizb Ut Tahrir Is Not a Gateway to Terrorism, Claims Whitehall

Report', *The Telegraph*, 25 July 2010, http://www.telegraph.co.uk/journalists/ andrew-gilligan/7908262/Hizb-ut-Tahrir-is-not-a-gateway-to-terrorism-claims-Whitehall-report.html, last accessed on 5 April 2013.

Gruen, Madeleine, 'Hizb-Ut-Tahrir's Activities in the United States', The Jamestown Foundation, http://www.jamestown.org/single/?no_cache=1&tx_ttnews%5Btt_ news%5D=4377, last accessed on 5 April 2013.

Hill, Evan, 'Libya Survivor Describes 1996 Prison Massacre', Al-Jazeera English, http://www.aljazeera.com/indepth/features/2011/09/20119223521462487.html, last accessed on 20 March 2013.

Jaffary, Shahab, 'Hizbut Tahrir Complicates Military's Terrorism Calculus', *Pakistan Today*, http://bit.ly/SYBVo6, last accessed on 30 October 2012.

Jordan, Michael J., 'Europe Cringes at Bush "Crusade" against Terrorists', *The Christian Science Monitor*, http://www.csmonitor.com/2001/0919/p12s2-woeu.html, last accessed on 3 April 2013.

—— 'Sex Charges Haunt UN Forces', *The Christian Science Monitor*, http://www. csmonitor.com/2004/1126/p06s02-wogi.html, last accessed on 3 April 2013.

Lambroschini, Sophie, 'Germany: Court Appeal by Hizb Ut-Tahrir Highlights Balancing Act between Actions, Intentions', Radio Free Europe, http://www.rferl. org/content/article/1055527.html, last accessed on 20 April 2013.

Malik, Shiv, 'For Allah and the Caliphate', *New Statesman*, 13 September 2004, http://www.newstatesman.com/node/148823, last accessed on 2 April 2013.

—— 'Watchdog Recommends Tory U-Turn on Banning Hizb Ut-Tahrir', *The Guardian*, 18 July 2011, http://bit.ly/qxtHLx, last accessed on 2 April 2013.

Massad, Joseph, 'The "Arab Spring" and Other American Seasons', http://www.aljazeera.com/indepth/opinion/2012/08/201282972539153865.html, last accessed on 19 April 2013.

MediaGuardian, 'Background: The Guardian and Dilpazier Aslam', *The Guardian*, http://www.guardian.co.uk/media/2005/jul/22/theguardian.pressandpublishing1, last accessed on 20 April 2013.

MRS/MMN, 'Turkey Arrests 200 Hizb Ut-Tahrir Suspects', Press TV, http://edition. presstv.ir/detail/101535.html, last accessed on 4 April 2013.

National Security Archive, 'Secret U.S. Message to Mullah Omar: "Every Pillar of the Taliban Regime Will Be Destroyed"', National Security Archive, http://www.gwu. edu/~nsarchiv/NSAEBB/NSAEBB358a/index.htm#7, last accessed on 19 April 2013.

Nordland, Rod, 'Files Note Close C.I.A. Ties to Qaddafi Spy Unit', *The New York Times*, 2 September 2011, http://www.nytimes.com/2011/09/03/world/africa/ 03libya.html?pagewanted=all&_r=0, last accessed on 3 April 2013.

Our Correspondent, 'Call to Revive Khilafat', *The News International*, 3 September 2005.

Perelman, Marc, 'Uzbek Unrest Shines Light on Leader's Ties to Jewry', *The Jewish*

*Daily Forward*, http://forward.com/articles/3544/uzbek-unrest-shines-light-on-leaderes-ties-to-je/, last accessed on 4 April 2013.

Reuters, 'Uzbekistan Torture Ignored by the West, Say Human Rights Group', *The Guardian*, 13 December 2011, http://www.guardian.co.uk/world/2011/dec/13/uzbekistan-torture-ignored-west, last accessed on 20 November 2012.

Schenker, David, 'One Year after the Cedar Revolution', The Washington Institute, http://bit.ly/RmsTzF, last accessed on 30 October 2012.

Sijjil, 'April Victims of the Gaddafi Regime', Tripod, http://sijill.tripod.com/victims/, last accessed on 27 October 2012.

Sloboda, John, and Chris Abbott, 'The "Blair Doctrine" and After: Five Years of Humanitarian Intervention', OpenDemocracy, http://www.opendemocracy.net/globalization-institutions_government/article_1857.jsp, last accessed on 18 April 2013.

Spyer, Jonathan, 'Hizb Ut-Tahrir: A Rising Force in Palestinian Territories', Global Politician, http://www.globalpolitician.com/default.asp?23871-palestine/, last accessed on 20 April 2013.

The Guardian, 'Tony Blair's Speech to the Foreign Policy Centre', 21 March 2006, http://www.guardian.co.uk/politics/2006/mar/21/iraq.iraq1, last accessed on 20 November 2012.

*The Nation*, 'Hizb Stresses Need for Khilafah', 3 September 2005.

Vallely, Paul, 'The Big Question: Why Are Dutch Soldiers Being Sued for the Massacre at Srebrenica?' *The Independent*, 19 June 2008, http://www.independent.co.uk/news/world/europe/the-big-question-why-are-dutch-soldiers-being-sued-for-the-massacre-at-srebrenica-849944.html, last accessed on 20 April 2013.

Williamson, Lucy, 'Stadium Crowd Pushed for Islamist Dream', BBC News, http://bbc.in/QNUYBG, last accessed on 20 April 2013.

# INDEX

# INDEX

www.ingramcontent.com/pod-product-compliance
Ingram Content Group UK Ltd.
Pitfield, Milton Keynes, MK11 3LW, UK
UKHW020753060225
454757UK00007B/86